The Cambridge Introduction to
Literature and Psychoanalysis

This volume is an introduction to the relationship between psychoanalysis and literature. Jean-Michel Rabaté takes Sigmund Freud as his point of departure, studying in detail Freud's integration of literature in the training of psychoanalysts and how literature provided crucial terms for his myriad theories, such as the Oedipus complex. Rabaté subsequently surveys other theoreticians such as Wilfred Bion, Marie Bonaparte, Carl Jung, Jacques Lacan, and Slavoj Žižek. This introduction is organized thematically, examining in detail important terms such as deferred action, fantasy, hysteria, paranoia, sublimation, the uncanny, trauma, and perversion. Using examples from Miguel de Cervantes and William Shakespeare to Sophie Calle and Yann Martel, Rabaté demonstrates that the psychoanalytic approach to literature, despite its erstwhile controversy, has recently reemerged as a dynamic method of interpretation.

Jean-Michel Rabaté is the managing editor of the *Journal of Modern Literature*. He is also founder and senior curator of the Slought Foundation in Philadelphia. Since 2008, Rabaté has been a Fellow of the American Academy of Arts and Sciences. He is also on the editorial boards of *Interfaces, James Joyce Quarterly, James Joyce Annual*, the *European Journal of English Studies, Modernism/Modernity, English Text Construction*, and *Word and Image*.

The Cambridge Introduction to
Literature and Psychoanalysis

JEAN-MICHEL RABATÉ

University of Pennsylvania

CAMBRIDGE
UNIVERSITY PRESS

CAMBRIDGE
UNIVERSITY PRESS

32 Avenue of the Americas, New York, NY 10013-2473, USA

Cambridge University Press is part of the University of Cambridge.

It furthers the University's mission by disseminating knowledge in the pursuit of education, learning, and research at the highest international levels of excellence.

www.cambridge.org
Information on this title: www.cambridge.org/9781107423916

© Jean-Michel Rabaté 2014

First published 2014

A catalog record for this publication is available from the British Library.

Library of Congress Cataloging in Publication data
Rabaté, Jean-Michel, 1949–
The Cambridge introduction to literature and psychoanalysis / Jean-Michel Rabaté.
    pages   cm. – (Cambridge introductions to literature)
Includes bibliographical references and index.
ISBN 978-1-107-02758-9 (hardback) – ISBN 978-1-107-42391-6 (paperback)
1. Psychoanalysis and literature.   I. Title.
PN56.P92R28   2014
801'.92–dc23   2014009938

ISBN 978-1-107-02758-9 Hardback
ISBN 978-1-107-42391-6 Paperback

Contents

Acknowledgments   *page* vii

Introduction: Why psychoanalysis matters   1

Chapter 1 Freud's theater of the unconscious:
           Oedipus, Hamlet, and "Hamlet"   25

Chapter 2 Literature and fantasy, toward a
           grammar of the subject   48

Chapter 3 From the uncanny to the unhomely   71

Chapter 4 Psychoanalysis and the paranoid
           critique of pure literature   93

Chapter 5 The literary phallus, from Poe to Gide   122

Chapter 6 A thing of beauty is a *Freud* forever:
           Joyce with Jung and Freud, Lacan,
           and Borges   150

Chapter 7 From the history of perversion to the
           trauma of history   174

Conclusion: Ambassadors of the unconscious   199

Keywords and Index of Authors   215
Bibliography   237
Index   249

Acknowledgments

I would like to thank Ray Ryan for his trust, support, and friendship.

I want to thank Jennifer Mondal who helped me edit the first draft of the book.

Two different versions of the Conclusion (pp. 204–214) have been published in collections, first as "L' image du tissage dans le tapis, de Holbein à Freud en passant par James" in *Decorum: Tapis et Tapisseries d'artistes,* edited by Anne Dressen, Manon Gingold, and Anna Fera, Paris, Musée d'Art de la Ville de Paris-ARC and Skira-Flammarion, 2013, p. 37–42, and then as "Freud's Textual Couch, or the Ambassadors' Magic Carpet" in *A Concise Companion to Psychoanalysis, Literature and Culture*, edited by Laura Marcus and Ankhi Mukherjee, Oxford, Wiley-Blackwell, 2014, p. 105–121.

The occasion for these essays was my collaboration with Mexican artist Santiago Borja, who was invited to work at the London Freud Museum. He replaced Freud's carpet with a hand-woven rug from the Wixarika community, also known as Huichol, in central Mexico. It was shown at the exhibition curated by Catalina Lorenzo "Divan: Free-Floating Attention Piece" in the Freud Museum from May to June 2010.

French artist Anne Deguelle had been working on a similar project independently and exhibited her work at the Freud Museum as "Sigmund's Rug: To Sleep to Dream No More" from November 2011 to January 2012. The cover illustration for the book comes from her series of "Composites" exhibited there. I thank Anne Deguelle warmly for allowing Cambridge University Press to reproduce it.

Introduction: Why psychoanalysis matters

In the field of literary studies, to say that psychoanalysis has had bad press is an understatement. Even if it remains strong at the field's margins, in film studies, in contemporary art history seminars, in queer studies, in trauma studies, in discussions of the Holocaust, in feminist and post-feminist approaches, in cultural critique and ideology critique following Lacanians such as Slavoj Žižek or neo-Marxist philosophers such as Alain Badiou or Jacques Rancière, when it comes to literature as literature, the invocation of Freud and disciples such as Marie Bonaparte, Oskar Pfister, Otto Rank, or Erich Fromm is most of the time a pretext for a good laugh before serious work begins.

Vladimir Nabokov has represented this tendency most forcefully, and he managed to summarize what he called the charlatanism of Freudians in just two quotes in *Pale Fire*: at one point, the mad commentator Kinbote quotes Oskar Pfister, who discussed the case of a young man who was unable to stop picking his nose, adding that he was obviously overcome by lust and knew no limits to his fantasies; he also quotes Erich Fromm who wrote that Little Red Riding Hood's cap of red velvet was an obvious symbol of menstruation.[1] It took a critic close to psychoanalysis such as Jeffrey Berman to point out that these observations were not as absurd in their original context.[2] However, when we see such flat-footed systems of equivalences, we can only laugh.

Nabokov was the most outspoken critic of a type of Freudianism that dominated in the United States just after World War II.[3] Then Freudianism was the rage in Hollywood; a mixture of Surrealism (mediated by Dalí) and second-generation Freudianism (Fromm is a good representative of this wave) had

---

[1] Vladimir Nabokov, *Pale Fire*, New York, Putnam, 1962, p. 271. Kinbote wonders whether these "clowns" believe what they teach, while he is, of course, psychotic and delusional.

[2] See Jeffrey Berman, *The Talking Cure: Literary Representations of Psychoanalysis*, New York, New York University Press, 1987, pp. 220–223. Berman points out that Pfister's *Psychoanalytic Method* discusses the case of a teenager's irrepressible tic betraying anxiety facing masturbation, whereas Fromm's *Forgotten Language* approaches the fairy tale as a story of coming of age teeming with signs of sexuality. Even if they do not offer ground-breaking interpretations, there is nothing absurd or scandalous in these readings.

[3] See Frederick John Hofman, *Freudianism and the Literary Mind*, New York, Grove Press, 1957, and Edmund Bergler, *The Writer and Psychoanalysis*, Garden City, Doubleday, 1950.

transformed literary criticism into a hunting ground for loose symbols, indiscriminate projections, and wild allegorizations. Nabokov was entirely correct in denouncing this practice as a return to medieval allegorism. In almost all his novels, memoirs, and lectures on literature, he repeats similar accusations: "I reject completely the vulgar, shabby, fundamentally medieval world of Freud, with its crankish quest for sexual symbols (something like searching for Baconian acrostics in Shakespeare's works) and its bitter little embryos spying, from their natural nooks, upon the love life of their parents."[4] Yet, if Nabokov impugns readings that pounce on random images to turn them into phallic symbols and sexual obsessions, why is *Lolita*, his most famous novel, the story of the passion of an adult for a twelve-year-old American girl? Why is *Ada* – the great, long novel of his maturity – a convoluted and fanciful tale of brother-sister incest?

Nabokov's rants conceal the deeper joke that the plot of *Lolita* literalizes the syntagm of "the child therapist" by transforming it into "the rapist." Humbert Humbert reminisces about the shortcomings of "the child therapist" in him who can casually regurgitate "neo-Freudian hash," yet "Lol" appears closer to the truth when she threatens him after they have sex: "I ought to call the police and tell them you raped me."[5] Proving perversely that Lolita is less of a child than Humbert Humbert, Nabokov betrays a troubling proximity to psychoanalysis. His repeated denunciations end up sounding more symptomatic than seriously accusatory. Still, his severe critique remains valid – most applications of psychoanalysis to literature have been either quite bad, or at least in bad taste.

One could believe that psychoanalysts are bad readers because they read too little – or mention glibly books they have not read. The situation is different in Europe, where psychoanalysts from Jacques Lacan to Adam Philips are intellectuals who intervene on cultural issues with relevance. I will turn to someone who is French and who happens to be both a professor of literature and a psychoanalyst. Surprisingly, his assessment is not very positive.

Apply here!

Like Nabokov, Pierre Bayard worries over the evolution of psychoanalytic literary criticism, and his book, *Can One Apply Literature to Psychoanalysis?*,[6] testifies to a certain crisis. Bayard, the praised author of *How to Talk about Books*

---

[4] Vladimir Nabokov, *Speak Memory*, rev. ed., New York, Putnam, 1966, p. 20.
[5] Vladimir Nabokov, *Lolita*, New York, Vintage, 1997, pp. 124 and 141.
[6] Pierre Bayard, *Peut-on appliquer la littérature à la psychanalyse?* Paris, Minuit, 2004. Hereafter abbreviated as PALP and page number.

You Haven't Read[7] – a freewheeling meditation on literary charlatanism and critical fabulation – here inverts the Freudian idea of applied psychoanalysis: when it comes to literature, he argues, one should reverse the classical paradigm and apply literature to psychoanalysis. The result is not as paradoxical as it seems, because a similar reversal had been anticipated by Jacques Derrida, Paul de Man, Hélène Cixous, Julia Kristeva, and Nicholas Royle, among others, yet it refutes Freud's belief that psychoanalysis could be applied to literature.

Bayard's ironical inversion is not entirely antagonistic to Freud. Indeed, Freud recommended a similar strategy when he listed literature as one of the fields that a psychoanalyst should master to be trained. This is clear in *The Question of Lay Analysis*, where Freud opposes medical training as a prerequisite for psychoanalysts and promotes the humanities: "[T]he analytical curriculum would include subjects which are far removed from medicine and which a doctor would never require in his practice: the history of civilization, mythology, the psychology of religion, and literature. Unless he is well oriented in these fields, the analyst will be unable to bring understanding to bear upon much of his material."[8] Freud is not simply alluding to a knowledge provided by personal contact with poems, novels, and plays with the term *Literaturwissenschaft*.[9] This word conflates personal literary expertise and something like the "science" of literature, which may include criticism. Thus, literature is an essential component of the training of a competent analyst. Freud, whose main distinction during his lifetime was a literary prize – the Goethe Prize awarded to him in 1936 – was extremely cultured. His essays are peppered with quotes from Goethe, Shakespeare, and Heine. Freud's library held more novels and plays and books about literature, mythology, and religion than treatises about psychiatric issues.

For Freud, the "science of literature" would encompass the idea of interpretation. There would be a general hermeneutics moving from the literary field to sexuality with its inexhaustible lore of examples, characters, situations, and even jokes that will refine individual diagnoses, dig more deeply into the complex dramas of the patients' lives, and finally look to the immemorial chronicles of gods, heroes, and mythical paradigms that will attest to the impact of transgenerational dramas. In Freud's view, literature is not a token of familiarity with great novels or a sign of cultural distinction, for the term implies knowledge, it informs a sense of pedagogy, and finally it underpins a training

---

[7] Pierre Bayard, *How to Talk about Books You Haven't Read*, trans. Jeffrey Mehlman, New York, Bloomsbury, 2007.

[8] Sigmund Freud, *The Question of Lay Analysis*, trans. Nancy Procter-Gregg, New York, Norton, 1950, p. 118.

[9] Sigmund Freud, *Die Frage der Laienanalyse* in *Schriften zur Behandlungstechnik*, Frankfurt, Fischer, 1982, p. 337.

bridging the gap between medical studies and the humanities. One might say that literature offers a privileged mode of entrance to "culture," a term that combines personal engagement with formalized modes of fiction (*Bildung*) with a compendium of the values defining a whole civilization (*Kultur*). Therefore, as Freud states, no psychoanalyst can ignore the benefits of its acquisition and subsequent mastery.

Is this what Bayard has in mind with his provocative title that postulates a reversal of "applied psychoanalysis"? In fact, he questions the usual critical methods elaborated in the name of psychoanalysis by simply "applying" psychoanalytic terms to literature. Like Nabokov, he criticizes the assumptions of standard psychoanalytic criticism. He agrees with the academic consensus that most schools of psychoanalytic criticism are obsolete today. It would be hard for any candidate to a good American graduate program to be accepted with a plan to study Hamlet's unconscious inhibitions or to assess the consequences of the castration complex in Dostoyevsky. Indeed, if we consider the overtones of the term "application" with Bergson's concept of laughter in mind, the idea of an "applied" discourse cannot but carry an ironical ring. There lurks a mechanical element in the very notion of something that has been *plaqué* – that is, mechanically applied – to literary interpretation. A knowing smirk is likely to greet "applications" of Oedipal patterns to literary works. Bayard is nevertheless more critical than sarcastic when he surveys how psychoanalysis has been applied to literature in the past.

Going back to excellent canonical Freudian explorations such as Sarah Kofman's book on Freud and art[10] or Jean Bellemin-Noël's exploration of a textual unconscious,[11] Bayard points out that Freud's theory always implied the preeminence of creative writers. Writers and artists were credited with having hit on Freud's concepts before he did. However, any awareness of the process was denied to them. Freud was surprised by the fact that if they had discovered the truth, it was without their knowing. Writers and artists did not know what they were doing when they were creating, thus they needed psychoanalytic interpretations to make full sense of brilliant intuitions. Whether these interpretations rely on psychobiography as practiced by Marie Bonaparte or Charles Mauron, or try to avoid it as Bellemin-Noël did when he presupposed a textual unconscious not identical with that of the author, Bayard remains equally critical. He does not spare Lacan, whose position is often modified: "Lacan does not seem to innovate on that issue, alternating critical texts in which the author is taken into account – as for Gide or Joyce – and texts in

---

[10] Sarah Kofman, *The Childhood of Art, An Interpretation of Freud's Aesthetics*, trans. Winfred Woodhull, New York, Columbia University Press, 1988.

[11] Jean Bellemin-Noël, *Vers l'inconscient du texte*, Paris, Presses Universitaires de France, 1979.

which the readings are not founded in any privileged manner on the life of the author, as with *Hamlet*" (PALP, p. 37). Lacan criticized biographical readings of Poe, to which we will return, apparently advocating the practice of "applying literature," yet he was a structuralist at heart and denied any agency or power to subjectivity. Lacan then returned to psychobiography when dealing with Gide and Joyce. In all these cases, the psychoanalytic schools, whether psychobiographical, structuralist, or textualist, reveal a belief in the superiority of psychoanalysis facing literature.

All psychoanalytical interpretations rely on a hermeneutics of suspicion deemed powerful enough to disentangle the hidden meanings lurking in the works. But this very power generates problems. Because these meanings are by definition unconscious, the author cannot control or even know anything of the dark forces that made the work happen. Hence the problem is that these readings yield only results that will conform to the initial theory and remain within the category of teleological interpretations. They function like religious readings: what is found in literary texts is less a product of the investigation than of its origins and of its presuppositions. Such a worry had been well expressed by Tzvetan Todorov regarding Biblical interpretations. Todorov noted that religious readings presuppose that the Bible can be made to confirm Christian doctrine. In the same way, canonical psychoanalytical readings only confirm the truth of psychoanalysis about the Oedipus complex, archaic fantasies, the primal scene, castration, childhood memories, and so on. This does not mean that the results are false. Simply, and more damagingly, they are entirely predictable. It is such a repetitiveness and predictability that has ended up generating boredom, finally leading to theoretical sterility.

To avoid this sterilization, Bayard suggests that psychoanalysis should be able to learn from literature, which entails a need to read literature differently, in such a way that it can be applied to psychoanalysis. One should meditate more comprehensively on the way literary texts reflect (on) psychic phenomena. Applied literature should focus on moments of emergence, on a new knowledge to be shared by the reader. However, this strategy will not convince psychoanalysts who will feel contested by it or critics from other schools who have no patience with psychoanalysis as such. As if to confirm these misgivings, the examples Bayard provided are not satisfactory. The plays or novels adduced, in which one recognizes his usual canon, Laclos, Proust, Maupassant, Agatha Christie, and Shakespeare, merely prove that literature "thinks" and is capable of staging complex psychological problems.

However, one has not waited for psychoanalysts to tell readers that literature "thinks." What do we gain from discovering that anger has been truly and deeply depicted by Homer in the *Iliad*? We may readily accept the idea that the invention of psychology has paralleled the developments of literature, just as it seems clear that Ibsen, Maupassant, Stevenson, and Nietzsche somehow anticipated Freud, which confirms that something like the *Zeitgeist* is operative and hardly qualifies as news. A more relevant position would entail a systematic historicization of these efforts. One might want to point out, for instance, the importance of the links between *Madame Bovary* and the invention of hysteria by French medical discourse, which culminated in Charcot's theories. Bayard notes that literature became a field of predilection for psychoanalysis at the time when psychoanalysis was being invented. Freud, Rank, Ferenczi, Jung, Bion, and others wanted to test their hypotheses by applying them to culture and thus to literature in general. Now that this discourse has been oversystematized, the issue is how to keep being inventive.

Given its riches, its diversity, and its subversive potentialities, literature would signal the disappearance of psychoanalysis as an interpretive paradigm, which makes one question its utility. Thus, the only chance of success of "applied literature" would be to acknowledge the paranoid side of all critical systems and to refuse to speak in the name of a method. Finally, a psychoanalyst reading literature should never say "we" but account for why she or he needs to speak in the first person. Are we not abandoning Freud's notion of a *Literaturwissenschaft* and throwing out the baby of culture with the dirty water of tainted hermeneutics? The debate about psychoanalysis and literature has not been satisfactorily resolved, because it has led Bayard to paint himself in a subjectivist corner, as the last paragraph of the book suggests. Bayard ends by evoking his reading habits, praising the ideal solitude inspired by Montaigne's famous library:

> It is not true indeed that literature, once it has once and for all delivered
> it knowledge about psychology, would have nothing to teach to
> ourselves.... It is wrong above all to imagine that my wish to listen to
> it would be destroyed by my own criticism, even when – for I keep my
> own reserve nevertheless – I have discovered a way that would allow me
> to be taught by books, in the tranquility found at last of the absence of
> dialogue, alone at last." (PALP, p. 173)

On the contrary, I will argue that once we have begun splicing literature and psychoanalysis, we cannot be left in contemplative peace; we will not continue to putter around the stacks in the meditative solace of a walled-in library. To promote a new restlessness linking literary theory and practice, we will have to review Freud's own program and show that his actual practice of reading cannot be reduced to "applied psychoanalysis."

My contention is that one can and will learn directly from Freud and that the "lessons" he provides rebound and resound when reading literature. This is not just to say that Freud is always a stimulating read, although this is undeniable. We need both to historicize Freud as a man of the nineteenth century, defined by a specific Jewish and Viennese cultural moment, and to seize on the multiple new insights that are disseminated in his books and essays. I will return in my Conclusion to Freud's library and to the specific space that he had constructed for psychoanalysis and, now, will just allude to his answer to the request that he should name ten "good novels." Freud wrote his response in November 1906; his letter was published in 1907, along with the responses of Peter Altenberg, Hermann Bahr, Hermann Hesse, Ernst Mach, Arthur Schnitzler, and a few others. Freud's response is deliberate, thoughtful, innovative, but also surprising in its choices. He lists his ten favorite books:

Multatuli, *Letters and Works*
Kipling, *Jungle Book*
Anatole France, *Sur la Pierre Blanche*
Zola, *Fécondité*
Merezhkovsky, *Leonardo da Vinci*
G. Keller, *Leute von Seldwyla*
C. F. Meyer, *Huttens letzte Tage*
Macaulay, *Essays*
Gomperz, *Griechische Denker*
Mark Twain, *Sketches*[12]

It is likely that none of these books will evoke anything in today's readers, save Kipling's *Jungle Book*. I can only refer to the meticulous glosses and summaries detailing the content of these ten books by Alexander Grinstein.[13] His compilation is a labor of love, and it is indeed crucial to know what Freud was reading in 1907, and why he chose these books. A recurrent feature in these books is their social, political, and humanistic side. For instance, Multatuli's work was made up of novels and letters that denounced the cruelty of the colonial system in Indonesia. Good books should teach a lesson, Freud states, and boldly tackle current issues such as anti-Semitism, colonial repression, and religious intolerance, as we see with demonized witches, also present in the *Leonardo da Vinci* book.

[12] Sigmund Freud, "Contribution to a Questionnaire on Reading" in *The Standard Edition of the Complete Psychological Works of Sigmund Freud, Volume IX (1906-1908)*, London, Hogarth Press, 1907, pp. 245–247.
[13] Alexander Grinstein, *Freud at the Crossroads*, Madison, CT: International Universities Press, 1990. See especially pp. 303–564.

At the same time, Freud insists that he is not listing the "ten best books ever" that he knows. If he was asked this, he adds, he would include Homer, the tragedies of Sophocles, Goethe's *Faust*, and Shakespeare's *Hamlet* and *Macbeth*. And if he had been asked to list the ten "most significant books," he would have named scientific books such as those of Copernicus, Johann Weier on the belief in witches, and Darwin's *Descent of Man*. Thus the terms that he uses to present his "ten good books" are revealing: they must be like "good friends"; these are books

> to which one stands in rather the same relationship as to "good" friends, to whom one owes a part of one's knowledge of life and view of the world – books which one has enjoyed oneself and gladly commends to others, but in connection with which the element of timid reverence, the feeling of one's own smallness in the face of their greatness, is not particularly prominent.[14]

Freud adds that he is interested by the possibility of throwing light "on the relation between the author and his work," which betrays the biographical bias often observed in applied psychoanalysis, to which I will return in the next chapters.

Freud's curiosity for history explains the mention of Dmitri Merezhkovsky's *The Romance of Leonardo da Vinci*. The novel became the model for Freud's "historical novels" and would give him the key to Leonardo's life and career – the political struggle between religion and paganism, Catholic intolerance, and Renaissance enlightenment, the iconoclastic rabble of Florence in the fifteenth century, and the elite groups admiring eternal beauty modeled on Greek artists provide couples of opposites that serve to frame the central enigma of Leonardo's *libido*. It is from this book that Freud derived the central image of a "vulture," introducing his tail into Leonardo's mouth that would underpin his 1910 *Childhood Memory of Leonardo da Vinci* and his connection between Leonardo and Machiavelli.

In what concerns Zola, Freud added that he could equally have chosen *Docteur Pascal*, and then he made a more surprising admission: "Genuinely creative writing of purely poetical value has been excluded from this list, probably because your charge – good books – did not seem exactly aimed at such."[15] Freud took the question literally: it was not about "aesthetic enjoyment" but about what "good books" can bring, hence about books that generate "edification." However, these ten books are not all badly written – some are, to be sure, but this cannot be said of Emile Zola, Anatole France,

---

[14] Freud, "Contribution to a Questionnaire on Reading," p. 247.
[15] Ibid.

Mark Twain, or Macaulay. The aesthetic quality comes after, even if it is not negligible. Literature therefore always occupies a certain function for Freud, and in this case, it is ethical and political. This is based on the fact that the practice of reading and of writing is never to be dissociated from a transferential movement. We will see this movement emerge in the conception of literature that Freud devises and refines in an exchange of letters with a close friend of his youth.

Freud's Spanish academy and "cynical" literature

There is no better place to observe the mastery of language and languages acquired by the young Freud than his ten-year correspondence with childhood friend, Eduard Silberstein. These letters were sent when Freud was between fifteen and twenty-five years old. What is curious is that entire sections of these letters were written in Spanish, bad Spanish indeed, but fluent enough – a Spanish replete with silly jokes, personal allusions, and grandiose schemes. Freud and Silberstein had read together Miguel de Cervantes's "El coloquio de los perros" (The Dialogue of the Dogs) in a primer of Spanish literature. This story was published in 1613 in *Exemplary Stories* (ES). Their juvenile enthusiasm for the text led Freud and his friend to invent an amusing "Spanish Academy" often abbreviated as "A. E." for "Academia Española." Neither had learned Spanish well, let alone owned a dictionary. This did not prevent them from writing to each other in garbled and fanciful Castillan. In his letters, because we have only his part of the correspondence, Freud keeps mentioning Seville and not Valladolid, where the dialogue is situated, which suggests that he never read the whole text. However, most of the adventures narrated by Berganza to Scipion occur in Seville, including a dreamlike section with a witch. In their exchange, Freud chose for his part the persona of Scipion and left to Silberstein the other dog, Berganza. From the start, Freud planned that he and his friend should enter into an epistolary pact and arrange weekly confessions:

> Hence my proposal amounts to stipulating that every Sunday each
> of us, the two sole luminaries of the A. E., send the other a letter that
> is nothing short of an entire encyclopedia of the past week and that
> with total veracity reports all our doings, commissions and omissions,
> and those of all strangers we encounter, in addition to all outstanding
> thoughts and observations and at least an adumbration, as it were, of the
> unavoidable emotions. In that way, each of us may come to know the
> surroundings and condition of his friend most precisely, perhaps more

precisely than was possible even at the time when we could meet in the same city. Our letters, which, when the year had passed, may constitute the ornament of the A. E. archives, will then be as diverse as our very lives. In our letters we shall transmute the six prosaic and unrelenting working days of the week into the pure gold of poetry and may perhaps find that there is enough of interest within us, and in what remains and changes around us, if only we learn to pay attention.[16]

Curiously, Freud wanted their regular exchange to remain "in the spirit of romanticism" but double as a sort of "journal" that would require the "strict observance of the form" (LSFES, p. 58). Freud sweeps away the objection that they may not have enough time, insisting that it is worth sacrificing two hours a week if this time is used to examine how they live. And, above all, the result should be entertaining: "[O]ne should not question in advance one's ability to keep a critical diary and spice it with a bit of humor" (LSFES, p. 58).

Indeed, Freud was following a Romantic tradition marked by a mixture of humor, fantasy, and poetry, whose main predecessor was none other than E. T. A. Hoffmann, whose tale of "The Sandman" would become the main literary evidence for a definition of the Uncanny, as we will see later. Hoffmann published "News from the Most Recent Fate of the Dog Berganza"[17] in 1814 in his groundbreaking *Fantasy Pieces in the Manner of Callot*. This collection of stories was introduced by Jean Paul (Richter), a Romantic writer who is mentioned in Freud's letters.[18] Jean Paul and Hoffmann provided obvious stylistic models for the younger Freud.

In Hoffmann's version, the first-person narrator listens to Berganza who continues the narrative of his fanciful adventures. Berganza had lived in a hospital and met witches as in Cervantes's tale, and in this spirited sequel, he learns music with a composer, he becomes a poet and an actor, and he rails against the foibles of society ladies who opt for bad marriages. At the end, he nevertheless turns back into a dog. It is a Romantic "portrait of the artist as young dog," *avant la lettre*. Freud's letters are written in the spirit of Jean Paul and Hoffmann, as they are self-consciously humorous and critical at the same time. To these combined influences one can add that of the humorist Lichtenberg – a letter from 1874 quotes him at length. Freud, who had recently been reading his works and the famous aphorisms, copies Lichtenberg directly to enlighten and amuse Silberstein. He gives a catalogue of imaginary objects mentioning

---

[16] *The Letters of Sigmund Freud to Eduard Silberstein, 1871–1881*, ed. Walter Boehlich, trans. Arnold J. Pomerans, Cambridge, Harvard University Press, 1990, pp. 57–58. Hereafter abbreviated as LSFES and page number.

[17] E. T. A. Hoffmann, *Fantasiestücke*, Frankfurt, Deutscher Klassiker Verlag, 2006, pp. 101–177.

[18] Freud suggests that they can do like Siebenkäs and Leibgeber, two characters of a novel by Jean Paul, who at some point exchange their names (LSFES, p. 118).

Lichtenberg's famous "knife without blade, handle thereof missing" (LSFES, p. 73.) He quotes pieces loaded with pointed political allusions, as a mention of a "large whip" used for the conversion of the Jews (LSFES, p. 74). These witty sentences provide a rich material that will be tapped later in Freud's book on jokes in which Lichtenberg is frequently quoted. In some letters, Freud sounds more censorious but is always a shrewd judge of character. At one point, he comments on the fact that Silberstein, who was barely eighteen then, had been seduced by a sixteen-year-old and that the affair was apparently approved or arranged by her mother, who sent the daughter to dancing lessons and tried to turn her into a coquette. He judges sternly the "collusion" between mother and daughter and warns his friend that he has walked into a trap:

> In short, your part in the whole business was that of a dressmaker's dummy masculine generis, that is, of a tailor's dummy. If there is anything to console your injured self-esteem for this discovery, it can only be the realization that she has been playing no nobler part in your eyes. You were plainly rehearsing the role of the tragic lover that you intend to enact one day. So much for my opinion. Quite honestly, I would like you the better were you to shed the last remnant of your "Sturm und Drang." No doubt you will do this soon without greatly missing it later. (LSFES, p. 98)

Here, the tone has changed, because Freud denounces *Sturm und Drang*, the late eighteenth-century proto-Romantic movement promoting an unleashing of emotions. He announces the detective work deployed in later case studies, such as the Dora case, to which we will return. Romantic irony à la Jean Paul is replaced with a Socialist critique of religious illusions that Freud had encountered in Ludwig Feuerbach. At the time, Freud was reading the works of Feuerbach and said that he "revered" him (LSFES, p. 96). The impact of the left-Hegelian critique of religion and ideology adds a new edge to his tone. Freud came close to ideology critique at the time. In the same letter, Freud adds an important codicil: for now on, the two correspondents will only call themselves "dogs," and to be a "dog" will be an honorific title. I quote the original Spanish: "Llámanse los miemb. D. l. A. E. 'perros,' que es su mayor título" (LSFES, p. 99).

However, the jocular tone of the exchange is kept throughout, especially when Freud harps on his adolescent, and apparently unrequited, love for a pretty young neighbor, Gisela Fuss. Early on, she metamorphoses into "Ichthyosaura," via an obscure allusion to a poem by von Scheffel. However, the antiphrastic turn of phrase turns more anxious when Freud learns that the object of his attention is to be married. He immediately sends Silberstein a droll and sad poem in bad hexameters, entitled "Epithalamium," still signed by a "Homerian of the Academia Espanola" (LSFES, p. 135). These halting verses transform his frustration into mock praise: first, the young woman is made to look spherical, then, she seems deprived of any intelligence. Finally, even if she appeared as the "crowning glory of Madrid and Seville," even if she might prepare nice kosher dinners for her hubby, it is certain that she lives in a place where the "Spirit" is lacking. Thus the half-hearted Epithalamium ends with a Parthian shaft:

> And so may they both live out their allotted span,
> Like the insects and worms that inhabit the earth,
> Blessed with splendid digestion and lungs
> Never plagued by the *Spirit*, such is the Academia's wish. (LSFES, p. 138)

The irony of history is that Freud's vengeful poem ended up being effective: in fact, Gisela did not marry the happy rival then, but only a few years later. Freud's draft of the poem contains funny equivocations about the marriage that is due to take place in Lemberg, but meanwhile he must go soon to Cracow.[19] Such a calculated hesitation resurfaced later, when Freud wrote his book on jokes in the wake of the *Interpretation of Dreams*. He analyzed what he called the genre of "cynical jokes" (*zynische Witze*) – jokes that attack social conventions, most of the times "sacred institutions" such as that of marriage[20] – and also the "skeptical jokes" (*skeptische Witze*). The latter attack the root of our certainty and our trust in truth. The best example of the latter category is, "Why do you tell me you are going to Cracow to make me believe you are going to Lemberg, when I know you are going to Cracow?"[21] Given Freud's personal investment, it seems that the original form of the joke was, "Why do you tell me that you are going to be married in Cracow to make me believe you are going to be married in Lemberg, whereas I know that you are going to be married in Cracow?" The performative power of the ironical poem was such that it magically prevented the realization of the marriage. The belief in any "reality" was lost as in those jokes, all the while helping Freud forget poor "Ichthyosaura," who was soon advantageously replaced by the bloodied eels that he would dissect in Trieste to discover their testicles.[22]

The spirit of burlesque, whimsy, and satire displayed here derives its ultimate inspiration from Cervantes's tale in which two dogs named Scipio and

[19] These details are introduced by Walter Boehlich, LSFES, pp. xxi–xxii.
[20] Sigmund Freud, *The Joke and Its Relation to the Unconscious*, trans. Joyce Crick, London, Penguin, 2002, p. 105.
[21] Freud, *The Joke and Its Relation to the Unconscious*, p. 110.
[22] See LSFES, pp. 142–155, for hilarious accounts of Freud's stay in Trieste, with funny drawings as illustrations.

Berganza converse endlessly about everything under the sun. In the letters, Freud had taken the role of Scipio (he always signs "Cipion.") In the original tale, Scipio has a more authoritative voice and leads the conversation while Berganza spins endless yarns – shaggy dog stories, as it were. Scipio listens and interjects sharp comments while Berganza gushes forth. One cannot help thinking of the forthcoming psychoanalytic cure. Here, it is not so much a "talking cure" as a "writing cure." Freud believed from the start that their joint effort had to keep a sense of form if the result was to be like a work of art. This is stated in a humorous passage when Freud justifies the fact that God took a week to create the world because he could easily have made it in a second. Freud then compares the very letters they exchange with a work of art: "The self-same order must also be reflected in our letters, but it must not be artificial or lifeless, rather that of a work of art, whose parts are not merely distinct but also closely interrelated" (LSFES, p. 48). The comment accompanies one of the most complex letters, because it is built like an edifice, evoked as a whole palace with three floors. One of these "floors" includes a summary of Carlyle's *Sartor Resartus* – a book that had struck Freud as "part parody, and part witty reflection" – that he compares with those of Jean Paul, the great model in the first letters (LSFES, pp. 49–50).

For Cervantes, Berganza embodies the *pícaro*, for his risky adventures always end badly, whereas Scipio is the one who derives philosophical meaning from the anecdotes. Scipio mocks Berganza, who boasts about his knowledge of Latin. Scipio knows Greek and gives the correct etymology of "philosophy." As a philosopher, he belongs to the school of the cynics, as we know from this passage: "You slander philosophy? So that's what we're about! Make a virtue, Berganza, of the cursed plague of gossip and give it whatever name you like, for it will earn us the title of cynics, which means slanderous dogs. For your own sake, shut up and proceed with your story." To which Berganza replies quite sensibly: "How am I to proceed if I must shut up?"[23] Cervantes has anticipated the useful category invented by Gregory Bateson of the "double bind": the double message containing a contradictory injunction.

The invective and moralistic tone of Scipio's interjection does not conceal the fact that both dogs judge humans severely. Freud's juvenile effort at creating a Spanish Academy should be inscribed under the banner of what Peter Sloterdijk has called a "critique of cynical reason."[24] The cynic is the philosopher who disguises himself as a dog. Having abandoned the pretense of social

---

[23] Miguel de Cervantes, "The Dialogue of the Dogs" in *Exemplary Stories*, trans. Lesley Lipson, Oxford, Oxford University Press, 1998, p. 267. Hereafter, abbreviated as ES and page number.
[24] Peter Sloterdijk, *Critique of Cynical Reason*, trans. Michael Eldred, Minneapolis, University of Minnesota Press, 1987.

disguise, he engages in exercises of brutal honesty. Diogenes, the founder of the Cynical school, also claimed that he belonged to no city but was first a "cosmopolitan" – a claim Freud echoes in the course of his career and exemplified by the decision to write in a different language.

The core of the *Coloquio* is a scene narrated by Berganza in which he is mistaken for the son of an old woman lying in the hospital of Montilla. She wants to kiss him on the mouth, which he finds disgusting. The woman believes that Berganza is Montiel, the son of a witch called Montiela, metamorphosed into a dog by an enchantress. Then the witch anoints her body with a magical unguent that leaves her unconscious (ES, p. 289). Berganza pulls her by his teeth into the open to revive her, but her hairy and nude body attracts attention and outrage from the onlookers. When she comes to, she curses him, in consequence of which he is taken for a demon (ES, p. 291). After having heard this rambling fantastic tale, Scipio gives his most extensive tirade. He cannot believe that a baby can turn into a dog, but then assumes that there must be an allegorical meaning in the fanciful narrative: "[T]he words are meant to be taken in a sense I've heard called allegorical, where the meaning is not what the words literally say, but something which, although different, may be similar" (ES, p. 292). He develops the trope of "Fortuna," which leads his friend Berganza to conclude that all his adventures have been like a dream. If it was a dream, however, it could be interpreted through human speech: "I've reached the conclusion that everything we've experienced until now, and what we're experiencing at the moment, is a dream and that we're dogs. But that should not prevent us from enjoying this blessing of speech and the great honour of human conversation for as long as we can" (ES, p. 293). Scipio agrees and wants to narrate his own story, which he never does. The dialogue reveals its one allegorical impossibility while highlighting the power of language to make sense of absolutely everything.

What stands out in Freud's letters to Silberstein is the wish that, under the aegis of the Academia Española, the two friends should narrate to each other their day-to-day lives as candidly as possible. Although they never fully fulfilled this intention, at least judging from the letters we have, Freud's insistence evokes the program of guided transferential friendship in which we recognize Freud's recurrent practice of self-analysis via dialogue with an intimate friend. Cervantes's "The Dialogue of the Dogs" struck a chord in Freud when he was sixteen because the dialogue stages dogs who soon morph into the couple of *pícaro* and philosopher. The "pseudo-couple," a concept invented by Samuel Beckett and to which we will return, offers the idea of a confidential exchange between two persons who will discuss everything that they have experienced to extract a truer meaning from their interaction; this chimes in with the plan of an "examined life," for, indeed, Freud agreed from the start with Socrates that an "unexamined life" is not worth living.

In suggesting something that looks like a "contract" in the "Colloquy" of these Viennese "dogs," Freud stipulated strict rules of exchange mediated by another language, Spanish, in which, moreover, none of the interlocutors was proficient. These were not the immature outpourings of "best friends," because the dialogue was mediated by a foreign language. By highlighting a sense of style, by choosing a specific tone and an exotic idiom, he imagined a sequence of witty and detailed narratives. Their cumulative effect would lead to a critical and cathartic "examination" of life. Dialogue offered the key to a new form of introspection. Paradoxically, communication can be all the more intimate as it is mediated by another language, an idiom different from the mother tongue. We often see Freud struggling to find the correct Spanish word (he is without a dictionary, which adds a constraint, and is also part of the "contract") as he strives to articulate the exact nuance of thought. Then and only then can a felicitous turn of phrase illuminate all the rest. This setting curiously anticipates the verbal insight of a young Viennese hysteric, called Anna O. by Freud's friend Breuer. Her lasting contribution to psychoanalysis was having coined the phrase "talking cure," using the English language that replaced her native German, made inaccessible by her hysteria. The establishment of a comparable estrangement of language in a cure that nevertheless only uses language (and not hypnosis or medication, for instance) was to become the trademark of psychoanalysis.

Moreover, because the "contract" stipulates regular reports regulating male effusiveness, we see here the blueprint for Freud's passionate attachments to a series of male correspondents: after Silberstein (their correspondence lasted more than ten years), there would be Breuer, then Fliess, finally replaced by Jung, and later by Ferenczi. The exception was his daughter Anna, the last of the series, after she took up the profession of psychoanalyst and never married so as to remain close to her beloved father. In all these exchanges, as in these juvenile letters, Freud managed to overcome, discipline, or criticize romantic attachments that marked his earlier years. However, this was a gesture of which Silberstein was incapable.

A personal drama revealed an ominous sign of his blindness. A few years later, Silberstein married a young woman, Pauline, soon to realize that she was troubled by melancholia. In a sign of trust in his old friend's healing power, he sent his wife to Freud for a consultation. This took place in May 1891. Instead of going up to Freud's consulting room, the twenty-year-old woman threw herself to her death from the third floor of Freud's building at Maria-Theresienstrasse 8. A few months later, Freud moved to Berggasse 19. He was to occupy the large ground floor apartment; this remained his address for the rest of his years in Vienna. Silberstein remarried soon afterward, and his second choice was the right one.

As we know, the critique of romantic illusions is the main theme of Cervantes's masterpiece. We see Freud reading *Don Quixote* regularly in 1875 and attempting to send a copy to Silberstein (LSFES, p. 81). He praises to his friend chapter 47 in book II in which Sancho confronts the doctor Pedro Rescio de Tirteafuera, who prevents him from eating the delicacies heaped on his plate for fear of diseases or his diet: Freud describes this as an "idyllic moment" (LSFES, p. 87). A little earlier, Freud had alluded to his own "chivalry" in response to a flattering remark by Silberstein about his being a "jewel":

> While my chivalry is thus reduced to hollow illusions, you must still
> strip its image of several falsehoods intended to elevate it to a position
> beyond anything it might wish for itself or one you could defend before
> God or your conscience. Strip it of its lures, its artifices, its serpentine
> wiles, and its charms, it is still far from being an Armida. (LSFES, p. 83)

In this deliberately mixed cultural reference, Freud superimposes Cervantes's knight and the seductress from Torquato Tasso's *Jerusalem Delivered*. Freud is both the deluded *caballero andante* and Rinaldo in his enchanted bower, as manifested in a letter in which he deplores his stiffness and lack of ease with young women. Nevertheless, pushed by the "spirit" lacking with Gisela and all the other temptresses, Freud identifies with the delirious knight-errant in pursuit of high deeds while feeling some complicity with the astute, rational, and down-to-earth servant. He would try to fight the windmills of cultural obscurantism and sexual prejudice with the very cunning of Sancho Panza.

Freud finished reading *Don Quixote* some time in 1875. One will recall that the second book ends with Don Quixote's death. However, the *ingenioso hidalgo* does not die as Don Quixote, because "Don Quixote" must first die a metaphorical death before a mortal one, which is the condition for his true immortality. He dies only as Alonso Quixano, his real name. His death is not caused by illness or old age but is triggered by a depression that engulfs him after he has seen through his past delusions. His friends blame this disease on his "disenchantment" with Dulcinea and the loss of the chivalric names bestowed on neighbors or objects. When they realize that he may die of such melancholia, they try to revive him by pretending to believe in the old chivalric code, but to no avail. Sancho, who has undergone a sort of "quixotization," even urges Don Quixote to go back to his previous adventures:

> [T]he greatest madness a man can commit in his life is to suffer himself
> to die, without anybody's killing him, or being brought to this end by
> any other hand than that of melancholy. Be not lazy, sir, but do get out

of bed, and let us be going to the field, dressed like shepherds, as we agreed to do: and who knows, but behind some bush or other we may find the lady Dulcinea disenchanted as fine as heart can wish?[25]

One of the most endearing twists of Cervantes's novel is that it ends with a paradoxical appeal to romantic fiction after it had been rendered impossible. Romanticism is now deemed obsolete, unfashionable, and delusional. Quixano, restored to sanity, can admit his previous madness. However, this does not help him live better. Freud would meditate on this paradox, alerted by Cervantes to the fact that some illusions are necessary to keep the wish to live, whereas other delusions are detrimental to one's health.

My main contention in this book is that we can learn a lot about literature when focusing on Freud as a writer more than on Freud as a theoretician. Early on, he was aware of the lack of scientific status of his texts. Close to the end of his detailed account of his treatment of Elizabeth von N., Freud notes:

> I have not always been a psychotherapist. Like other neuropathologists, I was trained to employ local diagnoses and electro-prognosis, and it still strikes me myself as strange that the case histories I write should read like short stories [*Novellen*] and that, as one might say, they lack the serious stamp of science. I must console myself with the reflection that the nature of the subject is evidently responsible for this, rather than any preference of my own. The fact is that local diagnosis and electrical reactions lead nowhere in the study of hysteria, whereas a detailed description of mental processes such as we are accustomed to find in the works of imaginative writers [*Dichtern*] enables me, with the use of a few psychological formulas, to obtain at least some kind of insight into the course of that affliction.[26]

This is also true of his treatment of the Dora case, a text of which he was rightly proud and that he could present in those terms to his friend Wilhelm Fliess: "It is the subtlest thing I have written so far and will put people off more than usual."[27] Indeed, what makes this book so singular is that Freud is both foregrounding the fact that he only presents "fragments" from an analysis and maintains that his text looks like a *"roman à clef."*[28] I will discuss this

[25] Miguel de Cervantes, *Don Quixote*, trans. Charles Jarvis, Oxford, Oxford University Press, 1998, p. 941.

[26] Sigmund Freud and Josef Breuer, *Studies on Hysteria*, trans. James Strachey and Anna Freud, New York, Basic Books, 2000, pp. 160–161.

[27] Letters to Fliess, Jan. 25, 1901, *The Complete Letters of Sigmund Freud to Wilhelm Fliess, 1887–1904*, trans. and ed. Jeffrey Moussaieff Masson, Cambridge, Harvard University Press, 1985, p. 433.

[28] Sigmund Freud, *Dora, An Analysis of a Case of Hysteria*, New York, Collier, 1993, p. 3. See also *Fragments of an Analysis of Hysteria*, in Sigmund Freud, *The Psychology of Love*, trans. Shaun Whiteside, London, Penguin, 2006, p. 5.

book, taking my point of departure in a link between the first book on hysteria co-written with Breuer and the Dora case.

All accounts of the invention of psychoanalysis begin with Anna O., whose real name was Bertha Pappenheim, the young hysteric we have met. She was treated by Josef Breuer, Freud's older and established colleague. Anna O.'s symptoms included the projection of a second self, a woman who could only speak in English and had forgotten her native German. Next to her calling therapy a "talking cure," she also described the whole process in English as "chimney sweeping."[29] She suffered from hallucinations, absences, contractures of the limbs, and paralyses. Breuer soon stopped hypnosis and would just let her speak (in English). This improved some symptoms but not all, but ultimately Breuer had to abandon his patient, as his own wife was getting jealous of his attention to the young, pretty, vivacious, and intelligent Bertha.

One night, Bertha declared that she was in the throes of a pregnancy and was going to give birth to a child conceived by Breuer. According to Freud's account (which became more critical as years passed), immediately after, Breuer "fled" to Venice with his wife. In a 1932 letter to Stefan Zweig, Freud still regrets that Breuer had not resolved the incident psychoanalytically. Breuer interrupted the transference with Bertha when he chose to take flight and have a second honeymoon trip with his wife.[30] Freud's negative assessment was reiterated by Ernest Jones in his 1953 biography of Freud. According to Jones, Breuer was so shocked by the hysterical childbirth that "he fled the house in a cold sweat." He adds: "The next day he and his wife left for Venice to spend a second honeymoon, which resulted in the conception of a daughter; the girl born in these curious circumstances was nearly sixty years later to commit suicide in New York."[31] It looks as if Jones had distorted everything, perhaps unintentionally.

The historical investigation recently conducted by Louis Breger yields a different story:

> The truth is that Breuer did not flee from Bertha but remained involved
> with her treatment for several years. He and his wife did not vacation
> in Venice that year; his daughter Dora was born in March 1882, three
> months before the end of the cathartic treatment of Bertha; and she did
> not commit suicide in New York, but rather stayed in Vienna after 1938
> to help her sister's family. She died at the hands of the Nazis in 1942.[32]

[29] Freud and Breuer, *Studies on Hysteria*, p. 30.
[30] Stefan Zweig, *Briefwechsel mit Hermann Bahr, Sigmund Freud, Rainer Maria Rilke und Arthur Schnitzler*, ed. Jeffrey B. Berlin, Hans-Ulrich Lindken, and Donald A. Prater, Frankfurt, Fischer, 1987, p. 200.
[31] Ernest Jones, *The Life and Work of Sigmund Freud*, vol. 1, New York, Basic Books, 1953, p. 225.
[32] Louis Breger, *A Dream of Undying Fame: How Freud Betrayed His Mentor and Invented Psychoanalysis*, New York, Basic Books, 2009, p. 42.

Now we are indeed back to a Nabokovian plot: Is this a tale of an older therapist whose work had been stolen by a younger and eager scholar? In fact, as Breger notes, even if Freud's narrative is unfounded, it remains true to one fact: after the treatment of Bertha, Breuer refused to use the cathartic technique, and above all he rejected Freud's emphasis on the sexual side of neurosis and hysteria. If Freud stole the discovery of the "talking cure" from Breuer, he apologized by giving the name of Breuer's daughter, a Dora who never committed suicide, to his next heroine. This is how the real life Ida Bauer became "Dora." Such a symbolic baptism made her into another daughter of Breuer. As such, Dora was to embody a gift – the gift of speech and interpretation – taking her cue from Anna O.'s cure and bringing it to bear on Dora's dreams of femininity.

The novel of Dora: Bringing the dangerous gift of literature

Within the huge literature on Dora's case, I will follow the lead of Jacques Lacan, who discussed her in 1951 in "Presentation on Transference," then returned to her case six years later, changing his assessment of the cure completely to become much more critical of Freud's approach. The differences between this 1951 text and his 1957 seminar testify to the huge impact made by Lévi-Strauss on his work, especially when it came to a systematic rereading of Freud. Lacan gave a talk on Dora in 1951 at a conference of French-speaking psychoanalysts, later published in the *Revue Française de Psychanalyse* in 1952.[33] His starting point was Freud's remark to Dora that she had played the part of an accomplice in the sexual comedy of betrayals in which she had been involved and "had dismissed from her mind every sign which tended to show its true character."[34] Or again, "it was quite certain that the reproaches which (Dora) made against her father of having been deaf to the most imperative calls of duty and of having things in the light which was most convenient from the point of view of his own passions – these reproaches recoiled upon her head." (DA, p. 31) Freud proceeded to turn against Dora the charges that she had leveled against her father – that is, exploiting his bad health to further an illicit amorous liaison. Freud wanted Dora to take a good look at herself and at her situation. This she did, which led to the only successful moment in her treatment. Dora immediately complained of gastric pains, and Freud easily identified these as

---

[33] In Jacques Lacan, *Ecrits*, Paris, Seuil, 1966, pp. 215–226, and *Ecrits*, trans. Bruce Fink, New York, Norton, 2006, pp. 176–185. For the discussion of the Dora case, see pp. 178–184.
[34] I follow *Dora, An Analysis of a Case of Hysteria*, subsequently abbreviated as DA and page number. Here, DA, p. 29.

imitative symptoms, looking for their models in Dora's married cousin. He then asked: "Who are you copying now?" Alas, his triumph was to be short-lived. Freud had "hit the mark" (DA, p. 31), but only once.

In a series of dialectical reversals, Freud turned the tables against Dora in three moments. First, Freud made Dora aware of her unexamined function in the "quadrille" by linking her to Mr. K., Frau K., and her father. This eye-opening disclosure forced Dora to be aware of her objective collusion in the sexual exchange of partners. The second moment is when Freud asked Dora to understand that her jealousy facing her father's love for Mrs. K. concealed something else. The third moment corresponded to her infatuation with Mrs. K., her father's mistress. This unreciprocated love belied what was really at stake – namely, her fascination for the mystery of femininity.

In his approach of Freud's treatment of Dora, Lacan began by a detour via Hegel's dialectics so as to get a better concept of the case. He perceived a striking similarity between Dora's predicament and the character called by Hegel a "beautiful soul." Indeed, Hegel's analysis corresponds point by point to Dora's situation. Dora protests of her purity, denounces the confusion outside while remaining blissfully unaware of her own murky role and obvious contradictions. In his famous portrait, Hegel was thinking of his sister's pathology (she ended up institutionalized).[35] The evocation of "beautiful soul" in *The Phenomenology of Spirit* alludes also to Molière's *Misanthrope*: in the play, Alceste exemplifies the *schöne Seele*. For Hegel, the only outcome for the "beautiful soul" is madness:

> The "beautiful soul", lacking an *actual* existence, entangled in the
> contradiction between its pure self and the necessity of that self to
> externalize itself and change itself into an actual existence, and dwelling
> in the *immediacy* of this firmly held antithesis …, this "beautiful
> soul", then, being conscious of this contradiction in its unreconciled
> immediacy, is disordered to the point of madness, wastes itself in
> yearning and pines away in consumption.[36]

A "beautiful soul" is thus someone who, for "sentimental" reasons, refuses to see the economic circuit in which he or she is caught. The "beautiful soul" remains blind to the actual interactions of commerce in real or symbolical realms. Sentimentalism veils the cruel realities underpinned by a symbolic system, therefore denying social relationships.

[35] See Daniel Berthold-Bond, *Hegel's Theory of Madness*, Albany, State University of New York Press, 1995.
[36] G. W. F. Hegel, *The Phenomenology of Spirit*, trans. A. V. Miller, Oxford, Oxford University Press, 1957, p. 407.

In January 1957, Lacan returned to Freud's treatment of the Dora case and added to Hegel's dialectics a few concepts borrowed from Lévi-Strauss's structural anthropology.[37] They provided a new critical leverage. Instead of praising Freud's clinical expertise in the handling of transference, Lacan expressed his astonishment at Freud's blunders, the first of which was Freud's confusion as to Dora's true object of desire. In an embarrassed footnote, Freud admitted that he had missed her homosexual attachment to Mrs. K. (DA, pp. 95–96). This mistake was predicated on Freud's unanalyzed assumption that Dora should "normally" have been attracted to Mr. K. Her disgust when being forcibly kissed was just another proof of hysteria. At this point, it seems that Freud had forgotten the lessons conveyed by literature, since we may remember that Berganza found the kisses of the old woman in the hospital of Montilla totally disgusting. However, Freud tells us that one cannot discard Mr. K. from an analysis of Dora's convoluted desire. The key will be given later: hysterics love by proxy, therefore they refuse to be an "object" of desire; wanting to be a "subject" and not an "object" of desire, the hysteric chooses an object that is fundamentally homosexual – thus, perhaps Berganza had been in love with Scipio all along.

In Dora's dialectics of desire, Mrs. K. derived her importance from the fact that, beyond her election to the status of object of desire and the narcissistic investment that Dora's *Verliebheit* entails, she embodied Dora's question: What is a woman? For Dora, what was of prime importance was that her father, although rich (*vermögend*), was supposed to be impotent (*unvermögend*). Dora's father should have been the agent who bestows symbolically the missing object or the phallus, but in this case, Dora's father could not give it because he did not have it. The phallic lack of the father generated a new twist in the dialectics of giving. Dora remained exclusively attached to a father whose virile gift she could never possess, accept, or even refuse.

Dora loved her father all the more as she believed him to be wounded, deficient or impotent. Love for the maimed father was inversely proportional to the diminution of his status. This can be generalized to include the status of fiction, hence of literature as such; if being able to write is a "gift," it functions according to the libidinal circuit of hysteria. A writer "gives" us lives he or she has not lived – in Dora's case as in literature, there is no greater gift than the gift of something that one does not have. Psychoanalysis teaches us that the true sign of love is to give what one does not have. Following this paradigm, literature will present dangerous gifts of love (or passion, or transferential attachments, or pure hatred) in a symbolic economy it creates.

---

[37] Jacques Lacan, *Le Séminaire IV: La Relation d'objet*, Paris, Seuil, 1994. I will refer to it as RO followed by the page number.

Anthropologist Marcel Mauss showed that gifts circulate feely but are compensated by counter-gifts,[38] and Lacan's interpretation of the Dora case was filtered by Lévi-Strauss's structuralist anthropology. Lévi-Strauss's basic rule of kinship leading to exogamic exchanges can be summed up by the formula: "I have received a wife and I owe a daughter." Such a principle of exchange underpinning the symbolic economy of culture transforms any woman into an object of barter, which is precisely what Dora refuses with utmost energy. Dora could not stand being excluded as an active agent from the laws governing the gift. As soon as she saw herself reduced to a pure object, Dora rebelled and concluded that her father was selling her short to cover up for his extramarital intrigue. Trying to untangle this, Dora attempted to extract herself from metaphors that trapped her. One was the metaphor of a court (*Hof*), which recurred in her dreams, in which we find a jewel box and then *Bahnhof, Friedhof*, and *Vorhof* (DA, p. 91). These signifiers kept repeating – *hof*, a multivalent "courtyard." They multiplied because Dora was prevented from situating herself in any economy. She did not know who she was any longer because she had lost her place in her family. In her structural lability, she was unable to fathom what love might mean for her.

We can understand better Freud's mistake: he blundered when he tried to convince Dora that she was in love with Mr. K. Freud failed to see that the introduction of Mr. K. as a normalizing object of heterosexual love was Dora's last attempt to comply with the law of symbolic exchange. Because Dora could only accept the idea of being an object of desire once the riddle of femininity was solved, what she was looking for in Mrs. K. was less an object of same-sex desire than the answer to the riddle of how one can be an object of desire at all. Thus one of the keys to the case is founded on the reversibility of "giving" and "taking." In the end, Freud surmised that Dora's mother might have been the real key to the riddle of Dora's desire. In an exchange with Dora about one of her dreams, Freud states:

> As you say, the mystery turns upon your mother. You ask how she comes into the dream? She is, as you know, your former rival in your father's affections. In the incident of the bracelet, you would have been glad to accept what your mother had rejected. Now let us just put "give" instead of "accept" and "withhold" instead of "reject." Then it means that you were ready to give your father what your mother withheld from him; and the thing in question was connected with jewelry. (DA, p. 62)

[38] Marcel Mauss, *The Gift: Forms and Functions of Exchange in Archaic Societies*, trans. Ian Gunnison, New York, Norton, 1967.

The "jewel-case," understood as part of a series of "return-presents" (*Gegengeschenke*),[39] had to represent female genitals. When Freud told this to Dora, she replied, we can imagine, wearily: "I knew you would say that." Undeterred, Freud pushed what he thought was his advantage: "That is to say, you knew it was so" (DA, p. 61.) Here, therefore, Freud appears insensitive to nuances that will become clear to a reader who will have to be, as Nabobov insisted, always a "re-reader."[40] And psychoanalytic rereaders will have to become sleuths. In fact, this is what Freud expected when he wrote his "fragments." It is up to us to piece together the revealing features and create a better picture of Dora than he did. Freud's misguided insistence that Dora should have loved Mr. K. because he reminded her of her father was a fictional premise that Nabokov exploited fully and perversely in *Lolita*.

The choice of "Dora" as a fictional name for Ida Bauer was Freud's lasting stroke of genius and hence his true gift to literature.[41] The *dora* in the plural in Greek means not only "gifts" but also "retaining fees" or "bribes." The legal overtones of the Greek plural hint at accusations against those who take bribes. However, if a gift involves the obligation to give back, which gift will not turn into a bribe? As long as Dora can be given the father's "nothing," a nothing that condenses the impossibility of a "pure" gift, she maintains her function in a structure of exchanges that allows her to participate in her father's love in the double sense of the genitive, both objective and subjective. However, when another type of "nothing" was presented to her by Mr. K.'s admission that his wife was "nothing" to him, she was forced to renounce the phallic substitutes that had come along the symbolic chain. All at once, when Dora realized her position as an object of exchange, she fell from the structure and was reduced to the function of bribe.

Given the dilemma of bribe or bride, Dora forces our admiration in refusing the most basic form of alienation, commodification, and reification via social barter. She could say like Laokoon: "*Timeo Danaos et dona ferentes.*"[42] The problem for her was that those "Greeks" would have referred to her family and her closest friends. She was not killed by snakes sent by the gods but chose the coils of hysteria as an escape. Freud's interpretation was condensed into the perfect choice of a pseudonym for his rebellious patient. By making her

---

[39] Sigmund Freud, "Bruchstücke einer Hysterie-Analyse," in *Studienausgabe, VI, Hysterie und Angst*, Frankfurt, Fischer, 1971, p. 141.

[40] Vladimir Nabokov, *Lectures on Literature*, New York, Harcourt, 1980, p. 3.

[41] The curious anonymity to which Freud consigns the real Peppina Zellenka and her husband, his decision to use the simple initial K (which happens to be the initial of the most neglected character in the whole story recounted by Freud – Dora's mother was named Katharina or Käthe Bauer) seems to announce Kafka's fictional alter egos.

[42] Virgil, *Aeneid*, II, 49, meaning: "I fear the Greeks, especially when they bring gifts."

allegorize the concept of "gifts" in the plural, Freud managed to conflate all at once language with all its historical layers, a whole cultural unconscious, and an abbreviation evoking socioeconomic patterns of exchange.

Moreover, the plot of *Dora* shows that Freud had been wrong to "apply" his own theories to the predicament of his reluctant heroine. Freud himself only understood what had happened after he wrote his book, then rewrote it, and annotated it. This is why, in *The Psychopathology of Everyday Life*, he comments on the fact that there was no other name that came to his mind when he chose that of "Dora": "Only a single name came into my mind: the name *Dora*."[43] He even rebaptized the children's nanny Dora, although her real name was Rosa. Obviously, Freud felt compelled by the fictional name, which suggests a case of Dora *sub rosa*.

Like a good account of a perfect parapraxis, the Dora case is a novel that follows the quester, Freud, in his fantastic wild goose chase. Like Don Quixote, Freud appears as an easily misled sleuth, a stubborn but often deluded detective. His windmills are the signs of an attraction between an older married man (a Humbertian Mr. K.) and a nymphet (Dora as Lol) that he keeps harping on, missing the obvious lesbian elements in Dora's makeup. He gets lost in semantic investigations that soon reach a dead end. Nevertheless, because of his obstinacy and honesty, he manages to let us know where and when he has been led astray. He provides thus, among other things, a perfect indictment of applied psychoanalysis. Freud's clinical failure turns then into a triumph of literary and psychological analysis. Indeed the treatment was a failure, yet still today makes great literature. Like all engrossing novels, it includes the author's delayed admission of why he was stupidly wrong and why we can become more intelligent in the end: we just need to pay attention to the details that he missed, and are sure to be granted the gift of insight if only we reread the text another time.

---

[43] Sigmund Freud, *The Psychopathology of Everyday Life*, trans. Anthea Bell, London, Penguin, 2002, p. 230.

Chapter 1

Freud's theater of the unconscious: Oedipus, Hamlet, and "Hamlet"

Let us begin our rereading process with a few of Freud's "ten best books ever." Two on this list are by Shakespeare. Freud, who read and spoke English fluently, had a lifelong passion for Shakespeare. He quotes more than twenty plays in his various works, often from memory, which over time produced a number of revealing slips. One could even assert that Shakespeare became Freud's guide on the path of discovering a cultural unconscious.[1] Freud felt that he was Shakespeare's contemporary – at a certain distance from the classical theater of the Greeks and not fully attuned to the work of the Viennese avant-garde. Already at the age of seventeen, he could pun on a line from *Twelfth Night* I, 1, in a letter to Eduard Silberstein: "'Frances is the key to the heart,' you say, adapting Shakespeare, who said the same of music. 'Young ladies are boring, ergo they are cure for boredom, poison being the best antidote'" (LSFES, p. 40). Here, "Frances" means the French language, and Silberstein and Freud outplay each other in the conceit that an excess of love will cure this disease by surfeit.

Freud and Hamlet

Then, in an important letter to his friend Fliess dated September 21, 1897, Freud suggested that he had wholly identified with Hamlet. This was the same letter in which he announced that he rejected his previous theory of neuroses; it was based on the idea that the perversion of the fathers – that is, their sexual seduction – would produce or precipitate the hysterical symptoms of the daughters. As we have seen, he had already changed his mind about this seduction theory during Dora's treatment. In 1897, Freud realized that most of these accusations were fantasy-based delusions. Yet, in the context of his letter, accounting for his decision to take a new departure, he slightly misquoted

---

[1] This is a point made cogently by Henriette Michaud in *Les Revenants de la Mémoire: Freud et Shakespeare*, Paris, Presses Universitaires de France, 2011.

Hamlet. Hamlet had said, "The readiness is all," but Freud writes, "To be in readiness."[2] Freud was aware of having produced a "variation" on the hero's famous words; a deeper identification is nevertheless obvious. Like Hamlet, Freud is full of doubts; the rosy picture of a future leading to "eternal fame" brought by scientific discoveries has faded away. Freud is like Hamlet in that he has to question the very root of desire and to find that desire is founded purely on "psychological" determinations.

The Shakespearean quote leads to a cryptic Jewish *Witz*, one of those Freud was collecting for his book on jokes. He nevertheless did not use this joke in the book, and we are not sure what it is; we only have the climax, when the bridegroom tells the prospective bride, "Rebecca, take off your gown, you are no longer a bride" (LWF, p. 266). Halfway between the dark Prince of Denmark facing betrayal and murder and the disposed Jewish bride, Freud feels like someone left in the lurch. Yet, he does not despair: in spite of the "collapse" of all his certainties, "the psychological alone has remained untouched" (LWF, p. 266). The psychology of uncertainty remains a fixed touchstone; because Hamlet provided a paradigm for the investigator of the unconscious, Freud soon overcame his initial disappointment and understood that more discoveries lay in wait for him.

Indeed, the first explicit mention of an original theory about Hamlet and Shakespeare's unconscious followed soon after. It was presented to Wilhelm Fliess less than a month later in a very frank letter in which Freud analyzed his sexual desire for his own mother and his jealousy of his father:

> I have found, in my own case too, [the phenomenon of] being in love with my mother and jealous of my father, and I now consider it a universal event in early childhood, even if not so early as in children who have been made hysterical. [...] If this is so, we can understand the gripping power of *Oedipus Rex...* [...] Fleetingly, the thought passed through my head that the same thing might be at the bottom of *Hamlet* as well. I am not thinking of Shakespeare's conscious intention, but believe, rather, that a real event stimulated the poet to his representation, in that his unconscious understood the unconscious of the hero. (LWF, p. 272)

Here is the foundation of Freud's theory of the unconscious: a universal law of repression prohibits the erotic tension linking parents and children of the opposite sex. A personal drama gave birth to the whole idea of the Oedipus complex, which became the keystone of his theory. It is important to note that

---

[2] Sigmund Freud, *The Complete Letters to Wilhelm Fliess (1887–1904)*, p. 265. Hereafter abbreviated as LWF and page number.

the edifice of psychoanalytical concepts is founded on literary texts, from a well-known play by Sophocles to Shakespeare's dark prince. Moreover, we have another key to understand Freud's relation to the authors he reads: he tries to bypass conscious intentions to reach the Unconscious itself. This Unconscious, however, is not, as with Jung, a collective Unconscious. It is particular to one author, hence Freud's recurrent need to find a confirmation of his insights in the author's biography. In this case, Freud acquired his knowledge from Georg Brandes's influential biography of Shakespeare in which he saw that *Hamlet* was composed shortly after the playwright's father had died.

What remains less clear is the link that Freud seems to presuppose between his own hysteria (recently analyzed thanks to the transference with Fliess) and that he thinks he recognizes in the hero of Shakespeare's play: "How does Hamlet the hysteric justify his words, "Thus conscience does make cowards of us all"? How does he explain his irresolution in avenging his father by the murder of his uncle – the same man who sends his courtiers to their death without a scruple and who is positively precipitate in murdering Laertes? How better than through the torment he suffers from the obscure memory that he himself had contemplated the same deed against his father out of passion for his mother, and – "use every man after his desert, and who should 'scape whipping?' "(LWF, pp. 272–273). Freud's untimely "precipitation" appears in the curious mistake he makes by replacing Polonius with Laertes.[3]

It is indeed Ophelia's father who is dispatched with remarkable swiftness and equanimity by Hamlet, whereas he ends up being killed at the end in the fatal duel with Laertes. This belongs to the long series of slips of the pen in which Freud betrays his uncertainty facing male genealogies and may be linked to his particular family structure. Freud's older half-brother was an obvious rival in the affection of his young and attractive mother, who was the second wife of his older father. In the chapter on "Making Mistakes" of *Psychopathology of Everyday Life*, Freud discusses two mistakes on names he had made in *The Interpretation of Dreams*: he had mixed up Hasdrubal and Hamilcar Barca as the father of Hannibal, and he had written that Zeus had castrated his father Kronos, whereas it was Kronos who had castrated his father Uranus.[4] The confusion on Laertes and Polonius is clearly of the same type.

The passage from the letter to Fliess contains the main insight on which Freud's theory of desire will be established; it will be systematized more solidly in *The Interpretation of Dreams*. A section on "typical dreams" devoted to dreams of dead parents develops the implications for psychic life provided by

---

[3] See *Les Revenants de la Mémoire*, pp. 52–54.
[4] Sigmund Freud, *The Psychopathology of Everyday Life*, trans. Anthea Bell, New York, Penguin, 2002, pp. 208–209.

Oedipus Rex. Then a long footnote, already present in the first version of the text, develops the comparison between Sophocles and Shakespeare:

> Another great creation of tragic poetry is rooted in the same soil as *Oedipus the King*: Shakespeare's *Hamlet*. But the change in treatment of the same material reveals the difference in the inner life of these two cultural periods so remote from each other: the advance of repression over the centuries in mankind's emotional life. In *Oedipus* the child's wishful fantasy on which it is based is out in the open and realized – as it is in dreams; in *Hamlet* it remains repressed, and we learn of its existence – as we learn of a neurosis – only through the inhibiting effect it produces.[5]

Shakespeare's play is a universal masterpiece not only because it offers an interesting riddle about murder and revenge, a detective plot for us to decipher, but also because it teaches something fundamental about human sexuality, desire, and the evolution of culture. If we understand *Hamlet*, we can be aware of a deep change or progression in morality and ethics. In this view, the Greeks would be less susceptible to repression than us "moderns," like Hamlet. Oedipus' automatic accomplishment becomes quasi-impossible for Hamlet, and in turn for us. This is why the plot's most obvious feature – the apparently meandering tale of hesitation, procrastination, and sadistic games interrupted by sudden outbursts of violence – can touch a nerve in us all. Freud continues his analysis in the same footnote:

> Hamlet can do anything – except take revenge on the man who removed his father and took the latter's place beside his mother, the man who shows him his own repressed infant wishes realized. The revulsion that should urge him to revenge is thus replaced by self-recrimination, by the scruples of conscience which accuse him of being, quite literally, no better than the sinner he has to punish. I have translated into conscious terms what is bound to remain unconscious in the hero's psyche; if anyone wants to call Hamlet a hysteric, I can only acknowledge that it is an inference my interpretation admits. The sexual revulsion which Hamlet expressed in the dialogue with Ophelia is congruent with it.[6]

Freud has no qualms in discussing the "unconscious" of a character. Literature becomes all the more valuable when it can represent, or stage, the psychic opacity of a given person, whether alive or fictional. Why should Hamlet be called a (male) "hysteric," then? Above all, it is because of his well-known

---

[5] Sigmund Freud, *The Interpretation of Dreams*, trans. Joyce Crick, Oxford, Oxford University Press, 1999, p. 204.
[6] Ibid.

revulsion to sexuality. If his "conscience" conceals the unconscious knowledge of his incestuous desire for his mother, he will be defeated by his own moral awareness: he is no better than his uncle, who at least had the courage to act and achieve the same desire. On the other hand, his sexual coldness facing Ophelia, whom he seems to take pleasure in torturing, his rejection of paternity and begetting, and finally his displacement of aggression from his father/uncle to the feminine pole embodied by Ophelia are, for Freud, typical signs of the hysteric's structure. In a sense, Hamlet is a male version of Dora: he does not grasp the role he is supposed to play in a perverted sexual exchange, and he will precipitate a crisis instead of solving the issue. As Freud notes, in the end, he brings down the punishment on himself, dying in the same way as his father, poisoned by the Oedipal rival, which confirms the identification to the father that marked Dora's symptoms.

Thus Hamlet, both the character and the play, stand for modernity insofar as the treatment of repressed desire is concerned. *Hamlet* finds its most intimate root in the Oedipus complex:

> [T]he changed treatment of the same material reveals the whole difference in the mental life of those two widely separated epochs of civilization: the secular advance of repression in the emotional life of mankind. In *Oedipus* the child's wishful phantasy that underlies it is brought into the open and is actualized as it would be in a dream. In *Hamlet* it remains repressed; and – just as in the case of a neurosis – we only learn of its existence from its inhibiting consequences.[7]

This would remain Freud's thesis for *Hamlet* throughout, even after he changed his mind over the identity of the author. He confided in a bold footnote added in 1930 that he no longer believed that "the man from Stratford" was the author of the plays. As the French humorist Alphonse Allais quipped, Shakespeare never existed. His famous plays had been written by an unknown writer who simply happened to bear the same name. Jorge Luis Borges (we will come back to him later) upped the ante by asserting that Shakespeare was a cultural memory that could be downloaded at will, much as an anonymous Homer was a compendium of myths, tales, and genealogies for the Greeks.[8]

Freud nevertheless returned to *Hamlet* in later years, less in connection with hysteria than with melancholia. In "Mourning and Melancholia" (1915), Hamlet embodies the histrionic self-abasement typical of protracted melancholia. Freud quotes the play in a rather humorous passage:

---

[7] S. Freud, *The Interpretation of Dreams*, trans. James Strachey, New York, Avon Books, 1965, p. 298.
[8] Jorge Luis Borges, "Shakespeare's Memory" in *Collected Fictions*, trans. Andrew Hurley, New York, Penguin, 1998, pp. 508–515.

> When in his exacerbation of self-criticism (the patient) describes himself as petty, egoistic, dishonest, lacking in independence, one whose sole aim has been to hide the weaknesses of his own nature, for all we know it may be that he has come very near to self-knowledge; we only wonder why a man must become ill before he can discover truth of this kind. For there can be no doubt that whosoever holds and expresses to others such an opinion of himself – one that Hamlet harboured of himself and all men /"Use every man after his desert, and who should 'scape whipping" (II, 2)/ – that man is ill, whether he speaks the truth or is more or less unfair to himself.[9]

In this essay, Freud opposed mourning, which is defined as a process through which the lack or absence of the loved object becomes accepted after a certain time. Subjects then invest new objects with libido and melancholia, and therefore become entrenched in their loss, unable to overcome it. Narcissism provides a key, because the melancholic identifies his or her ego with the abandoned or lost object. This steady identification stymies the process and freezes time.

Apart from this important character analysis, if one concentrates on plot and structure, Freud's psychoanalytical thesis does not change. His future biographer, Ernest Jones, gave himself the task to systematize Freud's theory of *Hamlet*. The result was the essay "The Oedipus Complex as an Explanation of Hamlet's Mystery," published in the *American Journal of Psychology* in 1910 and later expanded as a book on *Hamlet and Oedipus*.[10] The 1910 essay had important repercussions for modernists, such as T. S. Eliot and James Joyce, who read it. Joyce owned a German version of the book from 1911 that he bought while in Trieste and had with him when he was preparing lectures on Shakespeare.[11] This suggests how fast Freudian interpretations had spread then.

Jones offered few new ideas in his convenient summary, save the one chapter devoted to "matricide." There he asked whether Hamlet should want to kill his uncle or his mother, whose hurried remarriage hints at her guilt, a guilt akin to "incest" in the language of the time. If "incest" is a perversion shared by Gertrude and Hamlet, albeit with different meanings, then Hamlet's task may be different from the injunction issued by the ghost.[12] Fundamentally, *Hamlet* has to be understood within the structure provided by Sophocles. Oedipus indeed kills his father and sleeps with his mother, while Hamlet dithers and postpones the revenge expected from him. His inhibition stems from

---

[9] S. Freud, "Mourning and Melancholia," in *General Psychological Theory*, pp. 167–168.
[10] Ernest Jones, *Hamlet and Oedipus*, (1949), New York, Doubleday, 1954.
[11] See Richard Ellmann, *The Consciousness of Joyce*, London, Faber, 1977, pp. 54 and 114.
[12] Jones, *Hamlet and Oedipus*, p. 109. Jones refers to Dover Wilson's influential reading of *Hamlet*, J. Dover Wilson, *Hamlet*, 2nd ed. 1936, first entitled *What Happens in Hamlet*, Cambridge, Cambridge University Press, 1959.

his unconscious recognition that his uncle had accomplished before him what he most intensely desires: to kill his father and marry his mother. This theory is posited as a cornerstone of psychoanalytical dogma and should escape any reproach of "psychologization" because it derives from an unconscious structure.

The impatience of Hamlet

A subtle variation on the theme came from a British psychoanalyst Ella Freeman Sharpe. She had been a schoolteacher before being trained in London by James Glover and Hanns Sachs, and had worked on Shakespeare. She remained a visible member of the third group – that is, the psychoanalysts who refused to choose between Melanie Klein and Anna Freud. Her 1929 paper on Hamlet reverses the usual pattern: whereas most commentators insist on the indecision of the hero, she foregrounds his haste and precipitation. Sharpe's provocative thesis is that to describe *Hamlet* as the tragedy of procrastination is misleading. It makes more sense to characterize it as the "tragedy of impatience,"[13] by which she means that, in spite of the protracted denouement of the last act, the main symptom exhibited by the play's eponymous hero is melancholia caused by a failed mourning.

   Indeed, mourning requires time, and melancholia even more time; this period of bereavement is denied to Hamlet and to all the other protagonists, which accounts for the curious accelerations in the plot, the various untimely murders committed by Hamlet, culminating in the final general slaughter. Even then, time is lacking for a proper account because Hamlet finally exclaims:

> Had I but time--as this fell sergeant, death,
> Is strict in his arrest – O, I could tell you –
> But let it be. (V, 2, 314–16)[14]

Hamlet is thus the "tragedy of impatience" (IH, p. 203) even though the plot can be described as a "long drawn-out delay in doing a deed" (IH, p. 203). For Sharpe, the parallels between Ophelia and Hamlet are important, because we see her as mad, whereas we see Hamlet as waging war against madness (IH, p. 208). Ophelia is the feminine side of Hamlet, and the mother is the castrator (IH, p. 209). There are "traps" everywhere; hence castration is lurking under

---

[13] Ella Freeman Sharpe, "The Impatience of Hamlet," in *Collected Papers on Psycho-Analysis*, London, Hogarth Press, 1950, p. 20. Hereafter abbreviated as IH and page number.

[14] I am using the New Cambridge Shakespeare edition of *Hamlet*, ed. Philip Edwards, Cambridge, Cambridge University Press, 1985, p. 240.

every apparently insignificant detail. In a very Kleinian analysis, Sharpe sees "oral frustration, oral impatience and oral sadism" as inseparable (IH, p. 211).

Sharpe resists any direct equation between Shakespeare and Hamlet:

> The poet is not Hamlet. Hamlet is what he might have been if he had not written the play of *Hamlet*. The characters are all introjections thrown out again from his mind. He is the murdered majesty of Denmark, he is the murdered Claudius, he is the Queen, Gertrude, and Ophelia. He is Hamlet. He has killed them and himself by writing the play. (IH, p. 205)

This insight underpinned her subsequent practice. As Sharpe explains in her 1930 lectures "The Technique of Psycho-analysis," Shakespeare's famous play can depict a whole life as a creation: writing on *Hamlet* made her understand that "Hamlet" could only be understood in terms of "Shakespeare."[15] The Elizabethan playwright enacted what every patient probably confronts, an entire life plotted like a play. The analyst will have to begin by saying: "It is all yours. You made the plot, you invented the characters. It is your show, you must be the showman and the stage manager. You must command these creatures, not they you."[16]

Joyce's and Eliot's Hamlet theories

Sharpe's position is similar to that of Joyce, who has his younger alter ego, Stephen Dedalus, expatiate on Shakespeare in one episode of *Ulysses*. Joyce's theory is mostly based on *Hamlet*, because he had noted that the playwright took the part of the ghost in the first performances of the play. With this insight, as well as the loss of Shakespeare's son, Hamnet, who died at the tender age of eleven, Freudian intuitions from the "Viennese school," and theological speculations borrowed from Aquinas, Stephen develops a theory in which Shakespeare becomes both his own grandfather and his own grandson thanks to the act of writing:

> When Rutlandbaconsouthamptonshakespeare or another poet of the same name in the comedy of errors wrote *Hamlet* he was not the father of his own son merely, but, being no more a son, he was and felt himself the father of all his race, the father of his own grandfather, the father of his unborn grandson who, by the same token, was never born.[17]

---

[15] Sharpe, *Collected Papers on Psycho-Analysis*, p. 27.
[16] Ibid.
[17] James Joyce, *Ulysses*, ed. H. W. Gabler, New York, Random House, 1986, p. 171.

One would have to read all of *Ulysses* to see how crucial Joyce's *Hamlet* theory is to his view of literature in general. A dream quoted by Richard Ellmann throws light on the Irish writer's fascination with *Hamlet*:

> At a performance in the theatre
> A newly discovered play by Shakespeare
> Shakespeare is present
> There are two ghosts in the play
> Fear that Lucia may be frightened.

> *Interpretation*: I am perhaps behind this dream. The "new discovery"
> is related to my theory of the ghost in Hamlet and the public sensation
> is related to a possible publication of that theory or of my own play.
> The figure of Shakespeare present in Elizabethan dress is a suggestion
> of fame, his certainly (it is the tercentenary of his death) mine not
> so certainly. The fear for Lucia (herself in little) is fear that either
> subsequent honours or the future development of my mind or art or its
> extravagant excursions into forbidden territory may bring unrest into
> her life.[18]

The date is significant: Joyce had this dream in 1916, during the tercentenary of Shakespeare, as he was writing *Ulysses*. This dream was truly prophetic: Joyce's fame was to rival that of Shakespeare, yet he paid for it dearly when his daughter Lucia began exhibiting signs of dementia during the next decade. Lucia had begun very early to identify with her father, and his increasing fame was hard for her to bear – she had to participate in it, but did not know how. The profusion of her father's gifts slowly pushed her to a joint megalomania. We will see how Jung tried to explain this to her father.

Throughout the years, Joyce kept believing in his own theory about *Hamlet*, much more it seems than his character Stephen Dedalus, who, when confronted by one of his interlocutors, recants and denies his own theory.[19] When Joyce later befriended the French academician Louis Gillet, who had also written on Shakespeare, he kept expounding his *Hamlet* theory, to the point that Gillet thought that it contained the "clue to the book."[20] Here is how Gillet synthesizes Joyce's take on the play:

> Joyce maintained that the true hero in *Hamlet*, the main character, the
> one that dominates everything, was not Hamlet but the Ghost: not
> the living but the Other, not the mortal but the immortal. It was his

[18] Richard Ellmann, *James Joyce*, rev. ed., Oxford, Oxford University Press, 1982, pp. 436–437.
[19] See Joyce, *Ulysses*, p. 175.
[20] Louis Gillet, "The Living Joyce," in *Portraits of the Artist in Exile: Recollections of James Joyce by Europeans*, ed. Willard Potts, Seattle, Wolfhound Press, 1979, p. 191.

> apparition that set the whole drama in motion; it was he who led and
> delayed, controlled and hastened the action (in the sublime scene of
> the Third Act). And his weakling child appeared only as a ghost of the
> Ghost, whose gestures it repeated meekly on earth.[21]

This interpretation owes a lot to Freud's logic, and it manages to combine it
with the symbolist view of the play as the clash between a self-centered hero
who reads "the book of himself," as Mallarmé, quoted by Joyce, wrote, with
the surprising crescendo of murders at the end, in what was a "sumptuous and
stagnant exaggeration of murder."[22]

T. S. Eliot was similarly indebted to Freud's reading. His reference to *Hamlet*
as early as the first drafts of "The Love Song of J. Alfred Prufrock" and his
acquaintance with Freudian concepts confirm this.[23] His essay on *Hamlet* in
the *Sacred Wood* starts from a different question: Is *Hamlet* a good play or
not? Eliot's answer is negative. For him, *Hamlet* fails as a work of art because
Shakespeare attempted to do too much at once: "Shakespeare's *Hamlet*, so far
as it is Shakespeare's, is a play dealing with the effect of a mother's guilt upon
her son; [...] Shakespeare was unable to impose this motive successfully upon
the 'intractable' material of the old play."[24] Unlike Joyce who stressed the paternal lineage in the plot, Eliot theorized that the mother was the key. For him,
the drama positions a perturbed son against his guilty mother: "The essential
emotion of the play is the feeling of a son towards a guilty mother.... Hamlet is
dominated by an emotion which is inexpressible, because it is in excess of the
facts as they appear."[25] He concludes from this emotional excess that the play
is an artistic failure; in fact, it is too "pathological" – a point made by Freud in
an essay on "Psychopathological Characters on Stage," to which I will return.
If we should leave *Hamlet* to the "pathologist," we should not preclude the disclosure of some "unconscious knowledge" in the play.

For Eliot, such excess is blamed as betraying a lack of artistic control:

> The intense feeling, ecstatic or terrible, without an object or exceeding
> its object, is something which every person of sensibility has known; it
> is doubtless a study to pathologists. It often occurs in adolescence: ...
> We must simply admit that here Shakespeare tackled a problem which
> proved too much for him. Why he attempted it at all is an insoluble
> puzzle; under compulsion of what experience he attempted to express

---

[21] Ibid.
[22] Stéphane Mallarmé, *Oeuvres Complètes*, ed. H. Mondor and G. Jean-Aubry, Paris, Gallimard, Pléaide, 1945, p. 1564.
[23] See the poem from 1915 "Suppressed Complex" in *Inventions of the March Hare, Poems 1909–1917*, ed. Christopher Ricks, New York, Harcourt and Brace, 1996, p. 54.
[24] T. S. Eliot, "Hamlet and His Problems," in *The Sacred Wood*, London, Methuen, 1972, p. 98.
[25] Ibid.

the inexpressibly horrible, we cannot ever know…. We should have, finally, to know something which is by hypothesis unknowable, for we assume it to be an experience which, in the manner indicated, exceeded the facts. We should have to understand things which Shakespeare did not understand himself.[26]

Ironically, this is exactly Freud's position, but for Freud, the assessment is positive. Eliot, for his own part, requires that art should sublimate the feelings of ineffable horror on which it is founded. Joseph Conrad had managed this feat in "Heart of Darkness" by putting between Kurtz's awareness of the African "horror" and his British audience the urbane skepticism of a narrator like Marlowe. Eliot's all-too-strong reaction confirms Freud's first insight: Eliot's own hysteria was not triggered but at least was reinforced by his reading of the play. Freud was able to look at it without flinching and to continue interpreting.

Hamlet as the tragedy of desire

Lacan's recently published seminar VI, *Desire and Its Interpretation*,[27] has significantly displaced the usual Freudian reading of *Hamlet* as an Oedipus one removed. This seminar is important because it shows that Lacan had come closer to Melanie Klein, whom he then engaged with and quoted repeatedly. In that British context, he started reading Ella Freeman Sharpe's works, including her various essays on Shakespeare. The impact of the Kleinian school had a determining effect on Lacan's sly subversion of the Freudian model. I will trace this very rich seminar's progression, because it seems that Lacan did not realize that his reading contradicted both classical Freudian canons. Following Ella Sharpe's lead, Lacan stresses the function of haste, hence of time, in elaborating an interpretation.

In the seminar of March 4, 1959, Lacan moves from Ella Sharpe's dream to a famous passage in *The Interpretation of Dreams*, in which Freud mentions a patient who relives his father's death in his dreams shortly after the incident. Freud's dream is summed up as such: "*His father was alive once more and was talking to him in his usual way, but* (the remarkable thing was that) *he had really*

---

26 Eliot, "Hamlet and His Problems," pp. 102–103.
27 Jacques Lacan, *Le Désir et son Interpretation*, ed. Jacques-Alain Miller, Paris, Editions de la Martiniere et la Champ Freudien, 2013. The sections devoted to Hamlet in the Seminar had already been published by Jacques-Alain Miller in *Ornicar*, numbers 24, 25, and 26. The text of *Ornicar* is often significantly at variance from the version of 2013, and I follow the latter. I refer to the French text by S. VI and page number.

died, only he did not know it."[28] To account for the apparent absurdity of the dream, Freud needs to connect it with a "stirring up of the dreamer's earliest infantile impulses against his father" and the idea of emotional ambivalence facing dead people. The full syntax of the unconscious thought of the dream is simply: "[H]e did not know that I wished him to be dead." A dreamer who dreams of his own death and the dreamer who dreams of his father's death have something in common, besides being projections of Freud's psyche. We know how much of the *Interpretation of Dreams* owes to his own father's death. Similarly, as we have seen, Freud's interpretation of *Hamlet* hinges on the fact that Shakespeare wrote the play shortly after his father's death. Shakespeare and Freud are both haunted by the precariousness of the barrier between life and death. They are forced to see the deceased as a potential ghost that attests to the tenacious survival of unconscious desires. Or, as Freud often writes, quoting Horatio, "there needs no ghost, my Lord" to announce the inevitable return of the Unconscious.

Lacan's interpretation focuses on ignorance – the "he did not know" works both for Freud and for Hamlet; however, he does not grudge his admiration for Freud, stating that his approach is "so just, so balanced."[29] Surprisingly, in view of what follows, Lacan promises that he will not move Hamlet from the place in which Freud put him! (S. VI, p. 283). The play revolves indeed on the return of the ghost, which announces the Other in the Unconscious. It is because "the Father did not know that he was dead" that Hamlet will have to discover what the Other cannot know. Lacan thus contrasts the Ghost in *Hamlet*, who knows he is dead, and Oedipus, who "did not know" and whose tragedy originated from his relentless desire to know the truth. Some commentators believe that the incestuous crime of Oedipus was accomplished consciously, as Sophocles's text remains ambiguous about the role of the oracle.[30] In Shakespeare's play, the crime is denounced from the start, but the origin of the denunciation (the ghost betraying the possible damnation of the dead king) is uncertain. Leaving this discussion for later, Lacan focuses on the core of Freud's argument, the idea that Hamlet could not kill Claudius because Claudius is a successful rival. The question is thus not "Why cannot Hamlet act?" but rather "What has happened to Hamlet's desire?" Thus the whole play could be condensed in Hamlet's unspoken request: "Give me my desire back!"

[28] Freud, *The Interpretation of Dreams*, 1965, p. 466. This section was added to the original text later.
[29] Lacan, *Le Désir et son Interpretation*, p. 283.
[30] See Patrick Guyomard, *La jouissance du tragique: Antigone, Lacan et le désir de l'analyste*, Paris, Aubier, 1992.

It is Ophelia, one of the most fascinating creations of Shakespeare, who allows us to catch a glimpse of Hamlet's waxing and waning desire, at least because she has been, at some point, the object of Hamlet's desire. However, she also unleashes in Hamlet a paroxystic expression of his "horror of femininity" (S. VI, p. 292). Then Polonius intervenes as a "wild psychoanalyst" who jumps to hasty conclusions when he believes that Hamlet's melancholia has been triggered by a forbidden love for Ophelia. Lacan jumps to a different conclusion, stating: "Hamlet's act is not Oedipus's act, in so far as Oedipus's act underpins his life and turns him into the hero he was before his downfall, as long as he does not know anything. Hamlet, for his part, is from the start guilty of being. For him being is unbearable" (S. VI, p. 293). Lacan then quotes the "To be or not to be" monologue and goes back to what the Father tells the son when asking for revenge: that he has been killed while a mortal sinner, "Cut off even in the blossom of my sin" (I, 5, 76).

Finally, Lacan highlights the scene of Hamlet about to dispatch Claudius, whom he sees full of remorse after the "play" and lost in his prayers (III, 3, 72–82). Hamlet cannot kill him, because he knows that his own father is either in Hell or in Purgatory. Lacan comments: "The whole *to be or not be* is entirely to be found here. He is concerned with the eternal *to be* of Claudius, and this is why he leaves his sword in its sheath" (S. VI, p. 314). The notion of a being surviving after death announces the concept of a "second death," which will later be taken by Lacan as the key to *Antigone* in the *Ethics of Psychoanalysis*. Antigone is condemned to be buried alive in a tomb – a Greek allegory showing her status as hovering between life and death. In a Christian world, however, the issue is salvation of damnation of the soul.

In *Antigone* as in *Hamlet*, the play's ontology is underpinned by desire. The analysis shifts from being or not being to desiring or not desiring, but desire needs an anchor, a foundation in the Other. Linking a Freudian primal scene and Hamlet's uncertainty facing desire, Lacan continues: "Hamlet explains very clearly that he would like to catch [Claudius] in the excess of his pleasures, that is to say in a rapport with the Queen. The key-point is the desire of the mother" (S. VI, p. 314). Lacan has found his central insight. His formula of "the subject's desire is the desire of the Other" will displace the Freudian thesis.

Thus Lacan revisits critically Freud's central insight that Hamlet presented a modern day version of an older, starker, and more uninhibited Oedipus. A close reading of *Hamlet* – the play and not the character – allows him to hit on a snag in the usual Freudian reading: its reliance on an unexamined and questionable psychology. Lacan saw that Freud's Oedipal model was predicated on a psychological reasoning that could be reversed. Here is what he has to say about the Freudian theory concerning *Hamlet*:

> What does the psychoanalytic tradition tell us? That everything hinges around the desire for the mother, that this desire is repressed, and that this is the cause for which the hero could not approach the act that is requested of him, namely the revenge against a man who is the current possessor, how illegitimate because a criminal, of the maternal object. If he cannot strike the person who has been pointed out for his vindication, it is because he himself has already committed the crime to be avenged. In as much as there is in the background the memory of an infantile desire for the mother, of the Oedipal desire to murder the father, Hamlet would in a sense become an accomplice of the current owner, *beatus possidens*, in his eyes. He could not attack this owner without attacking himself. Is this what they mean? – or he could not attack this possessor without reawakening in himself the old desire, felt as a guilty desire, in a mechanism that one feels everywhere in the play. (S. VI, p. 330)

Lacan pushes his advantage, questioning the pseudo-evidence:

> However, should we remain fascinated by the aura of such a non dialectical scheme? Couldn't we say as well that everything can be reversed? If Hamlet was to jump immediately on his father-in-law, could one not say that he finds in this an opportunity to quench his guilt finding a culprit outside of himself? (S. VI, p. 330).

Quite deliberately, Lacan has punched a hole in Freud's central contention that Hamlet could not kill his uncle as a revenge for his father's murder because Claudius, the "happy owner" (*beatus possidens*) of Gertrude, has enacted his repressed incestuous wishes for his mother. This thesis, for Lacan, is "non-dialectical" because it rests on a psychology of imitation that might lead to different outcomes. Freud's psychologization of the main characters' French triangle (as Joyce would say in *Ulysses*) founded as it is on a commonsensical view, could easily turn into its opposite. It is not a stretch of the imagination to suppose that Hamlet would want to punish a successful and "happy" rival precisely for having achieved what he could not do.

Such a reversal was brought home to Lacan in the thirties when he studied the "mirror stage" and the role of aggression in psychoanalysis. Lacan's shift from a subjective genitive (in which the "mother's desire" means "desire for the mother") to an objective genitive (for which the "mother's desire" is read as "her desire for another man") is a "dialectical" reversal, and it refutes a psychology of mimetic desire that assumes that one cannot punish someone who has acted out one's deepest longings. In this reversal, Hamlet's inhibition is seen to stem from an archaic desire for his mother but not as an object; the mother is truly the source of alterity and desire, a source that will concern Lacan. Hamlet's paralysis ultimately derives from his bafflement facing the riddle of his mother's desire for another man, whether he be an uncle or his father.

To avoid relying an intuitive psychology, Lacan argues that one needs to read the text itself in the original language more carefully and pay attention to recurrent signifiers. One of these signifiers is rather obvious for a psychoanalyst: it is the echo between Ophelia and phallus, which turns into a verbal point of connection, similar to the "Knotenpunkte" repeatedly mentioned by Freud in the *Interpretation of Dreams*.[31] A good psychoanalytical reader will start from such literal signifiers before embarking on a phenomenology of the desiring subject. Hamlet's first failure as a desiring subject is explained by the fact that he questions the very source of desire: Is the ghost telling the truth when his mother may be lying? How would Ophelia be honest if all women can be suspected of sexual treachery? If pondering the source of an Other desire in his own mother is the inevitable solution to the riddle, then the price to pay for a true insight will be nothing less than his own life. Hamlet's progression will make him overcome this earliest object of desire to confront the complex reversals of the phallic object of heterosexual love. Then and only then will he reach an awareness of the place of the Other as determining his desire. Much more than a textual hermeneutics, this complex phenomenology leads to an ethics of difference and desire. Freud's intuitive psychology will be replaced by an ontology of being as desiring being. The subject has to go beyond a first object before reaching an awareness of the place of the big Other that determines desire. Just a little later, Lacan will displace the ontology of desire toward an ethics of desire.

In Lacan's reading, therefore, the key scene of *Hamlet* is not the play within the play. We know of the "mouse-trap," the play composed by Hamlet to catch the "conscience" of Claudius; this reflexive moment in *Hamlet* became crucial for Ella Sharpe. Lacan prefers to foreground the scene that immediately follows, when we see Hamlet alone with his mother and with the ghost of his father. Now, Hamlet may have managed to touch his uncle's feelings in such a way that he seems to repent, but a different scene is played with this mother: this time Hamlet fails to have her repent or experience guilt. It is the famous and harrowing scene (III, 4) in which Hamlet argues both with Gertrude and with the ghost of his father, who may or may not be visible to the audience, and

---

[31] See Sigmund Freud, *Die Traumdeutung*, Studienausgabe II, Frankfurt, Fischer, 1980, pp. 286, 310, 336, 492, 505, 565.

may appear either in battle dress or in night attire, that has posed countless problems to directors. The ghost had said, "O, step between her and her fighting soul" (III, 4, 112), which echoes a previous "between" mentioned by Hamlet in his reply to Ophelia who had said, "You are as good as a chorus." Hamlet had responded: "I could interpret between you and your love if I could see the puppets dallying" (III, 2, 222–224), which calls up his earlier bawdy remark pointing to sexuality as one main site of dereliction: "That's a fair thought to lie between maids' legs" (III, 2, 105).

Here, clearly, Hamlet fails to penetrate this particular "between." Obviously, the recurrent signifiers imply that he has been denied access to the intermediary space that would lead him to an understanding of female sexuality. Thus, he fails with his mother as he fails with Ophelia, and because of these failures, he can assess the lability and the weakness of his own desire. It looks as if Hamlet had reached the limit of his fantasy. He does not know what he wants because his fantasy has abandoned him. Lacan's seminar attempts to sketch a new grammar of fantasy in which the barred subject might learn to link desire with an object that will "cause" it. Such an object would "bite" on him, but also force him to act accordingly.

Following Eliot's remark on the "inexpressibly horrible" aspect of Hamlet's desire, Lacan reopens the issue of Hamlet's dependence on his mother's desire. This is how he sums up his central hypothesis: "[W]hat Hamlet is affronted to, and all the time, what he struggles with, is desire. This desire has to be considered where it is in the play. This desire is quite far from his own. It is not his desire for his mother, it is his mother's desire" (S. VI, p. 332). The key resides in a further decentering of the hero's plight. Just as Eliot performed a curious slip of the pen that made him title his essay "Hamlet and *His* Problems," although he wished to treat the play as a text and not as a psychological documents (having rightly noticed that all commentators tend to project themselves into the hero, Goethe seeing him as a Werther, and Coleridge as Coleridge), Lacan might speak of "Hamlet and *its* problems." Perhaps one should even call Lacan's entire interpretation "*Hamlet* and *her* problems," because *Hamlet* as a play not only articulates how desire and fantasy work together but also shows human desire as determined by the mother's desire. Desire is not to be reduced to fantasy, because fantasy aims at the phallus concealed in the missing, shifting, and elusive *objet petit a*.

Lacan sums up his progression by identifying the big Other, the Locus of the Unconscious, with the Mother – a striking departure from Freud's stubborn patro-centrism: "Our first step … was to express the extent to which the play is dominated by the Mother as Other, i.e., the primordial subject of the demand. The omnipotence of which we are always speaking in psychoanalysis is first of all the omnipotence of the subject of the first demand, and this omnipotence must be related back to the Mother" (S. VI, p. 374).[32] Such maternal omnipotence (as felt by Hamlet) appears clearly in the scene of moral torture in which Hamlet tries to make Gertrude renounce Claudius. It is when Hamlet seems to have won and has forced his mother to confess, "Oh Hamlet, thou hast clef my heart in twain" (III, 4, 157), when Gertrude seems ready to follow his advice ("What shall I do?" III, 4, 181), that he suddenly and violently sends her back to the lover he despises:

> Let the bloat king tempt you again to bed,
> Pinch wanton on your cheek, call you his mouse,
> And let him for a pair of reeky kisses,
> Or paddling in your neck with his damned fingers,
> Make you to ravel all this matter out... (III, 4, 182–187)

Hamlet's previous tone of censorship was marked by restraint until the moment when his discourse collapses and recoils. He has been caught up in the imaginary power of the sexual fantasy. Lacan puts this quite bluntly, as he says that for Hamlet, Gertrude is a "gaping cunt." She thinks only "when one has gone, here comes the other" (S. VI, p. 339). At any rate, it looks as if Hamlet had been overwhelmed by his mother's *jouissance*, an excessive enjoyment of genital lovemaking that he cannot fathom or from which he cannot move her.

A farcical slip of the tongue in the exchange between Hamlet and Claudius at a later point confirms ironically the power that Gertrude has over her son. Hamlet has agreed to leave Denmark with Rosencrantz and Guildenstern and asks:

> **Hamlet**: For England?
> **Claudius**: Ay Hamlet.
> **Hamlet**: Good.
> **Claudius**: So it is if thou knew'st our purposes.
> **Hamlet**: I see a cherub that sees them. But come, for England! Farewell dear mother.
> **Claudius**: Thy loving father, Hamlet.
> **Hamlet**: My mother. Father and mother is man and wife, man and wife is one flesh, and so, my mother. Come, for England. (IV, 3, 44–49)

Is this Hamlet feigning madness in mixing up his Others? Do we see his ruse at work, or is it a simple slip of the tongue, a parapraxis? It is because of the common fantasy among children who believe that their parents have been

---

[32] Jacques Lacan, "Desire and the Interpretation of Desire in Hamlet," in *Literature and Psychoanalysis. The Question of Reading: Otherwise*, ed. Shoshana Felman, Baltimore, Johns Hopkins University Press, 1982, p. 12. Hereafter abbreviated as LP and page number.

"combined," as Jones thinks?[33] Whereas Claudius woodenly and obstinately enacts the consequences of his own speech on fathers (I, 2, 87–117), insisting on a literal gendering of authority, Hamlet's "mad" speech alludes both to Denmark as his "motherland" and to the riddle of an "incestuous" couple whose illicit desire stems from the puzzling mother. The solution will only come from another term in the Freudian equation: the phallus as the signifier both of phallic power and castration.

Ophelia and the phallus

In the logic of the plot, Hamlet retrieves his desire and then acts at the end, when he returns from his voyage and sees Laertes in Ophelia's open tomb. Hamlet cannot stand a rival who expresses mourning better than him; he recaptures his desire and even signs it as he shouts the passionate cry: "This is I, Hamlet the Dane" (V, 1, 223–224). By this time, indeed, Ophelia has become mad and has drowned. Ophelia has fulfilled her role as impossible object of desire when she dies: she literally embodies the phallic overtones of her name and chooses a string of erotic names for the flowers out of which she wove her funeral garland. Ophelia becomes the phallus. Homer used *ophelio* to mean "swell, make bigger" (S. VI, p. 343). The staging of the phallus always hesitates between comedy and tragedy. If the phallus is that part of the body in which "vital tumescence" is symbolized (S. VI, p. 381), then indeed Ophelia's very name condenses this function, while her imaginary role for Hamlet could be evoked in terms of the dire consequences of the sexual act: "[w]hy wouldst thou be a breeder of sinners?" (III, 1, 119).

Ophelia carries a crucial role in the play because she is, as we have seen, Hamlet's first or explicit object of fantasy. She not only is identified with the missing phallus, but also is Hamlet's *objet petit a*, the object which causes desire. However, soon, Hamlet loses any interest in Ophelia even if he confesses that he "did love" her once. She has turned into a mere symbol and will be associated with other images like flowers called "dead men's fingers," to which "liberal shepherds give a grosser name" (IV, 7, 170). Indeed, these "wild orchids" were commonly associated with testicles because of the shape of their roots; or, they were conflated with mandrakes, those roots that sprout where the sperm of a hanged man had fallen. The lush imagery is symbolic; Ophelia has become a phallus that has been expelled by Hamlet as a symbol

---

[33] See Jones, *Hamlet and Oedipus*, p. 113.

of life. One should not forget that at the time of her madness, she intones ribald song-fragments:

> Young men will do't if they come to't--
> By Cock, they are to blame.
> Quoth she, "Before you tumbled me,
> You promised me to wed." (IV, 5, 60–64)

Claudius just asks: "How long has she been thus?" (IV, 5, 66) hinting that a double madness runs in the family.

We see here a variation on Ella Sharpe's thesis about the impatience of Hamlet, but with a major difference. Lacan's analysis of Hamlet's desire has to be inscribed in a symbolic logic underpinned by the Other. Now, for Hamlet, all his actions are determined by "the time of the Other": "Hamlet is always at the hour of the Other" (LP, p. 25). Time following a logic of which Hamlet has no control is another manifestation of his having lost his grip on desire. First, there was the unshakeable desire of his mother, then the time of his revenge scheme eludes him, until he crosses the limit separating life from death. It is only when Hamlet jumps into Ophelia's freshly dug tomb that he can mourn the *objet a*. Then he can escape from the power of his mother's desire and recapture a desire for his lost object – an object not "of desire" but *in* desire" (LP, p. 28). The price to pay will be, as we have seen, his own death, a death that finally allows the expected revenge by answering to the ghostly father's demand. Because of the original "haste" evinced by every protagonist, the dead father has reached the kingdom of the dead with an open wound and an open debt. The father appears as supported by the barred Other; the only hope is that this hole can be closed at the end by a resolution, but it will also mark the triumph of death.

When surveying the last scene of the lethal duel, Lacan notices a special emphasis on the swords used by the fighters. The term Shakespeare uses is "foil" ("Let the foils be brought" V, 2, 155) so as to allow for a pun in Hamlet's mouth: "I'll be your foil, Laertes. In mine ignorance / Your skill shall like a star i' th' darkest night / Stick fiery off indeed" (V, 2, 227–229). While glossing on the prevalence of punning in Shakespeare – which attests to the domination of the signifier over the signified – Lacan surmises that *foil* is derived from *feuille*, and means a material, such as velvet or tinfoil, which was used to set off jewels in a box. Hamlet pretends then that Laertes is a better swordsman and also more handsome than he is. One could conclude that we have come back to a mirror stage in which Hamlet and Laertes are still caught in an imaginary rivalry based on a more overarching deception. This is because the phallus has undergone its last metamorphosis: like a deadly letter completing its circuit, it will unite Hamlet and Laertes, and also the guilty King and innocent Queen: "In this pun there lies ultimately an identification with the mortal phallus." (LP, p. 34) This deadly phallus appears as a way of stopping the hole in the real that has opened for Hamlet when he jumped into Ophelia's tomb.

Thus the hole created by death will appear as identical to the hole left by the letters of literature, to allude to a conceit elaborated by Lacan with Gide, in analysis to which we will return. Such a gaping hole rephrases the gaping hole of the mother's open genitals – a baffling sight that has to be rejected – and allows for the projection of a missing signifier without which desire cannot find its place:

> Just as what is rejected from the symbolic register reappears in the
> real, in the same way the hole in the real that results from loss, sets the
> signifier in motion. This hole provides the place for the projection of the
> missing signifier, which is essential to the structure of the Other. This
> is the signifier whose absence leaves the Other incapable of responding
> to your question, the signifier that can be purchased only with your
> own flesh and your own blood, the signifier that is essentially the veiled
> phallus. (LP, p. 38)

By a neat structural homology, what is revealed by literature has the most momentous consequences for any individual desire. Lacan knew that for the Elizabethans the signifier "will" implied in the repeated question, "What do you want/will?" (or "*Che vuoi?*," which is the Italian sentence by which the devil makes himself known to Cazotte's hero in the *Devil in Love*), was also a coded term referring to the phallus as the organ of generation. The lethal "foil" hides the deadly "will" of the phallus.

The hysterical will to truth

In the end, Lacan ends up reconciling his interpretation with the main tenets of Freudian theory. If *Hamlet* is both the "tragedy of desire" – if desire is shown to fail because of an insufficient mourning – the key consists in the link between mourning and the phallus. Quoting Freud's late text on the "decline of the Oedipus complex" (1924),[34] Lacan shows that the only way for the subject to accept castration and "resolve" the Oedipus complex is to "mourn the phallus": "[T]he Oedipus complex goes into its decline insofar as the subject must mourn the phallus" (LP, p. 46). The phallus as Freud sees it would be

---

[34] Sigmund Freud, "The Passing of the Oedipus-Complex," in *Sexuality and the Psychology of Love*, ed. Philip Rieff, New York, Collier, 1963, pp. 176–182.

determined by the narcissism that the subject is ready – or not – to abandon; in Lacan's terminology, it is less an imaginary object than a "veiled" object that only appears in brief flashes, in sudden "epiphanies" (*phanies*) (LP, p. 48). Then all the elements fall together:

> And doesn't it seem that this is the point around which Hamlet's action turns and lingers? His astounded spirit, so to speak, trembles before something that is utterly unexpected: the phallus is located here in a position that is entirely out of place in terms of its position in the Oedipus complex. Here, the phallus to be struck at is real indeed. And Hamlet always stops. The very source of what makes Hamlet's arm waver at every moment is the narcissistic connection that Freud tells us about in his text on the decline of the Oedipus complex: one cannot strike the phallus, because the phallus, even the real phallus, is a *ghost*. (LP, p. 50)

One cannot kill the phallus because, like Hamlet's king, it is a "thing of nothing." In other words, it exists only because it does not exist. Hamlet is able to desire and kill his rival after he has relinquished all his other narcissistic attachments. *Hamlet* is truly a ghost story: from the dead king to Ophelia, all the main characters of the play, including Gertrude and Hamlet, carry the burden of an immaterial and impossible phallus.

Mortally wounded, knowing that they are going to die, Hamlet and Laertes exchange mutual blessings. They want to prevent future deaths, unlike the situation of *Oedipus*, in which the tragic *Atë* (mischief, ruin) is perpetuated and passed on to the next generation. By positing a Hamlet who is caught up in his mother's desire until he traverses death and the phallus thanks to Ophelia and her sad fate, Lacan has offered an original reading of the play. His approach remains attentive to the interaction of key signifiers while reworking the usual interpretation of the play as a modern rendition of the Oedipus complex.

As Bruce Fink has indicated, Lacan does not interpret *Hamlet* so much as learns from the play.[35] Reading literature, as we have seen, remains a pedagogical process; it inscribes a learning curve for psychoanalysis. When Freud noted that poets had "preceded" him on the terrain of the Unconscious, he also thought that Hamlet was a hysteric. Literature has the positive function to "hystericize" us, forcing us to pose the question of our true desire with a new intensity. We can all identify with Hamlet for two main reasons, as Freud

---

[35] Bruce Fink, "Reading Hamlet with Lacan" in *Lacan, Politics, Aesthetics* ed. Willy Apollon and Richard Feldstein, Albany, SUNY Press, 1996, p. 182. See also Stanley Cavell, "Hamlet's Burden of Proof," in *Disowning Knowledge*, Cambridge, Cambridge University Press, 1987, pp. 179–191, and Julia Reinhard Lupton and Kenneth Reinhard, *After Oedipus: Shakespeare in Psychoanalysis*, Ithaca, Cornell University Press, 1993, pp. 60–118.

generalizes in "Psychopathological Characters on Stage." The protagonist suffers from a universal affliction, because all of us have supposedly been determined, one way or the other, by the Oedipal predicament, and he is not a neurotic before the play begins but becomes a neurotic as the action unfolds.[36] The result of these two factors is that we are hypnotized by the play: "[T]he spectator … is in the grip of his emotions instead of taking stock of what is happening."[37] The situation of the theater is not without evoking the analytic situation: resistance is diminished so that the spectator can let his emotions run their course. The repressed material may even come to our consciousness, in a way that normal life will not allow. The classical catharsis of negative emotions can take place, and we will perhaps share Freud's power as an interpreter: "After all, the conflict in *Hamlet* is so effectively concealed that it was left to me to unearth it."[38]

Freud's pride was justified. He had simply connected, as we saw, the plot of Oedipus with that of *Hamlet*. Was this the only key? Lacan doubted it. There was also the issue of a distance in time and in interpretive abilities. Oedipus had lived his unconscious unconsciously, it seems, whereas Hamlet lived his unconscious consciously.[39] As Heinz Politzer has observed astutely, the root of the problem lies in the term of "conscience." When Hamlet famously states that "[t]hus conscience does make cowards of us all," is he alluding to the sadism of the superego in which, for Freud and Ella Sharpe, the function of morality was condensed, or was he alluding to "consciousness" in the modern sense?

What distinguishes Hamlet from his grand-grandfather Oedipus is that the Greek hero is unable to interpret the signs that surround him. Oedipus needs Tiresias as a sort of detective to ascertain the hidden root of evil, whereas Hamlet combines Oedipus and Tiresias in one person. In Hamlet's case, the hero cannot act for most of the play, but his paralysis results in a series of violent parapraxes, often sanctioned by death. As Joyce wrote: "Khaki Hamlets don't hesitate to shoot," because in the end, "[n]ine lives are taken off for his father's one."[40] Not content with having invented concentration camps, according to Joyce,[41] Hamlet will also scheme, invent a play to set up a trap, feign

---

[36] Sigmund Freud, "Psychopathic Characters on the Stage," *Writings of Art and Literature*, ed. Neil Hertz, Stanford, Stanford University Press, 1997, p. 92.

[37] Ibid.

[38] Ibid.

[39] See Heinz Politzer, *Hatte Oedipus einen Oedipus-komplex?*, Munich, Piper, 1974, and *Freud and Tragedy*, trans. Michael Mitchell, Riverside, Ariadne Press, 2006, p. 25. One will find an intelligent problematization of the "Hamlet doctrine" announced by Nietzsche in Simon Critchley and Jamieson Webster, *Stay Illusion: The Hamlet Doctrine*, New York, Random House, 2013.

[40] Joyce, *Ulysses*, p. 154.

[41] "The bloodboltered shambles in act five is a forerunner of the concentration camp sung by Mr Swinburne." Ibid.

madness, or let himself be carried away by the murderous political psychosis that is rife all around him. Above all, however, he has to interpret words. The world has been replaced by words, which does not rule out guilt and bad conscience, with its "agenbite of inwit," as Stephen Dedalus says. However, when Hamlet asserts, "[t]he rest is silence," rather than leaving us in some sort of ethical awe, he bequeaths us a silence pregnant with meaning to the point that it will never stop speaking to us.

Chapter 2

Literature and fantasy, toward a grammar of the subject

Following Hamlet's structural indecision and strategic postponing, a psychoanalytic reading usually takes into account the time one needs to understand the riddle, a mystery postulated at the core of the text. As we have seen, Hamlet was more impatient than hesitant. So was Freud, especially when he seems to be going too fast in his reading of the famous play. This haste is inevitable for one main reason: literature implies a deferred temporality. This idea was first adumbrated by Freud when discussing short stories by Conrad Ferdinand Meyer, a prominent Swiss writer who also happened to be Wilhelm Fliess's favorite author. Freud wanted to prove to his friend Fliess that one could analyze the "unconscious" not only of people but also of literary characters, thus, he would find illustrations of psychoanalytical concepts in popular fiction. He wrote to Fliess: "I am reading C. F. Meyer with great pleasure. In *Gustav Adolf's Page* I found the idea of deferred action twice: in the famous passage you discovered, the one with the slumbering kiss, and in the episode involving the Jesuit, who insinuates himself as little Christine's teacher" (LWF, p. 316). This very letter was to introduce a key concept for psychoanalysis.

Deferred action

Freud's letter provides the first example of applied psychoanalysis, which derives from intense discussions about literature between Fliess and Freud. The concept of *Nachträglichkeit*, or "deferred action" – that is, the belated perception of an effect generated by a repressed trauma – operates remarkably in the tale. The plot of this historical novella is complex; the scene takes place in 1632, at the height of the Thirty Years War. The Protestant king of Sweden, Gustav-Adolf, is waging war on the Catholic forces of Wallenstein, who serve the Holy Roman emperor in the part of Germany controlled by the Habsburgs. The war, after an initial success, is not going well for Gustav-Adolf, who needs a new page because the previous ones have been killed in action. Thinking that he is doing him a favor, Gustav-Adolf asks the rich German merchant Leubelfing to send his son. Neither the merchant nor the son is enthusiastic at the honorable but dangerous prospect. However, their young cousin Gürtel, a girl who acts like a wild tomboy, happens to be in love with the king and thus volunteers to be the next page. She disguises herself as Gus, a boy page, and gives entire satisfaction to the king. Then, two parallel incidents threaten to expose her ruse. There is the discovery of the Slavonic mistress of duke Lauenburg, a noble man in their camp, who is married to one of Gustav-Adolf's cousins. She almost blows Gus's cover when she guesses that Gus is a woman. The other threat comes from an incident pairing the king's daughter, Christel, and a Jesuit who, disguised, had attempted to convert her to Catholicism secretly. When he discovers the plot, Gustav-Adolf is disgusted by such treachery but magnanimously decides not to kill the Jesuit. However, the Catholic Slavonic girl commits suicide in front of the king and the page, which triggers Lauenburg's bitter enmity for Gus and the king. Further tensions mount in the Swedish camp, and the page feels that she will be found out, so she rides away. She is rescued by an old colonel who reveals to her that when she was a young child, she had been kissed by the king. The page returns to the camp before the final battle at the end of which the king Gustav-Adolf is killed. A severely wounded page carries the king's body back. As the page dies, she reveals to the court and her family members that it was Lauenburg who had shot king Gustav-Adolf.

Freud finds in this historical melodrama two points of interest. There is first the idea that Gürtel/Gus has fallen in love with the king because of an ancient, quasi-archaic, seduction. The young woman had forgotten that as a child she was often kissed by Gustav-Adolf; nevertheless, this encounter later determined her wish to work for him as a page. Then there is the plot of the Jesuit who was hiding his religious mission, in the same way as she was hiding her gender. Freud knew that the whole plot was based on historical facts, because he adds: "In Innsbruck they actually show the chapel where she converted to Catholicism!" (LWF, p. 316). In both cases, an act of primary seduction (the king's kiss, the Jesuit's religious indoctrination) will have been forgotten only to take full effect much later. This illustrates Freud's doctrine of *Nachträglichkeit* – that is, the retroactive comprehension of a traumatic event that had remained unperceived or the deferred effect of a childhood trauma.

This term became central for Jean Laplanche, who devoted a whole seminar to it. The wording of how the colonel reveals Gus's forgotten seduction – what Freud calls "a famous passage" – is notable. The colonel states: "Kisses like that can sleep and then burst into flame when lips are fuller and more ready for them. You know, don't you, that the king took you out of my arms more than once? Cousin, he used to tickle you and kiss you with a great big smacking sound. You were a pretty lively and pretty baby."[1] Not knowing how to answer the colonel, Gürtel/Gus only blushes silently. Laplanche comments on the passage of the kiss in those terms: "There is here the pattern of a time-bomb. . . . The action has a mechanical unfolding, nothing can prevent or go against dialectically with the arrow of time going from past to present."[2] The ancient sexual excitation left by the adult's kiss on the baby's lips has left a crypted message, whose meaning will only be deciphered later, with the progression of sexual development. Although the idea was not discovered by Freud just then, because he had elaborated it in his study of hysterical repression, *Project for a Scientific Psychology* (1895), this is when he coins the expression. Having coined the term, he eagerly looks for its instantiations in the fiction he reads at the time.

One might say that the entire status of literature can be defined according to a type of *Nachträglichkeit*, a deferred action that introduces a recursive temporality. Literature is not the immediate jotting down of everyday events, but rather a staged delay. Such a delay is needed to understand, shape, process, and finally reflect on experience. The vexed question arises of whether *Dichtung* (literary creation) can accommodate *Wahrheit* (truth), to go back to Goethe's dichotomy. Discussing a text by Goethe in which the famous author reports a childhood prank that looks perfectly innocent, albeit somewhat naughty, Freud shows that the young genius was expressing his considerable annoyance at having siblings. The forceful expulsion of breakable objects – the pretext for Goethe's tale – is a metaphor for his wish to get rid of a new brother or sister.[3] Hence the *Dichter* (the poet) cannot display any "innocent" fantasy. Even Goethe will have to reckon with the *Richter* (the judge), whose gender may also be feminine.

The following letter to Fliess completes these insights when Freud delivers a detailed analysis of another story by Meyer, "Die Richterin." This too is a historical tale, set this time in the year 800, at the time of the coronation of Charlemagne. The action takes place in the mountains of Switzerland, where the hero, Wulfrin, the son of a dead count, returns to the castle managed by his father's former wife, Stemma, who is a reputed and charismatic judge. He has grounds to be suspicious of her and of her daughter, Palma, with whom he nevertheless falls in love quickly. We learn at the end that Stemma indeed killed the count. However, Wulfrin falls under the charm of her young daughter whom

---

[1] Conrad Ferdinand Meyer, "Gustav Adolf's Page," in *Complete Narrative Prose*, vol. II, trans. David B. Dickens, Lewisburg, Bucknell University Press, 1976, p. 57.

[2] Jean Laplanche, *Problématiques VI, L'après-Coup*, Paris, Presses Universitaires de France, 2006, p. 115.

[3] Sigmund Freud, "A Childhood Recollection from *Dichtung und Wahrheit*," in *Writings on Art and Literature*, pp. 182–192.

he considers as a sister. Sexual tension mounts steadily to his dismay until he screams openly: "I desire my sister."[4] The resolution comes when Stemma decides to atone for her past deed and becomes her own *Richterin*, indeed. As a female judge, she sets things straight: she accuses herself publicly and drinks the poison with which she had killed the evil count. Charlemagne, who is present, then accepts the marriage of Wulfrin with his half-sister: it is declared legal because they are not technically brother and sister.

Freud's lengthy commentary highlights the psychopathological elements of a plot dominated by incest:

> There is no doubt that this has to do with a poetic defense against the memory of a (sexual) affair with the sister. Strange, though, that this (defense) proceeds *exactly* as it does in neurosis. All neurotics create the so-called family romance (which becomes conscious in paranoia); it serves on the one hand the need for self-aggrandizement and on the other as a defense against incest. (LWF, p. 317)

He concludes: "Parental quarrels provide the most fruitful material for the romances of childhood. Resentment against the mother is expressed in the novel by turning her into a stepmother. Thus, in every single feature it is identical with the romances of revenge and exoneration which my hysterics, if they are boys, invent about their mothers" (LWF, p. 318). We catch Freud developing the thesis of the "family romances" of neurotics, especially those who wish to rewrite history. If a boy falls in love with his sister, the best solution is to construct a fantasy or a legend according to which she is not his sister: "If the sister is not one's mother's child, one is relieved of all blame" (LWF, p. 317).

This formulation describes adequately the twisted argument in the plot of "The Judge." The tale pairs Stemma, the strong woman who has usurped her dead husband's rights and privileges, and her lower servant, Faustina, who confesses very early on that she, too, has poisoned her husband. Stemma rejects her entreaties to be condemned to death and shows surprising clemency. In the end, both women confess similar murders, both die poisoned side by side. Noticing this somewhat clumsy literary construction, Freud praises it as symptomatic. He thus makes an important point about repetition: "In all analyses one therefore hears the same story twice: once as a fantasy about the mother; the second time as a real memory of the maid. This explains why in *Die Richterin* – who is in fact the mother – the same story appears twice without changes, a composition one would scarcely regard as a good literary accomplishment" (LWF, p. 317). The novel, by which he means Meyer's stories, and the "romances," by which he means the fantasies spun together in

---

[4] Meyer, "The Judge," in *Complete Narrative Prose*, p. 208.

some coherent but delusional plot by the neurotics, all obey the same logic. Repetition and fantasy combine to produce a certain type of subjectivity.

Family romances and daydreaming

Freud's 1909 essay on "Family Romances" (literally, the family novel, "Der Familienroman der Neurotiker") was written as a preface to Otto Rank's *The Myth of the Birth of the Hero*. This text opposes fantasies, daydreams, and "neurotic novels," which all revolve on projections of unconscious desires. One will dream of being the king's son or of coming from higher social backgrounds. However, this does not constitute a debasement of the real parents. On the contrary, as Freud notes at the end,[5] such grandiose delusions only return to a prior stage, when the father and mother were idolized. The fantasy returns them to the grandeur they lost when the child grew up. All novels could take as their title what Freud later discovered when he became interested in the works of Josef Popper-Lynkeus: *Fantasies of a Realist*.[6] Popper-Lynkeus had published *Phantasien eines Realisten* in 1899; this collection of short vignettes and prose meditations covers exactly the same ground as Freud's *Interpretation of Dreams*, as he became aware only later: Popper postulated that dreams have a meaning and that fantasies all contain an element of truth. Their strangeness derives from repression and censorship.

We should wonder what is meant by "fantasy"; another essay entitled "The Poet and Day-dreaming" (1907) will help. Freud describes children who are seriously engaged in playing, and daydreamers ensconced in their private images; for both, this is a serious activity: "The opposite of play is not serious-ness – it is reality. For all the emotion it is charged with, the child is well able to distinguish his world of play from reality and likes to connect the objects and situations he imagines to palpable and visible things in the real world. This link alone distinguishes the child's 'play' from 'fantasizing.'"[7] Freud shows that the writers of popular fiction find a way to go back to these states. Those writers create heroes with whom we immediately identify. We can identify all the more with the figure of the hero because, despite all the dangers braved, "nothing can happen to you!" To reach this insight, Freud quotes a popular author from his childhood, Ludwig Anzengruber, whose hero, Steinklopferhanns, is repeatedly

---

[5] Sigmund Freud, "Family Romances," in *The Uncanny*, trans. David Mclintock, London, Penguin, 2003, p. 40.

[6] See "My contact with Josef Popper-Lynkeus" (1932), in *Collected Papers*, vol. 5, ed. James Strachey, New York, Basic Books, 1959, p. 299.

[7] "The Creative Writer and Daydreaming," in Sigmund Freud, *The Uncanny*, p. 26. Hereafter abbreviated as CWD and page number.

told, "*Es kann dir nix g'schehen.*" Such a mark of invulnerability betrays "His Majesty the Ego, the hero of every daydream and every novel" (CWD, p. 30). Here, Freud seems to use indiscriminately "fantasy" and "daydream," although he provides a clear genealogy of fantasy. "Daydream" is a useful term because it establishes a bridge between nocturnal dreams and fantasies.

There is a specific temporality of fantasies, capable of knotting together capricious and captious networks of images and of weaving an oneiric tapestry, as it were, in which past, present, and future are interwoven.

> One could say that a fantasy hovers, as it were, between the three periods involved in our ideation. The subject's mental activity attaches itself to a current impression, an occasion in the present that has succeeded in arousing one of his major desires. From here it harks back to the memory of an earlier experience, usually belonging to his childhood, in which this desire was fulfilled. It now invents a situation, lodged in the future, that represents the fulfillment of this desire. This is the daydream or the fantasy, which has its origin in present experience and the recollection of the past: so that past, present and future are strung together on the tread of one desire that unites all three. (CWD, pp. 28–29)

This is why we need literature to be aware of the impact of *Nachträglichkeit* on our lives. Another novel by Meyer brings this home to Freud, who calls it his "most beautiful" creation. It is *The Monk's Wedding*, a gothic fantasy from 1884 that became a best seller thanks to its mixture of gore, pathos, and medievalism. It ends with the corpses of the monk Astorre killed by a friend and his would-be wife killed by the noble Diana.[8] The monk has been punished for his hubris and will be buried by Ezzelino, the tyrant of Padua, who inscribes their names in a tombstone.

A remarkable framing device is that the story is narrated by Dante, then in exile from Florence, to famous friends in Verona such as Can Grande. Dante, who saw the tombstone before, tells the sad story, thinking no doubt that he will use these characters in his *Commedia*. Freud comments on the reversible temporality of fantasy and takes the novella as an example:

> "The Marriage of the Monk" illustrates the process occurring in later years in the formation of fantasies – a new experience is in fantasy projected back into the past so that the new persons become aligned with the old ones, who become their prototypes. The mirror image of the present is seen in a fantasied past, which then prophetically becomes the present. (LWF, p. 320)

[8] Meyer, "The Marriage of the Monk," in *Complete Narrative Prose*, pp. 167–168.

Importantly, the monk, who technically should not marry, is pushed to this foolish action by various factors and remains a *brother*. Thus the fantasy of the author would be "a *frater* like me should not marry lest my childhood love take its revenge on my wife later on" (LWF, p. 320). As Freud writes in a later letter, the lessons drawn from the historical novels of Conrad Ferdinand Meyer have little to do with style, novelistic technique, or the depth of the imagination. What they achieve, however, is to present us "man with all his contradictions" (LWF, p. 346),[9] which is a sufficient.

Popular fiction functions mostly at the level of daydreaming by pandering to our most childish fantasies: if all the women fall in love with the hero in a totally unrealistic manner, we are flattered as if this happened to us. The difference between day- or night-dreamers on the one hand and novelists on the other lies in a sense of participation. We are generally bored or disgusted by the narratives of other people's intimate images or private fantasies. Freud wonders why fictional narratives, on the other hand, can provide such pleasure:

> How the writer achieves this is his most intimate secret; the true *ars poetica* lies in the technique by which he overcomes our repulsion, which certainly has to do with the barriers that arise between each single ego and the others. We can make a guess at two of the means used by this technique: the writer tones down the character of the egoistic daydream by modifying and disguising it, and bribes us with the purely formal – that is aesthetic – bonus of pleasure that he offers us in the way he presents his fantasies. (CWD, p. 33)[10]

Freud's theory of literature has been called reductive, yet his insight, although brutal, is powerful: the aesthetic function of art is a means to an end. It consists in overcoming the barriers that separate one *ego* from all others. The ultimate aim of literature is to release a deeper fantasy that can be shared by all.

Here, art is not simply reduced to a bribe or bonus; its "incitement premium" (*Verlockungsprämie*) provides a "fore-pleasure" (*Vorlust*) before any further ego trip can begin. What Freud states dispassionately and scientifically has been asserted with more pathos, violence, and negativity by Kafka just a few years before:

> I think we ought to read only the kind of books that wound and stab us. If the book we are reading doesn't wake us up with a blow on the head, what are we reading it for? … we need the books that affect us like a

---

[9] Freud quotes lines by Meyer: "Ich bin kein ausgeklügelt Buch, / Ich bin ein Mensch mit seinem Widerspruch." They are part of an epigraph to the poem *Hutten's letzten Tage* and may be translated as, "I am not an ingenious book, / I am a contradictory man."

[10] See also Sigmund Freud, "Der Dichter und das Phantasieren," *Studienausgabe X. Bildende Kunst and Literatur*, Frankfurt, Fischer, 1970, p. 179.

disaster, that grieve us deeply, like the death of someone we loved more than ourselves, like being banished into forests far from everyone, like a suicide. A book must be the axe for the frozen sea inside us.[11]

I will return to Kafka in the next chapter. Beyond all the metaphors, whether economical or geologic, the main point, for Kafka as for Freud, is the ability to share apparently ineffable and private fantasies.

Pleasure and displeasure

The theory of a "fore-pleasure" that sets literature in motion would hold true for the joke-work as well. As Freud explains in his *The Joke and Its Relation to the Unconscious*, the "form" of a joke is its ability to condense in few words a complex knot of affects, whether erotic or aggressive, and the pleasure elicited derives from the perception of a certain economy.[12] Freud's anatomy of the joke-work is too complex to be analyzed here; I want simply to point to the presence of a certain "formalism" in Freud's consideration of literature, insofar as his goal is to give a shape to universal fantasies. These fantasies are regrouped, organized, and regulated by a grammar of the cultural unconscious. To understand this better, I will return to Shakespeare, read by Freud on the "theme of the three caskets."

This short essay illustrates all the strengths and the weaknesses of Freud's method. It begins with a simple superposition. Two scenes seem to echo each other: one from *The Merchant of Venice* in which we see the suitors of Portia having to choose between three caskets, one in gold, one in silver, one in lead, and the other from *King Lear* who divides his kingdom between his three daughters, Goneril, Regan, and Cordelia. Each time the right choice is for the most humble, inconspicuous, unremarkable object or person. There are huge differences: Bassiano chooses the lead casket, and wins, whereas Cordelia is the mute and modest daughter who first loses her father's love. Freud adds to these two groups of three a series of motifs coming from folklore and comparative religion, including the judgment of Paris, Grimm's tale of the "Twelve Brothers," and "The Six Swans," and establishes a series of bold parallels and equations. Lead is the color of death, and silence its main manifestation.

---

[11] Franz Kafka's letter to Oskar Pollak, *Letters to Friends, Family and Editors*, trans. Richard and Clara Winston, New York, Schocken, 1977, p. 16.

[12] Freud, *The Joke and Its Relation to the Unconscious*, pp. 33–34. It is noteworthy that Freud gives the example of Hamlet's "joke" at the expense of his mother and uncle – "The funeral baked meats / Did coldly furnish forth the marriage tables" (I, ii, 180–181) – as a sign of verbal and psychic "economy" implied by wit.

Cordelia turns into the goddess of Death while the three sisters, taken together, are identified with the Fates: Lachesis, Clotho, and Atropos.[13]

A first objection can be raised: Why would one want to choose death as a bride? Freud's logic of the unconscious rolls on, unperturbed: "However, contradictions of a certain kind – replacement by the precise opposite – offer no serious difficulty to the work of analytic interpretation. We shall not appeal here to the fact that contraries are so often represented by one and the same element in the modes of expression used by the unconscious, as for instance in dreams" (TC, p. 118). The principle discovered in dreams echoes the idea developed in "Antithetical Meanings of Primal Words":[14] the fundamental ambivalence of primary images and their antithetical meanings (we can think of "host" or "to cleave" in English) generates semantic undecidability – that is, the impossibility of choosing between opposites; in turn, this requires a principle of equivalence or compensation.

Human imagination invented the goddess of Love, whereas Death (with its attendant goddess) had been perceived as an ineluctable limit: "[T]he replacements by a wishful opposite in our theme harks back to a primaeval identity" (TC, p. 118). The claims made for fantasy become enormous: "Choice stands in the place of necessity, of destiny. In this way man overcomes death, which he has recognized intellectually. No greater triumph of wish-fulfillment is conceivable" (TC, p. 119). This sketches a whole ethics of fantasy: man makes a choice, an unconscious choice to be sure, to replace Death with Love. The figure of horror is replaced, on its very site, by the most alluring figure of love and desire. However, the replacement is not always achieved smoothly – the fairest woman who replaces the goddess of Death keeps an intimate connection with the uncanny. It was precisely this uncertain border that allowed Freud to guess the nature of the reversal. In Apuleius's story, Psyche maintains a privileged link with death: her wedding is a funeral, and she descends into Hades. I will develop the theme of the Uncanny in the next chapter, noting simply that the uncanny prevents a too neat reversal of the contraries.

Finally, when it seems that Freud asserts the power of human fantasy to promise a future life geared to Love, the ending of *King Lear* suddenly makes him veer in the opposite direction. By a curiously counterintuitive inversion, Freud transforms the moving scene in which Lear walks carrying the body of Cordelia in his arms into its opposite – in fact, the goddess of Death carries him. Freud's prose waxes lyrical in this superb evocation: "Cordelia is Death.... She is the Death-goddess who, like the Valkyrie in German mythology, carries

[13] Sigmund Freud, "The Theme of the Three Caskets," in *Writings on Art and Literature*, ed. Neil Hertz, Stanford, Stanford University Press, 1997, pp. 109–121.p. 117. Hereafter, TC and page number.

[14] See *Writings on Art and Literature*, pp. 94–100.

away the dead hero from the battlefield. Eternal wisdom, clothed in the primaeval myth, bids the old man renounce love, choose death and make friends with the necessity of dying" (TC, p. 120). One may find this recreation of the scene fanciful, because it is Lear who carries her corpse, uttering the famous "Never, never, never, never, never!" and then dies immediately after. For Freud, Cordelia has turned into Mother Earth, and the three feminine figures embody one after the other the woman who gives birth, the woman who mates, and the woman who destroys. Freud still believes in the power of myth and does not trust human fantasy fully. It will take Adorno and Horkheimer to oppose myth radically in *Dialectic of the Enlightenment* – with Odysseus triumphing over the Sirens and leaving Hades alive, the endless resources of human cunning manage to defeat the ancient power of myth, thus undoing even the repetition of Death. Because the world of myth is characterized by ritualistic repetition, Death inhabits it as a hyperbolic condensation of the repetition compulsion. However, Freud will express the hope that this repetition compulsion can be defeated.[15]

The grammar of fantasy

This new development takes place after World War I, when the edifice of a new metapsychology is in place, which allows Freud to explore new points of view. It is to this period that Freud's latest elaboration of fantasy belongs. This is the essay on "A Child Is Being Beaten" (1919) in which we see the complexity of interrelated themes. The ostensible aim of this paper is to provide a "contribution to the understanding of the origin of sexual perversion," which is its subtitle, but it provides more readily a new grammar of fantasy. Condensing the accounts of more than six patients (four women and two men) who had a similar fantasy – a child was being beaten on his naked bottom, which produced intense sexual excitement – Freud shows that the fantasy can be decomposed into three successive stages. There is first the figure of the child who fantasizes about possessing the father's exclusive love. The child's fantasy is that the father beats another child who is hated by the subject. In this figure, the father beats the rival of the child, which generates pleasure because it confirms the incestuous father-child link. In the second figure, the subject is in the position of the beaten child, which corresponds to a masochistic enjoyment of the humiliation felt. In the third figure, the father is replaced with any authority figure, and the beaten child is an anonymous and male third party. In this sadistic

---

[15] I have discussed this in *Crimes of the Future*, New York, Bloomsbury, 2014 , pp. 125–147.

variation, the subject is sexually excited by the vision of a child or children being beaten. This last fantasy is more autoerotic, a conscious daydream.

The sequence of sentences making up the fantasy (*Phantasievorstellung*,[16] literally the "representation of fantasy") is as follows:

1. "The father is beating the child;"
2. "I am being beaten by the father;"
3. "I am watching little boys being beaten by an adult."[17]

When it would seem that (1) and (3) are almost identical, in fact, they correspond to very different positions. The first figure dates from the full-blown expression of the Oedipus complex, and the image of the father beating other children asserts that the subject is fully one with the father (or mother.) Here, beating means rejecting the extra sibling or unnamed rivals. The second figure usually takes place after the huge repression of sexuality has begun – that is, when the subject is closer to three or four years old. Then, a passive attitude dominates, with the experience of guilt linked to the repressed sexual content of the earlier stage; hence, in this figure, to be beaten means to be loved. The beating gesture is a regressive substitute for the hoped for Oedipal fusion in the first moment. In the third moment, we are back to an active role, but the fact that for men and women the child has to be male corresponds to an onset of perversion. Women who have the fantasy imagine themselves as boys, hence they project this sadistic activity on boys; for men, what counts is the anonymous feature, because it is any number of boys who are beaten up, and the perpetrator varies, shifting from the position of paternal substitute to that of any person who can embody the law. What counts then is the masturbatory activity triggered by the fantasy, and the old Oedipal content is at a further distance.

What makes these fantasies true fantasies is that the subjects did not enjoy watching children being actually beaten. Moreover, they themselves had not been beaten regularly by their parents, and one cannot argue that they repeated a trauma: "Being present at real scenes of beating in school provoked a curiously excited, probably mixed feeling in which opposition probably played a large part. In some cases the real experience of beating scenes was felt to be unbearable."[18] This is a point that Lacan has developed in his seminars – namely that a fantasy should always be marked by a detail that proves that it is not real. Slavoj Žižek has analyzed this with great finesse when he argues for an

[16] Sigmund Freud, "Ein Kind wird geschlagen," in *Studienausgabe VII, Zwang, Paranoia und Perversion*, Frankfurt, Fischer, 1973, p. 251.
[17] Freud, "A Child is Being Beaten," in *The Psychology of Love*, pp. 287–288.
[18] Ibid., p. 282.

"ethic of fantasy" at the conclusion of *Looking Awry*. Drawing on a short story by Patricia Highsmith, "The Stuff of Madness," the well-known film *Letter from an Unknown Woman*, and Mitchum's decision to cut a knuckle of his finger to apologize to a Japanese gangster whose wife he has seduced unaware of her status in the film *Yakuza*, Žižek combines two motives that are already in Freud: a fantasy is what makes us different from the others; it is our particular absolute, and yet the tendency is great to reject the other's fantasy as trifling and obnoxious. He concludes thus:

> Fantasy as a "make-believe" masking a flaw, an inconsistency in the symbolic order, is always particular – its particularity is absolute, it resists "mediation," it cannot be made part of a larger, universal, symbolic mediation. For this reason, we can acquire a sense of the dignity of another's fantasy only by assuming a kind of distance toward our own, by experiencing the ultimate contingency of fantasy as such, by apprehending it as the way everyone, in a manner proper to each, conceals the impasse of his desire. The dignity of a fantasy consists in this very "illusionary," fragile, helpless character.[19]

In other essays, Žižek insists on the political function of fantasy, because ideology in a Marxist sense relies on basic human fantasies and because any ideology critique will have to deconstruct the fantasmatic root of identifications. This is indeed what Roland Barthes accomplished in the fifties when he analyzed what he called "mythologies" – namely, the stuff of political oratory, of publicity advertisements and everyday beliefs, all tapping in our innate desire to trust a "nature" or an "essence." Thus we will buy one type of soap because we think it kills the detested germs, whereas we choose another because we hope that it will rejuvenate our skin.[20] As Žižek has argued, fantasy creates a "multitude of subject-positions," and even in the crudest of cases, as in pornographic films, it is not always with the active man on top that we identify.[21]

What remains to be ascertained in this "grammar of fantasy" is how to analyze the place of the subject. We have seen with Freud how labile the links between subject and verb can be. One can distinguish between a primary fantasy, always unconscious, and a secondary fantasy that can be brought to the psychoanalyst. The next example is the case mentioned by Freud of a man who had nursed his father through a long and lethal illness. In the months

---

[19] Slavoj Žižek, *Looking Awry: An Introduction to Jacques Lacan through Popular Culture*, Cambridge, M.I.T. Press, 1991, pp. 156–157.

[20] Roland Barthes, *Mythologies*, new translation by Richard Howard and Annette Lavers, New York, Hill and Wang, 2012, pp. 32–34.

[21] Slavoj Žižek, "Fantasy as a Political Category," in *The Zizek Reader*, ed. Elizabeth Wright and Edmond Wright, Oxford, Blackwell, 1999, p. 92.

following his father's death, the patient had a recurrent dream. In the dream, his father was alive once more and talking to him as usual; however, the patient found it excessively painful that the father was dead and yet did not know it.[22] Freud has no difficulty in completing the sentence that makes up the thought of the dream: what the father does not know is that the son has wished his death to bring a release. This wish derives from the primary fantasy generated at the time of the Oedipal death wish, subsequently repressed and erased.

Whether the fantasy is conscious or unconscious, it always posits a subject, even if this subject is an empty space. One can see this best in Samuel Beckett's play *Not I* in which a woman can talk about her deepest fears and obsessions only if she never uses the pronoun "I." In a similar manner, Christine Brooke-Rose, an experimental British novelist, decided that she could write her auto-biography only because she had found that it would be difficult to speak of herself in the third person – the constraint freed her, whereas before the free-dom to write "I" had had an inhibiting effect, which is how she wrote a witty and fascinating autobiography in the third person, entitled *Remake*.[23]

Fantasy and the Beckettian models for the unconscious

To show the relevance of this discussion to literature, I will take a literary example by analyzing briefly the function of fantasy in Beckett's work. Treating Beckett is justified because, among many reasons, he always displayed respect for other people's fantasies. His real-life experience with psychoanalysis fur-thermore grounds the application of psychoanalytic models to his work. Beckett resorted to psychoanalysis while he was in London and worked for two years with Wilfred Ruprecht Bion at the Tavistock clinic, beginning after Christmas 1933. Beckett suffered from severe anxiety attacks, and the cure greatly helped. It also helped resolve his writer's block.[24] Although a lot has been written on the topic, I want to restrict myself to the examination of Beckett's specific grammar of fantasy.

A first model that can be used productively to talk about Beckett's general attitude facing fantasy is that of Winnicott. This analysis has been done com-petently by Ciaran Ross, whose main source of inspiration was the French

---

[22] Sigmund Freud, "Formulierung über die zwei Prinzipien des psychischen Geschehens," *Studienausgabe III, Psychologie des Unbewussten*, Frankfurt, Fischer, 1982, p. 24. This dream was added to the *Interpretation of Dreams* in 1911; see *Interpretation of Dreams*, New York, Avon Books, 1998, p. 466.

[23] Christine Brooke-Rose, *Remake*, Manchester, Carcanet, 1996.

[24] See James Knowlson, *Damned to Fame: The Life of Samuel Beckett*, New York, Simon and Schuster, 1996, pp. 168–174.

psychoanalyst Didier Anzieu; Anzieu was himself obsessed with Beckett as a psychoanalyst and wrote several books on this topic. What triggered Ross's investigation was the manner in which Beckett interrupted the writing of the "trilogy" of *Molloy, Malone Dies* and *The Unnamable* to dash off *Waiting for Godot*. It was clear to Beckett that the oppressive meta-textuality that he was exploring in these French novels did not leave him enough space in which to breath and dream. With *Godot*, Beckett could explore a "transitional space" in which the simplest object, be it a carrot, a shoe, or a tree with a few leaves, acquires a double status: prop and allegory – a clown's decoys or symbols of finitude – neither fully one nor the other. I can only point to Ross's excellent theoretical recapitulation of the main tenets of Melanie Klein, W. R. Bion, and D. Winnicott, because he has masterfully shown how they apply to Beckett's theater.[25] One could even add that transitional objects can be relayed by transitional subjects. This is what Beckett himself deftly characterized as the "pseudo-couple." The first pseudo-couple to appear was in a novel written directly in French, *Mercier and Camier*, who are called "pseudo-couple" in *The Unnamable*, whose narrator sees two men appearing and then disappearing, adding: "I naturally thought of the pseudo-couple Mercier-Camier."[26]

The most famous "pseudo-couple" is of course Didi and Gogo. Beckett wrote *Waiting for Godot* as a diversion from the relentless probing of meta-textual paradoxes in *Molloy* and *Malone Dies*. One detail is precious[27]: the first draft of *En Attendant Godot* pairs two old men named Lévy et Vladimir.[28] Didi comes from Vladimir, a Russian name that evokes Lenin. Indeed, without Vladimir, Gogo-Lévy would only be a "little heap of bones,"[29] which evokes the death camps and the Jews' liberation by Russian troops. These two emblematic characters obliquely and discreetly allude to recent history marked by the Shoah and the emergence of communism. The brotherly solicitude doubled by constant bickering evinced by Didi and Gogo also echoes the last sequences of Renoir's famous 1937 film, *La Grande Illusion*. Two French prisoners manage to escape from a German jail: Maréchal (Jean Gabin) and Rosenthal (Marcel Dallo). Throughout all the drawbacks, it is their solidarity that allows

---

[25] Ciaran Ross, *Beckett's Art of Absence: Rethinking the Void*, Houndsmills, Palgrave Macmillan, 2011. I owe to Ciaran Ross, whose dissertation I supervised in another century, the opportunity to meet Didier Anzieu, whose personality one cannot forget. Ross provides an impressive list of books on psychoanalysis read by Beckett, p. 7.

[26] Samuel Beckett, *The Unnamable*, in *Three Novels*, New York, Grove Press, 1991, p. 297.

[27] Knowlson, *Damned to Fame*, p. 344. See Jackie Blackman, "Beckett Judaizing Beckett," *Samuel Beckett Today/ Aujourd'hui*, no. 18, 2007, pp. 325–340.

[28] Angela Moorjani, "Whence Estragon?" *Beckett Circle*, vol. 32, no. 2, 2009, p. 7.

[29] Samuel Beckett, *En Attendant Godot / Waiting for Godot*, New York, Grove Press, 1982, p. 13.

them to survive in the end. It is obvious that their pairing owes something to the "pseudo-couple" constituted by the psychoanalyst and the analysand. Bionian psychoanalysis would, in that sense, stage and enact a workable "great illusion."

The first transitional space explored by Beckett was the space of a language other than his mother's. Later, he would systematically retranslate his own texts into the other language, keeping this back and forth movement until he felt that *Worstward Ho* had reached such a degree of concision that it could not be translated at all. Beckett's works show to what extent fantasies find their specific space between playing and thinking, both activities done unconsciously. I will try to sketch a dialectical interaction between the intuitions of Winnicott, who puts forward the concept of "playing" so as to open up the freedom of a new creative space, and those of Bion, who, closer to Klein, insisted on the issue of thinking. Before confronting them, let us recall that Beckett's initial psychoanalytical model was proposed by Carl Gustav Jung. Most critics who have discussed *Murphy* point to the numerous similarities between the image of Murphy's mind provided in chapter six and the model of the psyche elaborated by Jung in London. Both models are divided into three zones going from grey to dark, because in the middle is the obscure core of the unconscious. The surrounding zone of fantasy is a more superficial layer: it combines forms from the world and wishful distortions: "Here the physical fiasco became a howling success."[30] This is the reworking of images in what Freud calls conscious fantasies. The second zone corresponds to unconscious fantasies. And for Murphy, they revolve around "contemplation" and a passive "Belacqua bliss," meaning the wish not to have been born or to remain forever in limbo as his model, Dante's Belacqua. The third zone is the darkest "matric of surds," a space in which Murphy was "a mote in the dark of absolute freedom" (M, p. 112).

It was to Bion that Beckett owed this capital meeting; Bion had decided to bring his analysand to hear a talk by Jung who had come to London. Jung's theories helped Beckett overcome his writer's block as he was struggling to finish *Murphy*. The key was the phrase that Jung had used about a little girl who had died young, having been unable to really live, so deeply immersed in her unconscious she was. She had "never been born properly," Jung said, which became a sort of mantra for Beckett. He wrote the phrase in the addenda to *Watt*[31] and used it again and again. However, this did not mean a sudden conversion to Jungism or to psychoanalysis. In October 1935, Beckett described

---

[30] Samuel Beckett, *Murphy*, New York, Grove Press, 1957, p. 111. Hereafter, M and page number.
[31] See Samuel Beckett, *Watt*, New York, Grove Press, 1953, p. 248.

to his friend McGreevy the famous meeting with Jung with distance and sarcasm:

> His lecture the night I went consisted mainly in the so called synthetic (versus Freudian analytic) interpretation of three dreams of a patient who finally went to the dogs because he insisted on taking a certain element in the dreams as the Oedipus position when Jung told him it was nothing of the kind! However he lost his neurosis among the dogs – again according to Jung. The mind is I suppose the best Swiss, Lavater & Rousseau, mixture of enthusiasm & Euclid, a methodical rhapsode. Jolas's pigeon all right, but I should think in the end less than the dirt under Freud's nails.[32]

The view of Jung's mind is both critical and appreciative; Beckett's bantering tome suggests a divided allegiance, a hesitation between Freud and Jung. It was indeed Bion's model, grounded as it was in Melanie Klein's elaborations of the objects of fantasy (good or bad breast, etc.), that would provide Beckett with a better theory, far from the Oedipal drama with his mother, at a remove from the exploration of collective archetypes. Bion would above all reconnect Beckett with a more productive practice of thinking (and writing). Beckett had read some Jung, because the latter's paper on "Psychology and Literature" was published in the summer issue of *Transition* from 1930, an issue in which Beckett's poem "For Future Reference" was included. Jung's talk was supported by a diagram with "the different spheres of the mind in gradually darkening colors, in circles of decreasing circumference, until the personal and collective unconscious was reached, shown as a black circle at the very heart of the drawing."[33] Jung concluded that when the individual sinks into this black hole at the center, he disappears and is "victimized" by it. It is just such a "victimization" that Murphy wants to avoid when he runs away to the safety of his rocker. The anarchic proliferation of fragmented images corresponds to the savage irruption of the collective unconscious into the life of a subject who fails to master it. The buzzing confusion of the ground turns into a nightmare, and the last vision of a face – be it that of Celia, of his mother, or his father, "all the loved ones" – is but a frail rampart against the disruptive negativity of a night of the soul.

Murphy dies an ambiguous death in "his" novel in which Beckett knowingly played games with psychoanalysis. In one of these, the hero wishes to cheat the restaurant where he eats, however minimally. Having gulped down the first cup of tea, he complains that the tea is from India and not China as he

---

[32] Samuel Beckett, *Letters*, vol. I, Cambridge, Cambridge University Press, 2009, p. 282.
[33] Ibid., p. 208.

had asked. Given a fresh cup of tea, Murphy asks for a refill and some milk. He adds these decisive words:

> "I am most fearfully sorry," he said, "Vera, to give you all this trouble, but do you think it would be possible to have this filled with hot?"
>
> Vera showing signs of bridling, Murphy uttered winningly the sesame.
>
> "I know I am a great nuisance, but they have been too generous with the cowjuice."
>
> Generous and cowjuice were the keywords here. No waitress could hold out against their mingled overtones of gratitude and mammary organs. (M, p. 83)

Murphy plays on the unconscious register of the waitress to swindle the caterer of a few pennies. His near starvation, which smacks of anorexia, is instrumental in transforming the psychological experiment into a struggle – however minimal it is – with the forces of capitalism on the one hand and the seductions of femininity on the other. Vera is described snidely as "a willing bit of sweated labour, incapable of betraying the slogan of her slavers, that since customer or sucker was paying for his gutrot ten times what it cost to produce and five times what it cost to fling in his face, it was only reasonable to defer to his complaints up to but not exceeding fifty per cent of his exploitation" (M, p. 83). Her Latin name inscribes her in the series of Beckettian feminine characters whose names end in *a*. She allegorizes a "truth" that is effective even though it is humiliated and exploited. The truth that her name contains can be interpreted in Kleinian or Bionian terms; it is the primitive link established between truth and the "good object" or "good breast." For Bion if the relation between the infant and the mother is lacking in truth, there is a premature weaning or starvation: "This internal object starves its host of all understanding that is made available. In analysis such a patient seems unable to gain from his environment and therefore from his analyst. The consequences for the development of a capacity for thinking are serious; I shall describe only one, namely precocious development of consciousness."[34]

Bion's "Theory of Thinking" opens with an analysis of the dire consequences of a mother's inability to engage in reverie, which often creates a perverse couple with her infant. The starvation of truth attacks the thinking process, which Bion normally explains in terms identical to those describing the digestion of healthy food: thinking can only take place if beta elements made up of inchoate impressions, early sense data and raw feelings of loss and anger

---

[34] Wilfred R. Bion, "A Theory of Thinking," in *Second Thoughts, Selected Papers on Psycho-Analysis*, Northvale, Jason Aronson, 1993, p. 115.

are transformed into alpha elements. Alpha elements are the conditions for mental categories that are deployed in dreaming, memorizing, and above all thinking *thoughts*.[35] Bion assumes that schizophrenic patients were deprived of an "experienced mother" – that is, mothers equipped of a capacity for reverie. The mothers failed to help infants transform their inchoate experiences into "thoughts." Bion's distinctive contribution to the Kleinian school was based on a neo-Kantian architecture of abstract categories, an a priori "grid" providing the conditions of possibility for both normal and pathological thinking. It is on such a grid that the notion of "thoughts without a thinker" is founded.

The paper "On Linking" examines patients eager to cut all links, especially the link connecting them to the analyst. One strategy, self-defeating as it is, consists of destroying language to achieve this end. "For a proper understanding of the situation when attacks on linking are being delivered it is useful to postulate thoughts that have no thinker."[36] Bion's argument compares thinking with the concept of infinity. For Bion, thoughts exist without a thinker because, as he puts it, the idea of infinity comes before any idea of the finite. Hence, the finite is "won from the dark and formless infinite."[37] The human personality is aware of infinity through the oceanic feeling described by Freud and becomes aware of limitation, "presumably through physical and mental experience of itself and the sense of frustration."[38] Such an analysis describes Murphy's plight, when he hesitates between surrendering wholeheartedly to the infinite that he discovers in himself and accepting the sense of limitation equivalent to castration.

The only model capable of reconciling Beckett's rationalistic Cartesian dualism with a psychoanalytical philosophy of desire is Bion's theory of thinking. Bion may not have been able to communicate all his thoughts to the reluctant patient who used to grumble that therapy led him nowhere, but it was with his psychoanalyst's help that Beckett could start "thinking" productively with a concept of the "Nothing." This proximity with negativity allowed him to transform the ineffable horror experienced by Murphy facing disjointed and threatening images into "thoughts without a subject."

In his syntheses, Bion kept foregrounding the function of Truth, called "O," that he distinguishes from the function of Knowledge ("K"). Such a distinction calls up Lacan's and Badiou's subsequent opposition of Truth and Knowledge. For Bion, O can be reached if one suspends memory, desire, and even understanding. One should approach O by a systematic annulment of K, in a sort of

---

[35] Bion, "A Theory of Thinking," p. 18.
[36] See J. S. Grotstein's preface to *Second Thoughts*, p. xi.
[37] Bion, *Second Thoughts*, p. 165.
[38] Ibid.

via negative, like what mystics experienced – and Bion invariably quotes Saint John of the Cross at this point.[39] O will thus emerge as a lack of form and a lack in form, because knowledge bears on "phenomena" and never the "thing-in-itself," to follow the Kantian terminology favored by Bion. A dialectical inter-action between "other-people-seen-by-me" and "Me-seen-by-other-people" adheres to the logics of forms. Bion's questions sound extremely Beckettian:

> It is possible through phenomena to be reminded of the "form." It is possible through "incarnation" to be united with a part, the incarnate part, of the Godhead. It is possible through hyperbole for the individual to deal with the real individual. Is it possible through psycho-analytic interpretation to effect a transition from knowing the phenomena of the real self to being the real self?[40]

The analyst will achieve this by creating a negative space that should release the mother's reverie inside him and in the analysand as well. The death of the *morphe*, or form, in the analyst will allow him to reconnect him with his mother, thus to reopen a shared creative reverie.

Indeed, Bion proposed a psychoanalytical theory of "thinking" that was lacking in Freud. For Bion, thinking cannot be restricted to Cartesian rational-ism or Enlightenment optimism. For Bion, thinking also includes daydream-ing and fantasy. Bion's theory of thinking offers a bold expansion of Freud's discussion on thought processes in the *Project for a Scientific Psychology* and finds an anchor in Melanie Klein's investigation of the young child's uncon-scious battles with pre-Oedipal monsters. The possibility of thoughts without subjects is a basic axiom for Bion. For him, human psyches are machines for thinking these thoughts; they begin operating early to deal with absence – the absence of the mother's breast being the first object of thought for the infant. Thinking is thus also dreaming, both activities working with a truth-function that is originally provided by the mother alone. Often, Beckett's texts use ani-mal images to represent thoughts without a subject. Animals are between the human and the natural realms and are literally "wild thoughts"; they may have to be tamed, to quote a book by Bion,[41] but they can also roam freely in a new textual unconscious.

This is most perceptible in "From an Abandoned Work," the first text ini-tially written in English after a long interruption (Beckett wrote in French first after *Watt*). John Pilling has evoked the "hysterical-obsessional structure" of this text, noting that it "seems at once to invite and discourage psychoanalytic

---

[39] See W. R. Bion's *Transformations: Change from Learning to Growth*, New York, Basic Books, 1965, pp. 158–159.
[40] Ibid., p. 148.
[41] W. R. Bion, *Taming Wild Thoughts*, London, Karnac, 1997.

interpretations."[42] Its autobiographical aspects are immediately obvious. We recognize the son's departure from a home in which the mother stays alone, wringing her hands in grief. The son exhibits Oedipal remorse because he feels that he has killed his father, which triggers a wish to escape "anywhere out of the world," when in fact he is going nowhere. The title puns on abandonment, from the birth trauma to leaving one's home as an adult, while describing its own status: Beckett never completed the draft.

The affects triggered by the status of being abandoned are marked by high ambivalence: given the tension between freedom and loneliness, they are marked by a mixture of rage and guilt, desire and disgust, all this leading to a curious mixture of haste and procrastination. There is both the libidinal release of pent up drives and the savage repression of the superegoic law. Meaning is opaque but concentrated in animal images that can make sense in a psycho-biographical narrative. We meet a white horse and then some stoats. These creatures suddenly emerge to block the progression of the narrator. The opening scene presents him as he leaves his mother's house: she is "weeping and waving," but soon his worry is deflected by the bad weather; when he might be changing his mind and turn back home, he is prevented by animals.

> Feeling all this, how violent and the kind of day, I stopped and turned. So back with bowed head on the look out for a snail, slug or worm. Great love in my heart too for all things still and rooted, bushes, boulders and the like, too numerous to mention, even the flowers of the field, not for the world when in my right senses would I ever touch one, to pluck it. Whereas a bird now, or a butterfly, fluttering about and getting in my way, all moving things, getting in my path, a slug now, getting under my feet, non no mercy. Not that I'd go out of my way to get at them, no, at a distance often they seemed still, then a moment later they were upon me. Birds with my piercing sight I have seen flying so high, so far, that they seemed at rest, then the next minute they were all about me, crows have done this. Ducks are perhaps the worst, to be suddenly stamping and stumbling in the midst of ducks, or hens, any class of poultry, few things are worse. Nor will I go out of my way to avoid such things, when avoidable, no, I simply will not go out of my way, though I have never in my life been on my way anywhere.[43]

On the one hand, these weird animals signal the narrator's paranoia (they resist, he attacks; they present vicious moving obstacles) while offering some

[42] John Piling, "From an Abandoned Work: All the Variants of the One," in *Samuel Beckett Today*, no. 18, *All Sturm and No Drang*, 2007, p. 176.

[43] Samuel Beckett, *The Complete Short Prose, 1929-1989*, ed. S. E. Gontarski, New-York, Grove Press, 1995, pp. 155–156. Hereafter, CSP and page number.

solace, if not a model. In a text propelled by long rhetorical surges, the imagery of animal life will be dominated by the opposition between motion and immobility:

> [N]o big birds at me, nothing across my path except at a great distance a white horse followed by a boy, or it might have been a small man or a woman. This is the only completely white horse I remember, what I believe the Germans call a Schimmel.... The sun was full upon it, as shortly before on my mother, and it seemed to have a red band, perhaps a bellyband, perhaps the horse was going somewhere to be harnessed, to a trap or such-like. It crossed my path a long way off, then vanished behind greenery, I suppose, all I noticed was the sudden appearance of the horse, then disappearance. (CSP, pp. 156–157)

This section had begun with "Enough of my mother for the moment." For a psychoanalyst like Bion, the horse stands for the mother, or more precisely for the mystery of the appearance and disappearance of the mother's breast. The hallucinatory presence and absence of the mother and the color white, associated with skin and milk, along with a German word calling up the image of a "shimmer" in the memory, all allude to what is both totally foreign and totally homely: the mother's body. The Schimmel exemplifies the main features of Freud's Uncanny. The dream vision is explained soon after: having evoked the onset of sudden rages that would blind him, the narrator moves on to more peaceful thoughts, remembering that he studied Milton's cosmology. He impressed his father with such knowledge during a trip to the mountains. He adds: "Never loved anyone I think, I'd remember. Except in my dreams, and there it was animals, dream animals, nothing like what you see in the country, I couldn't describe them, lovely creatures they were, white, mostly" (CSP, p. 158). There is a Freudian wink in this "I'd remember." Beckett knows about Oedipal wishes and their repression and how repression affects memory. The white animals are acceptable substitutes for the mother's body. She is both desired and rejected, much as in Freud's *Interpretation of Dreams* in which people with birds' beaks carry his mother, lead him *vögeln*, ("to have sex with the mother"), who is almost dead on a bed.[44] Freud interprets the anxiety generated by the dream as the product of a successful fantasy of having sex with his mother.

The second act of the Oedipal fantasy is the inevitable punishment meted out, because the narrator now thinks he has killed both father and mother, although he is not entirely sure: "My father, did I kill him too as well as my mother, perhaps in a way I did, but I can't go into that now, much too old and weak" (CSP, p. 159). Indeed, they have not been killed in the same way: the

---

[44] Sigmund Freud, *The Interpretation of Dreams*, 1965, p. 622.

father has been "killed" in Oedipal fantasies, whereas the mother was "killed" by the son's departure to live on his own. The son imagines his own demise in a vision split between the earth and the sky. The earth is the chthonian world beneath with its "conqueror worms." The realm above, with its white animals, keeps symbols of beauty. The narrator drifts a little, his fantasy makes him penetrate under the surface, drift through earth and rocks, down into the sea:

> A ton of worms in an acre, that is a wonderful thought, a ton of worms, I believe it. Where did I get it, from a dream, or a book read in a nook when a boy, or a word overheard as I went along, or in me all along and kept under till it could give me joy, these are the kind of horrid thoughts that I have to contend with in the way I have said. Now is there nothing to add to this day with the white horse and white mother in the window, please read again my descriptions of these, before I get on to some other day at a later time. . . . What happens now is I was set on and pursued by a family or tribe, I do not know, of stoats, a most extraordinary thing, I think they were stoats. Indeed, if I may say so, I was fortunate to get off with my life. . . . Anyone else would have been bitten and bled to death, perhaps sucked white, like a rabbit, there is that word white again. I know I could never think, but if I could have, and then had, I would just have lain down and let myself be destroyed, as the rabbit does. (CSP, p. 161)

One cannot miss the emphatic use of the verb "to think": first innocuously in "I think they were stoats," then reflexively in "I can think these thoughts." This is Freudian overdetermination in the domain of fantasy allied with Bion's theory of thinking. Here, thinking truly is daydreaming with images – mostly images of animals. The choice of this specific animal is less weird than it seems, because a pun links wild "stoats" with those stray "thoughts." Thoughts left in a wild state before rationalization occurs, rabid and fluctuating thoughts that need to be straightened by thought as thought. The color white signals as much the mother's beauty as a death associated with her, because the two meanings have now been blended. The recurrent image of a white horse leads to another pun: the association with a "hoarse" throat, which accompanies diminished hearing: "Throat very bad, to swallow was torment, and something wrong with an ear, I kept poking at it without relief, old wax perhaps pressing on the drum" (CSP, p. 163). Bion repeated that thoughts can be generated without our knowledge, even without any subject being present. Such a process also happens when the body does its duty unconsciously, which is actually what takes place most of the time. This was a moot point, a point made into a methodological principle of Occasionalism, for Arnold Geulincx, the post-Cartesian philosopher of humility in whom Beckett immersed himself in the

1930s. Freud, let us remember, had heard about Geulincx, at least because he had been advised by his philosophy teacher Franz Brentano that he had to avoid reading him.[45]

If I cannot ever know what happens when my limbs move, why not leave this thought to God or to the Other? The Other should be able to make sense of a process that is, anyway, not so important or significant. Otherwise, how will one avoid paralysis? Thus, Beckett's "abandoned" text ends without ending (its draft continued, Beckett added a few more sentences) but logically enough with a glimpse of mechanical autonomy. The world and the body can go on without the intervention of the narrator, but the text has to be cut at the right spot by the author: "[Y]ou could lie there for weeks and no one hear you, I often thought of that up in the mountains, no, that is foolish thing to say, just went on, my body doing its best without me" (CSP, p. 164). What would follow – if it could follow – would generate an autonomous text, a text continuing its infinite progress by itself. This is how fantasy can think itself, "doing its best" in ideally endless iterations, the perpetual reiteration of grammatical subjects devoid of subjectivity. Its mindless mind is sustained by the Other, the maternal word-hoard, a prodigious resource of vocabulary and affect. As Beckett wrote at the close of *Ohio Impromptu*: "What thoughts who knows. Thoughts, no, not thoughts. Profounds of mind. Buried in who knows what profounds of mind. Of mindlessness. Whither no light can reach."[46]

---

[45] "Of [Descartes's] successors, Geulincx, Malebranche, and Spinoza, none was worth reading." Freud's letter to Silberstein of March 13, 1875, in LSFES, p. 103.
[46] Samuel Beckett, *Ohio Impromptu*, in *The Complete Dramatic Works*, London, Faber, 1986, p. 448.

Chapter 3

From the uncanny to the unhomely

Beckett learned with Bion and Jung but kept paying homage to Freud, although he feared the reductive aspect of his theories.[1] Like many sophisticated writers and readers, he tended to deride a certain naivety shown by Freud facing literature. Such naivety is nowhere more evident than when Freud wrote to the German novelist Wilhelm Jensen asking if Jensen had read *The Interpretation of Dreams* and if he had a sister, given the brother-sister incest theme in his novella *Gradiva, a Pompeian Phantasy*. Jensen replied politely that he had not read Freud and that he had no sister. I will now discuss Freud's reading of Jensen's charming novella, a literary or belletristic exercise completed to please Jung, who had first pointed it out to Freud.

Gradiva / Gravida

Freud's book, *Delusions and Dreams in Jensen's Gradiva*, evinces such a lightness of touch and ease in style that one recognizes a transferential element: this was his gift to Jung, who praised it warmly in return. Freud expressed some regret at Jensen's lack of cooperation: "Soon after the publication of my analytic examination of *Gradiva* I attempted to interest the elderly author in these new tasks of psycho-analytic research. But he refused his co-operation."[2] In fact, Jensen had replied courteously to Freud when the latter had sent him the essay, but he insisted that the text had no foundation in his life or in science. It was just a

---

[1] Beckett quotes with approval Freud's objection to Kant in his second dialogue with Duthuit, and here Freud sounds very much like Beckett: "Following a well-known pronouncement of Kant's which couples the conscience within us with the starry Heavens, a pious man might well be tempted to honour these two things as the masterpieces of creation. The stars are indeed magnificent, but as regards conscience God had done an uneven and careless piece of work, for a large majority of men have brought along with them only a modest amount of it or scarcely enough to be worth mentioning." See Sigmund Freud, *New Introductory Lectures on Psycho-Analysis*, trans. James Strachey, New York, Norton, 1989, p. 77, quoted by Samuel Beckett, in *Disjecta*, London, Calder, 1983, p. 141.
[2] Sigmund Freud, "Delusions and Dreams in Jensen's Gradiva," in *Writings on Art and Literature*, p. 85.

fantasy.[3] Jensen, who gave the telling subtitle of *pompejanisches Phantasiestück* to his novella, had the right to insist on his "free" and "autonomous" use of the imagination. Freud looks like a bully when in his 1912 postscript he looks for clues, repetition compulsion, and the recurrent image of a brother-sister link in Jensen's fiction. Freud still believed that because Jensen saw "a sister in the woman he loves,"[4] he penned the story.

Jensen had alluded to the usual literary meaning of the word *phantasie* in German, a term originally borrowed from the French *fantaisie*, which suggests fancy, whimsy, eccentricity, extravagance, and even clownish or extreme delusion. Grimm's dictionary provides meanings that span the spectrum, from poetic fancy (the term was often used by Romantic writers) to the delusional state of falling in love.[5] Once more, it seems, Freud's scientific determinism clashes with the free associative power of creativity. However, Freud felt that he was praising Jensen for having independently understood the main mechanisms of psychoanalysis. If his novella had reached the same conclusions as Freud's patiently elaborated theories on verbal therapy had, was it a sign that literature could elucidate human passions? I will have to traverse Freud's reading of Jensen to suggest that the close reading of the text reveals much less about the process of "fantasy" than about the Uncanny.

Here is how Freud sums up Jensen's "phantasy." The hero, Norbert Hanold, is a young German professor in archeology from Northern Germany. Since the death of his parents, he shuns the society of men, and of women above all. He hides his social ineptitude by investing all his time and energy in the study of Greco-Roman antiquity, thus reproducing his father's academic career. His investigations focus on a relief showing a young woman who walks with her right foot lifted up at a right angle with the ground. In a dream, he sees himself alongside the woman in 79 AD, when Vesuvius covered Pompeii in ashes and killed its inhabitants. He feels that he has experienced the death of his beloved. This triggers a determined wish to go to Rome first and then to Pompeii in search of the traces of this woman to whom he gives the name of "Gradiva" (she who walks). Now his imaginary world entirely revolves around her. En-route to Pompeii, he falls into some kind of delirium or delusion (*Wahn*) and hallucinates her presence at various spots of the ruined temples. At length they talk, and he is not too surprised to discover that they can converse in German.

---

[3] Wilhelm Jensen's three letters to Freud from May 13, May 25, and December 14, 1907, have been published in *Psychoanalytische Bewegung*, no. 1, 1929, pp. 207–211. Freud read the first letter to the Viennese society of psychoanalysis on May 15, 1907. See Ernest Jones, *The Life and Work of Sigmund Freud*, II, *Years of Maturity, 1901–1919*, New York, Basic Books, 1955, p. 343.

[4] Freud, "Delusions and Dreams in Jensen's Gradiva," in *Writings on Art and Literature*, p. 86.

[5] See the useful introduction to *Unconscious Phantasy*, ed. Ricardo Steiner, London, Karnac, 2003, pp. 2–3.

A young German woman plays the part of the Roman girl and later reveals that she is none other than Zoe Bertgang, an old childhood playmate, a neighbor with a similarly academic and absent-minded father. Zoe and Norbert end up kissing and walking together hand in hand. Once Zoe has blended with Gradiva, they confess their reciprocal love and decide to marry; a similar trip to Italy is their honeymoon voyage. In the last scene, Zoe walks in front of Norbert, exhibiting her charming instep for her lovelorn fiancé.

In Freud's reading, the key to Norbert's delusions and hallucinations is simply sexual repression. Such repression is allegorized by Pompeii, perhaps the main character in the story and a constant modelization of the unconscious in Freud's works.[6] The remains of Pompeii consist in well-preserved corpses from the past, buried all at once by catastrophe, inaccessible without a systematic excavation. Jensen decided to situate his novella in Pompeii and not in Rome, where the original relief is kept (he had only seen a copy in Munich, in fact), to suggest that Norbert's forgotten childhood memories have the same status as the buried corpses. Zoe Bertgang understands all this, and she plays the game in an effort to bring Norbert out of his trance; she behaves like a psychoanalyst. Sexual repression had hidden the childhood love for the young neighbor, and Zoe digs up the past by enacting the part of the hallucinated Gradiva. Because she was already in love with Norbert, she uses transference to reinstate his capacity for love – for a living person that is, and not a statue. In this inversion of the Pygmalion myth (here, it is Galatea who comes to life to transform her "creator"), the novella illustrates Freud's main tenets – the therapeutic function of transference, the dynamic role of fantasy, the symbolic meaning of dreams, the sexual origins of repression – all the while offering an allegory of the unconscious as a field of petrified ruins that ghosts of the past stalk. Freud downplays only one factor in his account: he does not comment on the fact that Norbert has suffered a trauma linked less with sexuality (we know very little of it, except for its fetishistic character) than with an incomplete mourning of his parents.

By giving the name of Zoe Bertgang to the young woman, Jensen insists on her function as life-bringer. He also suggests, as Freud notes, that the delusion was nothing but the enactment of a translation: her name, which was known to Norbert as a child, means "who has a beautiful gait." Norbert vaguely remembers having seen someone walk like the woman in the relief, with a foot almost perpendicular to the ground – it was his neighbor, obviously, glimpsed

---

[6] It even reappears in one of the last papers, "Constructions in Analysis": "Here we are regularly met by a situation which in archeology occurs only in such rare circumstances as those of Pompeii or the tomb of Tutankhamen." Sigmund Freud, *Therapy and Technique*, ed. Philip Rieff, New York, Collier Books, 1963, p. 276.

74 *Introduction to literature and psychoanalysis*

at a time when he could not pay attention to her because of the repression. Fundamentally, *Gradiva* is the story of a repetition: when Zoe understands that Norbert has taken her for the ghost of a Pompeii woman, she plays the part, and leads him back to life. One recurrent semantic couple is thus the opposition between death and life, redoubled as darkness versus light, and also, with some help from Nietzsche, as Apollo versus Dionysius. The young woman's first name means "life" in Greek, and at the end of the "wild cure," Norbert exclaims that it is good to simply feel alive. He had been buried alive as a consequence of a trauma – most likely the sudden death of his parents about which we know nothing. Is this sufficient to explain the huge repression and his quasi-psychotic features? Freud wanted to obtain more details, but Jensen demurred. When he sees Gradiva for the first time, the text mimes his surprise with "And suddenly ..." and the next sentence in a new paragraph. When he sees Gradiva for the second time, a few minutes later, the language is truly proto-Freudian:

> Dadurch bot sie dem unbemerkt Herangekommenen, dessen Fußtritt sie offenbar erst eben vernommen, die Vollansicht ihres Antlitzes entgegen, das eine Doppelempfindung bei ihm hervorrief, denn es erschien seinen Augen zugleich als ein fremdes und doch auch als ein bekanntes, schon gesehenes oder vorgestelltes. Aber am Stocken seines Atemzuges und Aussetzen seines Herzschlages erkannte er als unzweifelhaft, wem es angehöre. Er hatte gefunden, wonach er gesucht, was ihn unbewußt nach Pompeji getrieben; die Gradiva führte ihr Scheinleben in der mittägigen Geisterstunde noch fort und saß hier vor ihm, so wie er sie im Traum sich auf die Stufen des Apollotempels niederlassen gesehn.[7]

I translate this literally:

> Thus she offered to the person who had stepped in without being noticed the entire vision of her face, which provoked in him a double impression, for to his eyes it appeared as something at once alien and familiar, whether seen before or imagined. But in the way his breath stopped and his heart missed a beat, he recognized without any doubt to whom it belonged. He had found what he was looking for, what had driven him unconsciously to Pompeii; Gradiva continued to live a semblance of life at noon, the time of the specters, and she was sitting in front of him as he had seen her in a dream on the steps of the temple of Apollo.

---

[7] Wilhelm Jensen, *Gradiva*, Leipzig, Kamm & Seemann, 1903, PDF version, Projekt Gutenberg, accessed August 18, 2013, p. 66.

The expression "at once alien and familiar," along with Norbert's delusion as to the return of a specter, corresponds with the main features of the Uncanny. The Uncanny reveals itself in this doubling of the strange and the familiar; the familiar has become strange, and vice versa. When Norbert becomes aware of this, he realizes that he has been "driven unconsciously" to Pompeii. The compulsion to repeat similarly replays the old tragic drama opposing Apollo, the god of sun but also of shining vision, and Dionysus, the dark god of frenzy, wine, and sacrifices. This is why we see Norbert get drunk at least twice in the novella. And the ending may not be such a "happy ending" if we want to insist on the perverse nature of the bond between Norbert and Zoe. The most uncanny moment occurs at the end, when we must assume Norbert has been cured of his delusion. Yet the story ends thus:

> Norbert Hanold hielt vor ihnen an und sagte mit einem eigentümlichen Klang der Stimme: »Bitte, geh hier vorauf!« Ein heiter verständnisvoll lachender Zug umhuschte den Mund seiner Begleiterin, und mit der Linken das Kleid ein wenig raffend, schritt die Gradiva rediviva Zoë Bertgang, von ihm mit traumhaft dreinblickenden Augen umfaßt, in ihrer ruhigbehenden Gangart durch den Sonnenglanz über die Trittsteine zur anderen Straßenseite hinüber.[8]

I translate:

> Norbert halted in front of them [the crossroad at the Herculanum door] and said, with something particular in the sound of his voice: "Please, walk across here!" A joyous smile of complicity played on the lips of his companion, and lifting a little her dress with the left hand, Gradiva rediviva Zoe Bertgang, whom he took in with a dreamy and insistent gaze, in her peacefully agile gait, passed on the flagstones through the sunshine to the other side of the street.

The most astute close reader of this text, Jean Bellemin-Noël, insists on the "uncanny" tonality of this last scene.[9] Norbert's eyes are said to be "traumhaft dreinblickenden Augen," something like "eyes gazing to inner side in a dreamy manner." Has Norbert gotten rid of his delusion or simply transferred his fantasy to his future wife? Because they become accomplices, should we imagine them joining a foot-fetishists' club back in Germany? Or given the sexualized role of animals such as flies and lizards, opening an archeological museum of zoophilia? The last word of the text is the adverb *hinüber*; it modifies the verb radical *schritt*, which comes three lines before. In this literal grammatical

---

[8] Ibid., p. 151.
[9] Jean Bellemin-Noël, *Gradiva au pied de la lettre*, Paris, Presses Universitaires de France, 1983, p. 256.

enjambment, a literal straddling cannot be rendered in English because we have to dissociate "pass" and "across," whereas the German verb *hinüberschreiten* gives a syntactical frame for the last part of the sentence, where we witness how the woman's peculiar gait triggers a peculiar look in the man. Their exchange may not end on a "peaceful" economy of desire: the remains of the "Uncanny" and the ruins of Pompeii still haunt the scholars of Germany.

Freud had not yet hit on the term of *unheimlich* in 1906, because his investigation dates from 1919, but one may say that the tale of *Gradiva* leads directly to Hoffmann's more distinguished fiction of the Sandman. If the "Uncanny" is marked by the theme of repetition, it has to include Freud in an almost literal repetition of the text in his essay. The suggestion is that there is a dangerous contamination or contagion of the Uncanny, as proved by this vignette added by Freud to his reading of Jensen's story to explain that Norbert's symptoms are not extravagant – Freud himself had a similar experience. Even in the way the anecdote is narrated, there is a rather "uncanny" split between the third and the first person:

> I know of a doctor who had once lost one of his women patients suffering from Graves' disease, and who could not get rid of a faint suspicion that he might perhaps have contributed to the unhappy outcome by a thoughtless prescription. One day, several years later, a girl entered his consulting-room, who, in spite of all his efforts, he could not help recognizing as the dead one. He could frame only a single thought: "So after all it's true that the dead can come back to life." His dread did not give way to shame until the girl introduced herself as the sister of the one who had died of the same disease as she herself was suffering from.... The doctor to whom this occurred was, however, none other than myself; so I have a personal reason for not disputing the clinical possibility of Norbert Hanold's temporary delusion that Gradiva had come back to life. (JG, p. 64)

We do find a similar temporary delusion reported by Freud in the Uncanny:

> I was sitting alone in my sleeping compartment when the train lurched violently. The door of the adjacent toilet swung open and an elderly gentleman in a dressing gown and travelling cap entered my compartment. I assumed that on leaving the toilet, which was located between the two compartments, he had turned the wrong way and entered mine by mistake. I jumped up to put him right, but soon realized to my astonishment that the intruder was my own image, reflected in the mirror of the connecting door. I can still recall that I found his appearance thoroughly unpleasant.[10]

[10] Sigmund Freud, "The Uncanny," in *The Uncanny*, p. 162 note.

This was Freud's encounter with his own "double," which was of course himself. This sudden and temporary dissociation of the mirror image can question one's very sense of identity. Lacan later made most of the "mirror stage" through which a little child constitutes an imaginary identity prematurely, before he or she can actually experience it as such.[11] For Lacan as for Freud, the lessons of this necessary "stage" in the development of subject are that the sense of identity is fluctuating, based on a flat bi-dimensional image that can fade away easily, and that because of this ontological weakness at the core of identity, a reaction of aggression is the most common way of warding off the intrusion of the "other."

Another of Freud's personal "adventures" is relevant in the context of *Gradiva*, because this is Freud's "uncanny" variation on the paradigm of the Italian journey:

> Strolling one hot summer afternoon through the empty and to me unfamiliar streets of a small Italian town, I found myself in a district about whose character I could not long remain in doubt. Only heavily made-up women were to be seen at the windows of the little houses, and I hastily left the narrow street at the next turning. However, after wandering about for some time without asking the way, I suddenly found myself back in the same street, where my presence began to attract attention. Once more I hurried away, only to return there again by a different route. I was now seized by a feeling that could only describe as uncanny, and I was glad to find my way back to the piazza...[12]

The mixture of unintentional repetition and absolute helplessness defines the Uncanny in this memory. Is it so different from what Norbert experienced in Pompeii? The compulsion to repeat clearly stems from a certain sexual repression in both cases. It seems at any rate that Jensen's Italian fantasy had given a perfect signifier to Freud – his *Gradiva* was indeed, by metathesis, a "pregnant" book if we decide to read the Latin name as *gravida*: Jensen's *Gradiva* gave birth to the idea of the Uncanny.

At home in the unhomely

Freud's concept of *das Unheimliche*, usually rendered as "the Uncanny," can also be translated as "unhomely," which is the solution adopted here and there by David McLintock in the 2003 translation for Penguin. *Unheimlich*

---

[11] Jacques Lacan, "The Mirror Stage as Formative of the I Function," and "Aggressiveness in Psychoanalysis," in *Ecrits*, 2006, pp. 75–101.
[12] Freud, *The Uncanny*, p. 144.

is indeed based on the radical of *Heim* (home) yet cannot be always rendered as "unhomely." By using "Uncanny," we can play on a couple like canny vs. Uncanny, whereas the French equivalent *l'inquiétante étrangeté*, neatly poetic as it is, cannot allow this. The first twelve pages of the essay are devoted to philological considerations: Freud maps out the semantic field of the term, follows its evolution, and teases out its meanings of "hidden" or "concealed" and also "dangerous" and "frightening" or "disquieting." He concludes that there is not a great difference between the two adjectives *heimlich* and *unheimlich*, which begs the issue of the translatability of the concept as a concept. More than once, we see how Freud is thinking in German, from a German corpus made up of dictionaries and literary works. This tends to prove, as Bruno Bettelheim,[13] Jacques Lacan, and others have noticed, that psychoanalysis bypasses its "metalanguage" – the lexicon of basic concepts such as the ego, the id, and the superego to which it is too often reduced – to work from within a natural language and a given culture. Freud's essay taps German culture with all its aspirations to universality, no doubt, and does not set a series of translatable terms, but rather poses the problem of translation from the start. This is why most English translations are so iffy. Can one really think in terms of "parapraxes" and "cathexes," whereas the original terms used by Freud are everyday words such as "failed action" and "investment"? It is clear that all those terms will have to be retranslated if one wants a useable "standard edition" of Freud's works.

In the case of the Uncanny, the semantic slippage may be less a result to problems of translation than to problems of definition. The term is notoriously slippery. Two excellent books have been written about the Uncanny, and they should be read side by side. Nicholas Royle's 2003 *The Uncanny*[14] stages in a dynamic manner the whole field covered by the notion, from Hoffmann's famous story "The Sandman" on which Freud bases his case, and Poe's stories of *Doppelgängers* like "William Wilson," to his own uncanny experience when he discovered that another Nicholas Royle had published fiction very similar to his own efforts. Finally, this turns into a book on Derrida; Royle presents the Uncanny as a variation of deconstruction itself. Because the familiar is constantly defamiliarized in the Uncanny, the conclusion that "[t]he Uncanny is (the) unsettling (of itself)"[15] sounds logical. The Uncanny underpins a mode of

---

[13] See Bruno Bettelheim's invaluable *Freud and Man's Soul*, New York, Knopf, 1982. Bettelheim's sharp observations on the mistranslations of Freud's main concepts are based on the idea that Freud wanted to use a simple style to make his readers experience their own unconscious. On top of that, Freud expected his readers to share the same culture, which was not the case in the United Kingdom or the United States.

[14] Nicholas Royle, *The Uncanny*, New York, Routledge, 2003.

[15] Ibid., p. 5.

spectral haunting that replaces any ontology with its "hauntology." Following his own principle, Royle's text often turns into an experimental intellectual journal in which he mixes dreams and fragments of personal memoirs with theoretical analysis. What Anneleen Masschelein gave us in 2011 with *The Unconcept: The Freudian Uncanny in Late-Twentieth-Century Theory*[16] could not be further away stylistically. She examines the concept of the Uncanny both in psychoanalytic literature and in literary theory in a cogent and consistent analysis of the meanings, uses, and applications of the concept to various fields. Masschelein's precise critical examination describes the historical emergence of a term that was first brought to the fore by Tzvetan Todorov and Hélène Cixous, before being absorbed by Derrida and deconstruction. Whereas Todorov attempted to align the Uncanny with the more usual definitions of the fantastic, a genre based on a continuous hesitation between the rational and the irrational, between the world of magic and spirit and the world of madmen and hysterics, Cixous radically transformed the text into a psychoanalytical novel in which all the recurrent obsessions of Freud were replayed. All of these critics revisit the Freudian term, making it indispensable to an approach to fiction today. However, it is quite clear that the Uncanny cannot be defined as a genre. If it often overlaps with the genre of the fantastic, or at times with the genre of the gothic, it is not identifiable with these. Neither is it a philosophical concept, as Masschelein has shown: the Uncanny is by definition the "unconcept"; it is a hybrid, a monster, a theoretical or a "quasi-transcendental," as Derrida would have it. Can we psychologize it as an affect? Not even, for it would be too simple or reductive to identify it with fear or anxiety – it is more a trigger leading to fear or awe. The Uncanny is, however, also an intellectual hesitation that leaves us stranded between competing explanations or between conceptual universes. Perhaps it is safer to historicize it: there would be the Uncanny before Freud, the "historical Uncanny," and the Uncanny "after Freud" – today's Uncanny.

All the critics who have written on the Uncanny name Frantz Kafka as one of the undisputed masters of the Uncanny. Kafka's unclassifiable texts seem to beg the term of the Uncanny. One of his best-known short stories, "The Judgment," can be adduced here. This is the only text Kafka expressed some satisfaction with, given the ease of the writing process (he wrote it without a break, in one sitting, and felt glorious about it) and the result: he remained proud of this one story, when he expressed doubts over almost all the others.[17]

---

[16] Anneleen Masschelein, *The Unconcept: The Freudian Uncanny in Late-Twentieth-Century Theory*, Albany, SUNY Press, 2011.

[17] See the documents gathered by Stanley Corngold's edition of *Kafka's Selected Stories*, New York, Norton, 2007, pp. 197–201.

He mentions having thought of Freud after having written it, and indeed the plot is heavily imbued with Oedipal elements focusing on the struggle between father and son. Many similar elements are to be found in Kafka's "Letter to His Father," such as the impression that his father disapproved of everything in his way of life. However, in the fiction, the many twists in the narrative generate the uncanny element. It all begins when Georg Bendemann writes to a friend living in Russia that he is going to marry, and it ends a few hours later when Georg rushes headlong to commit suicide by throwing himself from a bridge because he has been condemned to death by his father. The son is "judged" by his father for no other reason than his possible wish to supplant him in his role as a businessman, even though Georg proclaims his love for his father. The convoluted logic of "judgment" leads to a verdict that can only lead to a death sentence. Kafka universalizes his own conflict by making his readers feel that they still react to authority as "sons." We are caught in the Oedipal patterns of punishable desires. Love for one's parents is always ambivalent and may have to accommodate sudden outbursts of hatred. The apparently absurd condemnation has to be interpreted as the only logical resolution of Georg's plight.

This sketchy summary does not yet account for the emergence of the Uncanny. It derives from a number of contradictions that baffle both the reader and Georg. Georg's initial problem is how to disclose the good news of his impending wedding to his friend in Russia. At the end, we learn both that the father has been writing to the friend, denouncing his son behind Georg's back, and that the father questions the very existence of the friend. At first Georg sees his father as physically and morally diminished, then he appears as a giant, who doubles in size when he shouts his final verdict. The decision to marry a bride (who seems difficult and perhaps reluctant to marry) appears as a detour or a delusion whose main function was to conceal the real problem with the father. Contradictory details crop up in an apparently matter-of-fact third-person narrative: Georg wonders what he will write in his letter, but the letter is sealed, ready to be mailed. The beautiful vista from the window offering a glimpse of greenery soon turns into his father's stifling room with closed windows. What stands out is the powerlessness of the son, whose words are idle or empty if they have not been corroborated or sanctioned by those of the father. All the performative power of language is still entrusted to the father, this "giant" whose words can kill, and they do.

The post-Freudian Uncanny, which begins with Kafka, has become quotational and meta-textual. I will give one example of this: a baffling passage in Coetzee's *Life of Jesus*. The plot is apparently simple. Simon, a middle-aged man accompanied by a young child, David, has arrived to a new land where only Spanish is spoken. They look like refugees in quest of a better life, after some catastrophe that has taken place over there and a shipwreck. Arriving in this dystopic pseudo-paradise, Simon looks for a suitable mother for David, and soon finds one. Earlier on, David proves that he can sing and he intones a song that he says is in English:

> *Wer reitet so spät durch Dampf und Wind?*
> *Er ist der Vater mit seinem Kind;*
> *Er halt den Knaben in dem Arm,*
> *Er füttert ihn Zucker, er küsst ihm warm.*[18]

Most readers who have some German recognize the most famous poem in the language, Goethe's "Erlkönig." However, the text is not accurate. The original text goes like this:

Wer reitet so spät durch Nacht und Wind?	Who rides so late through the night and wind?
Es ist der Vater mit seinem Kind;	It's the father with his child;
Er hat den Knaben wohl in dem Arm,	He has the boy safe in his arm,
Er faßt ihn sicher, er hält ihn warm.	He holds him secure, he holds him warm.

In Coetzee's novel, "Dampf" (mist) has replaced "night," the third line is grammatically incorrect ("halt" should have an Umlaut) and the last line is a grotesque distortion, meaning, "He feeds him sugar, he kisses him warm." Why is this called an English poem? Obviously, because Simon does not know "English," he cannot distinguish between German and English either. However, what language did they speak before they learned Spanish? How can Simon be that ignorant, or else is he indulging David and knows better? These basic epistemic questions would be irrelevant to any other novel, but here, because we keep wondering whether David is a bright child perhaps endowed with prophetic powers, or a difficult, opinionated, if not quasi-psychotic child, who is indulged too much by his adoptive parents, it is important. The title gives away that David might be a new Christ in a world where apparently that kind of Christian legend based on the gospels has been deliberately repressed or simply forgotten. In fact, the gospels implied here look more like the gospels of pseudo-Thomas or pseudo-Matthew in which we discover a terrifying Jesus who can kill with one glance at the most minor provocation. At the end of the superb novel, we recognize the old paradigm of the older father, the Virgin mother, and the preternaturally gifted child leaving the colony to start "a new life." It is the same but totally different. The old paradigm is still there but completely transformed by the Uncanny.

---

[18] J. M. Coetzee, *The Childhood of Jesus*, London, Harvill Secker, 2013, p. 67.

The Uncanny as desublimation

Is David a true future Jesus, or is this a mere delusion, or is this a completely new situation? This example tends to show that the Uncanny resists straight-forward definitions, because it indicates a process that has not fully or logically been completed. Quite often, the Uncanny appears whenever the process of artistic or intellectual sublimation is shown to be imperfect, halfway, or onto-logically insecure. It seems thus that the post-Freudian Uncanny can be better apprehended by Lacan's theory of the Thing, which provides a better grasp on the endless paradoxes of the Uncanny. Lacan's own sense of the Uncanny made him resist Freud's too pat and easy concept of sublimation, of which Lacan pre-sented a devastating critique in his seminar on the *Ethics of Psychoanalysis*:

> Freud's text is very weak on the topic. The definition he gives of
> sublimation at work in artistic creation only manages to show us the
> reaction or repercussion of the effects of what happens at the level of the
> sublimation of the drive, when the result or the work of the creator of
> the beautiful reenters the field of goods, that is to say, when they have
> become commodities. One must recognize that the summary Freud
> gives of the artist's career is practically grotesque. The artist, he says,
> gives a beautiful form to the forbidden object in order that everyone, by
> buying his little artistic product, rewards and sanctions his daring. That
> is a way of short-circuiting the problem.[19]

These highly critical remarks come from a section devoted to the Beautiful, as a preamble to a systematic reading of *Antigone*. With this famous play, Lacan provides a counterpoint to *Hamlet* in presenting an example of the true ethical position. While Hamlet questioned desire, *Antigone* shows how desire can be purified not just by ethical issues but also by aesthetics. The tragedy provides a purification whose object is desire itself. Surprisingly, Lacan does not pre-sent the heroine as either a guilty or an innocent, but as a young, beautiful woman. Her beauty shines and catches fire, and this fire somehow singes the gazes of the spectators. In Lacan's variation on Aristotelian "catharsis" – the "purgation of the passions," which should be the main effect of terror and pity in tragedy according to Aristotle's *Poetics* and also to Freud's "cathartic method" – Antigone the character purges desire itself. Antigone fascinates, and her fascination destroys fascination itself because she offers herself as an image that surpasses itself. This very movement purifies vision and operates a *catharsis* of the imaginary: "[T]hrough the intervention of pity and fear ...

---

[19] Jacques Lacan, *The Seminar Book VII, The Ethics of Psychoanalysis*, trans. Dennis Porter, New York, Norton, 1992, p. 238. Hereafter, abbreviated as S VII and page number.

we are purged, purified of everything of that order. And that order, we can now immediately recognize, is properly speaking the order of the imaginary. And we are purged of it through the intervention of one image among others" (S VII, pp. 247–248).

By arguing that Antigone's "beauty" can in effect function as the sublime, Lacan deliberately avoids resorting to the analysis of the Kantian sublime. He dodges using the concept of the sublime because of its proximity to sublimation – or more precisely, the Lacanian Sublime sends us to Freud's Thing. Lacan's final definition of sublimation is the act of raising an object to the dignity of a Thing: the function of art is to ensure that "the object is elevated to the dignity of the Thing" (S VII, p. 112). An example of this process would be Marcel Duchamp's gesture when he transformed a banal urinal into a work of art by signing it, turning it upside down, and asking to have it exhibited in a group show. When the urinal becomes a Thing, it cannot be reduced either to its formal properties or to its inverted functionality.

Indeed, Freud almost surreptitiously introduced the term of *das Ding* into the core of the subject's psychic structure in an early text linking the issue of the "fellow-creature," the neighbor, to the emergence of the Thing:

> [I]t is on his fellow-creatures that a human being first learn to cognize (*erkennen*).... Thus the complex of a fellow-creature falls into two portions. One of these gives the impression of being a constant structure and remains as a coherent thing (*Ding*); while the other can be understood by the activity of memory – that is, can be traced back to information about the subject's body. This process of analyzing a perceptual complex is described as *cognizing* (*erkennnen*) it; it involves a *judgment* and is brought to an end when that has been achieved.[20]

We are in the midst of the intricate terminological problems of Freud's "Project for a Scientific Psychology" from 1895. This important draft was never published, but it contains the most ambitious attempts at connecting the life of the unconscious with a cognitive mapping of the brain, whose different neurons are the basis for this reconstruction of the subject's structure.

Just after the previous quote, Freud develops the concept of "the Thing" when tackling an important problem. If the aim of all thought-processes is to establish a state of identity, why is there a principle of reality? Why do we not hallucinate all the time, if we are ruled by an archaic unconscious whose single objective is the attainment of pleasure? It is because thought recognizes early

[20] Sigmund Freud, "Project for a Scientific Psychology," in *The Origins of Psychoanalysis*, trans. Eric Mosbacher and James Strachey, New York, Basic Books, 1977, pp. 393–394. Hereafter, abbreviated as OP and page number.

enough that there is something like reality and that it is mostly impervious to its encroachments. In the sexual domain, from which he elaborates all these categories, it is crucial to understand that "no sexual experience can produce any effect so long as the subject has no sexual feelings (*Sexualempfindungen*), that is, generally speaking, until the beginning of puberty" (OP, p. 395). There is thus a certain judgment about the reality of something based on sexual sensations and libidinal investments. Thus, the "judging … is in its origin a process of association between cathexes arriving from without and cathexes derived from one's body.… What we term 'things' (*Dinge*) are residues that have evaded judgment" (OP, pp. 395–396). Commenting on this passage, Lacan states that the Thing remains as a center of exteriority within the subject. It is an inner exteriority, the trace of the Other in us:

> *das Ding* is at the center only in the sense that it is excluded. That is to
> say, in reality *das Ding* has to be posited as exterior, as the prehistoric
> Other that it is impossible to forget – the Other whose primacy of
> position Freud affirms in the form of something *entfremdet*, something
> strange to me, although it is at the heart of me, something that on
> the level of the unconscious only a representation can represent.
> (S VII, p. 71)

Thus, one can say that the main function of the Uncanny is to make the Thing appear, often under the most banal or innocuous guises. Art is a good site for this troubling emergence. We will exemplify this process with a few photographs chosen by Roland Barthes, because they testify to the return of the dead in art, and also with an installation by Sophie Calle about the death of her mother.

How can there be an art of the Uncanny?

A photograph reproduced in the first part of *Camera Lucida* represents an old and dilapidated Mozarabic house from the Alhambra of Granada. It was taken in 1854–1856 by Charles Clifford, a Welsh photographer who worked mainly in Spain. This photograph "touches" Barthes deeply; however, for once he is unable to say whether the main effect derives from a hidden *punctum* (a telling or surprising detail) in the general composition or from the theme chosen: "[T]his old photograph (1854) touches me: it is quite simply *there* that I should like to live."[21] In an effort at elucidating such a wish to "inhabit" certain pictures,

---

[21] Roland Barthes, *Camera Lucida*, trans. Richard Howard, New York, Noonday Press, 1981, p. 38. Hereafter, abbreviated as CL and page number. I have developed this analysis in *The Ghosts of Modernity*, Gainesville, University Press of Florida, 1996, pp. 67–82.

Barthes links this place to a maternal function. It embodies a regressive desire to return to the mother's womb:

> Looking at these landscapes of predilection, it is as if I *were certain* of having been there or of going there. Now Freud says of the maternal body that "there is no other place of which one can say with so much certainty that one has already been there." Such then would be the essence of the landscape (chosen desire): *heimlich*, awakening in me the Mother (and never the disturbing Mother). (CL, p. 40)

Barthes highlights the Freudian plotting of this photograph: it embodies *his* fantasy. "This longing to inhabit, I observe it clearly in myself, is neither oneiric (I do not dream of some extravagant site) nor empirical (I do not intend to buy a house according to the views of a real-estate agency); it is fantasmatic" (CL, p. 40). Barthes describes with great precision the space of fantasy: a fantasy is neither a dream nor a conscious plan or project. It remains halfway, enjoying as it were a purely hypothetical location. The fantasy is endowed with the same temporality that Freud described earlier; it connects the past and the future while letting the present float in a pure imagination: "[I]t is fantasmatic, deriving from a kind of second sight which seems to bear me forward to an utopian time, or to carry me back to somewhere in myself: a double movement which Baudelaire celebrated in *Invitation au voyage* and *La Vie antérieure*" (CL, p. 40). He feels that he has lived in this place to which he longs to return. Indeed, this Spanish house is anthropomorphic; it resembles a tattooed body with its elaborate yet faded Arab fresco, the two windows serving as eyes, and the huge arch bringing to mind human legs. One needs some time to discover a young boy sitting on a stone against an outer wall, his back pressed against the right-hand side of the house. Dwarfed by the enormity of the building, the boy stares into the void. One can see behind, in the distance, a cypress tree and then, quite distinctly, three white crosses.

As a pure fantasy, this house is nothing but a passage, and quite literally too, it is an entrance to a cemetery visible in the background. Freud repeats it often: the *heimlich* already contains the *unheimlich* as the return of the repressed. This repressed meaning is here, inevitably, Death. What Barthes does not know yet is that his regressive longing announces the death of the mother. Death has been somewhat tamed by being incorporated into a regressive fantasy. Barthes sees himself as an old child who lives near a graveyard. Let us repeat: "*[H]eimlich*, awakening in me the Mother (and never the disturbing Mother)" (CL, p. 40). The translator could not render the exact nuance of "*heimlich*, réveillant en moi la Mère (nullement inquiétante)."[22] In French, the Uncanny is

---

[22] Roland Barthes, *La Chambre Claire. Note sur la photographie*, Paris, Gallimard/Seuil, 1980, p. 68.

always translated as *inquiétante étrangeté*, and Barthes betrays a desire to split the phrase and delete its worrying "inquiétude." In all this passage, Barthes is quoting Freud who writes this about the Uncanny:

> It often happens that neurotic men state that to them there is something uncanny about female genitals. But what they find uncanny is actually the entrance to man's old "home," the place where everyone once lived. A jocular saying has it that "love is a longing for home," and if someone dreams of a certain place or a certain landscape and, while dreaming, thinks of himself, "I know this place, I've been here before," this place can be interpreted as representing the mother's genitals or her womb. Here too, then the uncanny is what was once familiar. The negative prefix un- is the indicator of repression.[23]

The desire to bask in the pure quietude of the mother's love was, sadly, pro-phetic, in that it concealed a desire for "perpetual peace" – that is, the peace one finds in a cemetery, as Kant famously remarked. In stark contrast to his muted elegiac mode, the abrupt announcement of the mother's death marks a rupture and a new departure in the second half of the book: "Now, one November eve-ning shortly after my mother's death, I was going through some photographs" (CL, p. 63). The investigation of the essence of photography starts anew, its pro-cess now explicitly linked with mourning: "I had acknowledged that fatality, one of the most agonizing features of mourning, which decreed that however often I might consult such images, I could never recall her features (summon them up as a totality)" (CL, p. 63).

Yet the Mother's image, even more than her death, remains "undialectic." It cannot be shown; it cannot be transformed into a Hegelian negativity, or the Proustian search for a Lost Time, or even Sartre's capture of the *eidos* in a flash of the imagination: "The Photograph does not call up the past (nothing Proustian in a photograph)" (CL, p. 82). On the contrary, its two dimensions and glossy paper only testify to a certain "nevermore" of a reality that has been there. It is a simple "that has been." Barthes discovers in this personal odyssey the truth that something has taken place. There is, therefore, a realism of the Uncanny, in spite of all its private associations: "The realists, of whom I am one and of whom I was already when I asserted that the Photograph was an image without a code[24] – even if, obviously, certain codes do inflect our read-ing of it – the realists do not take the photograph for a "copy" of reality, but for

---

[23] Freud, "The Uncanny," p. 151. Here, I have not followed the translator's decision to double "uncanny" with "unhomely/homely" in brackets.

[24] See Roland Barthes, "The Photographic Message," in *Image-Music-Text*, trans. Stephen Heath, London, Fontana-Collins, 1977, p. 17.

an emanation of *past reality:* a *magic*, not an art" (CL, p. 88). This "reality" is haunted, doubled by emanations that can be recorded by a camera.

Historically, the invention of photography had combined two technologies: the optical apparatus of the *camera obscura* used by painters to follow the laws of perspective and the chemical discoveries of certain metallic emulsions capable of being modified by light rays. In his last book, Barthes downplays the optical side, which entails an ideological analysis of the framing mechanism. He eschewed this sort of ideological analysis because he had performed them too often before, when he would assess the semiotics of political or ethical choices presupposed by any shot, any angle, any frame. Here, he wishes to focus on the "magic" of photography, and this magic derives mostly from a chemical transsubstantiation:

> For the *noeme* "That-has-been" was possible only on the day when a scientific circumstance (the discovery that silver halogens were sensitive to light) made it possible to recover and print directly the luminous rays emitted by a variously lighted object. The photograph is literally an emanation of the referent.... A sort of umbilical cord links the body of the photographed thing to my gaze: light, though impalpable, is here a carnal medium, a skin I share with anyone who has been photographed. (CL, pp. 80–81)

Curiously, for Barthes, this light is above all white and black, which is why he almost never mentions color photography in his book; the only color photograph he reproduces is a blue-green tint of Boudinet's Polaroid. He narrates elsewhere his visit to a show of Daniel Boudinet's series of polaroids from which he chose the picture on the back page of the table of contents of *Camera Lucida*: a small triangular shape opens at the bottom of a double veil, against which a round cushion seems to force its way out, like a fetus being expelled from the womb. Its color matches that of the Mother's eyes, because in the early black-and-white pictures of his mother, he recognizes "quite a physical luminosity, the photographic trace of a color, the blue-green of her pupils" (CL, p. 66). By the same token, Barthes relishes the thought that the silver in the emulsion remains somewhat alive. Photography participates in some magical transubstantiation (light becomes metal), thus averring the consubstantiality of the gaze to its object.

The ghostly nature of photography sends us back to the *Unheimlichkeit* of the Thing. It is, as Lacan and Žižek both insist, a Freudian *Ding*, which entails that after it has been resurrected, it may not come back exactly at the same place or with the same gaze. This slight difference captures the thrill that Barthes expects to get when watching a photograph that moves him. In keeping with Balzac's innate fear that each photograph that his friend Nadar took of him would steal a layer of his precious spectral emanations, Barthes describes the triangle composed by the photographer, the object, and the observer as a sort of ghost dance:

> [T]he person or thing photographed is the target, the referent, a kind of little simulacrum, any *eidolon* emitted by the object, which I should like to call the *Spectrum* of the Photograph, because this word retains, through its root, a relation to "spectacle" and adds to it that rather terrible thing which is there in every photograph: the return of the dead. (CL, p. 9)

The exact reverse of Barthes's Uncanny was the underlying theme of an installation by Sophie Calle and, in fact, one of her most disturbing pieces. Early in the Spring of 2007, the French conceptual artist learned two things at once: she was invited to represent France at the Venice Biennale and her mother was dying of cancer and had only a few months to live. Calle promised her mother, who had deplored that she could not come to Venice to witness her daughter's triumph, that she would be with her anyhow, telling her: "You'll be in Venice." This promise was fulfilled through her installation *Pas pu saisir la mort* (Couldn't Capture Death), first shown in July 2007 at the International pavilion of the Venice Biennale, while her main installation, "Take Care of Yourself," occupied the French pavilion. It was seen as a taboo-breaking work because it depicted in grueling detail the death of the mother. Some immediately accused it of voyeuristic visual consumption. *Pas pu saisir la mort* has, even more than Calle's other installations, immediately generated controversy.[25] The video of her mother's dying moments was indeed hard to take. One might fear that it verged on the exploitative side of sentimentality facing the demise of loved ones.

No doubt, the negative reaction I had first was offset by my enthusiastic response to *Take Care of Yourself*, shown at the Paula Cooper Gallery in 2009.[26] In this multimedia installation, Sophie Calle reproduces a breakup message from a lover; it was sent to her as an email that announced that everything was over but that the unmade ex-lover asked her to "take care of herself." Not being sure of what was meant by this final valediction, Calle then asked more than

---

[25] See the survey of diverging opinions (including mine) gathered by Daphne Merkin in "I Think, Therefore I'm Art," *New York Times Sunday Magazine*, October 19, 2008, pp. 18–20.

[26] I am grateful to Marcelline Block with whom I discussed the exhibition at Paula Cooper gallery. See her excellent essay "Unburied Mothers: The Death of the Maternal in Simone de Beauvoir's *Une mort très douce* and Sophie Calle's *Pas pu saisir la mort*" in her edited collection *The Many Ways We Talk about Death in Contemporary Society*, Lewiston, NY, Edwin Mellen, 2009. The latest iteration of Sophie Calle's exhibition about her dying mother, called "Rachel, Monique," has been presented by Paula Cooper Gallery and Galerie Perrotin at the Episcopal Church of the Heavenly Rest in New York from May 9 to June 25, 2014.

100 women from various fields and with various competence to make sense of the famous breakup missive: "I asked 107 women (including two made from wood and one with feathers), chosen for their profession or skills, to interpret this letter. To analyze it, comment on it, dance it, sing it. Dissect it. Exhaust it. Understand it for me. Answer for me." The result was hilarious, savage, and witty, and everyone in the room was sooner or later convulsed by laughter, a laughter directed at the unnamed writer of the email, whose message was indeed dissected a hundred times, and also perhaps, at times at Calle herself, which was what her cunning installation had prepared, as we can witness when she stages a parody of "In Treatment" with a couple therapy specialist, who psychoanalyses the letter, sitting next to it in a chair.

The tonality of *Pas pu saisir la mort* was evidently darker. A few friends of mine who had visited the Biennale were much more touched than I was and responded very emotionally to the staging of mourning that was deployed in those rooms. Having seen *Pas pu saisir la mort* one or two of these viewers left the room and went outside to cry. One of them said that he had been moved by it as if he had witnessed the death of his own mother. Had my negative reaction been a defense reaction or was it attributable to ingrained French cynicism facing the exhibition of personal grief? Was I overcompensating in rejecting what I saw as a sentimentalist exploitation of personal grief? I felt that I was bullied into submission to the power of the death of a loved one and found instead only a dangerous descent into tear-jerking triteness. However, a doubt persisted – in fact, without knowing it, I was facing the paradoxes of our contemporary Uncanny.

Pas pu saisir la mort lists in a short introductory text all the final preparations made by Calle for her mother's death. We see then the mother's portrait when she was in the prime of her life along with family photographs. In the second room, a video loop represents the last thirteen minutes of her life recorded in real time. She is seen in profile, lying still with closed eyes; hence, we cannot tell whether she is asleep, awake, or dead. What has to be missed is the exact moment of her death. Calle was hoping to catch the instant of death and failed. For eighty hours, she had remained awake, changing the tape each hour, hoping to capture the moment of her death, in vain.

Calle shows that death cannot be "captured" even if one brings to bear all the technology available. However, some technology is indispensable if we want to re-experience the facts. Calle discusses this paradox in an interview with Louise Neri in April 2009.[27] She confirms that her quest, once preserved in a

---

[27] Louise Neri, *Interview Magazine*, April 2009, http://www.interviemagazine.com/art/sophie-calle/p.1, accessed August 5, 2009.

video, was more effective than her experience. In fact, she needed the delay of *Nachträglichkeit* to measure the extent of her loss: "It was only when *Pas pu saisir la mort* was installed and I went to look at it that I realized that this was my mother, and I started to cry." *Pas pu saisir la mort* undoes the fantasy in which she had been stuck for a while – that is, her initial wish to capture the moment of death on video so as to overcome the pain. The horrifying Thing, in which raw Death apprehended here and now consists, could not but fail to materialize. This suggests that the failure of the fantasy corresponds to a failure of the sublime Thing to appear.

This staged failure produced a totally uncanny feeling in me. What was Uncanny, first of all, was the decision of fixing the moment when the "soul" leaves the body. Are we not dangerously close to the trick photographs of ectoplasms and children's spirits, thus to all the sentimental Kitsch that the Victorians loved to produce and observe? However, as we soon learn from Calle, no object and above all no Thing can be interposed in an effort to minimize pain or abolish anxiety. The fantasy of a mourning that would be mapped, pinned down to a precise spot in time and space, is undone by a principle of reality that dismisses even the minimal pleasures provided by aesthetics. The notes explain that Calle's mother had been preoccupied with her appearance until the end. Trusting cosmetics to sublimate the sordid aspects of death, the mother wanted to look as beautiful as possible. She got a pedicure, so that her feet would "look nice when I go." Nevertheless, in the grainy video we see, the mother's body is reduced to her face in a profile, and all this posthumous beauty has vanished.

Here, however, the dying body, almost invisible to the viewer, never falls into the category of abjection, which is often the effect produced by films of artists dying of AIDs, as in Hervé Guibert's *La Pudeur et l'Impudeur*. In this film, shot by himself in 1990–1991, Guibert exposed the abjection of his weakened, emaciated, crippled body. For a man who had been proud of his good looks, this film constituted an exercise in anti-narcissistic flagellation, a literal mortification. In Calle's video, we were not allowed to perceive the ravaging effects of the cancer that led to the mother's demise. Her physical presence was sublimated, her wan face and static body offset by the dynamism of background music – Mozart's Clarinet Concerto in A Major – heard on the soundtrack while the video loop replayed images that revealed absolutely nothing of the very last minutes of her life.

When Calle's mother learned that she had only a few weeks to live, she prepared for her death. Her mortuary preparation included arranging the very installation at the Venice Biennale. Thus Calle followed her mother's wishes literally about when, where, and how the piece was to be exhibited. In a sense, the mother became the co-author of the piece, almost burying herself alive. For instance, she wanted her daughter to include her pre-funeral epitaph, which consisted of the sentence, "I'm getting bored already!" The jocular aside was actually engraved on her tomb. This defiant jest recalls Duchamp's tongue-in-cheek epitaph on his own tombstone: "Besides, it's always the others that die." Indeed, the mother appears already bored to death on the photo that she had selected for her own tombstone.

Had I reacted too fast to the personal drama that was displayed in the installation? Was I upset by what could appear as the "sick" exploitation of personal bereavement to make art? Had I had failed to see the "sublime" of the situation? Was I caught up in the reductive bourgeois *doxa* that art should not cross certain limits? Since the beginning, Calle's work always aimed at subverting the limits between the private and the public, between the confessional and the exhibitionistic. Can one bury one's mother in a video installation, or even let her bury herself in advance? As for me as a spectator, faced with the drab reality of death, I had no room to go, neither height nor depth. Whereas the installation on the failed breakup letter extolled the virtues of making sense at any cost, here no interpretation was possible. Facing *Pas pu saisir la mort*, I could neither sublimate the artist's pain nor introduce distance via irony. Neither could I construct my own narrative around Calle's mother's death, not because the installation was devoid of uncanny elements, but precisely because I found the artistic gesture too "canny."

It took me some time to realize that I had missed the point. If Calle, in the privileged position of the daughter intervening at the scene of imminent death with her usual apparatus, a camera recording day and night the forthcoming demise, having enlisted the help of a nurse and friends, failed to capture the moment of her mother's death, how could I imagine that I would succeed in catching anything? There were no obvious aesthetic markers to hold on to, no "beauty" to see in all this, except obliquely, in the mother's pathetic wish to retain markers of beauty thanks to her favorite music and icons. Here, however, beauty vanished in front of an ethical form of respect – or at least this is how I construed the daughter's accomplishment of her mother's last wishes. What was Uncanny then was the superimposition of the mother and the daughter, a double ghostly author united in a single gesture blurring the border between aesthetics and ethics, art and life. Thus the Uncanny had destroyed the fantasy; my ambivalence revealed that I was stuck in the logic of the original fantasy, the desire to master death via a single image, concept, or artistic gesture.

The Uncanny has been described by Freud as the struggle between our rationalist beliefs that the dead cannot come back to haunt us and the suspicion that, in exceptional circumstances, replayed by fiction or art, something weird can always happen. Freud explains why the return of the dead is not a realistic possibility but belongs to archaic beliefs that we have surmounted – only up to a point. "Yet we do not feel entirely secure in these new convictions; the old ones live on in us, on the look-out for confirmation. Now as soon as something *happens* in our lives that seems to confirm these old, discarded beliefs, we experience a sense of the uncanny."[28] If Calle's issue was to test the "material reality" of death as an event before concluding that it was impossible to "catch" it, she was both exhibiting a fantasy of mastery and destroying it at the same time. Hence, when I had worried that Calle's gesture was too "canny," I expressed the same hesitation that one can have facing works of art that attempt to produce the Uncanny by miming unconscious processes attached to it. However, my divided reaction to her powerful work on mourning and the impossibility of mourning had confirmed to me that the site of the Uncanny was the failure of sublimation. The Uncanny remains within art, yet hovers at its borders and tends to exceed them, appearing when deeper affects cannot be certain of having found a form, of being "expressed" fully just to be buried and forgotten once and for all. The Uncanny testifies to the resistance of affects, to a resilient haunting that dodges us beyond any formalist capture. If most powerful artworks produced today are not all variations of the Uncanny, they tend to grapple with the intractable problem of presenting the Thing, and with the ghostly survival of affects reemerging beyond the form of art. In that sense, the Uncanny might well be today's privileged mode of access to the sublime. As we know, however, there is a short step from the sublime to the pathetic or to pure bathos. This deep uncertainty will lead us to a problem that I will tackle in the next chapter, especially when dealing with Surrealism: how can artists or writers tap, use, or mine the unconscious?

[28] Freud, "*The Uncanny*," p. 154.

Chapter 4

Psychoanalysis and the paranoid critique of pure literature

When André Breton publicly discussed his conflicted rapport with Freud and psychoanalysis in *Communicating Vessels*, he began with an epigraph quoting the last lines of Jensen's *Gradiva*: "And lightly picking up her dress with her left hand, Gradiva Rediviva Zoé Bertgang, wrapped in the dreamy gaze of Hanold, with her step supple and tranquil, in the bright sunlight striking upon the pavement, passed on the other side of the street."[1] Left hand, right foot: there is always a body part that remains invisible. Indeed, the game of sunlight and buried darkness played so well by Gradiva had seduced Breton, to the point that he used her name to baptize the art gallery that he opened in Paris in 1937, at 31 rue de Seine. In his presentation, Breton had written about her magical name. He capitalizes it, "SHE WHO ADVANCES," and adds: "What can she be, 'she who advances,' if not the beauty of tomorrow, still masked to the crowd, who reveals herself once in a while next to an object, a painting, a book?"[2] Breton was always keen on being on the vanguard; he had to enlist this fictional creature to pursue his lyrical utopia of a more radiant future in which dream and reality would blend, released by the power of desire. By contrast, Freud never tried to be "in advance," and even if he knew that he was on the side of "progress," his view tended to a scientific enlightenment. These two models were bound to clash.

At entrance to Breton's tiny Gradiva gallery was a double door designed by Marcel Duchamp. It represented the dark silhouette of a man and woman embracing, a hulking double shadow directly cut out of glass panel. The slightly forbidding figure was modeled on the couple Norbert Hanold sees in Pompeii. We may remember that he had first taken them for a brother and a sister, only to realize later that they were a married couple on their honeymoon. This vision of happy sexual exchanges, relaying what he had heard at night in the adjacent room, led to the elaboration of a jealous fantasy. Indeed, soon after,

---

[1] André Breton, *Communicating Vessels*, trans. Mary Ann Caws and Geoffrey T. Harris, Lincoln, University of Nebraska Press, 1990, p. 1.

[2] André Breton, "Gradiva" in *La Clé des Champs, Oeuvres Complètes*, vol. III, ed. Marguerite Bonnet, Paris, Gallimard, Pléiade, 1999, p. 672.

Norbert imagines Gradiva in the arms of another man and is immediately ready to challenge him to a duel.

Obviously, the themes that attracted Breton and Duchamp to Jensen's story (Freud's book and the original story had only been translated into French in 1931) was the *Wahn*, the delirium, the systematic delusion, and the wild hallucinations tapping the dark realm of dreams and visions. This domain nevertheless appeared split between the irresistible seduction emanating from a woman bold enough to "pass" to the Other side of the Unconscious, risking her own mental health in the process (as Breton's Nadja ended up doing) and the more aggressive projection of unfounded suspicions facing the imaginary rival who embodies a perpetually elusive Other. This tension underpins Breton's ambivalent relationship to Freud, and one can translate it into the psychoanalytic vocabulary as a hesitation between hysteria and paranoia.

Breton and Freud

Our culture has adopted Surrealism and Freudianism with identical hyperboles. The 1998 exhibition, *Freud, Conflict and Culture*,[3] presented by the American Library of Congress exploited much more audio-visual documents than objects. Beyond illegible manuscripts in Gothic script and some realia – Freud's rings, his couch floating in the air – the exhibition's impact mostly came from well-chosen film excerpts from Hollywood classics. Freud's ideas have survived in a popular culture that it has shaped and permeated. This is why an astute Freudo-Lacanian-like Slavoj Žižek illustrates his books with film clips, thrillers, horror stories, science fiction novels, and television series. The same remains true of Surrealism today; its last public flowering was linked to the counterculture of the 1960s, but the 2013 Venice Biennale, *The Encyclopedic Palace* curated by Massimiliano Gioni, paid a notable homage to Breton and Surrealism in many ways. The face of Breton was represented by his death mask in the International Pavilion, and his concept of a museum of curios and ephemera from all over the world recurred in several rooms of the Arsenale. Using the example of Marino Auriti, a self-taught Italian-American artist who had made a blueprint for a universal museum in 1955, Gioni also included psychoanalysis in the huge show: a reproduction of Jung's *Red Book* occupied a whole room of the Central Pavilion. Surrealism is not dead, at least in the world of contemporary art, and psychoanalysis

[3]   See Michael S. Roth, ed., *Freud, Conflict and Culture. Essays on His Life, Work and Legacy*, New York, Knopf, 1998. This section condenses a chapter of *Given: 1° Art, 2° Crime. Modernity, Murder and Mass Culture*. Eastbourne: Sussex Academic Press, 2007, pp. 151–171.

survives as culture. We need to understand how Surrealism became a continuation of psychoanalysis by other means through Breton's early fascination with Freud.

Breton appealed to Freud when he pioneered psychic automatism, the unconscious dictation of the Unconscious, and hysteria as a revolutionary art form. However, Surrealism's initial enthusiasm for hysteria and automatism transformed itself into a theory and practice of paranoia. The correspondence between Breton and Freud one finds in *Communicating Vessels* documents a rapport that had been caught up in whirls of hysteria only to end in paranoid accusations. This ambivalence is partly a result of Breton's first occupation. He began his career as a medical student specializing in psychiatry and served in this function during the World War I. He read Freud closely then, at a time when French schools of psychiatry ignored Freud. Breton was sent to the neuropsychiatric ward of Saint-Dizier in August 1916, which was supervised by a former assistant of Charcot. There, Breton devoured all the psychoanalytic literature available. He copied entire pages for his friend Fraenkel, providing accurate syntheses of the main Freudian concepts such as resistance, repression, and sublimation.[4] Breton had to defend Freud's ideas against his friend's skepticism.[5] At the same time, he took many notes on the delirious speeches uttered daily by psychotic patients. His first exposure to war psychosis was followed by a forced encounter with hysteria when Breton was transferred to Dr. Babinski's service in 1917, where he would work with the doctor on the vexed issue of hysteria's nature.

Breton adhered for a while to Babinski's refutation of Charcot's theory of hysteria. However, his notebooks prove that it was Freud's impact that led him to trust the spontaneous production of language as a key to the unconscious. Some of the terms used by Breton refer to French pre- or anti-Freudian psychiatry as represented by Charcot, Janet, or Babinski, through the key insight that spontaneous utterances of hysterics allow access to the actual mechanism of psychic production derived from Freud. Breton acknowledged this in the first *Manifesto of Surrealism*:

> Completely occupied as I still was with Freud at that time, and familiar as I was with his methods of examination which I had had some slight occasion to use on patients during the war, I resolved to obtain from myself what we were trying to obtain from them, namely a monologue spoken as rapidly as possible without any intervention

---

[4] Quoted in Marguerite Bonnet, "La Rencontre d'André Breton avec la Folie: Saint Dizier, août-novembre 1916," in *Folie et Psychanalyse dans l'expérience surréaliste*, ed. Fabienne Hulak, Nice, Z'éditions, 1992, pp. 126–127.

[5] Ibid., p. 121.

on the part of the critical faculties, a monologue consequently
unencumbered by the slightesty inhibition and which was, as closely
akin to *spoken thought*.[6]

Freud is ubiquitous in this manifesto written in 1924, and his theories lead
to Surrealist experiments aimed at abolishing the borders between sleep and
waking life, and also between art and life.

In October 1921, Breton met with Freud and was disappointed. "Interview
with Professor Freud" (1922) is a curt account of the meeting published in
Littérature and *Les Pas Perdus* (1924). Breton betrays his bitterness by sticking
to a physical description: Freud's appearance is that of "an old man without
elegance who receives in the poor consulting room one would expect from a
local doctor." The article concludes ironically by quoting Freud's tepid endorsement: "Happily, we do count a lot upon the young."[7] The discrepancy between
Freud, the man, and Freud, the theoretician, weighed on Breton's attitude in
the following years.

Later interactions turned more aggressive when Breton entertained suspicions that the *Interpretation of Dreams* had plagiarized previous dream
theoreticians. In the summer of 1931, as he was drafting *Communicating
Vessels*, Breton read the French translation of Freud's *Interpretation of Dreams*
thoroughly. He took twenty pages of notes in a schoolboy's exercise book.
In response to Freud's critique of Delboeuf in the section on "Theories of
Dreaming," Breton jumped ahead and stated a connection between dream
activity and paranoia. He wrote in the right-hand marginalia: "Theories
of dreams. 1. 'The whole psychical activity of the waking state continues in
dreams.' (Delboeuf) (Very insufficient) Dream = Paranoia." He comments on
the left-hand side: "Theories. Delboeuf. Dream-paranoia. Valéry: 'The dream
goes on.'"[8] This refers to section E of *The Interpretation of Dreams*,[9] which
establishes a bridge or a resemblance between dreams and paranoia: "If I may
venture on a simile from the sphere of psychiatry, the first group of theories
construct dreams on the model of paranoia, while the second group makes
them resemble mental deficiency or confusional states."[10] This sentence struck
Breton who copied it twice, and then he checked references to other authors.
He wrote: "Volkelt's *remarkable* sexual symbolism," and on the left-hand side,

---

[6] André Breton, "Manifesto of Surrealism" in *Manifestoes of Surrealism*, trans. Richard Seaver and
Helen R. Lane. Ann Arbor: University of Michigan Press, 1972. See also "Manifeste du Surréalisme,"
in *Oeuvres Complètes* I, ed. Marguerite Bonnet, Paris, Gallimard, Pléiade, 1988, p. 326.

[7] Breton, "Les pas Perdus," in *Oeuvres Complètes*, vol. I, p. 256.

[8] See André Breton's notes reproduced in *Folie et Psychanalyse dans l'expérience surréaliste*, p. 155.

[9] See Freud, *The Interpretation of Dreams*, 1965, pp. 75–78.

[10] Ibid., p. 76.

"Volkelt, quoted by Freud *without references (?).*"[11] This led to a personal attack that wounded Freud deeply.

Breton had written that Freud omitted Volkelt's book on symbolism from his bibliography on purpose, implying that he borrowed more than what transpires in the rapid remarks of the *Traumdeutung*. Volkelt would have inspired the whole theory of sexuality in dreams.[12] This was a double attack: first, Freud would have stolen the idea of sexuality in dreams from an obscure writer; then, Freud was censured for having forgotten his monism and fallen into the trap of idealism when organizing dreams and reality into radically different realms. If this ferocious critique betrayed the contagion of the theme of "paranoia," from Delboeuf to Freud and to Breton, the latter relied less on dialectical materialism than on the post-Kantian theories developed by Schopenhauer about prophetic dreaming or "second sight." For Breton, one axiom is that reality is a single undivided continuum and that dreams belong to it. Dreams keep a productive and dynamic interaction with everyday life. He writes: "Freud is again quite surely mistaken in concluding that the prophetic dream does not exist – I mean the dream involving the immediate future – since to hold that the dream is exclusively revelatory of the past is to deny the value of motion."[13] To counter what he calls Freud's "passeism," Breton gives an example: he provides a complete interpretation of one dream he had had on August 26, 1931. Predictably, this dream, in which a tie is called "Nosferatu," revolves about Surrealism. The point is to contradict Freud's idea of an "umbilicus" or dark core of unknowability in dreams, because Breton plans to "exhaust" the contents of the dream through a thorough examination of its images and associations.[14] However, even if he rewrites Freud's principles of condensation and overdetermination in a materialistic language inflected by Marx and Lenin and gives a thorough account of most of the images, he never comments on the curious fact that, throughout this dream, he keeps clutching a loaded gun. He was clearly aiming at Freud, but somehow overstated his own vigilance.

Freud defended himself from insinuations of plagiarism by pointing out that the omission of Volkelt's name was a mistake made in the French translation of 1926. The name was present in the original German text. A second letter accounted for the missing reference. Volkelt's name was dropped by mistake after the third printing. The French version was based on a later version.[15]

---

[11] Facsimile reproduction in *Folie et Psychanalyse dans l'expérience surréaliste*, p 154.
[12] André Breton, *Communicating Vessels*, p. 11. *Les vases Communicants*, vol. I, in André Breton, *Oeuvres Complètes*, vol. II, eds. M. Bonnet, P. Bernier, E.-A. Hubert, and J. Pierre, Paris, Gallimard, Pléiade, 1992, p. 109.
[13] Breton, *Communicating Vessels*, p. 13.
[14] Ibid., p. 45.
[15] See the appendix with Freud's letters and Breton's response in *Communicating Vessels*, pp. 149–155.

Freud rejected Breton's hypothesis that he had been prudish in matters of sexuality and that Volkelt would have been more explicit about sexual symbols in dreams. The third letter ended with a barb; Freud pretended not to understand Surrealism at all: "Although I have received many testimonies of the interest that you and your friend show for my research, I am not able to clarify for myself what Surrealism is and what it wants."[16] We see how Freud tried to reduce Breton's paranoid reading to simple hysteria, asking not "What is wanting?" but "What do you want from me?" Freud was sending back to Surrealism a feminized version of itself, the Gallic version of *Was will das Weib?* or "What does a woman want?"

Breton, eager for a male-to-male confrontation, gleefully noted Freud's agitated and contradictory responses, the flurry of successive letters, and a vindictive denunciation of Surrealism. Breton may have indeed "touched on a rather sensitive point."[17] The irony is, of course, that Freud and Breton elaborated similar strategies of power and containment. Freud, who had to exclude Jung as we will see in more details, ended up choosing a "Committee" of selected and trusted disciples whose task was to protect the orthodoxy of psychoanalysis. It was comprised of the most loyal followers: Ernst Jones, Karl Abraham, Otto Rank, Hanns Sachs, and a few others.[18] They were given special rings by Freud and behaved like a secret society. In the same way, Breton and his friends had launched a "Bureau of Surrealist Research" that practiced and recorded verbal and visual experiments but soon became a "central" or a "cell" whose mission was to exclude dissidents: thus, Philippe Soupault for writing journalism, Antonin Artaud for directing plays, Georges Bataille and his friends for irreducible divergence of opinions about politics and materialism. Both groups dealt with "deviations" and enforced a certain dogma. In both cases, the model was a small group of radical experimenters ready to battle the rest of the world and ending up excluding the more independent personalities.

Praising hysteria so as to invent paranoia

If *Communicating Vessels* pits Freud and Breton in a struggle for mastery, which revolves around contested archives, missing annotations, faulty bibliographies, deliberate misquotations, and issues of literary ownership and intellectual propriety, we remain in a game of male domination. However, it

[16] Breton, *Communicating Vessels*, p. 152.
[17] Ibid., p. 155.
[18] See Phyllis Grosskurth, *The Secret Ring: Freud's Inner Circle and the Politics of Psychoanalysis*, London, Jonathan Cape, 1991.

seems that Breton's strategy worked: whereas Freud had claimed that he had succeeded where the paranoiac had failed, Breton proved that the paranoiac could succeed where the psychoanalyst had failed. Freud found himself caught up in the net, writing apologetically to rectify the picture, and finally rejecting the whole business of the avant-garde as not serious enough. However, when Salvador Dalí met Freud in London in 1938, Freud appeared more receptive to "the young" this time; he liked Dalí even though Dalí was named as a fellow-Surrealist in *Communicating Vessels*. However, Dalí would soon be excluded by Breton for his political drift to the right. Paranoia still reigned. We may wonder how Surrealism moved so abruptly from a strategy that promoted hysteria to a strategy that took paranoia as its main weapon and mode of vision.

A few years before, in March 1928, Breton and Louis Aragon's manifesto extolling the "Invention of Hysteria" had been published in *La Révolution Surréaliste* to celebrate the "fiftieth anniversary of the invention of hysteria." The invention was dated from 1878, which pointed to Jean-Martin Charcot. Hysteria was hailed as "the greatest poetic discovery of the latter part of the century."[19] Quite logically, this homage to hysteria rejected Babinski, who had reduced hysteria to suggestion. Charcot was praised less for the fact that La Salpêtrière was a theatrical scene in which he exhibited patients in front of a fashionable crowd than for having created the conditions for the vulgarization of hysteria. Freud was not spared. Breton and Aragon opposed his conservatism to what they found admirable in Charcot's set up: the fact that La Salpêtrière's interns would sleep with their beautiful hysterical patients regularly. "Does Freud, who owes so much to Charcot, remember the time when, according to the survivors' account, the interns of La Salpêtrière refused to separate their professional duty and their taste for love, and when night fell, the patients would either visit them outside or they would meet the patients in their beds?"[20] Freud would have been horrified by the insinuation that he might be associated with that unruly crowd. The living poetry embodied by female patients and young interns sleeping together culminated in the "passionate attitudes" photographed by Charcot. In these images, stunning, half-undressed women in curious poses indicated the possibility of a new "convulsive beauty."

This new beauty, created out of the ruins of older representations, would emerge from the dream world. What mattered for Breton as for Freud was

---

[19] Breton, *Oeuvres Complètes*, I, p. 948. The text is written in small capitals throughout. An English translation of a section of this manifesto is provided in Elisabeth Roudinesco, *Jacques Lacan & Co. A History of Psychoanalysis in France, 1925–1985*, trans. Jeffrey Mehlman, Chicago, University of Chicago Press, 1990, pp. 6–7.

[20] Breton, *Oeuvres Complètes*, I, p. 949.

that dreams provided considerable freedom and avoided moral concerns. In *Nadja*, Breton analyzes his inexplicable fascination for a bad melodrama entitled *Les Détraquées*. Its powerful impression on him was similar to a disturbing dream he had at the time. The dream's climax was a moss-colored insect about twenty inches falling into his throat; he had to pull the hairy legs out of his mouth. Meditating on the nausea that the memory triggers in him, Breton reflects on the porous border separating dreams and waking life:

> Since the production of dream images always depends on at least
> this double play of mirrors, there is, here, the indication of the highly
> special, supremely revealing, "super-determinant" – in the Freudian
> sense of the word – role which certain powerful impressions are made
> to play, in no way contaminable by morality, actually experienced
> "beyond good and evil" in the dream, and, subsequently, in what we
> quite arbitrarily oppose to dream under the name of reality.[21]

Breton introduces the Freudian concept of "overdetermination" – the idea that each element of a dream simultaneously means several things, often with contradictory meanings. "Overdetermination" entails positing an extra-moral site for dreams: because of their plurality of meanings, these images are beyond good and evil. Breton's *Nadja* argues that avant-garde poetry will change life by introducing a deliberate confusion of the domains of dream and reality. The idea is developed in a passage of the *Manifesto of Surrealism*:

> The mind of the man who dreams is fully satisfied by what happens to
> him. The agonizing question of possibility is no longer pertinent. Kill,
> fly faster, love to your heart's content. And if you should die, are you
> not certain of waking up from the dead? Let yourself be carried along,
> events will not tolerate your interference. You are nameless. The ease of
> everything is priceless.[22]

In the "otherness" of dreams, one must acknowledge that belonging to a different realm in which moral issues are irrelevant. This does not mean that dreams are worthless fantasies; on the contrary, one should not attempt to collapse the world of dreams with reality. Breton adds: "What reason, I ask, a reason so much vaster than the other, makes dreams seem so natural and allow me to welcome unreservedly a welter of episodes so strange that they would confound me now as I write? And yet I can believe my eyes, my ears: this great day has arrived, this beast has spoken."[23] The conflation of the two states, the waking state and the sleeping state, leads to a redefinition of reason

---

[21] André Breton, *Nadja*, trans. Richard Howard, 1960. New York, Grove Press, p. 51.
[22] See *Manifestoes of Surrealism*, p. 13. I have modified the translation.
[23] Ibid.

and of reality: reality has to be replaced by "surreality." One type of people who could testify to its impact on their bodies is the group of "hysterics" who were studied by Charcot at the end of the nineteenth century. Surrealism had to launch a praise and defense of hysteria as a poetic mechanism.

We have seen that in 1928 Breton and Aragon redefined hysteria by reject-ing its medicalization: "Hysteria is not a pathological phenomenon and can in every respect be considered a supreme vehicle of expression."[24] Thus Breton and Aragon insisted on the quasi-normalcy of a state seen as a limit-experience. For them, hysteria also ruled out any "systematic delirium," by which they mean classical paranoia. The phases of the classical hysterical crisis would lead to a "superb aura" in a magnificent theatralization before subsiding by a "simple resolution in everyday life."[25] Hysteria was identified with a mysti-cal and erotic ecstasy deriving from a fundamentally artistic impulse. Adding salt to the humdrum of everyday life, hysteria proved that the Surrealist ambi-tion to merge poetry and life was not a vain dream or a delusion. In their pamphlet, Breton and Aragon bid farewell to their former master Babinski for whom hysteria was a mimetic disease, an affection generated by a "sugges-tion" that could be eradicated by a counter-suggestion. His harsh treatment of male hysterics like shell-shocked soldiers back from the front during World War I was a form of medical abuse that involved electroshock therapy. Against this, Breton and Aragon promoted hysterical simulation as leading to poetry and art. For the Surrealists, simulation was a roundabout way of going back to Aristotle's mimesis while avoiding the "realism" it seems to presuppose. This appears explicitly in a text written jointly by Breton with Eluard in 1930: *The Immaculate Conception*. In "Possessions," the two poets recreate the dis-courses of debility, of mania, of general paralysis, of interpretive delirium, and of precocious dementia.[26] The introduction to this section, written by Breton, discusses the amphibology of the term "simulation." Breton links the tech-nical meaning of simulation in psychiatry, especially for war neuroses, to a critique of traditional poetic forms. An older and conventional poetry should be replaced by stylistic imitations of various types of psychotic speech: "This is to say that we offer the generalization of this device and that in our eyes, the 'attempts at simulation' of diseases that land you in a jail might advantageously replace the ballad, the sonnet, the epic, the nonsense rhyme and other genres now totally obsolete."[27] Linking the verbal production of the insane and of

---

[24] Breton, *Oeuvres Complètes*, vol. I, p. 950.
[25] Ibid., p. 949.
[26] Ibid., pp. 848–863.
[27] Ibid., p. 849.

poets are the same laws of composition, the same rhetorical patterns, the same tropes and stylistic devices. This general rhetoric leaves room for an alternative vision of reality.

Such a new vision was expressed forcefully when a young Catalan painter and poet named Salvador Dalí joined the group. The systematization of psychic disorder became his aesthetic credo. Dalí's painting, the *Lugubrious Game*, had been praised by Breton for its "hallucinatory" quality,[28] while the Surrealist dissident Georges Bataille took it as a new paradigm. In December 1929, *Documents* published Bataille's essay on "The Lugubrious Game" in which Bataille developed the idea of castration as a critical tool. For him, emasculation was presented by Dalí, as a parody with the shocking figure of a man with shitty breeches. Dalí, because of his allegiance to Breton, refused to allow Bataille to reproduce the painting and attacked Bataille directly, calling him "cretinous" and "senile," whose misreading derived from a wrong interpretation of Freud.[29] One can see Bataille, Breton, and Dalí reproaching one another for having misapplied Freudian ideas. These furious controversies paved the way for the emergence of Dalí's paranoid-critical method.

The Freudian source of these ideas stands out in Dalí's "The Moral Position of Surrealism" of March 22, 1930. Aligning himself with Breton's *Second Manifesto*, Dalí explained that next to going into the street with a revolver in hand and shooting people at random, his proselytizing activity aimed at propagating the "violently paranoid will to systematize confusion."[30] Freud's ideas had been watered down, and it was urgent to restore their "rabid and dazzling clarity." The text mentioned that he had written under a painting of the Sacré-Coeur: "I spat on my mother." Such a provocation, which was not taken lightly by his family, corresponded less with a systematic attempt at "demoralization" similar to that of Sade than with the idea of launching a method allowing one to see reality differently. This is what he called "paranoia":

> The particular perspicacity of attention in the paranoiac state must
> be insisted upon; paranoia being recognized, moreover, by all
> psychologists as a form of mental illness which consists in organizing
> reality in such a way as to utilize it to control an imaginative
> construction. The paranoiac who believes himself to be poisoned
> discovers in everything that surrounds him, right up to the most
> imperceptible and subtle details, preparations for his own death.
> Recently, though a decidedly paranoiac process, I obtained an image

[28] Breton, *Oeuvres Complètes*, vol. II, pp. 308–309.
[29] Salvador Dalí, "The Rotting Donkey," in *Oui. The Paranoid-Critical Revolution: Writings 1927–1933*, ed. Robert Descharnes, trans. Yvonne Shafir, New York, Exact Change, 1998, p. 117.
[30] Dalí, *Oui*, p. 110.

of a woman whose position, shadow and morphology, without altering or deforming anything of her real appearance, are also, at the same time, those of a horse.[31]

If we understand why paranoid mechanisms are exemplified by the man who imagines himself poisoned, this method of guided hallucination recalls the poetics of Rimbaud whose "systematic deregulating of all senses" generates teeming wild images. Even if Dalí adds that the process can become more "violent" or "intense" and yield three, four, or even thirty different images, his concept operates with images anchored to reality.

In "The Rotting Donkey," Dalí, stung by Bataille's account of his work in terms of castration anxiety, pushes his thesis further by radically collapsing conventional systems of representation and pure paranoid delirium. He returns to his example of a woman who is at the same time a horse, and a lion's head, explaining:

> I challenge materialists to examine the kind of mental crisis that such an image may provoke, I challenge them to examine the even more complex problem of knowing which one of these images has a greater number of possibilities for existence if the intervention of desire is taken into consideration, and also to investigate the more serious and more general problem of knowing whether the series of representations has a limit or whether, as we have every reason to believe, such a limit does not exist, or rather, exists solely as a function of each individual's paranoid capacity.[32]

The reversal of perspective is obvious: whereas paranoia seemed to open a door to another kind of visual perception, it now turns into a regulating principle that replaces the Marxist idea of a "material world" as a basis. The material world is just one type of simulacrum, which provides a sly way of debunking Bataille's "base" materialism.

Dalí chose Breton over Bataille, but meanwhile both camps criticized Freud's dualism because there was always a clash between the pleasure principle and the reality principle in classical psychoanalytic doctrine. To incorporate Freud's insights into a monist discourse, Bataille started from the materiality of the body, with its attendant notions of excess, waste, excrement, and abjection, whereas Breton and Dalí assumed that reality was made up of oneiric simulacra; however, these, in their turn, would be underpinned by a universal and productive desire. This debate proved formative for Lacan who came into contact with it as he was completing his doctoral dissertation on

---

[31] Ibid., p. 112.
[32] Ibid., p. 116.

paranoia. As Roudinesco has shown, it was the impact of Dalí's *Rotting Donkey* that allowed Lacan to break with the classical psychiatric theories of personality and constitution and to revisit Freudian metapsychology.[33] Lacan was translating Freud's 1922 article on "Certain Neurotic Mechanisms in Jealousy, Paranoia and Homosexuality" into French. This is an essay in which the thesis underpinning the analysis of Schreber, the main case of paranoia discussed by Freud, is developed: for Freud, the root of all paranoia is the return of a repressed homosexuality. In a case of a jealous delirium observed by Freud in a heterosexual patient, the delusional attacks followed successful sexual rapports between the man and his wife. By inventing imaginary male lovers that generated delirious recriminations, the husband facilitated the projection of his desires facing these men. Even though Lacan translated the essay, he ended up rejecting the validity of this interpretation for Schreber's case, as we will see later.

Thus one can observe that Lacan's first models were found in Surrealism, much more than in Freud. Just then Lacan contributed to a collective essay on "Inspired Writings" of 1931 in which the three authors analyze the psychotic ramblings of a teacher who was hospitalized at Sainte-Anne. Their description of the formal components of a grammar of mad utterance pays homage to Surrealism, because the authors quote the first *Manifesto of Surrealism* and look for a model of interpretation in Breton's and Eluard's imitations of individual styles of typical delirium in *The Immaculate Conception* published in 1930.[34]

Thanks to the convergence of interests among Bataille, Dalí, Breton, and Lacan, the second decade of Surrealism was dominated by the concept of paranoia, much as the first had been by automatism and hysteria. This was not a passing fashion: Breton's most comprehensive prose synthesis, his 1937 *Mad Love*, still affirms his belief that desire is the mainspring of all our dreams and actions while still making an important place for paranoia. Desire, no longer structured by hysteria, was to follow the lead of paranoia. In the fifth section, Breton reopens Freud's *A Childhood Memory of Leonardo da Vinci* before expounding the principle of paranoiac criticism or critical paranoia. A vulture hidden in the Virgin's dress had been seen by Oskar Pfister after Freud had analyzed its intellectual relevance. Once an interpretation generated a

[33] See Roudinesco, *Jacques Lacan & Co. A History of Psychoanalysis in France, 1925–1985*, pp. 110–112, for an account of their meeting, which had been instigated by Lacan, and also her *Jacques Lacan*, trans. Barbara Bray, Columbia University Press, 1997, pp. 31–32, for a more general assessment.

[34] Jacques Lacan with J. Lévy-Valensi and P. Migault, "Ecrits 'Inspirés': Schizographie" in Jacques Lacan, *De la psychose paranoïaque dans ses rapports avec la personnalité suivi de Premiers écrits sur la paranoïa*, Paris, Seuil, 1975, pp. 365–382. The authors quote Breton's first Manifesto of Surrealism p. 379 and *Immaculate Conception* p. 380.

new image in a previous one, it remained there, hovering between objectivity and subjectivity.[35] Visual hallucinations can be shared whatever one's opinions about the divide between madness and sanity may be. Whereas hysteria relies on mutual seduction to reach the truth of desire, paranoia articulates a system of signs whose pseudo-objectivity betrays flimsy foundations. The force of desire appears as the source of what had been shared, even momentarily. The extravagant gestures enacted by hysterics were pathetic attempts at aesthetic expression; these were staged differently by paranoia in a violently assertive discourse that would be shared not just by an elective master but by a whole confrontational and dialogical community, in a movement that tended more and more to political confrontation.

Surrealist doctrine shifted from a praise of hysteria disclosing sexual desire via seduction to a practice of guided paranoia that aggressively tried to change the world by providing a new system of interpretation. It thus merged with what David Trotter has called "paranoid modernism."[36] A profound shift in values marked the end of the 1920s. The hysterical style of modernism had posed the question of femininity and masculinity, thus causing panic for men and women. Hysteria's main question ("Am I a man or a woman?") was followed by a second question: "Whom am I imitating in my desire?" The couples implied took two shapes – the seduced interns (so-called masters) and the enraptured hysterics – to produce the ecstasies praised by the Surrealists. This shift had important consequences for high modernism, a modernism that allegedly attempted to distinguish itself from commodified mass culture.[37] Modernism would boil down to a male hysteria, compulsively rejecting feminine weakness in the name of the "hard" style of modern poetic practice. As Pound and Eliot insisted, the poet must become a professional and not a feminized dilettante dabbling in versifying. For Huyssen, who follows Adorno, the true modernist is a serious artist only insofar as his or her most threatening enemy is a defunct Victorian culture identified with a "bitch," the "botched" civilization that gave birth to the Great War. In fact, such a perspective should be qualified if not resisted, and the example of Surrealism leads to some reservations. If the role of the Great War is truly crucial, the main divide might not be 1914 and 1918, but 1929 and 1930.

These questions appeared more crucially when André Breton attempted to blend automatic writing with the imitation of psychotic speech. He had, of course, to stick to the belief that the second series of texts were just games, pure

---

[35] As noted by Breton in *L'Amour Fou* in *Oeuvres Complètes*, vol. II, p. 753.
[36] David Trotter, *Paranoid Modernism*, Oxford, Oxford University Press, 2001, pp. 284–325.
[37] Andreas Huyssen, "Mass Culture as Woman: Modernism's Other," in *After the Great Divide*, Bloomington, Indiana University Press, 1986, p. 45.

stylistic exercises, skillful imitations of psychiatric case studies. Much earlier, nevertheless, as we saw, Breton had encountered psychotic delusion. This was in Saint-Dizier, when he was discovering Freud. There, Breton chanced on a particular type of delirium: a soldier who was traumatized by battle. As a consequence, he stopped believing in the reality of war. For this shell-shocked patient, the only way to survive psychically was to treat the whole war as a simulacrum. Fields full of blood, smoking ruins, and mangled corpses were just an illusion that had been created by occult powers. As an illusion, it was successful because it succeeded in creating the effect of the "sublime." This delirious discourse akin to a paranoid projection had such a powerful effect on Breton that he transformed it into a prose poem, which happened to be his first prose piece.

In this text entitled "Subject," the soldier speaks in a sort of dramatic monologue. "Subject" begins with a double entendre on how to harden one's sensitivity while getting used to the idea of "war:" "How I wish I could harden myself (*m'aguerrir*) one day, with the help of God."[38] The speaking subject feels that all of humanity watches him. He is ready to become an experimenter who will sacrifice his reason for the good of all. He cannot refuse this call: "To what would my refusal serve. – Exploring the so-called murderous zone, it became child's play for me to denounce blatant imposture."[39] The denunciation of "imposture" takes on epic proportions when he evokes his experience in battle:

> Knocked out by gypsies, lost between ramps, a waltzer would fall once in a while, lifting his hand to his vermilion rose. Using the maximum of art, they have maintained me all that time under the empire of the sublime. And the apparatus of death has not been able to awe me as they thought. I have walked over corpses it is true. One can see such as these in any dissecting room. Quite a number could have been made in wax. Most of the "wounded" looked happy. As to the illusion of spilled blood, you see as well this in any province town when they stage Dumas's plays.... What does it cost them to make a whole company disappear little by little?[40]

The paranoid interpretation of the world follows an unassailable logic: How could one believe the spectacle of frenzied mass slaughter on such a huge scale? For Babinski, such a "subject" would have been called a simulator, and treated as such, although he is obviously not just a male hysteric. Breton's

---

[38] "Sujet," (April 1918), *Oeuvres Complètes*, vol. I, p. 24.
[39] Breton, *Oeuvres Complètes*, vol. I, p. 24.
[40] Ibid., p. 25.

astute title stresses the ambiguity of a "subject" who cannot be objectified by medical knowledge. The subject's refusal of the reality of war is radical. It goes further than the logics of persecution displayed by Yossarian in Joseph Heller's *Catch 22*, when the whole world has become a crazy simulacrum, which shows how little "reality" the world contains. "Subject" announces Breton's 1934 "Introduction to the Discourse on the Scarcity of Reality," an essay in which he asserts a refusal to believe in the tyranny of reality.[41]

This is the ontological basis of Breton's subsequent poetry. A verse poem from *Earthlight* (1923) rewrites this sense of being trapped in delirium yet somehow released, even if this freedom is a result of chance much more than to a poetic program of liberation; one recognizes Breton's trademark lyrical ease with flowing images:

> Stream of stars
> Who washes away the punctuation marks of my poems and those of my
>   friends
> You musn't forget that in drawing lots I wont liberty and you
> If she's what I won
> Who else but you comes here by sliding down a rope of frost
> The explorer grappling with the red ants of his own blood
> Right to the end it's the same month of the year
> Perspective which allows us to judge if we have to deal with souls or not
> 19… An artillery lieutenant is waiting in a trail of gunpowder[42]

The title is ominous: "There's No Way Out of Here." An earlier draft had "a *true* artillery lieutenant,"[43] which confirms that we are still in the realm of real figures versus simulacra, as exhibited by "Subject."

However, "Subject" is probably more powerful; it is also a prose poem, the first written as such by Breton. In 1918 "Subject" caught the attention of Paul Valéry and Jean Paulhan, who both believed that Breton had invented the work and based it on his interactions with several patients. In fact, he had transcribed the ravings of one patient over several days, condensing and rearranging them in a single monologue. The soldier's delusion that the whole world is a simulacrum generates a paranoid interpretation of reality, while producing a devastating critique of what is taken as "real" by those who have blindly accepted it. If Breton had started quoting Kraepelin and Freud at that time,[44] here they do merge. It is as if Freud presented us with a President Schreber who would not

[41] "Introduction au discours sur le peu de réalité," in André Breton, *Oeuvres Complètes*, vol. II, p. 278.
[42] André Breton, *Earthlight*, trans. Bill Zavatsky and Zack Rogow, Los Angeles, Sun and Moon Press, 1993, pp. 57–58.
[43] See the editor's textual note in Breton's *Oeuvres Complètes*, vol. I, p. 1203.
[44] In a letter to Tzara from 1919, quoted in Breton, *Oeuvres Complètes*, vol. I, p. 1105.

stop at transforming homosexual fantasies into a cosmic struggle against an evil God but went on to show the whole war as a sick joke, an improbable trick put on for his unique esthetic delectation. As Pascal said, there are situations when one would be very insane not to become insane; it is from this awareness that the text derives both its subversive power and its dark beauty.

The "paranoid style" developed by modernism multiplies levels of reality while addressing the locus of the big Other. The Other may be seen as the "enemy" that Lewis was so fond of creating for his own endless execration, or it might become a feminine Other, as when Joyce forced his writing to descend into the deepest recesses of female schizophrenia (the disease exhibited by his daughter to whom we will return) in the opaque polysemy of *Finnegans Wake*. Paranoia might have been the answer to the quandary in which hysterical high modernism had found itself: for, as both Salvador Dalí and Thomas Pynchon have shown, paranoia is one concept that can bridge effortlessly the old gap between high and low culture. Dalí's solution has been to project his archaic phobias, such as his fear of grasshoppers and rotting donkeys, into images that could acquire universal validity. They seduced Freud, who remarked in 1938 that Dalí showed an obvious talent, an admission that he never made facing Breton's poetry. He may have simply registered Dalí's incipient academism. Whatever the motivation, he could see that a paranoid style was shaping a world teeming with wilder fantasies than he had ever imagined, while interpreting it with a semblance of rational order.

Closer to us, a late modernist such as Pynchon has meditated (and keeps meditating, as one can see from his recent post-9/11 extravaganza, *Bleeding Edge*[45]) on the inexhaustible American fund of paranoid ideas and a "paranoid style" in politics, tracing the movement further back in time to a Puritan heritage obsessed with ideas of predestination or a new purity to be found in the wilderness. There again, the main danger lies in a feared but desired and necessary encounter with the Other. Oedipa Maas discovers another America through creative paranoia in *The Crying of Lot 49*,[46] while her psychoanalyst is a former Nazi whose job in the death camps was to render Jews catatonic. Because of his name, Doctor Hilarius, we should not take him too seriously – no more than the pyrotechnics of rockets launched from Nazi Germany hovering above our heads in *Gravity's Rainbow*.[47] Thus the issue of the joke will thus acquire more importance.

---

[45] Thomas Pynchon, *Bleeding Edge*, New York, Penguin, 2013.

[46] Thomas Pynchon, *The Crying of Lot 49*, New York, Harper and Row, 1986.

[47] See Richard Hardack, "Revealing the Bidder: The Forgotten Lesbian in Pynchon's *The Crying of Lot 49*," *Textual Practice*, vol. 27, no. 4, 2013, pp. 565–595. Hardack argues that Oedipa's main intellectual grounding is in an invisible lesbian counterculture.

Paranoid jokes

François Roustang understood the power of good joke in a psychoanalytic cure. His book *How to Make a Paranoid Laugh*[48] discusses a patient with marked paranoid tendencies. Roustang had noticed that the patient always left a pungent smell after his session on the couch; there was no way of getting rid of it after his departure. After a while, he realized that the patient used his bad smell to establish an aggressive distance with his psychoanalyst; his stink should have the power to force the psychoanalyst to berate, accuse, or counsel the deliberately unwashed man lying on the couch. No doubt, the difficult patient was conveying something like, "Vous ne pouvez pas me sentir, non? You can't stand me, that's it? Now, what are you going to do with that?"

This analysis found a positive outcome because of a shared joke. The patient had been getting better and felt that he was about to reach the goal of his therapy: to be able to write. He would talk about the texts he had in mind, adding that his inhibition stemmed from the suspicion that, as soon as he would publish them, his analyst was going to attack them. He would repeat this accusation angrily at each session, testing the psychoanalyst's limits. One day, as the patient was leaving, Roustang made a sarcastic intervention, telling him: "You're right; as soon as you publish one line, I am going to let all hell loose; and you know that my pen is sharp!" Then the patient laughed.[49] Hearing the tone of sarcasm, he saw that Roustang was not speaking seriously. Had he missed the tone of sarcasm, he would have remained a paranoid. Sharing in the joke, he could laugh about himself, seeing his own exaggerations in his paranoid rants.

Understanding that one can say one thing and mean another helped Roustang's paranoid patient get out of the tunnel vision of his paranoid accusations; his sudden laughter helped him tolerate ambiguity and appreciate a certain lability of truth. When we become aware of linguistic ambiguity, we discover that we do not master language but are spoken by it. If truth burns more than a lie – as Lichtenberg wrote, "It is almost impossible to carry the torch of truth through a crowd without singeing someone's beard"[50] – the half-lie or the "bullshitting" joke opens a space in between, a true *pseudos*, opening up the space of fiction or literature.

---

[48] François Roustang, *How to Make a Paranoid Laugh, or What is Psychoanalysis?* Trans. Anne C. Vila, Philadelphia, University of Pennsylvania Press, 2000.

[49] The story has been shortened in the French book and in its English translation. Here, I am quoting the original essay, "Comment faire rire un paranoïaque" in *Critique, Quatre Essais sur le Rire,* Janvier-Février, 1988, 488–489, p. 15. See also François Roustang, *Comment faire rire un paranoïaque*, Paris, Odile Jacob, 1996, pp. 14–16.

[50] Freud, *The Joke and Its Relation to the Unconscious,* p. 69. Hereafter, JU and page number.

This insight often comes in a sudden flash – speed and delivery tone are crucial for jokes like this. A *Witz* told by Freud allows us to understand the twisted economy of jokes:

> A gentleman goes into a pastrycook's and orders a cake; but he soon brings it back and asks for a glass of liqueur instead. He drinks this up and makes off without paying. The shopkeeper detains him. "What do you want of me?" – "To pay for the liqueur." – "But I gave you the cake for it." – "You didn't pay for that either." *But I didn't eat it.* (JU, p. 49)

The original contains a play on an anaphoric ja that makes it even tastier: "Für den habe ich Ihnen ja die Torte gegeben." – "Die haben Sie ja auch nicht bezahlt." – "Die habe ich ja auch nicht gegessen." If one laughs, it is because one sees a fault in the impeccable logic without being able to pinpoint it.

The logical mistake begs the issue of beginnings. When does an account begin to accrue? Is there a "before" in a commercial transaction? If the first order is considered as a free gift, the reasoning makes sense, and the owner has to accept the consequence. Had he written somewhere that this was a commercial establishment in which people were expected to pay for whatever they took? Probably not. Had he thought that he was selling a cake? In fact, he did not know that he was giving it, or treating a nice customer. Having been given a cake, the customer changes his mind and opts for liqueur instead. This joke provides an appearance of reason (who has not been in a situation in which one thinks one is given something, only to discover one has to pay for it?), but its faulty reasoning relies on a deliberately distorted use of semantics: the customer plays on the double meaning of "in exchange for." This is the usual logic of the Irish bull. Freud gives a good example in a footnote: "Is that the place where the Duke of Wellington spoke these words? – *Yes, that's the place, but he never spoke the words*" (JU, p. 80). Freud makes sense of this pleasure in nonsense that bypasses the rational censor.

This is why the most important Freudian joke is the *Witz* of the two Jews who lie by telling the truth, a joke that we have already encountered (albeit in a different version) in the letters to Silberstein: "Two Jews meet in a railway carriage at a station in Galicia. "Where are you traveling?" asks the one. "To Cracow," comes the answer. "Look what a liar you are!" the other protests. "When you say you're going to Cracow, you want me to believe you're going to Lemberg. But I know that you're really going to Cracow. So why are you lying?" (JU, p. 110). Freud comments by explaining the apparent absurdity, noting that the second Jew never contradicts the other's assumption that he had meant to lie by telling the truth. Is it because he is speechless in front of such a brazen accusation?

In spite of their absurdity, skeptical jokes and Irish bulls still imply some form of reason. One needs only to look at what Aristotle says about enthymemes to understand the important category of faulty logic reasoning. We can articulate independent chains of reasons that develop the unspoken part of the joke. These would belong to the category of the enthymeme because they are not strictly logical, but a "relaxed" formalization that allows for hypotheses, and often interprets the merely probable. An enthymeme is commonly described as an incomplete syllogism. Enthymemes must be brief (they often reduce the length of a syllogism by removing the central statement). They also exploit all the resources of culture and language: they use and abuse puns, verbal parallels, and mythological parallels. More fundamentally, for Aristotle, enthymemes underpin political rhetoric. Enthymemes are logics for the masses and not for philosophers; they therefore play a crucial function in political oratory.

Aristotle's enthymemes look very much like Freud's skeptical jokes. Here are a few examples, the first being a "topic" predicated on division: "There are always three motives for wrongdoing; two are excluded from consideration as impossible; as for the third, not even the accusers assert it."[51] This is a little like the old joke of "There are three types of people, those who can count and those who cannot." This joke corresponds to the specific type of economy of the enthymeme: it expresses in a condensed form what should be glossed by several syllogisms. This is the case of this remark by Agathon on the paradoxical probability of improbable events: "One might perhaps say that this very thing is probable, that many things happen to men that are not probable."[52] Another type of self-referential paradox is the remark made by Pithius that "the laws need a law to correct them."[53] Enthymemes thus have the flexibility of a pragmatic logic that accommodates exceptions, contradictions, and even deception. Aristotle states a principle that he deems universal: "[S]ince men do not praise the same things in public and in secret, but in public chiefly praise what is just and beautiful, and in secret rather wish for what is expedient…," one can always infer its exact opposite from any statement that has been made. We are not far from the guide to bad faith and logical tricks by which Schopenhauer taught his reader how to win an argument even when one is defeated.[54]

---

[51] Aristotle, *"Art" of Rhetoric*, II, xxiii, 10, trans. J. H. Freese, Loeb Classical Library, Cambridge, Harvard University Press, 1982, p. 305.
[52] Ibid., xxiv, 10, p. 335.
[53] Ibid., xxiii, 22, p. 319.
[54] Arthur Schopenhauer, *The Art of Always Being Right*, trans. T. Bailey Saunders, London, Gibson Square Books, 2009.

The hysterical proton pseudos

This discussion of Aristotelian logic sends us back to hysteria; we see this theme crop up in Freud's section about hysteria in the *Project*. Freud has demonstrated the existence of repressed chains of thought, rejected outside the conscious ego, that then fabricate specific and often bizarre obsessions. Hysterical repression operates through symbolization or simple "translations" of linguistic expressions that then become fixated on certain neurons. The force of this repression derives from libidinal investments, in last analysis, from the drives. Section 4 of the "Project for a Scientific Psychology," entitled "The Hysterical *prôton pseudos*,"[55] illustrates the Greek phrase borrowed from Aristotle's logic by a clinical example. It is that of Emma, who suffered from a particular inhibition: she could not enter a shop alone because of a memory dating from when she was thirteen. Then she had entered a store and was upset by the laughter of two shopkeepers. Their obscene mockery created a sense of panic that was repeated each time she entered a similar establishment alone. It was necessary for Freud to bring out an almost erased memory dating from when she was eight: twice Emma had visited a grocery whose owner caressed her genital organs through her dress. Yet she had come back, as if to provoke a new assault. She later understood that she had wished to trigger the illicit contact. What turned this erotic impulse into hysteria was, according to Freud's reconstruction, the emergence of disgust in place of sexual excitement.

Freud outlines a grammar of Emma's unconscious associations. He shows that they are dominated by parallel series of memories, each marked by positive and negative affects, and in the end the series intersect with each other. The laughter of the two shopkeepers recalls the smile of the grocer, and the fact that one of the two shopkeepers was attractive to Emma evoked her complicity in the first seduction scene. She understood this after the fact, which corresponds to the founding principle of *Nachträglichkeit* already discussed (OP, pp. 413–414). The hysterical structure allows us to understand the a posteriori reorganization of memories because of the delay of puberty and the erasure of the sexual excitations at the age of reason: "Every adolescent individual carries memory-traces which can only be understood after his own sexual feelings have appeared; every adolescent, accordingly, must carry within him the germ of hysteria" (OP, p. 413). However, it is only in a particular structure that we can speak of hysteria in the proper sense. The hidden memory causing displeasure

---

[55] Sigmund Freud, "Project for a Scientific Psychology," in *The Origins of Psychoanalysis, Letters to Wilhelm Fliess, Drafts and Notes 1887–1902*, ed. M. Bonaparte, A, Freud, E. Kris, trans. E. Mobacher and James Strachey, New York, Basic Books, 1954, p. 410. Hereafter abbreviated as OP and page number.

or inhibitions can be found in many other patients, but with a hysteric, it becomes a *prôton pseudos*. The Greek words are then abridged as "Pp."

Freud had found the expression in Aristotle, because it has been quoted in a congress on natural sciences, for which he was the secretary of the neurological division. Max Hertz, a Viennese doctor, had used it during his presentation. Freud continued to use it in his correspondence with Fliess; he did so in March 1901, after their friendship had cooled off.[56] Freud may not have read Aristotle's *Organon* attentively, however, he knew that this expression had a well-defined meaning and concerned the theory of the syllogism developed in the *Prior Analytics*. Aristotle affirms that "falsity in an argument rests on the first false statement (*prôton pseudos*) which the argument contains."[57] The error in one of the premises leads to a whole error of reasoning. Freud's demonstration borrows Aristotle's formalization; Aristotle shows that if C is proved by A and B, and if these are proved by D, E, F, and G, and if proposition A is false, this error (*pseudos*) emanates from that of one of the first propositions D, E, F, and G; Freud himself schematizes in A and B the series of images or memories that intersect in hysteria (OP, pp. 406–408).

Aristotle's expression concerns logical relations between different moments of reasoning. Just after having announced this axiom, Aristotle attacks the theory of Plato's *Meno* in which we learn that knowledge comes from reminiscence (*anamnesis*), otherwise described as the memory of the truths buried in the soul since birth.[58] Plato thought that the knowledge of a particular triangle would bring to Meno the definition of the triangle in general. Aristotle contradicts this and states that we only arrive at truth through knowledge founded on universals.[59] Freud echoes this critique to denounce a naïve confidence in the truth of a memory or a dream. As he shows in "Screen Memories,"[60] a dream always hides another dream and a memory opens onto another memory, often a screen memory that poses an obstacle to the truth. It is indispensable to arrive at indisputable general premises. This requires an effort at

---

[56] Freud speaks of a patient whose father cannot decide whether to finance his visit to care for his son who was staying in a sanatorium in Berlin or not. Similarly, Freud, who was elaborating plans for a meeting, cannot promise Fliess that he will come see him. He adds: "[T]he rub of the whole business, as a *proton pseudos*, is that my medical intervention is rather superfluous." Masson, *The Complete Letters of Sigmund Freud to Wilhelm Fliess, op. cit.*, p. 438. The expression is understood in a double sense, both as a logical error bearing on premises (because he is planning a trip in advance without knowing if it is possible) and as a suspicion of professional abuse that was coming into conflict with the medical code of ethics.

[57] Aristotle, *Prior Analytics*, trans. Hugh Tredennick, Loeb Classical Library, Cambridge, MA, Harvard University Press, 1967, book II, 18, p. 495.

[58] Aristotle, *Prior Analytics, op. cit.*, p. 503.

[59] Ibid., pp. 503–505.

[60] Sigmund Freud, "Screen Memories" (1899), in *The Freud Reader*, ed. Peter Gay, New York, Norton, 1989, pp. 117–126.

generalization, and the need for a theory of dreams, desire, and repression – in short, a whole metapsychology.

This examination of the Aristotelian intertext might suggest that the translators made a mistake when they rendered it as "the first lie." The *Standard Edition*, followed by the first French translators, translated the expression by "lie," following the annotation of the first German edition of the complete works. By leaving the expression in Greek whereas he could have used terms such as *Urteilstäuschungen* (errors of judgment), *Fehler des Prämissen* (faults in the premises), *logische Fehler* (faults of logic), or *Denkfehler* (faults of thought), as is done in the passage from the *Project* already cited, Freud plays on the complex of meaning contained in *pseudos*. *Pseudos* means "lie," "logical error," and also "pseudo," the "not true" defining the space of fiction – thus giving free reign to the imagination. Freud is writing a scientific treatise in the technical jargon of his times, which is why he assigns Greek letters to the diverse neurons (ψ, φ, ω). In the hysterical phenomenon, he discerns a particular kind of undecidability between lie, creation, and error, between deception and simulation, wayward syllogism, and simulated faults in logical reasoning.

What logical error was Emma guilty of committing? She had put herself in a position of not knowing, while her body spoke for her by refusing to work. Her symptom spoke for her and in her place, but in a confused way. She did not know that the affect of displeasure, even of horror, that she experienced was hiding an affect of pleasure. The pleasure was linked with transgression that had been forgotten for a long time but of which the spur of jouissance had not disappeared. She lied to herself because the two series reconstituted by Freud, with the shopkeepers, the laughter, the grocer, the attack, the clothing, the sexual discharge, were struck by a repression that recalls primary repression – that is, the entire machinery of the Freudian unconscious. Thus the *prôton pseudos* refers to a myth of origins that explains everything while dissolving it into a paradoxical temporality, fundamentally determined by the logic of *Nachträglichkeit* with its perpetual revisions, subtending a primary repression that forbids access to the "source" once and for all. Similar enthymemes will be used to produce a delirium like that of Judge Schreber. In this case, truth itself will be interpreted as a delirium. There, however, Freud will analyze not a person, but a text – the published memoirs of President Schreber.[61]

[61] Daniel Paul Schreber, *Memoirs of My Nervous Illness*, trans. Ida MacAlpine and Richard A. Hunter, New York, New York Review of Books, 2000. Hereafter, MNI and page number.

Schreber as Schreiber: Writer at work

Freud's discussion of Schreber's *Memoirs of My Nervous Illness* is his only systematic engagement with paranoia.[62] It was in this hefty book that Schreber explained how he had received his truth directly from God. The first chapter of his *Memoirs* is entitled "God and Immortality" and begins with a dogmatic statement: "The human soul is contained in the nerves of the body" (MNI, p. 190). Schreber describes the extraordinary fineness of these nerves that are connected with the brain on the one hand, with God on the other hand. These nerves cause unspeakable pleasures and also generate "miracles" and apparitions. Indeed, Schreber's God is entirely made up of nerves and is therefore incorporeal, a conception that accords well with most religions. Schreber's twist is to add that his God is obsessed with pleasure and that his obscene jouissance has focused on Schreber. Thus God will not even let him defecate in peace. God has no other wish than to transform poor Schreber into a woman by a "miracle." Then He will copulate with him to recreate a better human race. As Freud asserts, "the delusion of sexual persecution was retroactively transformed into religious megalomania" (SC, p. 11). For Freud, Schreber's main wish is to be turned into a woman to engage in same-sex fantasies with his doctor, Flechsig. The only way that such a forbidden desire can be made acceptable to his consciousness is the creation of a whole mythology, with an evil God who cannot really understand what life means, in a weird parody of Manicheism that veils a fundamentally homosexual position. His "miracles" tend to emasculate poor Schreber, who must "think" without stopping to struggle against a feminization that shames him, but that he secretly desires.

Confronted with such a perfect case of paranoia, Freud's thesis is simple: everything derives from the homosexual libidinal charge linking Schreber to his doctor Flechsig, and then to his father, the formidable Dr. Schreber, an educator and social reformer well known in Germany. The enjoying and abusive father of his fantasies provides a clear parody of the dominating Victorian father. The only way Schreber found to make these homosexual fantasies acceptable is to imagine that God forces him to be transformed into a woman. He creates an entire mythology, with Manichean features echoing Ormuz and Ahriman. Freud cannot fail to evoke Nietzsche's Zarathustra when he reconstructs an interpretation of the case, which consists, in fact, of a reading of the *Memoirs* published by Schreber. Freud demonstrates that the elaboration of the delusion has not only a meaning but also a curative value that allows

---

[62] Sigmund Freud, *The Schreber Case*, trans. Andrew Weber, London, Penguin, 2002. Hereafter, SC and page number. I have discussed Schreber's case in the context of lies in *The Ethics of the Lie*, New York, The Other Press, 2007, pp. 321–331.

Schreber to replay long ago traumas inflicted by his father, who shared many of the unwholesome God's traits.

This was not Lacan's view, and we see him repeating what he did with *Hamlet* – that is, grounding his theories in an ontology of desire. When Freud points to libido as a principle, Lacan postulates the big Other, and everything that derives from it: the jouissance of this obscene God in which the absence of paternal symbolization has left its ravages. Whereas Freud saw a transformation of repressed homosexuality into a delirium of redemption, Lacan insisted on Schreber's perverse, hysterical, and transsexual dimension. Lacan refused the idea that the key was Schreber's repressed homosexuality, a repression that led him to create a world of his own. Reluctant to accept Freud's thesis of a repressed homosexuality that would find the detour of paranoia, Lacan writes in "On a Question Prior to Any Possible Treatment of Psychosis": "Homosexuality, which is supposedly the determining factor in paranoiac psychosis, is actually a symptom articulated in the psychotic process."[63] Against Freud's projection thesis, Lacan preferred to speak of "transsexualist" practices[64] related to perversion and opening onto an "other" type of jouissance.

Before reaching that point, Lacan had to struggle with the issue of the Oedipal structure. Schreber's end-of-the-world "catastrophe" had to be situated in the domain of the Real. What counts for Lacan, fundamentally, is that the effect of the name of the father is not symbolized. In the end, Schreber is redeemed not only because his *Memoirs* sketch a tripartite system in which the Real appears simply in hallucination but also because Schreber is a Romantic rebel against the lies of the fathers. Schreber exemplifies the child's disgust facing his own parents' childishness. Here is how Lacan concludes his peroration on the sins of fathers:

> Further still, the father's relation to this law must be considered in its own right, for one will find in it the reason for the paradox whereby devastating effects of the paternal figure are found with particular frequency in cases where the father really functions as a legislator or boasts he does – whether he is, in fact, one of the people who makes the laws or presents himself as a pillar of faith, as a paragon of integrity or devotion, as virtuous or a virtuoso, as serving a charitable cause whatever the object or lack thereof that is at stake, as serving the nation or birth rate; safety or salubrity, legacy or law, the pure, the lowest of the low, or the empire. These are all ideals that provide him with all too many opportunities to seem to be at fault, to fall short, and even to be fraudulent – in short, to exclude the Name-of-the-Father from its

[63] Lacan, *Ecrits*, 2006, p. 455.
[64] Ibid., p. 474.

position in the signifier. // This result can be obtained with still less, and
no one who practices child analysis will deny that children see right
through hypocritical behavior, so much so that it can be devastating
to them. However, who articulates that the lie thus perceived implies a
reference to the constitutive function of speech?"[65]

Who? The answer is of course Lacan. Had it not been Lacan, it would have
been Schreber, who writes his name as *Schreiber* (writer) to expose the lies
of the Father's law. Schreber has been well educated, and he wrote poems
for his mother and his family. His style is quite remarkable, crisp, lucid,
gripping even when he documents his own hallucinations, such as his own
Brüllenwunder, the "bellowing miracle" issuing suddenly from his mouth, or
God's *Grundsprache*,[66] an antiquated but vigorous German. He reproduces
perfectly the demotic energies of the cryptic utterances issued by the birds sent
as messengers by God, including their mystifying distortions of normal words
and phrases.[67] Breton would have loved Schreber's idea that all these utterances
coming from God worked via "miracles" and "rays" connected with sexual
libido. The whole world is animated, shot through by stunning verbal creations
that reveal a mystical jouissance. Given the wealth of details and the precision
of this deviantly reconstructed universe, how could one make Schreber laugh?
He would have to realize that the "nonsense" he means to "abolish" is his only
available sense. Can one abolish a whole counter-theology, given the fact that
his nonsense reaches the limits of the whole world and that even encompasses
God? As Freud noted, his delirium was an attempt at a recuperative cure. A
way out might be to push Schreber closer to hysteria.

The psychotic Schreber is not far from Hegel's "beautiful soul," especially
when we see Schreber assuming that "it would be *beautiful* to be a woman
submitting to the act of copulation." The function of beauty is underlined
by Lacan.[68] A hystericized Schreber would have no difficulty in recognizing
the *prôton pseudos* that Freud saw as the root of the genesis of hysteria in the
Project for a Scientific Psychology. In their different genetic accounts, Lacan
and Freud betray their different styles. Freud looks much more like a novelist, a modernist novelist to be sure, close to Henry James or Conrad, one
who is attuned to ambiguities and reversals and who never trusts any narrative fully. Freud had defined the Unconscious as an "other scene" or "stage,"
which is a precondition of all interpretations. However, Lacan's model is less

[65] Ibid., pp. 482–483.
[66] Daniel Paul Schreber, *Denkwürdigkeiten eines Nervenkranken*, ed. Samuel Weber, Frankfurt, Ullstein, 1973, p. 77.
[67] Ibid., pp. 235–236.
[68] Lacan, *Ecrits*, 2006, p. 455.

the twisted psychological narratives of a Dostoevsky (one of Freud's models) than Breton, who criticized Dostoevsky in the first *Manifesto of Surrealism* for having recourse to long descriptions of furniture and bedrooms. Lacan, who never describes anything, and rarely provides case studies, began his career in synchrony with an avant-garde that abandons all narratives and prefers the direct metaphorical verticality and the unleashing of the unconscious via automatic writing.

The book as a performative sieve

What is remarkable is that Schreber, by writing his *Memoirs*, succeeded not only in freeing himself from his asylum but also in convincing Freud of the soundness of his allegations. Freud elaborated his theory of the libido and of God seen as a paternal projection on the basis of the Schreber case. Before having written this study, he had announced, in a letter to Ferenczi: "I succeeded where the paranoid fails," recognizing a curious proximity between paranoids as builders of delirious systems and his own tendency to elaborate theories on all subjects. Thus Schreber's book was successful, almost as early as it was published in 1903. He had proved that he should be released from the asylum even if he did not want to abandon any of his beliefs (like the fantasy that, even free, he could stare at the sun like an eagle without being blinded.) He could demonstrate that his beliefs were not that different from what religious people think as true and is often not very rational; after all, there are other people who believe in miracles. Moreover, whatever their foundation, his beliefs in a counter-God and the rest would not harm any other human being. Was Schreber the precursor of Thomas Szasz and all the militants of anti-psychiatry, or more darkly, as Elias Canetti[69] and Eric Santner[70] have argued, a prototype of Adolph Hitler? They insist on his dedication to saving the human race and peopling the world with a superior type of humanity.

Freud, who would address the issue or religion as an "Illusion," had showed that this delirium, like any other delirium, has a meaning and holds a function. Not only does it permit a fantasy to hold, but also it replays old traumas with a tyrannical father who has lent many of his features to this unhealthy God. The link between Schreber, his wife, and his doctor Flechsig is obscure, and certain parts of the *Memoirs* have been deleted, censored, so that there is a huge blur

---

[69] See Elias Canetti, "Schreber I and Schreber II," in *Crowds and Power*, trans. Victor Gollancz, New York, Farrar, Strauss and Giroux, 1984, pp. 434–464.

[70] Eric L. Santner, *My Own Private Germany: Daniel Paul Schreber's Secret History of Modernity*, Princeton, Princeton University Press, 1996.

on the very concept of "soul murder" that looks so crucial for Schreber.[71] Freud detected something of his own homosexual transference in Fliess, Jung, and a few others so as to elaborate his theories. The essay on Schreber is Freud's first psychoanalysis at a remove because this is a text analyzing another text.

A Freudian "Discourse on Method" emerges from his interpretation of paranoia, unless it is a more Kantian *Critique of Pure Reason*. This is revealed by Freud in a pointed and witty reference to Kant:

> The two principal elements of Schreber's delusion, the transformation into a woman and the privileged relation to God, are linked up in his system by the feminine disposition towards God. An inevitable task for us will be to prove an essential, *genetic* relationship between these two elements; otherwise our elucidations of Schreber's delusion would lead us to play the role described by Kant in the famous image from the *Critique of Pure Reason* as that of the man who holds the sieve under a billy-goat (*Bock*) while another milks it. (SC, p. 23)

Here, just before beginning the synthetic or theoretical part of his essay, Freud alludes to one of Kant's neat jokes in the first *Critique*. Kant debunks the philosophers who begin by asking directly: "What is truth?" This question can only be asked and answered if one understands the categories that will be used for the answer. To show his ironical rejection, Kant quotes an old joke from the Cynical tradition. The whole question embarrasses and misleads, and one has the "ridiculous sight (as the ancients said) of one person milking a billy-goat while the other holds a sieve underneath."[72] Freud's reference to Kant at this juncture is tantalizing.

We do find a curious alliance between Freud and Kant, who is mentioned in the introduction to *Totem and Taboo*: "[T]aboo still exists in our midst. To be sure, it is negatively conceived and directed to different contents, but according to its psychological nature, it is still nothing else than Kant's "Categorical Imperative" which tends to act compulsively and rejects all conscious motivation."[73] In 1920, Freud complements Kant's theory that time and space are "necessary forms of thought" when he includes the timelessness of the Unconscious into the process.[74] The very last notes that Freud ever wrote contained an attempt at distinguishing his metapsychology from Kant's system: "Space may be the projection of the extension of the psychical apparatus.

---

[71] Morton Schatzman, *Soul Murder: Persecution in the Family*, London, Penguin, 1973.
[72] Immanuel Kant, *Critique of Pure Reason*, trans. and ed. Paul Guyer and Allen Wood, Cambridge, Cambridge University Press, 1998, p. 197. See the translators' note pp. 723–724 alluding to Lucian of Samosata's dialogue *Demonax* as a source.
[73] Sigmund Freud, *Totem and Taboo*, New York, Random House, 1946, p. x.
[74] Sigmund Freud, *Beyond the Pleasure Principle*, New York, Norton, 1989, p. 31.

No other derivation is probable. Instead of Kant's a priori determinants of our psychical apparatus. Psyche is extended; knows nothing of it."[75] In fact, Freud is interested in promoting a neo-Kantianism of the Unconscious: he posits a Reason that does not know. Our psychical apparatus knows nothing about death, because it believes in its own immortality, and it does not know that it has a spatial quality. And besides, it does not know either that it is writing all the time.

Freud betrays his awareness that there are numerous links between Schreber, Kant, and himself: all three erect a whole system. As Schreber repeats, in an apotropaic sentence he tries to interpose against God and his dirty little miracles: "*Aller Unsinn hebt sich auf.*"[76] All the nonsense will be cancelled – that is, dialectically sublated. Freud's reference to Kant, often suspected of being an impenitent moralist complicit in the formation of the superego – as in the *Interpretation of Dreams*, where Freud openly mocks philosophers who want to leave a place for morality while an amoral or supra-moral unconscious is speaking[77] – takes on a symptomatic value when what is at stake is paranoia. Paranoia is a "reasoning delirium" or a "delirium of interpretation," a delirium that preserves all the appearances of rationality. Indeed, the term "paranoia," if it is not found in the classification of deliriums and mental illnesses of Kant's *Anthropology*, is attributable to Heinroth, who was himself a Kantian physician-philosopher.[78]

Finally we may wonder whether there such a difference between Schreber's *Memoirs* and the treatises of mystics or founders of religions. This was the argument used by President Schreber to get himself released from the asylum. He surely had curious beliefs, in reality similar enough to those of a number of compatriots, but he could prove that they were not dangerous for others and only concerned himself. Even if he persisted in the belief that God had elected him to become transsexual and then give birth to a regenerated human race, that belief, outlandish as it sounds, could in no way disturb public order.[79]

---

[75] Freud, "Findings, Ideas, Problems", in *Standard Edition of the Complete Psychological Works of Sigmund Freud*, June 1938, vol. 23, p. 299.

[76] Schreber, *Denkwürdigkeiten eines Nervenkranken*, p. 334.

[77] Freud, *The Interpretation of Dreams*, op. cit., p. 100: "[Those] who believe that the 'categorical imperative' extends to dreams, should logically accept unqualified responsibility for immoral dreams. We could only hope for their sake that they would have no such reprehensible dreams of their own to upset their firm belief in their own moral character."

[78] In his *Anthropology*, Kant distinguishes *amentia* (simple mental confusion), *vesania* (perturbation of thought), and *dementia* (a type of methodical madness). See Pierre Fédida, "La paranoïa comme théorie de la communication," in *Le Temps de la réflexion*, V, Paris, Gallimard, 1984, pp. 111–124.

[79] See the Judgment of the Royal Superior Country Court of Dresden of 14th July 1902, in Schreber, *Memoirs*, pp. 405–440. The French revolutionary date may have had an impact on the positive decision of the judges.

Schreber would continue wearing feminine apparel and undergarments from time to time, but their rationale had been accounted for in the *Memoirs*, which had the right to be published. Schreber was finally freed from tutelage, having won his case legally; although recognized as "insane" and suffering from paranoia, he became a legal subject again. He should be feted as the first hero of anti-psychiatry. He demonstrated that writing could become a singular absolute capable of changing life, but in a different sense from Breton's poetic practice. If Breton was still enamored with a Gradiva who crossed to the Other side, he also followed in the steps of a *Schreiber* who wrote, wrote, wrote, until the gates of the asylum opened.

Chapter 5

The literary phallus, from Poe to Gide

If Schreber's famous *Memoirs* can be considered as "literature," this has important consequences for literary criticism. Literature can open up and include the innumerable autobiographical documents of madness and survival often classified as nonfiction or true testimonies in the "recovery" sections of bookstores and libraries. Literature can again be a province of biography or autobiography. Indeed, all the details provided by Schreber about his family, his wife, and the plan of his rooms are "true." At the same time, we have understood that his delirium was "true" because it disclosed a fundamental principle of psychoanalysis: writing adheres to the symptom while keeping an intrinsic connection with extreme libidinal enjoyment, or the sublimation of terror and pain. This leads us to the vexed issue of "psychobiography" and the controversies to which the concept has given birth. After Freud's own experiments with figures such as Jensen, Goethe, Shakespeare, Dostoevsky, Michelangelo, and Leonardo da Vinci, it was an American poet who bore the brunt of classical psychoanalytic investigation. Marie Bonaparte, one of the founders of the French psychoanalytic movement, and a personal friend of Freud, was the great-grand-niece of the emperor Napoleon; her enlightened assistance proved vital to Freud when it came time for him to leave Austria after the Nazis had taken over. Her monumental psychobiography of Poe was published in French in 1933 and prefaced by Freud, who praised it in glowing terms:

> In this book my friend and pupil, Marie Bonaparte, has shone the light of psycho-analysis on the life and work of a great writer with pathologic trends.
>
> Thanks to her interpretive effort, we now realise how many of the characteristics of Poe's works were conditioned by his personality, and can see how that personality derived from intense emotional fixations and painful infantile experiences. Investigations such as these do not claim to explain creative genius, but they do reveal the factors which awaken it and the sort of subject matter it is destined to choose. Few

tasks are as appealing as enquiry into the laws that govern the psyche of exceptionally endowed individuals.[1]

Freud approves the project of a psychobiography: even if Poe was considered by some as a madman or a genius, or both, a patient analysis of his works buttressed by a reconstruction of his personal traumas and neuroses would disclose universal psychic laws.

Marie Bonaparte's poetics of the phallus

Bonaparte's voluminous Poe book (more than 700 pages) begins with a substantial biography of the American author and then tackles the works one after the other. They are illuminated by a few central insights: Poe was a compulsive necrophiliac, in love with dead women who all looked like his adored mother; his stern adoptive father John Allan was the model for all his persecuting doubles; he was impotent most of the time and reacted violently against threats of castration; and he found solace in drink and opium, a source of inspiration and the symbolic equivalent of his own death. This general interpretation of the "life and works" of Poe, as her title has it, opens up general vistas on "Literature: Its Function and Elaboration." Here again, the main themes and concepts are borrowed from Freud: literature follows the same laws as dreams, daydreams, and fantasies. Just as an author's "personality" will be split among different characters whose variations are ruled by the techniques of condensation, displacement, and overdetermination, every subject tends to reenact roles fixed by various alter egos every night. One finds a certain pleasure in the works of poets whose dream world can be shared. These formations replay a few infantile fixations infinitely; and one should hope that the neurotic factors thus exhibited will fade away, especially if literature allows one to understand better their source in affects and drives, as well as to master the dominant principle of a compulsion to repeat.

Bonaparte is faithful to the Freudian dogma of an "applied psychoanalysis" that brings some knowledge to the field of art and literature. A thorough understanding of Poe's life and works will thus yield the same lessons as a good perusal of Freud's complete works. The second part of this chapter ("Poe's Message to Others") is less predictable. It focuses on Baudelaire as Poe's heir and translator. Bonaparte provides a condensed version of

---

[1] Marie Bonaparte, *The Life and Works of Edgar Allan Poe: A Psycho-Analytic Interpretation*, trans. John Rocker, London, Imago, (1934) 1949, p. xi.

Baudelaire's life, focusing on his passionate and difficult relationship with his mother. The French poet found a "brother-soul" in Poe because he offered a model that gave him the courage to confront his own narcissism, his own necrophilia, and his own sadism. Poe's message survived in his French heir. Such a message can be expressed by Baudelaire's phrase, taken as a motto: "What matters the eternity of damnation to him who, for an instant, finds the infinity of joy!"[2]

Bonaparte thus reads all the stories and poems in an unabashed biographical manner. The old man who roams the streets of London in "The Man of the Crowd" is none other than John Allan, who rejected his adoptive son after he discovered the latter's addiction to drinking and gambling. All the murder scenes, and they are numerous, have to re-elaborate Poe's primal trauma, for he must have witnessed his parents having intercourse. How can Marie Bonaparte be so sure about this? In this case, she is merely projecting her own past, remembering how Freud reacted when she showed him her childhood notebooks, especially the notebook she had entitled "Mouth Pencil" (in English). In all her childhood tales (she wrote a lot), there was a monster, a sort of scary bogeyman with a strange name, *Sarquintuié*, or *Serquintué*.[3] This frightening character, looking like a huge train going at full speed, was also present in a series of recurring nightmares. After having glanced at the notebooks, Freud immediately concluded that she had witnessed a fellatio when a baby. The princess, shocked at the suggestion, flatly denied that such a primal scene had been possible, because her mother had died when giving birth to her. However, after she had interviewed her former babysitters Pascal and Mimi, she realized that everything had happened as Freud had reconstructed it. The *Sarquintuié* slowly revealed its secret: it was a compound made up of echoes of her mother's death, because she could have been taken away in a train and a coffin (*cercueil*), mixed up with distorted memories of the sexual act, followed by Mimi's "little death" that she had witnessed. To these were added the old accusations that her father might have killed his wife to inherit her fortune – silly or true gossip that she had overheard. She wrote in her commentary: "Thus, like an ancient people who raises to an epic the humble beginnings of its history, I had used universal symbols to sing my first impressions and my first excitations."[4] Freud's uncanny ability to guess her secret

---

[2] Ibid., p. 689. Note that Baudelaire's original ends with "l'infini de la jouissance", a term dear to Lacan. See Baudelaire's "Le mauvais vitrier" in *Petits Poèmes en Prose, Oeuvres Complètes*, vol. 1, Paris, Gallimard, Pléiade, 1961, p. 240.

[3] See the file reproduced in *Genesis, 8, Psychanalyse*, ed. Daniel Ferrer and Jean-Michel Rabaté, Inédit Marie Bonaparte, "Cahiers d'enfance, séquence du Crayon de Bouche, Vaga et les petits cahiers noirs," ed. and intro. Jean-Pierre Bourgeron, Paris, CNRS, 1995, p. 145–177.

[4] Quoted by Jean-Piere Bourgeron, *Genesis, 8, Psychanalyse*, p. 150.

made Bonaparte turn into a staunch supporter of psychoanalysis. However, such a revelation became universal; here, we see how much she projected her own trauma on Poe.

Savage murders hallucinated as moments of violent coitus accounted for the gothic violence that recurs in Poe's tales. The most excessive version is to be found in "The Murders in the Rue Morgue" in which the corpses of two women, Madame de L'Espanaye and her daughter Camille, are found murdered: the mother decapitated and thrown into a backyard and the daughter throttled to death and wedged head down into a chimney. Dupin solves the enigma when he speculates that because the testimonies of those who heard witnesses to the guttural utterances in a strange idiom did not know the language they thought they heard, it must have been an unleashed animal that imitated human language. In the same way, the animal imitated his master when shaving (no doubt, like Kafka's Red Peter, he tried to shave his red hairs to try to pass as human). Thanks to an advertisement, Dupin had no trouble finding the owner of the unchained Ourang-Outang who had murdered the two women. Here is Bonaparte's final interpretation:

> We have seen that the room stands for the mother's body and, by a similarly frequent symbolic transposition, the chimney will represent the maternal vagina, or rather *cloaca* – as anus and vagina are figured in infantile sexual theories and survive in the unconscious. In thus ramming the girl up the chimney and, so firmly, that four of five men are needed to draw her out, the ape thus symbolically does something equivalent to implanting, by coitus, a child in the woman.[5]

The stage is set for Poe's drama: Poe, who was traumatized at two and one-half years old by the loss of his mother, whom he saw bleed to death. Later, his wife died very young from consumption. Poe unconsciously thought that coitus was lethal, which made him impotent, so that he had to find a refuge in drink and writing as sort of superior intoxication. His poetic creations had the task of restoring his potency. The bloodthirsty but mimetically bumbling ape represents a hallucinated father-murderer whose terminal coitus killed the castrated mother. This explanation, willfully hardcore and improbable as it sounds, derives from a whole network of biographical "proofs" and provides a strict interpretive framework for the other Dupin stories. Thus, "Marie Rogêt" has to be murdered by a naval officer of "dark and swarthy complexion," who recalls the Ourang-Outang of the other story, and they all fit the "universal symbolism of the ravishing of the sea-mother."[6] It did not matter to Bonaparte

---

[5] Bonaparte, *The Life and Works of Edgar Allan Poe*, pp. 454–455.
[6] Ibid., p. 448.

that Poe had changed his mind as he was serializing the story and then realized that the alleged "murder" was the result of a botched abortion.

When it comes to the "Purloined Letter," the summary is also slightly reductive. Bonaparte assumes that the royal personage whose letter is stolen by the unscrupulous minister is obviously the Queen of France, although she is never named as such. Bonaparte thinks that we know nothing of the writer of the letter, whereas the initial of his name is given at the end of the story, when we are told the old letter had a small red seal with the "ducal arms of the S – family."[7] The twist of the plot is that the Queen, if we take her to be so, has seen the minister stealing the letter. She cannot do anything because the King is present, for the minister can impudently blackmail her. All the attempts by the police to retrieve the letter fail. Dupin intervenes, distracts the minister, and takes the letter from the place he had guessed: openly displayed. And there it is, simply inverted inside out with another address and different seal, hung in a card rack "from a little brass knob just beneath the middle of the mantelpiece."[8] Dupin can then steal the compromising letter and leave a similar one in its place. Here is the core of Bonaparte's interpretation:

> Let us first note that this letter, very symbol of the maternal penis, also "hangs" over the fireplace, in the same manner as the female penis, if it existed, would be hung over the cloaca which is here represented – as in the foregoing tales – by the general symbol of fireplace or chimney. We have here, in fact, what is almost an anatomical chart, from which not even the clitoris (or brass knob) is omitted. Something very different, however, should be hanging from that body! // The struggle between Dupin and the minister who once did Dupin an 'ill turn' ... represents, in effect, the Oedipal struggle between father and son, though on an archaic, pregenital and phallic level, to seize possession, not of the mother herself, but of a part; namely, the penis."[9]

One scene draws Bonaparte's interest, the discovery of the letter's hiding place. Once the letter is identified with the mother's penis, the Freudian mechanism falls into place. The Oedipal solution intervenes like a predictable *deus ex machina*. Dupin and the minister are father and son, and they fight for the possession of the mother's body coveted penis. However, is this her penis, or rather her phallus? Immediately after, Bonaparte quotes Karl Abraham's *A Short Study of the Development of the Libido* to define this "partial love" for a simple organ as a stage in the infant's libidinal development. She used the same

[7] Edgar Allan Poe, "The Purloined Letter," in *The Complete Tales and Poems*, Harmondsworth, Penguin, 1983, p. 220. Hereafter CTP and page number.
[8] Ibid., p. 220.
[9] Bonaparte, *The Life and Works of Edgar Allan Poe*, p. 483.

essays from 1921 and 1924 by Abraham in her later book on *Female Sexuality*, an offshoot in many ways of her book on Poe (she explains that the book on female sexuality was planned in 1933–1934 and published first in a French psychoanalytic review in 1949;[10] her book on Poe was published in French in 1934). This second book finds its point of departure in Freud's notion of bisexuality, his *Three Essays on Sexuality*, and the debate on femininity that was raging in psychoanalytic circles in the twenties. Although one finds this distinction in Freud's texts, Bonaparte is the first to clearly articulate what distinguishes the penis and the clitoris from the phallus in the evolution of the little boy and girl:

> The general activity now aroused soon flows, however, towards the phallus, the active erotogenic zone which, in its turn, seems destined to a later awakening. Ordinarily, beginning with the later sadistic-anal stage, that is, after earlier anal freedom is repressed, the child returns to true masturbation which, for the boy, ends in the active, positive, masculine Oedipus complex, and for the girl, in the same active Oedipus complex, (though femininely negative), both of which acknowledge the mother as an object and doubtless, also, the same main executive organ, the penis, or its diminutive homologue, the clitoris.[11]

Her point of reference is what Karl Abraham called "the phallic stage with exclusion of genitals (phallus)," or in her terms, "the phallic stage after the traumatic effects of the castration complex" (FS, p. 21).

We understand better why it makes sense to talk of a "feminine phallus": if the clitoris cannot be taken for a phallus as such, the practice of feminine masturbation shows that "phallus" refers to a mode of enjoyment that has been curtailed by castration. It is in the name of the phallus that the little girl accepts the loss of a penis she never had, or the parallel idea that her mother does not have a penis either. The phallus appears very clearly as the figuration of the organ of pleasure, and as Rudolf Loewenstein (who was Jacques Lacan's analyst in the thirties and also the princess's one-time lover) wondered, it makes sense for cultural representations, as we know with the Greeks and above all with the Romans, to always show an erected phallus (he is quoted FS, p. 42). Here, the apotropaic function of the tumescent organ is clear: the rigid and immense phallus wards off the evil eye.

Similarly, Bonaparte studies the many rituals of female excision throughout the world and concludes that what is cut off is the female phallus, which is often felt to be a threat in a masculine culture. At the same time, her study

---

[10] Marie Bonaparte, *Female Sexuality*, New York, International Universities Press, 1953, p. vi.
[11] Ibid., pp. 20–21. Hereafter, FS and page number.

of obsessive masturbation in some women leads her to assert that an intense clitoral pleasure can be obtained by women even after they have had the organ surgically removed. One woman would rub the stump of her clitoris as frequently, compulsively, and successfully in terms of orgasms as before (FS, p. 157). Because of the "intensity and tenacious fixation of the libido," the removal of the organ had not rendered the spot, defined as "the scar of the glans clitoris," insensitive – far from that. The phallus marks off a body that is not reduced to the organic body; it is a cultural body, above all. This kind of observation will lead Lacan and later psychoanalysts to a systematic analysis of the phallus as the site of the lack, a lack that is required to make desire possible.

In the conclusion to her section on "Female Mutilation among Primitive People," Bonaparte compares her anthropological survey with what takes place in our Western societies: what replaces archaic genital mutilation is a "psychological mutilation" of women, whose societal repression often produces frigidity and sterility. Marie Bonaparte was an expert in this domain: in 1924, frustrated at her inability to achieve vaginal orgasm, she published a study on the difference between women whose clitoris is close to the vagina and those whose clitoris is too far. She then had twice an operation to have her clitoris brought closer to her vagina, which did not produce any result. After that, Bonaparte consulted Freud, and the psychic nature of her problem appeared.

A few years before, she had been monumentalized as a phallus herself. In 1919, she had modeled for the Rumanian sculptor Constantin Brancusi, who had been her lover. Irritated by her incessant sexual demands, Brancusi portrayed her as "Princess X," a shiny phallus, with two round bulbs at the bottom and one for the head. When the sleek bronze sculpture was exhibited at the Salon of 1920, it created quite a scandal. Even today, in the Philadelphia Museum of Art where it is kept, it continues attracting embarrassed stares. Having been publicly represented as a huge phallus, Marie Bonaparte was obviously aware that a phallus is not the organ of sexuality but its exaggerated distortion or representation. This notion will be central in Lacan's reworking of psychoanalysis.[12] Even though Lacan was to attack her violently in his seminar on Poe a few years later, he could not but agree with her definition of a man's love for a woman: it was "to be able to love a whole being with phallus excluded" (FS, p. 22), a formulation that is not far from Lacan's own about the Dora case that we have discussed earlier. As we will see, however, the phallus will return like a ghost one cannot lay to rest in the series of conflicted readings of Poe's purloined letter.

---

[12] See "The Signification of the Phallus" in *Ecrits*, pp. 575–584.

Charles Mauron and the science of X

The perverse nature of Poe's cunning tale is such that if forces its reader to want to assign a specific meaning to the details or characters of the plot. If we look for roots in literary history, we will find them. For instance, one model was that of Alexandre Dumas who invented the convoluted plot of the *Three Musketeers* in which Georges Villiers, the English lover of the Queen Ann of Austria, is in danger of being discovered by the French king because of a gift of jewels. The novel *The Three Musketeers* was serialized in March and July 1844 in *Le Siècle*. By a strange coincidence, Poe's tale was first published in an abridged and, hence, unauthorized version in an almanac called *The Gift* in September 1844. If there is an echo of Dumas's context, however, Poe's story is remarkable precisely because it avoids the trappings of the genre of the swash-buckling adventures typical of historical romances. Most critics have observed that the Dupin trilogy of "Murders in the Rue Morgue," "The Purloined Letter," and "The Mystery of Mary Roget" had been instrumental in establishing the genre of the detective novel. Those tales may also have invented the more dubious genre of the psychoanalytic novel.

Poe's French antecedents are clear, even if the genre was American at first. The name "Dupin" was borrowed from Vidocq's spurious but entertaining *Memoirs*, translated into English just after having been published in French in 1828. Vidocq referred in passing to "that great prognosticator M. Charles Dupin."[13] As we have seen, Poe's Dupin engages in endless prognostications and calculations when not solving chess problems. A critic who is a specialist of the genre of detection like Messac decided not to take this idea too seriously: "*The Purloined Letter* is algebra if one wants, but then it is really elementary algebra."[14] Poe may flaunt his scientific knowledge or allude to mathematical computations, yet most of the time the only science he adduces is psychology. We saw this with the calculations of schoolboys who play a game of odd and even; in fact, as Poe's narrator concluded, it was "merely an identification of the reasoner's intellect with that of his opponent."[15]

What, then, is hidden by not being hidden at all? The fundamental thesis of "The Purloined Letter" is that one hides best by not. Dupin guesses this truth when he hears that the police, despite a systematic scrutiny of the minister's house, are unable to find the hidden letter. By pure deduction, not observation, Dupin predicts that the letter will have to be fully visible. Poe also owes

[13] Régis Messac, *Le "Detective Novel" et l'influence de la pensée scientifique*, Paris, Honoré Champion, 1929, p. 350.
[14] Ibid., p. 354.
[15] Poe, "The Purloined Letter," CTP, p. 215.

his main conceit to Vidocq's *Memoirs* in which one reads: "If you are forced to leave your home for some time, find a place to hide your most precious possessions; the most conspicuous place is quite often the place that no-one will want to search."[16] This is a practical tip, but for Poe it becomes a whole allegory of the depths that can be hidden at the surface, as with the libidinal body.

Poe's science owes little to calculus and algebra; it relies more heavily on Humean and Lockean laws of association of ideas. Mathematics is replaced by pseudosciences such as physiognomy. The sleuth's sagacity needs as a protective disguise the parading of scientific jargon. Dupin provides the archetype of the *détective en chambre* playing chess with himself or his alter ego, a type that surfaces again with Sherlock Holmes and Hercule Poirot. A critic like Charles Mauron followed in their steps; he began his career as a scientist and soon attracted the attention of British critics such as Roger Fry. Mauron had begun a career as a researcher in chemistry, but in 1921, his incipient blindness forced him to stop and devote his time to translations and literary criticism. Thanks to his friendship with Fry, he knew the whole Bloomsbury group and participated in their discovery and promotion of Freud's ideas. His welcoming house in Provence was often visited by Fry and his London friends. Like Roger Fry, Mauron evinced a penchant for a mixture of formalism and biographical approaches. He was led to this by a method that he thought was scientific: the superposition of many texts by one single author would allow the critic to find repetitive patterns, recurrent networks, and recursive fantasies. It could be a repeated sequence of images, or one main obsessive metaphor. This network of images gave access to a structure generated by archaic dramas; finally, such metaphors condense the personal "myth" by which an author formalizes family conflicts and unconscious wishes.

Mauron's first books were devoted to the poetry of Stéphane Mallarmé and immediately had great success. His *Mallarmé l'Obscur*, published in 1941, uses the new biography of the poet by Charles Mondor to focus on one event in the poet's life that had not been known or made much of: the death of his sister aged thirteen when he was fifteen. This traumatic event was to have organized the basic attitudes of the poet facing death, obscurity, sublimation, creation, and mourning. When Mauron revisited the methodology of his first book in a new publication, *Introduction to the Psychoanalysis of Mallarmé*, he began by stating the "scientific" character of his investigations.[17] If this is a science, it was

---

[16] Vidocq's *Mémoires*, Paris, Garnier, ch. XLVI, vol. II, p. 330, quoted by Messac, *Le "Detective Novel" et l'influence de la pensée scientifique*, p. 357.

[17] Charles Mauron, *Introduction to the Psychoanalysis of Mallarmé*, trans. Archibald Henderson, Jr, and Will L. McLendon, Berkeley, University of California Press, 1963, p. 1. Hereafter, abbreviated as PM and page number.

invented by Freud and then developed by Marie Bonaparte, to whom Mauron duly pays homage: "The work of Bonaparte on the American poet is a veritable monument" (PM, p. 41). Not only are their methods identical; we know that Mallarmé was enormously influenced by Poe. Mallarmé's and Poe's unconscious have much more in common, because both were obsessed with a dead woman (the mother for latter, the sister for the former), whereas Baudelaire was in love with a living mother. If this is a science, it has to be given a name, and it is Mauron who coins it: "psychocriticism," or even "comparative psychocriticism" (PM, p. 1).

Mallarmé's "personal myth" will thus be associated with a dead feminine presence haunting his verses. The reconstruction of the myth works by a network of associations, recurrent symbols, and interrelated fantasies in which the role of death, lack, or castration is central. The idea of castration is undeniably present in poems such as "Igitur" and "Hérodiade," which is why Mauron's readings gained so much credibility so quickly. The decapitation of St. John the Baptist, which is a recurrent theme in these texts, clearly exemplifies this threat. As always with Mallarmé, the whole of nature participates and the dying sunset adds pathetic echoes to the castration complex. Mauron, who evinces more delicacy than the bold and unflappable Princess Bonaparte, apologizes to her readers for having used such an ugly word as castration: "I should like to say one word for the reader who is shocked by the crudeness of the term 'castration.' We cannot avoid it in explicating the classic myths.... It is certainly the scythe of Kronos that we find in *Cantique*" (PM, pp. 125–126). All these readings, still in the wake of Bonaparte's reading of Poe, culminate with *A Throw of the Dice*, a revolutionary poem without any punctuation, developed like a score on the page and in which the Oedipal complex is recognizable: "Let us note, in support of the unconsciously sexual character of this symbol, that the Mater of *Coup de d*és merges with the sea in a death which is also a marriage" (PM, p. 139). The true heir of Mauron was the American critic Robert Greer Cohn, whose 1949 book, *Mallarmé's Un Coup de dés: an exegesis*, was to influence Jacques Derrida's reading of Mallarmé.[18] For Cohn, every word, every letter of the poem should be read closely: their very shapes, phallic l's and vaginal u's, will disclose the same dialectical drama in which Hegel and Freud are blended, a drama underpinned by an interminable conflict between life and death, castration and resurrection, negation and affirmation. *Un Coup de dés, Finnegans Wake*, and Hegel's *Phenomenology of Spirit* all reiterate the same seasonal dramas, finally testifying to the survival of the glorious letter of literature.

---

[18] Robert Greer Cohn, *Mallarmé's Un Coup de dés: an exegesis*, New York, AMS Press, 1949.

And yet it is about the question of "mythology" that Mauron begins to show reservations facing Freud's theories, precisely because the latter's thinking is said to be "mythological." In a curious aside for a book that flaunts its Freudian affiliations, Freud is criticized not for being a creator of myths, on the contrary, but for being neither enough of a poet nor enough of a metaphysician: "Freud's errors do not arise from the fact that he was too much the poet or metaphysician, but precisely because he was not enough of either" (PM, p. 195). Not being enough of a poet, he tended to confuse poetic sense with a repressed libido, or "the poem with the symptom." Mauron believes that he stays closer to poetic beauty by paying attention to the repetition of analogous structures or chains of symbols, which ultimately disclose the same tension between life and death. It is true that he is a stylist, in ways that may have eluded Freud at times. However, in rejecting Freud snidely at a moment when his entire method rests on Freudian concepts, he is sawing the branch on which he sits. He ends up launching an "unconscious psychology" (PM, p. 205) that aims at reconciling Mallarmé's unconscious and his conscious associations. His formalist structuralism, allied with a quest for obsessive images, taps at a poet's fundamental affects and not necessarily his Unconscious. Alas, Mauron's method turned quickly into a thematic associativism. It was also too close to the formalist Modernism of his friend Roger Fry, who believed in the "purity" of art. Fundamentally, Mauron's theories confirmed Fry's earlier insight about Mallarmé:

> [N]othing is more contrary to the essential esthetic faculty than the dream. The poet Mallarmé foresaw this long before Freud had revealed the psychological value of dreams, for in his poem in memory of Théophile Gautier he says that "the spirit of Gautier, the pure poet, now watches over the garden of poetry from which he banishes the Dream, the enemy of his charge."[19]

Fry's and Mauron's formalism relied on a myth of "purity" that made room for the pleasure of the viewer but excluded the logic of the drives and sublimation.

In one of the most confusing discussions of his second Mallarmé book, Mauron inserts a revealing subtitle: "Unconscious Ego – Conscious Ego and X" (PM, p. 205). His main presupposition is that if there is any beauty, any remarkable form in a poem, this cannot be the product of what he calls an "unconscious ego." He adds: "The idea implicit in many psychoanalytic works, according to which the poem was created in the void and effected a sort of

---

[19] Roger Fry, "The Artist and Psycho-Analysis," in *A Roger Fry Reader*, ed. Christopher Reed, Chicago, University of Chicago Press, 1996, p. 361.

compromise between conscious thought and unconscious drives, will not stand up" (PM, p. 205). His solution, if it solves anything, is to add an X to the equation; of course, Mauron puns here on the famous "Sonnet in X" by Mallarmé, this "Sonnet allegorical of itself."[20] Its key signifier is the "Styx," the river of the dead to which the Ego descends only to return rejuvenated. To keep the rare rhyme-scheme throughout, Mallarmé was forced to invent a French word, "ptyx." Although it exists in Greek, Ptyx, a sort of conch or shell we take it, is called here an *aboli bibelot d'inani*té *sonore* (literally "Abolished trinket of echoing nothingness"). The lines that underpin Mauron's commentary are between parentheses in the poem: "(For the Master has gone to draw tears from the Styx / With this sole object that Nothingness attains)."[21]

Mauron implies that like the poet, the critic needs only draw some material from the well of the Unconscious but should not tarry there – its contents may prove to be too "negative." Only the conscious personality of the poet will know what to do with the poetic Nothingness. What a far cry from Princess Bonaparte, who had, willy-nilly or against her will, perhaps, figured a bronze Phallus as "Princess X"! Here, in this "Master X," or, better, "Prince X" (because the Prince and the Master are opposed in an eternal duel by Mallarmé in *Un Coup dés*), another image is proposed for the critic: the critic, obsessed by the poet's "obsessions," ends up seeing only his own mirror image at the bottom of the well. Once he perceives it, he draws back, full of anguish. Orpheus has to rush back home to the reassuring world of light and beauty. To state that any equation in a science that includes the Unconscious will end up stating "equals X" was no doubt the price to pay for the too genteel foundation of "psycho-criticism."

Why the letter is not the phallus

Lacan dramatizes his rejection of psycho-criticism in several texts on Poe; at the same time, he continues elaborating a theory of the letter in the Unconscious. His first reading of Poe's "Purloined Letter" comes as a detour in the seminar of 1954–1955, devoted to *The Ego in Freud's Theory and in the Technique of Psychoanalysis*. Then he rewrites it to provide a general and programmatic introduction to *Ecrits* in 1966. In the first seminar, Lacan was brought to Poe's tale by way of cybernetics. His point of departure was Poe's excursus on

---

[20] See Henry Weinfield's note in Stéphane Mallarmé, *Collected Poems*, trans. Henry Weinfield, Berkeley, University of California Press, 1994, pp. 217–220.
[21] Mallarmé, *Collected Poems*, p. 69.

mathematics, when Poe accounted for Dupin's particular method of detection. As we have seen, Dupin remembers a game from his schoolboy days, when a boy of eight years of age would always win at the game of even and odd by guessing correctly whether the number of marbles held in another person's hand was even or odd. He relied on a systematic identification with his opponent; the boy's skill consisted in assessing whether the other was naïve or cunning. This remark led Lacan to play at this game with the seminar's participants for a full hour. Only later did he realize the allegorical potential contained in Poe's apologue.

The second version provided by *Ecrits* does its best to keep an oral and dialogical status as it begins *in medias res*: "Our inquiry has led us to the point of recognizing that the repetition automatism (*Wiederholungszwang*) finds its basis in what we have called the *insistence* of the signifying chain." A note indicates that the text reproduces one session seminar pronounced on April 26, 1955,[22] which corresponds to the session of *The Ego in Freud's Theory*.[23] Lacan gave a detailed reading of Poe beginning with a series of mathematical speculations concerning odd and even, plus and minus. The two texts have markedly different styles. This is perceptible when Lacan opposes the letter to writing:

> When one considers one of those proverbs attributed to the wisdom of nations – the wisdom of which is thus denominated by antiphrase – one is sure to light upon a stupidity. *Verba volant, scripta manent.* Has it occurred to you that a letter is precisely speech which flies (*vole*)? If a stolen (*volée*) letter is possible, it is because a letter is a fly-sheet (*feuille volante*). It is *scripta* which *volant*, whereas speech, alas, remains. It remains even when no one remembers it any more. (S II, pp. 197–198)

In the written version, first published in *La Psychanalyse* in 1956, then taken up at the beginning of *Ecrits*, this passage becomes

> *Scripta* manent: in vain would they learn from a deluxe-edition humanism the proverbial lesson which the words *verba volant* conclude. Would that it were the case that writings remain, as is true, rather, of spoken words: for the indelible debt of those words at least enriches our acts with its transfers. // Writings scatter to the four winds blank checks of a mad charge. And were they no loose sheets, there would be no purloined letters.[24]

---

[22] *Ecrits*, 2006, p. 33.
[23] Jacques Lacan, *Seminar II: The Ego in Freud's Theory*, trans. S. Tomaselli and J. Forrester, New York, Norton, 1998. Hereafter, S II and page number.
[24] *Ecrits*, pp. 18–19.

Condensation, allusiveness, and verbal paradoxes have rendered the second version more cryptic. Both versions are full of puns and difficult to translate; the seminar clearly relies on a spoken rhetoric when elaborating on a paradox, the reversal of the old proverb: *Scripta manent, verba volant*, whereas the written one sends us back to a whole library.

Both seminars try to get to the core of Poe's parable: What is the function of a letter when we do not know its content? What is the point of having the letter without being its addressee? Quite early in Seminar II we find an insight as to the feminized position occupied by whoever is the owner of the letter. Lacan comments on the particular way the minister has disguised the letter, making sure that the police would not recognize it. He has turned the letter over (it was a single sheet of paper with a seal.) The minister then stamped it with his own seal. Noting that the minister has replaced the bold hand of the original letter with his own diminutive hand, he adds:

> The letter undergoes a sudden feminisation, and at the same time it enters into a narcissistic relation – since it is now addressed in this sophisticated feminine hand, and bears his own seal. It's a sort of love-letter he's sent to himself. This is very obscure, indefinable, I don't want to force anything, and in truth if I mention this transformation, it is because it is correlative of something else far more important, concerning the subjective behavior of the minister himself. (SII, p. 199)

Lacan makes a pause here, and it is only three pages later that he returns to the same idea: "Isn't there some echo between the letter with a feminine superscription and this languishing Paris? ... [I]n order to be in the same position vis-à-vis the letter as the Queen was, in an essentially feminine position, the minister falls prey to the same trick as she did" (SII, p. 202). Here, Lacan finds the main conceptual handle: the notion that all the characters in the story go round in a circle or a triangle and systematically exchange their positions one after the other, thus exhausting a combinatory. The written version of the seminar, manifestly denser and tighter, is also more polemical. Lacan recalls Poe's initial observation that the most difficult names to read on a map will not be the small print names but large names spaced out across the expanse of a country or continent. This is linked with Vidocq's paradox that the best dissimulation is no dissimulation:

> Just so does the purloined letter, like an immense female body, sprawl across the space of the Minister's office when Dupin enters it. But just so does he already expect to find it there, having only to undress that huge body, with his eyes veiled by green spectacles. // This is why, without any need (nor opportunity either, for obvious reasons) to listen in at

Professor Freud's door, he goes straight to the spot where lies and lodges what that body is designed to hide, in some lovely middle toward which one's gaze slips, nay, to the very place seducers call Sant'Angelo Castle in their innocent illusion of being able to control the City from the castle. Lo! Between the jambs of the fireplace, there is the object already in reach of the hand the ravisher has but to extend.... Whether he seizes above the mantelpiece, as Baudelaire translates, or beneath it, as in the original text, is a question that may be abandoned without harm to inferences emanating from the kitchen. (*Ecrits*, p. 26)

This is clearly a parody, and the discussion of Baudelaire's translation gives away its victim, who is none other than Marie Bonaparte. Indeed Bonaparte had corrected Baudelaire's mistranslation, because for her the clitoridian nature of the spot was crucial. She may well have had Freud's ear but is reduced to a cook in her overinterpretation. Lacan's main aim in his reading is to avoid the kind of hasty equivalences and equations. Although Derrida, as we will see, repeatedly accuses Lacan of distorting Bonaparte's argument and thus of missing the teachings of psychobiographical criticism, like that reading of images that migrate from story to story,[25] a number of later critics, among whom Barbara Johnson has been the most brilliant, have pointed out that Lacan is careful not to translate the letter with the phallus taken either as a concept or an object.

In the final version of the seminar, the salient feature of the story is its logical structure: it follows a pattern of almost identical repetitions. Three scenes are therefore entirely superposed. In the first scene, which can be called the primal scene of the theft, we have a blind King, who embodies the law but is unable to understand that anything is happening at all, a seeing Queen who remains impotent while the daring minister profits from the interaction between the first two. He puts his own letter on the table and leaves with the coveted prize, knowing that the Queen cannot request it without waking up her spouse's suspicions.

The second scene consists of the doomed efforts by the police to retrieve the letter on behalf of the Queen. This time, the blind character is the prefect of police and his men. They cannot find the letter because they assume that it must be hidden, projecting into reality what they think "hiding" means. The "seeing" character who cannot do much, in this case at least facing someone who is his equal like Dupin, is the minister: he basks in the imaginary

---

[25] For a compendium of the readings of Poe by Lacan, criticized by Derrida, and then criticized by Barbara Johnson and a few others, see *The Purloined Poe: Lacan, Derrida and Psychoanalytic Reading*, ed. John P. Muller and William J. Richardson, Baltimore, Johns Hopkins University Press, 1988. Hereafter, PP and page number. Here, see PP, pp. 187–190.

security brought by the letter's possession. The active agent is Dupin, because he identifies with the minister, reconstructs his mental process, prepares an exact double of the stolen letter, and devises the strategy by which he will distract the minister.

The third scene, Dupin's intervention and theft, reverses the first theft. The minister has now turned into the blind man unaware of what is happening. Dupin, who indeed acts, nevertheless signs his substitution. He leaves a similar letter that quotes the lines by Crébillon that will identify him when the minister decides to check the contents of the letter. Caught up in brotherly rivalry, Dupin seems animated less by feelings of honor or greed (although he will be handsomely paid) than by the wish to settle an account. He exposes himself to the all-seeing gaze of the author, Poe, or his readers, including Lacan, all of whom are in the position of a psychoanalyst. We just need to reconstitute the plot's logic and understand its psychical economy so as not to fall into the trap of allegorizing the letter by stealing its meaning once more.

What matters in Lacan's reading is not a series of imaginary projections triggered by each place but the mapping of a symbolic structure that determines each subject's position facing the others and the Other. This structure determines a series of effects determined corresponding to the revolving displacement of a pure signifier, the letter. The letter allegorizes the itinerary of a signifier whose signified remains inaccessible. The subjective places that the characters or readers are meant to occupy cannot escape from a repetition automatism that literally ensures that the letter will come back to the same place at the end. In a famously violent attack, Derrida objected to this postulated economy. In an essay published in 1975 in the journal *Poétique*, reprinted in *The Post Card*,[26] Derrida develops a critical program facing Lacan that he had outlined in *Positions* in 1972. Fundamentally, Lacan is taken to task for his glib use of Hegelian categories, his undeclared idealism even though he flaunts the "materiality of the signifier," and a simplification of the nuances and endless intertextual plays contained in Poe's texts. The main objection is that Lacan translated the absence of content of the letter into a "truth," the truth of psychoanalysis according to Lacan: it is marked by the return of the phallus as the empty signifier that ultimately represents castration. Finally, Derrida categorically refuses Lacan's assertion that "a letter always reaches its destination." Derrida observes that it happens that letters get lost, stolen, or even

---

[26] See the long endnote 44 in Jacques Derrida, *Positions*, trans. Henri Ronse, Chicago, University of Chicago Press, 1982, p. 107–113. It sketches the entire program that Derrida followed three years later in 1975 when attacking Lacan's "phonocentism" and Hegelian idealism. See Jacques Derrida, "Le facteur de la vérité," in *The Post Card: From Socrates to Freud and Beyond*, trans. Alan Bass, Chicago, University of Chicago Press, 1987, pp. 413–496.

burned and destroyed. He demonstrated this idea in *The Postcard* in a series of performatives, and the main text, "Envois," is based on the remains of a destroyed correspondence.

The strength of Lacan's scheme was such that it leads to its own undermining. Who can prevent another turn of the screw and stop the permutations? The last triangle cannot provide a resolution or an end to the dialectics of blindness and seeing. This is also why, when Derrida accuses Lacan of translating a mute letter into its content (the phallus) – a content that would offer the truth of the letter revisited by psychoanalysis – he, too, caught in the game, tends to "see" too much. He translates into his terms and reduces the stylistic play of Lacan's text, which, as we have seen, is no less "literary" than Poe's own. At least, this was Barbara Johnson's famous imputation.[27]

Let us return to Lacan's argument. It is inseparable from an analysis of the essence of a letter. For Lacan, a letter remains a single entity no matter what happens to it. A letter is said to be "uncuttable." In a semantic analysis of French idioms, he points out that if one can speak of "letters" in the plural, one cannot say that "there is letter"* or "there is some letter,"* as one might say "there is time" or "there is butter here." The letter, be it singular or plural, cannot be divided. Even if it were cut materially, the fragments would still make up one letter. We understand better the basis of the police's deluded assumption that the minister's room can be divided into smaller units, which includes all its objects, books, frames, table legs, and so on. They repeat Zeno's paradox: if a line is endlessly divisible, then progress in movement is impossible. Thus Achilles may run faster, he will never catch up to the tortoise, he will only approach it asymptotically.[28]

In a similar way, a "letter" in French and English is based on a homophony that does not work in languages such as German. A "letter" (*Brief*) can be made up of "letters" as so many written signs (*Buchstaben*), but even if it has been destroyed, it remains present by its absence as a letter. Lacan refuses to distinguish the meanings, and the police proves a contrario that the indivisibility of the letter creates its invisibility. Because their categories cannot assimilate the idea of a reversed and re-signed paper, for them the letter "is missing in its place," to use the expression by which libraries notify that a book has been lost by being misplaced. Seeing only what they can divide into smaller units they miss the entity spread out in front of their eyes.

---

[27] See Barbara Johnson, "The Frame of Reference: Poe, Lacan, Derrida" in *The Purloined Poe*, pp. 213–251.
[28] See Slavoj Žižek, *Looking Awry, op. cit.*, pp. 3–9 for a discussion of Zeno in Lacanian terms.

Lacan had already conceded that the materiality of the signifier was "singular" or "odd,"[29] quoting Poe's term. Derrida goes further in his denunciation of Lacan's gesture:

> Now for the signifier to be kept in its letter and thus make its return, it is necessary that in its letter it does not admit "partition", that one cannot say *some* letter but only a letter, letters, the letter. It is against this possible loss that the statement of the "materiality of the signifier," that is, about the signifier's indivisible singularity, is constructed. *This "materiality," deduced from an indivisibility found nowhere, in fact corresponds to an idealization.* Only the ideality of a letter resists destructive division. (PP, p. 194)

Yet, the argument that the alleged "indivisibility" is "found nowhere" repeats the gesture of those who look for something without finding it. However, by placing himself strategically on the terrain of empirical evidence when he argued that one can always tear up a letter into small pieces, Derrida blinds himself to the common paradox that the materiality of a single letter does not entail its being "present" here and now. Derrida did not ignore the inevitable process of "idealization" performed by whoever goes beyond the pure materiality of the signifier to produce a concept. Neither had Poe, who had added this German epigraph to the second Dupin tale, "The Mystery of Marie Rogêt," whose imperfect translation is given as "[t]here are ideal series of events which run parallel with the real ones. They rarely coincide. Men and circumstances generally modify the ideal train of events, so that it seems imperfect, and its consequences are equally imperfect. Thus with the Reformation; instead of Protestantism cam Lutheranism."[30] Here, however, the concept at hand is not the translation of the letter into its meaning (as the phallus or castration), but it is simply the concept of the letter – the allegory of the letter, if you prefer.

Derrida's objections to the letter's economy as a circuit determined by an ideal teleology are more damaging. Why indeed should the letter always return to its original place? Does Lacan imply that all mislaid letters end up in their rightful owner's hands? If I play with Lacan's terms, however, the answer can be found: if I can relate to the letter in some way, I am the answer, or any reader can be. This was Žižek's argument in *Enjoy your Symptom!*[31] Countering Derrida's accusations of idealism and teleology, Žižek showed that Lacan's

---

[29] Here, Jeffrey Mehlman and Bruce Fink are at odds. See Lacan's seminar on the "Purloined Letter" trans. Jeffrey Mehlman in PP, p. 38, and in *Ecrits*, p. 16.

[30] Edgar Allan Poe, "The Mystery of Marie Rogêt," *Complete Tales and Poems*, p. 169. The quote is from Novalis' *Morale Ansichten*, and its first sentence could be rendered: "There are series of ideal occurrences that run parallel to Reality."

[31] Slavoj Žižek, *Enjoy your Symptom!*, New York, Routledge, 1992, pp. 1–28. Hereafter, EYS and page number.

formula should work at three levels defined by the registers of the Real, the Imaginary and the Symbolic. At an imaginary level, a letter always reaches its destination means that "its destination is wherever it arrives" (EYS, p. 10). For anyone to mention the letter, it must have had at least one recipient, even if she or he is not the original addressee.

This trajectory at several levels is exemplified by Lacan's deliberate transformation of the lines from Crébillon that Dupin copies in his substitute letter. At the end of his essay, he replaces the *dessin* by *destin*: "*Un destin si funeste / S'il n'est digne d'Atrée, est digne de Thyeste*."[32] A change of a letter has transformed the "design" (*dessin*) of teleology into a "fate" (*destin*) determined by repetition with which the minister, the letter's new owner, will now play. Crébillon's play revolves around a letter informing King Atreus of his betrayal by his brother Thyestes. The letter discloses that his son is the son of Thyestes and triggers the usual roll call of incest, parricide, and even cannibalism. Like Poe who wrote deliberately the exact inverse of the Romantic historical novels by providing directly a blueprint of the economy of exchanges underpinning fantasies, Lacan makes us witness a letter that cannot be returned to an empirical sender while nevertheless reaching its destination. Its destination is the locus of the Other, the birthplace of all desires and fantasies. The agency of the letter at work in Poe's tale is not limited to the ideality of a closed economy, as Derrida contended, but guarantees that the workings of language displaces identities thanks to the constant sliding away of the signifier. Poe leads us to Freud, who elaborated the notion of an Unconscious made up of letters.

We find this in Freud's earlier writings in which he struggles to articulate a model for unconscious processes that come close to a psychic "writing," because the main idea is that there is an interaction of "mnesic traces." Such an insight already underpinned Freud's pre-analytical essay on aphasia in which he had postulated memory traces or "paths" that could be written over. By a strange coincidence, given the context of the discussion, the most relevant text by Freud is a letter to Fliess from December 1896:

> As you know, I am working on the assumption that our psychic mechanism has come into being by a process of stratification: the material present in the shape of memory traces being subjected from time to time to a *rearrangement* in accordance with fresh circumstances – to a *retranscription* (*Umschrift*). Thus what is essentially new about my theory is the thesis that memory is present not once but several times over, that it is laid down in various kinds of signs (*Zeichen*).[33]

---

[32] *Ecrits*, 2006, p. 29. Italics in the text.
[33] Masson, *The Complete Letters to Wilhelm Fliess*, *op. cit.*, p. 207, translation modified. One finds a systematic commentary of this letter in Jacques Derrida's "Freud and the Scene of Writing" in *Writing and Difference*, trans. Alan Bass, Chicago, Chicago University Press, 1978, pp. 206–207.

Freud illustrates this with a schema that describes different "retranscriptions" as connected but distinct. The first layer is constituted by perception neurons that register consciousness without keeping a memory of it; then come neurons that register the perceptions, followed by a second re-elaboration of these traces in such a way that they become inaccessible to consciousness. These can be called unconscious traces. Finally, the neurons of the preconscious system intervene and offer a third transcription with a stress on "verbal images" and links to the "official ego" before reaching consciousness. This model of psychic writing corresponds to the synthesis that Freud was elaborating in his "Project for a Scientific Psychology."[34] Derrida and Lacan fundamentally agreed on the idea that there was an "archi-writing" and that it constituted the Unconscious. It is on such a unique basis that the later bifurcation between oral speech and writing can be established. The Unconscious is fundamentally a type of writing. Such writing can be illustrated by letters, hence the Greek letters chosen by Freud to distinguish between the phi and the psi neurons. It can also be allegorized by literature, and it was Poe's genius to sense this.

Lacan developed this point when he was asked to discuss literature and literary criticism in 1971. He sent an essay entitled "Lituraterre" that went back to his Poe reading, explaining why he had decided to open *Ecrits* with an interpretation of the "Purloined Letter." Poe had meant to stress the lack of content of a letter that is "purloined." Lacan distinguishes there the letter from the signifier it carries to reject the sort of psychobiography produced by Bonaparte. The fact that Poe never reveals the content of the famous letter cannot authorize one to project meanings borrowed from the author's life:

> Thus, the kind of psychoanalysis that has cleaned up all the other texts of Poe declares that its housecleaning meets a limit.... It is sure that, as always, psychoanalysis receives from literature a less psychobiographic conception even when taking repression as its main source. // If I propose to psychoanalysis the idea of a letter in sufferance, it is because this shows its own failure. And here is where I bring light: when I invoke the enlightenment, I demonstrate where it makes a *hole*. This is well-known in optics, and the recent physics of the photon is underpinned by it.[35]

Lacan's interpretation of the works and life of André Gide can help us understand why the letter is defined by a hole and also under which conditions a psychobiography is possible.

---

[34] See the discussion of the previous chapter. Freud's *Project* was published as part of Sigmund Freud, *The Origins of Psychoanalysis*, 1954, pp. 347–445.

[35] Jacques Lacan, "Lituraterre" in *Littérature*, n. 3, Paris, Larousse, 1971, p. 4. My translation.

Gide and the jouissance of the letter

Lacan's discussion of André Gide focuses on his relationship with letters. A key moment in Gide's life was the devastation he described at length, after his wife had burned all their correspondence. Gide never fully overcame the destruction of his letters by Madeleine, who, furious that he had betrayed her with a male friend, destroyed what was most precious to her, as we will see. Lacan analyzes this central event in "Gide's Youth, or the Letter and Desire," an essay originally written as a homage to Jean Delay's psychobiography of Gide. For once, Lacan approves Delay's monumental psychobiography, noting that it had remained faithful to Gide's project of exploring in depth a person to reach the central core of a human being. The issue was to throw light on "the *rapport between man and the letter*."[36] Delay had written 1,300 pages about Gide's life between 1869 and 1895 in an effort to analyze the life and career of the French author. Lacan approved this project, because with Gide, as with Joyce or Proust, one cannot separate the substance of the novels from the author's life:

> The only thing that counts is a truth derived from what is condensed by the message in its development. There is so little opposition between this *Dichtung* and the *Wahrheit* in its bareness, that the fact of a poetic operation should rather bring us back to a feature that is forgotten about every truth, namely that it is produced as truth in a structure of fiction. (E, pp. 741–742)

This tallies with Gide's attitude when he derided de Gouncourt's timidity: his realism forced him to give the "proof," as it were, of what he narrated, as if he had to adduce the reality of everything he writes (quoted by Lacan, E, p. 742, n.1).

Gide's works probed the complexities of human sexuality with a rare candor. His ambivalence facing his wife was acknowledged almost shockingly in the text published after the death of Madeleine, *Et nunc manet in te*.[37] Gide felt an obstinate desire to marry his older cousin, who was like a sister for him. Gide's mother objected, sensing that this was tantamount to incest. Gide's main desire was to protect this cousin, who had been traumatized by the scandalous behavior of her own mother, a beautiful, flighty, and sensual woman, who first brought lovers to the family home before deserting it. She had also made a sexual overture to her nephew André, which triggered his flight. The

---

[36] *Ecrits*, p. 739. Italics in the text.
[37] André Gide, "Et nunc manet in te," in *Souvenirs et Voyages*, ed. Pierre Masson, Paris, Gallimard, Pléiade, 2001. Hereafter, SV and page number.

riddle of his love for Madeleine posed an enormous problem for him. How could Gide, whose sensuality had bloomed early and whose homosexuality was not closeted, decide to marry – in an almost incestuous union – a cousin whose own sexual urges would remain unsatisfied? Gide believed in a "mystical love" based on sexual renunciation, one that divorced pure love from sexual satisfaction in adolescents. The unconsummated marriage exacted its toll on a Madeleine who was kept in the dark about her husband's sexuality. *Et nunc manet in te* unflinchingly documents how drained and aged his wife Madeleine had become; in public, they were regularly mistaken for a mother and her son (SV, p. 952).

In 1918, however, Madeleine acted. She burned Gide's letters to her after he had left with Marc, a young male friend, to spend some time in England. Gide's reaction to this loss was excessive: he cried for one week, stating that it was as if he had lost a child (SV, p. 961). For Madeleine, too, these letters were a treasure: "her most precious possession." Gide had been in the habit of writing about ten pages a day to her since they were in their teens. The letters, to which both had access, filled a large drawer in an unlocked chest. However, Madeleine had felt the need to "do something" after she had been left alone. She reread each letter one by one, and then burned them (SV, p. 961). Comparing himself to Oedipus after he had blinded himself, Gide even wrote: "Maybe there never was a more beautiful correspondence" (SV, p. 962, note). In the wake of this personal tragedy, Gide's decision to write a frank autobiography can be understood. He needed to portray his "passions" in the cold light of analytical writing and move away from the transference to an idealized feminine addressee.

Lacan quotes the last page of a diary appended to *Et nunc manet in te*, admitting that he has been guilty of a misreading. In 1939, Gide had written in his own diary:

> Before leaving Paris, I was able to revise the proofs of my *Diary*. Rereading it, it appears to me that the systematic excision (until my mourning at least) of all the passages concerning Madeleine have in a way *blinded* the text. The few allusions to the secret drama of my life thus become incomprehensible because of the absence of what could throw light on them. Incomprehensible or inadmissible, the image of my mutilated self I give there, offering only, in the burning place of the heart, a hole. (SV, p. 977)

Lacan first thought that Gide alluded to the burnt correspondence, then realized his mistake, finally to conclude that he was correct in his inference: Gide's text points to the same structural function. This is the point where Gide's famous irony, so visible in many novels, finds a limit – the limit of the letter as such. Lacan goes on: "The letters in which he placed his soul had ... no carbon copy (*double*). When their fetishistic nature appeared it gave rise to the kind of laughter that greets subjectivity caught off guard. // It all ends with comedy, but who will put a stop to the laughter?" (*Ecrits*, p. 641). Lacan's laughter aims at deflating Gide's overevaluation of a correspondence into which he had poured his heart on a daily basis, gushing forth all his emotions to a cousin who became his wife in a sexless marriage.

Madeleine, the addressee of the letters, had been well placed to observe the outbursts of her husband's libido. She noticed with horror how passion would suddenly distort his features, as in a scene that took place during their wedding trip to Algiers. Gide, sitting next to his wife, would go to the window and caress the arms and shoulders of seductive little Arab boys. "You looked like a criminal or a madman," she told him (SV, p. 948). In Lacan's view, however, Gide's "perversion" does not come from his sexual desire for young boys. What he desires is to recreate what he himself was as a little boy, a desired child who had been the object of his aunt's attentions. Gide as a child was caught in a triangle with the mother and the father as polar opposites. Gide loved his cousin, later his wife, but following Lacan's formula, his love meant that he would give her what he did not have. In this case, it meant not having sexual intercourse. Gide's theory of love was entirely divorced from physical desire. This wife whom he did not desire would embody a supreme, mystical love. Their letters had replaced desire; they were left in the place of a desire that had vanished, and as symptoms, they could not avoid the question of the phallus.

Gide's symptoms had started early; he had been expelled from public schools because of an inveterate habit of masturbating in public. Having lost his father when he was eleven, he experienced a series of unbearable fits of anxiety about the death of loved ones. Then he discovered a truth about himself: he was "not like the others." The early disappearance of the father prevented him from laying down the law, but his main heritage was a well-stacked library, a cultural treasure trove that the young man was allowed to enter when he turned sixteen only. Once established in the library, Gide would not leave it. He kept wondering whether the pact that he had made with himself early – namely, an effort to tell the truth – could be sustained. If his commitment to truth had led to a transgression of accepted norms, could it resist becoming perverse in its turn? Did Gide not take a perverse pleasure in pushing the envelope of sincerity? Gide attempted to deal with this issue by establishing a stark contrast between the two halves of his celebrated memoir, *If it die....* The first section, which looks very much like a traditional *Künstlerroman*, leads to a meditative pause, during which Gide expatiates on the impossibility of actually telling the whole truth: "My intention has always been to say everything," he writes but adds, "I am a being of dialogue; everything in me fights and contradicts itself. Memoirs are never more than half sincere, however great one's wish to tell the truth: everything is half more complicated that one says. It may even be that one approaches truth best in a novel."[38] Such a narrative hinge was necessary before reaching the sexual aspect of the memoirs. It is accompanied by a number of disclaimers as to the exact correlation of his memories, complemented by corrections of erroneous details later provided by a cousin (SV, pp. 328–329).

The second section of *If it die...* is more daring and centers around the figure of Oscar Wilde, whereas the first part was dominated by Mallarmé, the pure poet, and a model of artistic devotion found with de la Nux, a devoted piano teacher. In the second part, we meet the perverse, outrageous, almost satanic (given Gide's belief in the devil highlighted in the first part) figures of Wilde and Lord Douglas – yet it was to them that Gide owed the revelation of his sexuality. What had remained partly hidden at the beginning of *If it die...* (the memoir begins with two boys playing under a table, concealed by a cloth, enjoying their "bad habits," i.e., mutual masturbation) comes to the fore crudely in the intense sunlight of Algeria, a colonial locale less repressive than metropolitan France. The sharp glare of Africa banishes the shadows of bourgeois childhood, dispels the puritanical gloom and the "devils" hallucinated there, wipes away studious boredom and the pseudo-artistic *chiaroscuro* of Parisian interiors. Like Nietzsche's blinding light of noon, it annihilates the ghosts of the religious past. Gide's nature is revealed to him when he has sex with the handsome young Mohammed, one of Lord Douglas's "mignons" lent to Gide by Wilde for an unforgettable night of pleasure. The narrative becomes lyrical when evoking the transports and intense joy that come close to pure phallic jouissance.

Gide confides that he had five orgasms with his partner and then had to keep masturbating several times before he could regain his composure and return to his "normal self" (SV, p. 310). Gide had finally discovered pure pleasure in a sexuality that was not tainted by love, guilt, or marked by religious repression. Thus love and desire would be at odds, and this became Gide's truth. Before, in other attempts, as with the young female prostitute Meriem, whom he shared with his friend Paul, he had felt "foreclosed" (SV, p. 284) from pleasures that he imagined more intense for the others. The absolute truth reached in a climax of sexual jouissance transgressing all limits provides a secure foundation, almost a neo-Cartesian *"gaudeo ergo sum."*

---

[38] André Gide, "Si le grain ne meurt," in SV, p. 267. All translations are mine.

It is on the strength of this night masterminded by Wilde that Gide assumed the sexual orientation that he always called "pederasty." It implies a phallic worship of young men who are consenting partners. Thanks to this newly gained confidence, Gide parted ways with Proust, who had been mentioned at the end of the first part, and also with Wilde, even though his presence recurs in those pages. Gide strongly opposed Proust's decision to hide his sexuality in *La Recherche*. His 1921 diary records his indignation when *Sodom* was published: this constituted an "offense against truth" and was a sign of moral cowardice.[39] He disapproved of the transposition of his fascination for young men into the beautiful evocation of "young girls in bloom," which he understood as hypocrisy, and he loathed the portrait of Charlus as a sodomite monster in the last sections of his magnum opus.[40] Gide's furious attack in his diary established the "transposition" theory. Gide quotes Proust as having told him that he transcribed his homosexual encounters into the narrator's infatuation for young women, those *jeunes filles en fleur* whose own sexuality later appears more than ambiguous.

In the same way, he objected to Wilde's effeminate affectation and to his irrepressible histrionic tendencies; this may be why he gave a truly tragic vision of Wilde, who, seen just weeks before his fateful trial, seemed to know that he was courting disaster (see SV, p. 305). Wilde takes on a quasi-satanic personality, and Gide notes Wilde's sinister and uncontrollable laughter just before bringing his young French friend to the tryst with Mohammed (Wilde probably laughed at the good trick he was playing on Lord Douglas). What stands out is that in overtly confessing the truth about his homosexuality, Gide rejected donning a fake femininity and disavowed the myth of a "race of inverts" of Sodom and Gomorrah. Gide felt that he could truly present himself as a manly and healthy man, one "reborn" after a grave illness, who enjoyed having sex with boys or younger men. This frankness extends to observing gay friends; he does not hide his own astonishment when his friend Daniel engages in robust sex with the same Mohammed, who does not seem to mind being sodomized brutally. He compares this discovery to the lessons brought to him by Remy de Gourmont's *Natural Philosophy of Love* (SV, p. 312). The book, which had so much impressed Ezra Pound that he translated it in 1922, taught Gide that jouissance is always particular. If one observes the variously inventive and baroque ways in which animals copulate, one understands that despite the sameness of the aims and function, everyone acts differently in selecting

---

[39] André Gide, *Journal 1889–1939*, Paris, Gallimard, Pléiade, 1951, p. 705. *Gide's Journals*, trans. Justin O'Brien, New York, Knopf, 1948, vol. 2, p. 267.

[40] See Elisabeth Ladenson's *Proust's Lesbianism*, Ithaca, Cornell University Press, 1999, for a critical reevaluation of the "transposition" theory.

his or her modes of enjoyment. Hence, the absolute "difference" experienced as anxious *Schaudern* in early youth by Gide turns out to be a normal feature marking each subject's position in sexuality. There was no need to hide the phallus, Gide says: it can be shown, at least in literature, and it may not be reduced to castration.

Thus, it was only after having published *The Immoralist* that Gide could became an immoralist himself. The hero, Michel, has an unhappy wife whose death forces him to "confess" to his friends; he is just a half-hearted Nietzschean who has not shaken off the specters of religion and morality. Curiously, the death of Michel's wife in the novel anticipates the untimely death of Gide's wife, Madeleine, on whom the fictional character was based. The later memoir of *If it die…* ends with a different loss, the death of Gide's beloved mother. In spite of the pain, Gide exhibits a strange ambivalence. Because his mother was everything to him, he experienced a sort of absolute freedom when he felt plunged into "an abyss of love, despair, and freedom" (SV, p. 326). This was a first step toward the freedom the young Gide had longed for, but the decision to write a frank confession was triggered by the famous crisis of 1918, when Madeleine burned their letters.

The two losses, that of the mother and that of the correspondence with the wife, had hollowed out a double abyss in Gide. More important, perhaps, was the loss of the letters, because this left a deep "hole" in his heart. It was in this hole that he could then capture the depth of phallic jouissance. Such jouissance was never far from a symbolic death, a death replayed in fiction as evinced by the portrayal of Boris, the perturbed adolescent of *The Counterfeiters*. Boris commits suicide at the end, and the psychoanalyst who treated him briefly, Sophroniska, whose name may echo "wisdom," only makes matters worse by trying to have him stop masturbating. Her name barely hides Eugénie Sokolnicka-Kutner, the Polish psychoanalyst who introduced Freudian psychoanalysis to France. As a young woman, she had attended Pierre Janet's lectures in Paris, then worked with Jung and with Freud. In 1919, she had treated a young Jewish boy who suffered from obsessional neurosis in Warsaw, which constituted one of the first examples of a child analysis. She arrived in Paris in 1921 and organized "Freud sessions" that were attended by Jacques Rivière and André Gide. Gide had a few sessions with her and depicted her in 1925 as Doctoress Sophroniska in *The Counterfeiters*. If Boris's symptoms are clearly modeled on Gide's own (Boris masturbates with friends, believing that they are doing some magic and reaching a "state of hallucination and ecstasy, floating over an empty void"[41]), then what is more revealing for Gide himself is that

---

[41] André Gide, *The Counterfeiters*, trans. Dorothy Bussy, New York, Knopf, 1972, p. 190.

Sophroniska asserts that Boris has "nothing of the mystic."[42] This judgment, no doubt given by Eugénie Sokolnicka about Gide himself, helped him reject the idea of a "pure" or "mystical" love.

Gide, who had been introduced to psychoanalysis around 1919 or 1920 remained wary of Freud, whom he would call an "idiot of genius" responsible for a "wave of oedipedemics." At the same time, Gide had left room for the unconscious in his writings early on, before his discovery of psychoanalysis, as attested by the novel *Paludes* from 1895. This Virgilian satire makes fun of the symbolist literary milieu he knew so well and also evokes in *If it die....* In *Paludes*, Gide asserts that his readers are free to make sense of an open text:

> Before explaining my book to others, I wait for others to explain it to me ... what interests me is what I have put there without knowing it, – that part of Unconscious that I would like to call God's part. – A book is always a collaboration, and whatever it is worth, the more the scribe's part is small, the more God's welcome will be great.[43]

After Gide abandoned his religious mysticism, he still needed the function of a big Other. Hence, the "pact"[44] usually entailed by autobiographical writing of the kind he was to employ more and more implied that the dialogue between author and reader would invoke a third factor: the figure of truth, an absolute Other that did not have to be embodied by the God of his Protestant family. In the end, for Gide, this Other would be buttressed on the issue of phallic jouissance as opposed with and linked to castration. It was in the name of the truth discovered in sexual enjoyment that Gide would go further and probe more deeply the recesses of human sexuality.

Madeleine, the ideal addressee of his letters but never the object of his desire, could truly understand the horror of her husband's desire. However, Gide's "perversion" was not reducible to his desire for young boys. What he desired most was to recreate the little boy he had been, the boy who had once been the object of his aunt's sexual attentions, which led to his anguished flight, then followed by a wish to compensate by marrying the aunt's daughter, his future wife. Gide's perversion consisted in an autoerotic graphomania aimed at perpetuating a family drama, at rebuilding endlessly a private theater of unlimited adoration. On this incestuous theatrical stage, he would remain the hero of the plot no matter what happened. This mirroring process, keeping him as always

---

[42] Ibid., p. 189.
[43] André Gide, "Paludes," in *Romans et Récits*, vol. I, Paris, Gallimard, Pléiade, 2009, p. 259.
[44] See Philippe Lejeune, *Autobiographical Pact: Le pacte autobiographique*, Paris, Seuil (1975), 1996, expanded version, pp. 165–196. on Gide.

desiring and desired, was buttressed on the correspondence that was like the loving heart of his work.

Gide truly loved his cousin, the pure Madeleine (Alissa in *Straight Is the Gate*), yet this love followed the Lacanian formula: he gave to her what he did not have – namely, desire, a desire that remained pure and unconsummated. Gide understood the rationale of the strange couple they formed only after Madeleine's death and once the "letters" had been metamorphosed by the redeeming function of autobiography. Gide would then become a "man of letters" whose truth could be shared with the general reader. After the ordeal of the burned letters, Gide reached his true maturity and became a fully engaged and committed intellectual. He went with Marc to Africa, visiting Congo, which led to his powerful indictment of the French colonial system. Gide's attack triggered soul-searching debates followed by public controversy in France. His notorious trip to the Soviet Union had a similar effect; it turned into a scathing denunciation of Stalin's cult of personality. It was the first French account to be so outspoken. Gide had to tell the truth, even if it clashed with the Communist cause for which he was a militant. Gide was still a "man of letters," letters that implied a transgression of accepted norms, yet he avoided the trap of falling into mere perversity. The transgression pushed the envelope of sincerity but also destroyed the fetish of a literary phallus by playing with castration. Revealing everything about himself led to a universalizing disclosure and turned him away from literary narcissism, which is why Gide is still read and taught today as a true contemporary.

Chapter 6

A thing of beauty is a *Freud* forever: Joyce with Jung and Freud, Lacan, and Borges

Gide left us with the question of the specific enjoyment deployed and conveyed by literature. We have seen that most psychoanalytic readings tend to link this enjoyment with the phallus as a symbolic marker of lack, hence of desire, whereas the later Lacan insists on an absolute and transgressive *jouissance*. These interpretations attempt to situate enjoyment in relation with letters, either as literal letters (the "literariness" of literature or its literalness), or as allegorical letters, like the letters whose sum constitutes the essence of a "man of letters." The dual nature of the letter as opening up to absolute enjoyment and as constituting a personal myth of the author can be condensed in a symptom. This notion should lead us to James Joyce, who became for Jacques Lacan the "symptom of literature," whereas a little earlier he had been presented by Carl Gustav Jung as symptomatic of a modern tendency toward the splitting of consciousness – in other words, of schizophrenia. I will begin this chapter with a discussion of Jung's reading of Joyce's works to assess the main difference between Jung and Freud in terms of sexual dynamics. I will end with two parallel interpretations of Joyce's figure as a man of letters, one by Lacan – closer to Freud but with a tendency to overlap with Jung's theses – and the other by Jorge Luis Borges – definitively closer to Jung. Joyce will serve as a "strange attractor" for a variety of psychoanalytic discourses about literature, whose enjoyment has been enacted in advance by the Irish writer's very signature.

Jung's reading of *Ulysses*

There is a hushed silence in the abundant secondary literature about Joyce concerning Jung's notoriously bad-tempered essay on *Ulysses*. He published it in 1932, ten years after the novel's publication, at a time when Joyce's book was hailed as a modern masterpiece, receiving quasi-universal critical acclaim. It is rare to see a famous psychoanalyst, who by that time had founded his own school, rant for more than twenty pages about a novel that he claims not to like and not to understand and whose main interest comes from the fact that it looks very much like the ravings of schizophrenics. One must know the genealogy of the complex links between Jung and Joyce to make better sense of this odd diatribe.

It all began during World War I in Zurich where Joyce had sought refuge with his family. There, he met an American patron of the arts, Mrs. McCormick, who generously awarded him a subsidy that helped him write leisurely. As she was an ardent devotee of Jungian psychoanalysis, she suggested that Joyce would benefit from a psychoanalytic cure from the Swiss doctor. Joyce refused indignantly, and then suddenly, without any explanation, Mrs. McCormick withdrew her support and closed the account. At first, Joyce blamed this financial catastrophe on his friend Ottocaro Weiss, a psychoanalyst close to Jung, but Weiss was innocent. The sudden reversal may have been because of Jung's negative comments: he had heard that Joyce was drinking too much and was wasting his talent.[1] At the time, Joyce had not met Jung, but Jung had heard of him without having read him.

When Lucia, Joyce's daughter, started to show signs of schizophrenia in the early thirties, Joyce consulted many specialists, to no avail. In 1932, he had gone to Zurich for an eye operation, and he arranged for Lucia to come as well. However, Joyce was reluctant to have Lucia consult with Jung, whom he did not trust. During this time Joyce had read the negative review of *Ulysses* and felt that the tone was excessive yet could serve as promotion given the reputation of Jung. Two years later, they were all in Zurich once more. Lucia, whose symptoms had grown worse, was sent to the Burghölzi clinic, where she was treated by Jung. Jung's treatment was successful at first: Lucia became more talkative and expressed herself more rationally. She even wrote a long letter to her father in Triestine dialect that Jung had translated. Alas, it looked like a love letter to Joyce, almost every sentence beginning or ending with "Father." Here is a typical sentence: "Father, if ever I take a fancy to anybody, I swear to you on the head of Jesus that it will not be because I am not fond of you."[2] Jung, who had no difficulty in diagnosing an irreversible schizophrenia, saw the futility of therapy. He told this to Joyce, who was relieved in a way yet distraught in another. Jung explained to Joyce that no one could understand Lucia except her father; a psychoanalytic treatment could make her worse and even provoke a catastrophe.[3]

Jung understood Joyce's delusional attitude facing his daughter: as all his letters testify, and as many witnesses have confirmed, Joyce insisted for as long

---

[1] For all this, see Ellmann, *James Joyce*, pp. 422 and 466–469.
[2] Quoted by Ibid., p. 676.
[3] Ibid., p. 681.

as he could that Lucia was not insane but an expert linguist and inspired seer, whose gift of second sight could be verified in countless instances. He thought that he shared with her a new linguistic code along with the ability to intuit the world differently but truly. Hence, for Jung, Lucia had become her father's muse, her *anima inspiratrix*. Joyce was the stronger "animus" who had survived a deep dive into the waters of the Unconscious, while the weaker "anima" was drowning in them. A long and heated controversy surrounding Lucia's symptomatology has followed the publication of Carol Shloss's biography, *Lucia Joyce: Dancing at the Wake.*[4] Shloss's thesis is that Lucia was mostly victimized by the Joyce family madness. Indeed, Lucia was forced to renounce a career as a talented dancer, young men would come to her home not for her but for her famous father (as Beckett did), and she was preyed on by her brother's ambivalent care, laced with disguised hostility. Even Jung was attacked on this account for having trained too specialized an eye on Lucia. The debate is still raging. Here, focusing on the links between the writer and the psychoanalyst, I want to begin by a paradoxical detail. Around Christmas 1934, Joyce had not only dismissed Jung's assault in the latter's review of *Ulysses* as ill-tempered but also inscribed a copy of the same novel to him, mentioning that he was grateful for his advice. Joyce, who was often vindictive, could forgive or forget when his attitude was linked with the plight of his daughter.

Joyce's remarkable leniency and patience facing Jung were not simply tactical but also a result of the fact that he had read Jung's essays about paternity, incest, and madness quite early. He owned them in Trieste before the war, but having used them in the composition of *Ulysses* for all they were worth, he forgot about their conclusions and did not seem to have learned much from them for his own sake. It seems that Joyce bracketed them off in his conscious life, preferring to believe that his daughter was not psychotic. Joyce owned, as we have seen earlier, Jones's book on Freud and Hamlet translated into German and the original version of Jung's *The Significance of the Father in the Destiny of the Individual.*[5] This slim book of about fifty pages, originally published in 1909, reprinted in 1926 and revised in 1948, offers a veritable palimpsest of Jung's evolving terminology. It reveals the distance that Jung took from his Freudian beginnings, while throwing an important light on Joyce's conception of paternity. The first version belongs to what is often called Jung's "Psychoanalytic period"[6] – that is, a moment when Jung still pays homage to Freud while

[4]   Carol Loeb Shloss, *Lucia Joyce: Dancing in the Wake*, London, Picador, 2005.
[5]   Carl Gustav Jung, *Die Bedeutung des Vaters für das Schicksal des Einzelnen*, Leipzig and Vienna, Deuticke, 1909.
[6]   Carl Gustav Jung, "The Significance of the Father in the Destiny of the Individual," in *The Psychoanalytic Years*, trans. R. F. C. Hull, Princeton, Princeton University Press, 1974, pp. 94–116.

inserting rather modest qualifications. What was fascinating for Joyce was the number of accurate vignettes collected by Jung, who was skilled in the art of condensing a case study into a few pages. Thus, Jung mentions the sad story of an unconsciously incestuous father who wanted to marry his daughter only to the most stupid and ugly of men. Concluding his analysis of this case, Jung generalizes about fate and destiny, words that we often invoke to hide more embarrassing admissions. Facing psychic dramas, we have the sense that an "autonomous personality" rules our lives, be it a daemon, a god, or a devil.

In additions inserted in 1948 to this case, Jung added sentences that echoed his interpretation of Joyce's predicament. Against Freud's exclusive determinism in terms of the parents and the child, Jung introduced his theory of "archetypes" – that is, pre-existing patterns of behavior that are inherited and derive from a collective unconscious. One of these is the belief in the absolute power of the father; for Jung, when some fathers identify with it, they become monsters: "The more a father identifies with the archetype, the more unconscious and irresponsible, indeed psychotic, both he ands his child will be. In the case we have discussed, it is almost a matter of 'folie à deux.'"[7] Indeed, in many ways, Joyce's attitude toward his daughter was a "folie à deux," because her delirium was constituted mostly by megalomaniac delusions: her main ambition was to get Ireland to recognize the genius of her father. Her mission in life was to "reconcile" James Joyce and Ireland, as she reiterated in her letters, and for this aim she was ready to enlist the Pope himself. On the other hand, Joyce's increasingly obscure writing – that mimed the "language of the night, immersed in dreams to such an extent that it plumbed the depths of some form of collective unconscious – did its best to prove that Lucia was not insane. If she spoke and wrote like the characters of *Finnegans Wake*, this only proved that she obeyed the dictation of preexisting unconscious archetypes.

In the original version of the 1909 book owned by Joyce, Jung was talking about "original sin," stating that one should not blame one's parents for everything, as Freud would do too often. In the final version, it is simply the Unconscious that gets demonized: "They do not know what they are doing, and they do not know that by succumbing to the compulsion they pass it on to their children and make them slaves of the parents and of the unconscious as well.... 'They know not what they do.' Unconsciousness is the original sin."[8] These ideas, so strongly expressed, are echoed in *Ulysses*, even more in *Finnegans Wake*, a book that Joyce declared to be founded on one main mythical paradigm: original sin.

---

[7] Ibid., p. 109.
[8] Ibid., pp. 109–110.

We must now turn to Jung's review of *Ulysses* to understand better his position facing Joyce. In this essay, Jung vents his frustrations at discovering that "nothing happens"[9] in 736 pages, adding snidely that one can read the book backwards: the plot will be same. He grudgingly praises Joyce for the wealth of sensory details (SMAL, p. 112) but relates this performance to Janet's description of idiots who can only perceive reality and never think. Because the book does not aim at representing anything (SMAL, p. 113), it is amorphous and unfolds like a gigantic tapeworm! Jung had tried to read it in 1922, had stopped, utterly bored, and experienced the same boredom in 1932 (SMAL, p. 115). Some clinical language follows: the book resembles "the schizophrenic mentality" (SMAL, pp. 116 and 117, where Jung compares Joyce with Van Gogh, who was clearly schizophrenic) and expresses the "disintegration of the personality into fragmentary personalities" (SMAL, p. 117). An artist's aim is to reproduce a collective mentality, to give voice to a collective unconscious; Joyce does this, but negatively. In its perversely Catholic medievalism, *Ulysses* has the function of an emetic, a purgative; in this it resembles Freud's works – books that have been inspired by *Ulysses* "have in common with Freudian theory, that they undermine with fanatical one-sidedness values that have already begun to crumble" (SMAL, p. 119). The book's main effect is similar to that of Nietzsche: for both, negativity cannot be stopped; they keep destroying values in a perpetual gesture of "creative destruction" (SMAL, p. 119). Jung's painstaking caviling spares nothing.

One reason for this unleashed flak barrage is soon provided. Several times, Joyce is compared to Freud: "And it is because Joyce's contemporaries are so riddled with medieval prejudices that such prophets of negation as he and Freud are needed to reveal to them the other side of reality" (SMAL, p. 121). Finally, the main image that Jung retains of the book is that of Moses: "Looked at from the shadow-side, ideals are not beacons on mountain peaks, but taskmasters and gaolers, a sort of metaphysical police originally thought up on Sinai by the tyrannical demagogue Moses and thereafter foisted upon mankind by a clever ruse" (SMAL, p. 122). Jung may have known that one of Joyce's favorite passages in *Ulysses* was the passage from the "Aeolus" chapter with a highly rhetorical peroration by John Taylor, who compared Irish with the Jews about to be freed by Moses. This is the single passage of *Ulysses* that Joyce recorded on a disk. Here, obviously, Moses stands for Freud: the inflexible, dogmatic leader, who would have to be killed by his followers.

---

[9] Carl Gustav Jung, ""Ulysses": A Monologue," in *The Spirit in Man, Art and Literature*, Princeton, Princeton University Press, 1972, p. 109. Hereafter, SMAL and page number.

Through the ambiguous image of Moses, Jung betrays his ambivalence facing one master (Freud, the Father who will be dethroned), and another master (Joyce, the victim of Irish Catholicism whose consciousness merges with a whole collective culture). He presents universal culture as a "dunghill, but, lo!, out the dunghill noble treasures still emerge" (p. 129) Finally, Jung concedes that the "microcosm of Dublin" on June 16, 1904, can nevertheless emerge from "the chaotic macrocosm of world history" (SMAL, p. 130.) The review ends with an impassioned invocation: "O *Ulysses*, you are truly a devotional book for the object-besotted, object-ridden white man! You are a spiritual exercise, an ascetic discipline, an agonizing ritual, an arcane procedure, eighteen alchemical alembics piled on top of one another, where amid acids, poisonous fumes, and fire and ice, the homunculus of a new, universal consciousness is distilled" (SMAL, pp. 131–132). Jung has managed to introduce alchemy into his interpretation, and this single fact leads to a last-minute reconciliation – an atonement valid for the whole process.

Freud against Jung: The law of Moses

We need to understand under which conditions Joyce can be linked so closely to Freud in Jung's highly critical reading. We will need to go back to the moment of their falling-out. It can be dated from the years 1911–1913. In 1913, Freud published *Totem and Taboo*, which launched his "mythical" period, because he stated in this book his belief in an unverifiable original drama at the root of all cultures, societies, and religions: the murder of the father. This would of course include Moses, the Egyptian legislator later murdered by the rabble of the freed slaves. Already in 1911, Freud announced that he was working on the "psychology of religious faith and ties."[10] His already ancient interest in comparative religion had been reawakened by Jung's ongoing investigations in the domains of myth and ritual. Freud wanted to emulate his chosen heir – Jung had been installed President of the International Psychoanalytical Association in 1910, at Freud's insistence.

Above all, Freud was intent on correcting theoretical deviations. Jung, elected Freud's "crown prince" because he was not Jewish, which would dispel accusations that psychoanalysis was a "Jewish" fad, had focused more and more on myths and symbols gathered from many religions, with the aim of nuancing what he saw as a Freudian dogma. What Jung rejected was the idea

---

[10] Ernest Jones, *The Life and Work of Sigmund Freud: Years of Maturity 1901–1919*, vol. 2, New York, Basic Books, 1955, p. 350.

that everything hinged on the Oedipus complex and sexual repression in the early years. Jung's analysis of primitive religions and anthropological accounts of rituals found its expression in *Metamorphoses and Symbols of the Libido* from 1911–1912, but the term of "Libido" was used differently by Jung, often in a nonsexual sense. It became more "symbolic," "energetic," or "dynamic," because sexuality strictly understood led to a "regressive" insistence on the most archaic determinations of the patient. Jung was also reducing the incest taboo to a mere fantasy, whereas for Freud it was a cornerstone of his doctrine. One can see how the school of Melanie Klein, which was starting at the same time, took a parallel but opposite position: everything would revolve around pre-Oedipal dramas enacted in the first two years that then stamped adult neuroses with the positions adopted in infantile sexuality.

Jung made the mistake of boasting of his American success to Freud in a letter from September 1912. There, as he confided, his lectures had been applauded because he had downplayed the sexual themes that created too much discomfort for their Puritanism. Freud was annoyed and invited a gathering to sort out their differences. Freud and Jung apologized to each other for real or imagined slights, when Freud had a fainting attack. In the aftermath, Jung waxed paternalistic, reminding Freud that during their trip to the United States in 1909, the latter had refused to discuss personal details in a dream that Jung was analyzing because Freud did not want to lose his authority. In several letters, Jung pointed to the neurotic element in Freud's personality, and Freud concurred but reassured Jung that his neurosis had never impaired him. The truce lasted until December 14, 1912. On that day, Jung concluded a letter to Freud with a revealing slip of the pen: "Even Adler's cronies do not regard me as one of *yours*," when he meant obviously "one of theirs."[11] Freud wrote back and pointed out the slip, asking whether Jung could be "objective enough" when he betrayed such an ambivalence. Jung exploded in the following letter:

> I am objective enough to see through your little trick. You go around sniffing out all the symptomatic actions in your vicinity, thus reducing everyone to the level of sons and daughters who blushingly admit the existence of their faults. Meanwhile you remain on top as the father, sitting pretty. For sheer obsequiousness nobody dares pluck the beard of the prophet and to inquire for once what you should say to a patient with a tendency to analyze the analyst instead of himself. You would certainly ask him, "Who's got the neurosis?"[12]

[11] *The Freud/Jung Letters*, ed. William McGuire, abridged, Princeton, Princeton University Press, 1994, p. 251.
[12] *The Freud/Jung Letters*, p. 252.

Jung added: "I am not in the least neurotic – touch wood!"[13] In the following exchange, Freud controlled his anger and tried to remain above the fray but concluded that they should abandon personal relations. He threw a last shaft: "But one who while behaving abnormally keeps shouting that he is normal gives ground for the suspicion that he lacks insight into his own illness."[14] This terminated their friendship and their collaboration soon ended.

When he did not have to hide his many affairs, Jung was often brutally frank. Freud appeared more political, while unwilling to yield on doctrinal points. Freud tried a conciliatory attitude for a while, hoping to bring peace in the increasingly fractious and divided kingdom of psychoanalysis. *Totem and Taboo* was to reveal who was on his side; its thesis should "serve to make a sharp division between us (Jews) and all Aryan religiosity."[15] The book would "come at the right time to divide us as an acid does a salt."[16] Freud never had been as elated writing a book since his masterpiece *The Interpretation of Dreams*. Once *Totem and Taboo* was published new doubts crept in. The central hypothesis of the ritual killing of the father was to explain the origin of the patrilineal religions. The leader of the primitive horde tried to keep all the women until the sons united and murdered him; then their guilt found an outlet in the divinization of the murdered king. Moses was a good example of this metamorphosis: he had been killed by the rebellious Hebrews and then turned into a holy intermediary with God's word.

This thesis underpins Freud's essay on the Moses of Michelangelo, marked by the struggle with Jung. First published anonymously in 1914 as "The Moses of Michelangelo," it concludes a series of hermeneutical efforts dating from 1901 when Freud discovered the monumental statue of Moses that he visited repeatedly. In September 1913, Freud stayed alone for three weeks in Rome and lost himself in contemplation of Moses's statue every day.[17] Finally, he guessed the secret of the statue and wrote his essay, no doubt thinking of Jung as well. His ambivalence toward Moses stemmed from his own sense of kinship with the rabble of unbelievers whose idolatry triggered the fury of the prophet: "How often have I mounted the steep steps from the unlovely Corso Cavour to the lonely piazza where the deserted church stands, and have essayed to support the angry scorn of the hero's glance!"[18] Freud both stages his wish for intellectual control and his empathy with the rebellious

[13] Ibid., p. 253.
[14] Ibid., p. 255.
[15] Jones, *The Life and Work of Sigmund Freud*, p. 353.
[16] Ibid., p. 354.
[17] See Peter Gay, *Freud: A Life for Our Time*, New York, Doubleday, 1988, pp. 314–315.
[18] Ibid., p. 124.

and ultimately murderous rabble, helped by his theory of the murder of the father in *Totem and Taboo*.

Freud listed previous interpretations of the statue and found all of them contradictory. By narrowing his gaze to Moses' right hand, Freud perceived that Moses' thumb was hidden while his index finger pressed the beard. Then, he did exactly what Jung threatened to do to him: to "pluck the beard of the prophet." This time the prophet is Moses, and his lengthy analysis of Moses' beard yields a series of movements from which he deduces a whole inner drama. Moses was resting on his throne with the tables of the law when he was startled by the screams of the crowd carrying the Golden Calf. Seized by indignation, he was going to destroy the idolaters and the tables, then mastered himself and decided not to annihilate them but to give the law instead. This interpretation fits with Michelangelo's conflicted relationship with Pope Julius II, whose tomb the statue adorned. Both the pope and the artist had a violent temperament, and Michelangelo carved his Moses "as a warning to himself, thus rising in self-criticism superior to his own nature."[19] However, the calm following a storm hid another storm. In 1914, Freud would conclude that Jung's theories were incompatible with his and recommended that the Viennese group and the Zurich group should part their ways: the contested libido had reached the end of its "metamorphoses" and other distorted symbols.

In spite of the proximity of Freud and Joyce in Jung's view, it is obvious that the cultural milieu in which Joyce worked in the thirties was more Jungian than Freudian. We have seen how Breton reacted aggressively against Freud, and in the context of *transitions* spearheaded by Eugène and Maria Jolas, Jung and not Freud was the major prophet of a psychoanalytic syncretism, which is why so much of *Finnegans Wake* alludes to Jung's theories of the animus-anima, of the archetypes, and of universal symbols of all religions. Eugène Jolas published Jung's influential "Psychology and Literature" as "Psychology and Poetry" in transition number 19/20 (June 1930). This was a foundational text for the ideology of transition. Once more, Jung attacks Freud for his insistence on personal neuroses and the reduction of religion and philosophy to obsessional neurosis. For him, the artist is precisely someone who can transcend individual personality:

> The artist is not a person endowed with free will who seeks his own ends, but one who allows art to realize its purposes through him. As a human being he may have moods and a will and personal aims, but as an artist he is "man" in a higher sense – he is "collective man," a vehicle and moulder of the unconscious psychic life of mankind.[20]

[19] Ibid., p. 146.
[20] Jung, "Psychology and Literature," in *The Spirit in Man, Art, and Literature*, p. 101.

This Romanticism, relayed by Goethe and Carus (Jung quotes his theory of the Genius who can express the Unconscious of a period), shaped durably the ideas on which the avant-garde magazine was founded.

Jolas concluded that "a mystic Romanticism is the only refuge."[21] Jolas expressed his faith in the "new mythos" that would embody the "international psyche" in at least three languages: German, French, and English. This led to his deification of what he called the "Language of the Night," which also echoed Jung, who had written: "The ordered cosmos [man] believes in by day is meant to protect him from the fear of chaos that besets him by night – his enlightenment is born of night-fears!"[22] Jolas's multiple manifestoes and critical pronouncements established a strong link between Modernism and Romanticism. Jolas's model of Romanticism was not the British type; rather it derives from the earliest program of German Romanticism and corresponded to Lacoue-Labarthe's and Nancy's concept of the *Literary Absolute*.[23] Jolas was aiming deliberately at completing the unfinished program of German Romanticism, which gave itself the mission of founding a new "mythos." It is the Romanticism of the young Hegel, Hölderlin, and Schelling, and also of Novalis and the Schlegels. It colors Jolas's endorsement of Jung's collective unconscious; this anti-Freudian Unconscious is desexualized and expresses itself in universal archetypes, bridging the gap between individual dreams and ancient religions.

"Yung and easily Freudened":[24] From Jungian modernism to Lacan

Although Lacan kept invoking Freud, he may have been closer to Jung in the fifties, partly because of his Surrealist connections, or partly because of his own contrarian bend. Lacan visited Jung in 1954, at a time when he had been ostracized by the classical Freudians. He owed to Jung the now famous anecdote of Freud's cynical statement on arriving in the New York harbor. On seeing the Statue of Liberty, Freud quipped: "They don't realize we are bringing

---

[21] Eugène Jolas, *Critical Writings, 1924–1951*, ed. Klaus H. Kiefer and Rainer Rumold, Evanston, Northwestern University Press, 2009, p. 58.

[22] Jung, "Psychology and Literature," in *The Spirit in Man, Art, and Literature*, p. 95.

[23] Philippe Lacoue-Labarthe and Jean-Luc Nancy, *The Literary Absolute: The Theory of Literature in German Romanticism*, trans. Philip Barnard and Cheryl Lester, Albany, State University of New York Press, 1988.

[24] James Joyce, *Finnegans Wake*, London, Faber, 1939, p. 115, lines 22–23. Here, Joyce is parodying William Empson's psychoanalytic reading of *Alice in Wonderland* in *Some Versions of Pastoral* (1935).

the plague."[25] This sentence is now regularly attributed to Freud, whereas as Rouninesco notes, Lacan is the only interlocutor who claims to have heard it from Jung. One can believe Lacan, or then if it is invented, ben trovato. As Lacan added, fate turned this sentence against Freud, who was punished for the "hubris whose antiphrasis and darkness do not extinguish its turbid brilliance."[26] Thus Lacan never met Freud, to whom he constantly alluded, but he met Jung; he also met Joyce as a young man. That was at Shakespeare and Company on December 7, 1921, as Joyce was present at the readings in French from *Ulysses*.[27]

Joyce was to become Lacan's literary symptom and the symptom of literature par excellence. It is important to retrace the genealogy of the fascination exerted by Joyce on Lacan. Michael Thomas Davis discovered that Lacan had borrowed a book, *Shakespeare and Co.*, by Joyce from Sylvia Beach's lending library in 1941.[28] However, this was not a book by James Joyce but by Patrick Weston Joyce. On October 15, 1941, Lacan borrowed *A Concise History of Ireland from the Earliest Times to 1922*, a potted Irish history written by the erudite Irish polygraph. Lacan returned it on December 1 of that same year. Roudinesco's biography evokes his anglophilia at the time, his reading of American novels in Marseilles, and his translating of T. S. Eliot's poetry. Lacan had opened an account at Sylvia Beach's lending library two months before it closed for good – the closure brought about by the suspicious interest for Joycean items from a German officer who was threatening to confiscate the books.[29] Joyce's recent demise (January 13, 1941) may have motivated Lacan to read *Ulysses* in English with the help of Stuart Gilbert's *James Joyce's Ulysses, A Study*, because Joyce's *Concise History* is mentioned by Gilbert in his commentary on Joyce's use of Irish history.[30] Gilbert mentions the successive waves of conquerors that invaded Ireland, some of Grecian origins, others Semitic. Among them, the Milesians would have come from Scythia via Egypt and Spain. Ireland would owe its specific spirit and culture in part to ancestors of the Wandering Jew. Lacan had started studying *Ulysses* seriously in 1941. He may have been intrigued by the coincidence of this Irish homophony – from one Joyce to the other! Reading *Ulysses*, he was led back to the famous lending library where he borrowed the book, a bookstore that he used to go to as a young man.

---

[25] Roudinesco, *Jacques Lacan, op. cit.*, p. 265.
[26] *Ecrits*, p. 336.
[27] Roudinesco, *Jacques Lacan*, p. 13, and Ellman, *James Joyce*, p. 523.
[28] Michael Thomas Davis, "Jacques Lacan and Shakespeare and Company," *James Joyce Quarterly*, vol. 32, no. 3–4, Spring-Summer 1995, pp. 754–758.
[29] See Noel Riley Fitch, *Sylvia Beach and the Lost Generation*, New York, W.W. Norton, 1983, p. 405.
[30] See Stuart Gilbert, *James Joyce's Ulysses, A Study*, New York, Vintage, 1955, pp. 65–66.

Lacan had been invited to open the James Joyce International Symposium in June 1975 but, before that date, had often quoted *Finnegans Wake* in his seminars. In *Seminar XX*, Joyce is mentioned not only as one of the main authors defining modernity but also as someone who can give lessons to psychoanalysts:

> What happens in Joyce's work? The signifier stuffs the signified. It is because the signifiers collapse into each other, are recomposed and mixed up – read *Finnegans Wake* – that something is produced that, as a signified, may seem enigmatic, but is clearly what is closest to what we analysts, thanks to analytic discourse, have to read: the slip of the tongue.[31]

Joyce teaches psychoanalysts how to read thanks to his use of polysemic idioms in which the signifiers float and mean something else as they slip between languages and between oral speech and writing. These features dominate in the sentence that Lacan takes as an example in his June 1975 lecture, "Joyce the Symptom." In *Finnegans Wake*, one hears a feminine voice asking: "Who ails tongue coddeau, aspace of dumbillsilly?"[32] Joyce scholars identify this sentence as presenting courtship in the context of sexual wars leading to a Viconian marriage. Lacan admits that he would not have recognized the French sentence ("Où est ton cadeau, espèce d'imbécile!") hidden under English words without Jacques Aubert's help. This expression is the ritual phrase prostitutes use to ask for money from a customer. It rings ironically like the procedure of «*la passe*», then recently instituted as a competitive examination for graduating psychoanalysts of Lacan's school. Lacan comments:

> What is unbelievable, is that this homophony, here of a translinguistic kind, is only borne by letters that conform to English spelling.... There is something ambiguous in this phonetic usage, I am tempted to write faunic: the faunesque of the thing derives entirely from letters, that is something that is not essential to language, something that has been woven by the accidents of history. That someone may use this in such a prodigious manner forces us to question the very nature of language.[33]

In fact, Lacan's very wonder may cause some wonder, although it would be rash to mount a philosophical critique in the Derridian mode. Jacques-Alain Miller has stated in a commentary of his edition of the *Sinthome* that Lacan

---

[31] Jacques Lacan, *Seminar XX, On Feminine Sexuality, The Limits of Love and Knowledge*, trans. Bruce Fink, New York, W. W. Norton, 1998, translation modified, p. 37.

[32] Joyce, *Finnegans Wake*, p. 15, line 18.

[33] *Joyce avec Lacan*, ed. Jacques Aubert, Paris, Navarin, 1987, p. 26. Henceforth, abbreviated as JAL.

had been unfair to Derrida, whom he quotes.[34] However, one should not rush to a Derridian condemnation of Lacan's irrepressible "phonocentrism," a logocentrism made manifest when he adds that the letter is not essential to language, because throughout his Joyce seminar, Lacan stressed the role of equivocation in writing. It is true, while claiming his precedence to Derrida in this theoretical debate. Derrida had introduced his concept of writing only after psychoanalysis had shown him the way. Lacan remained somehow deaf to Derrida's idea that writing is constitutive of thinking, that it hollows out the link that we take for granted between our most intimate thoughts and the voice we believe we hear when we think. In the Joyce seminar, he appears to stick to the difference between the vocal substance of the signifier and the written effects of language.

Surprisingly, at the end of his seminar, Lacan concludes that for Joyce, writing had been essential to the constitution of his Ego. Joyce's Ego would absorb all cultures, encompassed by a world reduced to language. The writing process set in motion can work endlessly, because it aims at reconstituting a writer's Ego that grows into the dimensions of our linguistic and cultural universe. This is in fact not far from Derrida's own perception of Joyce's impact in philosophy. As Derrida had noted as early as in 1962, in his thesis on Edmund Husserl's *Origin of Geometry*, Joyce's project in *Finnegans Wake* can be described as the exact opposite of Husserl's phenomenology, with its wish to reduce equivocity to univocity. Joyce uses "a language that could equalize the greatest possible synchrony with the greatest potential for the buried, accumulated, and interwoven intentions within each linguistic atom, each vocable, each word, each simple proposition, in all worldly cultures and their most ingenious forms."[35]

While Derrida had been working with Joyce since as early as 1962, Lacan's original fascination for Joyce (when both were young men) was reawakened by his association with Philippe Sollers, who looms out large in Jacques-Alain Miller's endnotes. When Lacan and Derrida began quarrelling, Sollers and his friends at *Tel Quel* had to choose between the two in terms of friendships and allegiances. Sollers and Kristeva chose Lacan, much as Jolas chose Joyce over Gertrude Stein at the time of transition. Thus, we verify that Joyce's name came to mean more than the simple reference to a person or an author. Joyce allowed Lacan to re-translate Freud once more and perhaps for the last time.

[34] See "Derrida et le noeud," in Jacques Lacan, *Le Séminaire XXIII, Le Sinthome*, Paris, Seuil, 2005, pp. 232–236.
[35] Jacques Derrida, *Edmund Husserl's Origin of Geometry: An Introduction*, trans. John P. Leavey, Jr., Lincoln, University of Nebraska, 1989, p. 102. See also the excellent collection *Derrida and Joyce: Texts and Contexts*, eds. Andrew J. Mitchell and Sam Slote, Albany, State University of New York Press, 2013.

Lacan's French language was indispensable to move from German to English, much as Daniel Brody had blamed the animus *Ulysses* evinced in Jung on the author's name. He had told Joyce: "Translate your name into German."[36] That "Joyce" can be rendered, as "Freud" in German, is a reminder that the break between Freud and Jung left a deep impact. When he arrived in Paris in the summer of 1920, soon to be seen by a very young Lacan in Sylvia Beach's lending library, Joyce told John Rodker that the name Joyce "meant the same thing in English as Freud in German."[37] Whereas Joyce experienced this translation as an objective joke that sealed something like a fate, a young French medical student was ready to catch the joke at the first rebound.

The conceit of translating one's name into a common noun meaning "joy" was not unknown to Freud: he discusses an instance of forgetting in the *Psychopathology of Everyday Life* in which he had distorted the name of a French character, Monsieur Joyeuse, whom he had called Jocelyn, and also invented a whole episode. Freud comments: "*Joyeux* (the man's surname being the feminine form of the adjective) is the way my own surname would translate into French."[38] This was a game played by Joyce too, because he was in the habit of mentioning the coincidence of his family name with that of Freud. Ellmann describes Joyce arriving to Paris in the summer of 1920 and blurting out to John Rodker "that the name Joyce meant the same thing in English as Freud in German."[39] Joyce shared the fate of Samuel Beckett who was acutely aware of the fact that his name had been translated from a French noun ("becquet"). In Joyce's case, the translation brought along with its sense of fun something like a fate. It was precisely such a fate decreed by onomastics linking Joyce to Freud, a coupling now inseparable from the history of high modernism. According to Gorman's first biography of Joyce, Joyce's lively humor and pervasive sense of fun were justified by the fact that his hero was simply being true to his name, as we learn that "[t]he name is obviously of French extraction – Joyeux."[40] The earliest Joyce we know of to have come to Ireland was an Anglo-Norman settler who came from Wales in the twelfth century. He would have spoken Norman French and not Gaelic.

What would Freud have thought of changing his name to Joyce? Would he have wished to translate Jung as "Young" (and thus more easily "freudened" to quote *Finnegans Wake*) or "Le Jeune"? Lacan insisted on the fact that Freud's name had been translated in a lecture on Freud he gave in May 1956

---

[36] Ellmann, *James Joyce*, p. 628.
[37] Ibid., p. 400.
[38] Freud, *The Psychopathology of Everyday Life*, p. 141.
[39] Ellmann, *James Joyce*, p. 400.
[40] Herbert Gorman, *James Joyce*, New York, Farrar and Rhinehart, 1939, p. 8.

for medical students – in presence of Jean Delay, the author of the famous biography of Gide.

> I will begin by saying … that Freud's name signifies joy (*joie*). // Freud himself was conscious of this, as is demonstrated by a good number of things – an analysis of a dream that I could adduce, dominated by a sum of composite words, more especially by a word of ambiguous resonance, both English and German at the same time, and in which he enumerates the charming little spots in the environs of Vienna.…
> I'm recalling that his family, like all families of Moravia, of Galicia, of the outlying provinces of Hungary, owing to an edict of 1785 by Joseph II, had to choose this name from a list of names – it's a feminine first name, in fairly frequent use at the time. But this name is a much older Jewish name which throughout history one already finds translated differently.[41]

The world of dreams explored by Freud is a world of puns and onomastics in translation.

Freud had authored the invention of psychoanalysis when he changed his first name, a name that he deliberately changed by shortening it from Sigismund to Sigmund, to let echoes of "Sieg" (victory) and "Siegfried" ring clearer. As to his family name, "Freude" does not appear to be a crucial concept in canonical psychoanalytic literature – and psychoanalysis is only now tackling the issue of affects. One will not find "joy" in the index to the *Standard Edition*. It took Lacan to transform a key Freudian term – "Lust" – into French as "jouissance." Having started this process, Lacan needed the assistance of Joyce to provide a living signature, which implied that he had to "borrow" Joyce's name. Lacan was retranslating Freud into French as the inventor of jouissance while translating Joyce into a revised and revisited Franco-Irish Freud. In the end, Joyce literally replaced Freud as a "founder of discursivity" (to quote Michel Foucault) for Lacan: Joyce became the only "author" who could lead to an understanding of psychosis and then turned quite logically into the psychoanalytic Symptom as such, in the sweeping equation of James Joyce with Mister *Sinthome*.

I want to tarry for a while with this mixture of bafflement and of jouissance, or more simply, of an untranslatable joy migrating between texts, bodies, and languages. When Lacan began his seminar on Joyce, he declared that he was taking a new departure because he had wanted to go beyond the Trinitarian scheme that underpinned the logic of Borromean knots elaborated so far. He had, up to the R, S, I Seminar of 1974–1975, toyed with the possibility of

---

[41] Jacques Lacan, *Seminar III, The Psychoses*, trans. Russell Grigg, New York, Norton, 1993, pp. 232–233.

organizing the three "registers" of the Real, the Symbolic, and the Imaginary in such a way that they are, on the one hand, well "knotted together" and can call up the signifier of "heresy" (the capitals R, S, I, sound like *hérésie* in French). Then Lacan discloses his main insight:

> [I]f Joyce is completely caught up in the sphere and the cross, it is not only because he read a lot of Aquinas thanks to his education with the Jesuits. You are all as caught in the sphere and the cross. Here is a circle, the section of a sphere, and within the cross.... But no-one has perceived that this is already a Borromean knot.[42]

Lacan illustrates Joyce's cross, depicting it as two curves that are also the sections of two interlocking circles. What Clive Hart had described as the basis of Joyce's world view in *Finnegans Wake* – a grid made up of the interlocking of a sphere and a cross – is a structure that accounts for a looped linguistic universe (the first words of *Finnegans Wake*, "riverrun, past Eve's and Adam's" continue the last words of the last page: "... along the"[43]), and yet it keeps generating new meanings as a solution for the paradox of the quadrate circle – that is, "circling the square." Lacan made his the thesis of *Structure and Motif in Finnegans Wake*[44] and used numerology and topology to justify it. When Jacques Aubert invited Lacan to give the major address at the 1975 International Joyce Symposium, he could not guess that he would be luring Lacan into regions that would durably change his theory. All the new elements introduced in the early seventies – the Borromean knot of the Real, the Symbolic, the Imaginary, the emergence of the Symptom in the real, the new importance given to jouissance in its connection with writing, the idea of writing as making holes in reality, the theory of the lack of sexual rapport, the new figure of the Father as a perverse father – forcibly recur in the Joyce seminar, a seminar in which they find a last re-plotting, a re-knotting, in fact.

Listening to Lacan's lecture at the Sorbonne in 1975 (JAL, pp. 21–29), most Joyce scholars were disturbed by this mixture of brilliant insights and trite biographical explanations. The main idea of "Joyce le symptôme" was that Joyce embodied the "symptom" as such, a symptom rewritten *sinthome* to follow an older form of the word. This was the spelling used by Rabelais, a writer who was also a physician and Joyce's predecessor in verbal experimentation. Having morphed into the *Sinthome*, Joyce became a literary Saint, a depiction that in fact accords quite well with Joyce's habitual self-presentation to posterity. After Jean Genet in Sartre's masterful critical biography, it was Joyce's turn

---

[42] Jacques Lacan "R.S.I.," *Ornicar?*, no. 5, Paris, Winter 1975–1976, p. 37.
[43] James Joyce, *Finnegans Wazke*, London, Faber, 1939, pp. 3 and 628.
[44] Clive Hart, *Structure and Motif in Finnegans Wake*, London, Faber, 1962.

to become the "saint and martyr" of literature. Joyce would be the symptom of literature, a man who, as Claudel remarked, had let himself be devoured by letters: Joyce wished to be one with Literature.

In spite of the barbs he hurls at psychobiography, Lacan's reading of Joyce remains biographical, firmly founded on Richard Ellmann's authoritative *James Joyce*. Lacan presents Joyce's choice of an artistic career as originating in a wish to compensate for a lack on his father's part. John Joyce was the absent, lacking, and failing father. His elder son's writing was to supplement this fundamental deficiency. By becoming a writer, Joyce burdened himself with a symbolic paternity because there had been a "mistake" in the writing of the Unconscious of the Joyce family: the three circles of the Real, the Imaginary, and the Symbolic had not been properly tied together. Writing would splice together these partially loose rings or circles. James Joyce was caught up in his father's symptoms even while rejecting him: father and son were spendthrift, heavy drinkers, and incapable of keeping their families sheltered from disaster. Although John Joyce imagined that he had "killed" his exhausted wife, who died of cancer quite young, Joyce's cross was his daughter, Lucia, who started showing sings of derangement in the late twenties and was institutionalized in 1934. Lucia's fate confirms Joyce's flirtation with psychosis.

Thus in many ways, surprisingly enough, Lacan's reading of Joyce corresponds with Jung's view of *Ulysses*. Like Jung, Lacan stresses Joyce's wish to defend Lucia against psychoanalysis so as to ward off any suggestion that his own writing could be seen as "schizophrenic" or "psychotic." Like Jung he admits that Lucia drowns in the black waters of the Unconscious while the more experienced swimmer reaches the surface.[45] Besides, Lacan denounces Joyce's tendency to fall into Jungian archetypes in his universal history, much as Jung thinks that it is dangerous to fall under the sway of the archetypes. And finally, Lacan spent some time wondering whether Joyce was not a psychotic. The question of Joyce's potentially psychotic structure remained a riddle for Lacan – he never reached a single answer. Such caution was of little use, because Joyce would subsequently be used by Lacanian psychoanalysts as a "case," a stepping stone to approach psychosis. Lacan once noted that Joyce would not have been analyzable, not just because he was too much of a perverted Catholic but also because he loved his symptom too much.[46] In the "end," however, we cannot avoid a reminiscence of Lucia Joyce who figures as the trace, the remainder of the symptomatic formation: she was psychotic and also a central character in the *Wake* (Issy) and the main addressee of the book.

---

[45] Jung's diagnosis about of James Joyce and Lucia Joyce is given by Richard Ellmann in *James Joyce*, pp. 679–680.
[46] Lacan, Le Séminaire, *Livre XXIII, Le Sinthome*, p. 125. Hereafter, S XXIII, and page number.

Joyce is the symptom of a universal literature that he rewrites according to his *sinthome*, while staying at the cusp between psychosis and neurosis. Writing is essential to the constitution of the subject. The Ego is no longer accused of being an ideological or metaphysical illusion, but rather it turns into a useful tool: it is an artifice, the effect of writing because it permits a braiding, a knotting of the Borromean rings. With Joyce, one moves between the "original sin of the father" and writing as an overcoming of the sin, not a sublimation, but rather a translation to the level of the symptom, which takes us back to Joyce's earliest insight, to the time when he described Dublin portrayed on *Dubliners* as a "hemiplegia," a paralysis. At the time, Joyce declared that he saw symptoms everywhere.[47] Joyce had forced Lacan to transform his theory of the Ego. The later Ego knots writing and symptoms in a knot performed by letters that replace paternity. To be sure, the concept of the ego proposed here is not a "natural" one; this new Ego destroys the old self. It is made up of writing; it is, as Ezra Pound wrote in the *Cantos*, an "Ego Scriptor."[48]

Borges's Joyce: A joy forever

Lacan's main themes facing Joyce find similar expressions in Jorge Luis Borges's readings of Joyce. Borges expresses poetically the idea that Joyce's name slips a key, an allegorical key to be sure, because it embodies enjoyment of a specific literary type, and he agrees that given the possibility of sharing this enjoyment thanks to the miracle of literature, the old Ego will be replaced with pure writing. Moreover, like Lacan, Borges remains closer to Jung than to Freud, even though he quotes Freud once in a while. In an often quoted interview with Richard Burgin, Borges declared that he had "always disliked" Freud, whom he considered as a "kind of madman ... a man laboring over a sexual obsession."[49] On the other hand, he felt a strong proximity to Jung: "I've always been a great reader of Jung. I read Jung in the same way as let's say, I might read Pliny or Frazer's *Golden Bough*. I reads it as a kind of mythology, or a kind of museum or encyclopedia of curious lores."[50] As Harold Bloom has remarked, Borges is a gnostic, and gnostics "feel at ease with Jung," while they tend to be "very unhappy with Freud."[51] This has not prevented Julio Woscoboinik

---

[47] James Joyce, *Selected Letters*, ed. R. Ellmann, London, Faber, 1975, p. 22.
[48] Ezra Pound, *The Cantos*, London, Faber, 1986, p. 472.
[49] Richard Burgin, *Conversations with Jorge Luis Borges*, New York, Holt, Rinehart and Winston, 1969, p. 109.
[50] Ibid.
[51] Harold Bloom, "Introduction," *Bloom's BioCritiques: Jorge Luis Borges*, Philadelphia, Chelsea House, 2004, p. 1.

from giving us a very useful psychobiography of Borges or from claiming that Borges worked most of the time as a psychoanalyst. Woscoboinik even stages a convincing dialogue between Freud and Borges.[52] Thus Borges's ambivalent relation to psychoanalysis, split between the "unpleasant facts" of sexuality on which Freud keeps harping and the wonderful lore of myths and legends collected by Jung, has an impact on his reading of Joyce. I will address this by taking my point of departure in what I interpreted as a posthumous joke. As we will see, for Borges as for Lacan, Joyce means "joy" in a curious tautological apocope[53] laced with irony, paradox, and ambivalence.

This joke can be found in the preface written by Borges for the first volume of his collected works in the prestigious French Pléiade series. The text is dated May 19, 1986, from Geneva. Borges died on June 14, 1986, which makes this essay one of his last writings. A last riddle is hidden in a literary testament. As always, Borges states the importance of quotations and intertextuality, asserting that his book is just "made up of other books," but he introduces a different note:

> Eliot wrote that it is less important to know what one wants than what the century wants. He claims this, as if drunk on universal history. Is it necessary for me to say that I am the least historical of men? The circumstances of history touch me like those of geography and politics, but I think that I am an individual, above and beyond these temptations. // *A thing of beauty is a joyce for ever*, John Keats wrote memorably. In order to enjoy (*jouir*) any work adequately, we have to situate it in its historical context. There are nevertheless, as Keats wished it, felicities (*des bonheurs*) that are singular and eternal.[54]

Why, when he rejects Eliot's notion of a universal history in the name of Keats's sensual enjoyment of "eternity in the instant," does Borges slip Joyce's name almost invisibly? The pun was performed so cunningly that no copy editor of the Pléiade, a series that prides itself on absolute accuracy, noticed it. The sentence is highlighted by the roman characters setting it off as a quote, as the rest of the text is printed in italics. One imagines a discrete footnote reading: "Read *joy* instead of *joyce*. Borges may have wished to pay an ultimate albeit ironic homage to the Irish writer who has often inspired him." Of course, this note does not appear in the preface in which Borges lists a

---

[52] Julio Woscoboinik, *The Secret of Borges: A Psychoanalytic Inquiry into His Work*, trans. Dora Carlisky Pozzi, Lanham, University Press of America, 1998, pp. 4–6.

[53] An apocope is a rhetorical figure referring to the "cutting" or loss of a sound at the end of a word, such as "psycho" for "psychotic" or "schizo" for "schizophrenic."

[54] Jorge Luis Borges, *Oeuvres Complètes*, ed. Jean Pierre Bernès, vol. 1, Paris, Gallimard, Pléiade, 1993, p. x. The preface, translated from the Spanish by the editor, is printed in italics. The double slash indicates a paragraph break.

compendium of the literary canon with the names of Bacon, Burton, Browne, Keats, Coleridge, Wordsworth, Flaubert, Hopkins, and Emily Dickinson, all in less than two pages. Joyce is not there, but because he remained for Borges the great producer of polyglottic puns, his name had to be punned, mixed up with Keats's "joy for ever." The joke has often been made by mischievous students, but we know that Borges was not above low puns in his own life: when he was dismissed from his post as a librarian at the time of the Peronist dictatorship in 1946 and "promoted" to a post as an inspector at the *Direccion de Apicultura* (the Department of Beekeeping) – a name judged vague, ineffectual, and poetic enough for a literary person – Borges decided to read this as *Direccion de Avicultura* (Department of Poultry). The story that went round Buenos Aires was that their famous writer would hence inspect chickens! The joke was so irresistible that even Peronist newspapers endorsed the changed designation.[55] Borges resigned of course, knowing as little about bees as about chickens, which was a sly gesture of political resistance.

The Pléiade preface develops other themes than bees and chicken. This passage, with a series of variations on the motif of joy, announced to posterity the deep joy experienced by Borges at the end of his life, a joy generated by the union with Maria Kodama (their marriage was made official on April 26 and leaked to journalists on May 12, 1986.)[56] This sense of cheerful elation gained at the last moment and against all odds merges with his immersion in the collective dream of universal literature. This happiness does not preclude literary *bonheurs*, which evokes stylistic felicities. Borges gives examples, all of which appear as linguistic epiphanies, sudden glories of expression: "*Lux umbra Dei*," "The Himalayas are Siva's laughter" and "Mastering me God, giver of breath and bread." A happy man is a happy reader, and a happy reader is a happy writer. "Enjoyment" requires a "historical sense," to quote Eliot's "Tradition and the Individual Talent," and ahistorical postulations like an exit from history – a flight into timelessness by merging with universal archetypes: "Each new sheet is an adventure on which we must stake our all. Each word is the first word uttered by Adam."[57] This thesis about language explains why Borges needs the transformation of "joy" into the plural of "joys" via Joyce's name.

When Lacan transformed the key Freudian term of *Lust* into French as "jouissance," he needed the assistance of Joyce – or borrowed Joyce's name because it also translated to the name of Freud. Lacan translated Freud into French as the inventor of jouissance at the same time as he was translating Joyce into a new, revised and revisited Franco-Irish Freud. For Lacan, Joyce

---

[55] See Edwin Williamson, *Borges: A Life*, New York, Viking, 2004, pp. 293–294.
[56] Ibid., pp. 484–486.
[57] Borges, *Oeuvres Complètes*, vol. 1, p. ix.

became the only author who could lead to an understanding of psychosis, and in the process he became the psychoanalytic Symptom as such. One could pun on Borges's name in the same way and note that something like pervasive borderlines *goces* (in the plural) seem to be anagrammatically scrambled in the letters of his name.

Joyce was singled out for praise by Borges in a number of poems and essays.[58] It is necessary to reopen the stories of Pierre Ménard, the French poet and essayist author of the *Don Quichote* (1939), and of "Funes the Memorious" (1942) to understand what motivated Borges's testamentary connection between Joyce and "joy" via Keats and beauty. Before commenting on these well-known *ficciones*, one can take a cue from an essay written at the time Borges was still a fellow member of the Spanish and Argentinean avant-garde: "The Nothingness of Personality" from the first issue of *Proa*. This Argentinean avant-garde review was published in 1922, the year when *Ulysses* and the *Waste Land* were published. It is the first essay Borges later acknowledged as his own work, and it was used as the introduction to the 1999 *Selected Non-Fictions* translated by Eliot Weinberger. In this vehement proclamation, Borges attacks "The Futility of the Cult of the Ego" and rejects the Romantic theories of creative genius that he saw looming large with Whitman and Picasso. Borges aimed at debunking the "misprision" of the concept of the self: "I propose that personality is a mirage maintained by conceit and custom, without metaphysical foundation or visceral reality."[59] He reiterates that "[t]here is no whole self." Included in the critique of the self is a critique of the concept of memory: memory does not offer a sufficient basis for the constitution of personality.[60] Borges's meditation on the paucity of subjective memory follows a complex course before reaching a provisional conclusion: there is no way one can posit a strict boundary between the self and the not-self, especially when we talk about cultural manifestations. The self is contained by writing, the indefinite and a-subjective space defined by a library shelf and not by the bones of our skulls. One can understand why Borges attacks *modernismo* in the name of an *ultraismo* that he will soon reject, while being close to Eliot's thesis on impersonality that underpin Anglo-American modernism.

As César Augusto Salgado has shown, while most South American writers found in Joyce a revival of baroque esthetics, thereby claiming him as a Latin-American writer of some sort, Borges provided with "Funes the Memorious"

---

[58] See César Augusto Salgado's essay "Barocco Joyce: Borges's and Lezama's Antagonistic Readings," in *Transcultural Joyce*, ed. Karen R. Lawrence, Cambridge, Cambridge University Press, 1998, pp. 63–93.

[59] Jorge Luis Borges, *Selected Non-Fictions*, trans. Eliot Weinberger, New York, Penguin 1999, p. 4=. Hereafter, SNF and page number.

[60] Borges, SNF, p. 4.

a parody of the modernist fascination for past models and a critical allegory denouncing the hubris of Joyce's project. Borges discovered *Ulysses* early, and he enlisted Joyce among the inspirers of the *Proa* project. As early as 1924, he entertained the project of doing for Buenos Aires what Joyce has achieved with Dublin. If he was enthusiastic then, by 1927 he had grown disillusioned with the avant-garde and found in Ortega y Gasset's strictures against the "decadence of the novel" reasons to return to classicism. *Ulysses* starts appearing as a colossal failure, sounding the death knell of the nineteenth-century realistic novel. In 1939, a short but dismissive review of *Finnegans Wake* is even more pointed. One needs exegetes such as Stuart Gilbert to find one's way in the labyrinthine text; its "concatenation of puns" cannot but appear as "frustrating and incompetent" (SNF, p. 195).

Without displaying the anger evinced by Jung, Borges multiplies critical remarks, until the tale of Funes, the poor and crippled *compadrito* living in Fray Bentos in 1884, whose memory is simply photographic, total, absolute. Funes forgets nothing; he can compare the shapes of clouds seen in April 1882 to the veins of a marbled book glimpsed during his childhood. Borges explained that this story had been suggested to him by sustained meditations on *Ulysses* and *Finnegans Wake*:

> My story's magical *compadrito* may be called a precursor of the coming race of supermen, a partial Zarathustra of the outskirts of Buenos Aires; indisputably, he is a monster. I have evoked him because a consecutive, straightforward reading of the four hundred thousand words of *Ulysses* would require similar monsters. (I will not venture to speak of what *Finnegans Wake* would demand; for me, its readers are no less inconceivable than C. H. Hinton's fourth dimension or the trinity of Nicaea.)" (SNF, pp. 220–221)

The tale provides a commentary on Joyce's works, and beyond that on literature itself, because Joyce is described as "less a man of letters than a literature" (SNF, p. 221). Lacan could not agree more with this view.

The conclusion of Borges's obituary has a Benjaminian ring to it: "[F]or Joyce every day was in some secret way the irreparable Day of Judgment; every place, Hell or Purgatory" (SNF, p. 221). The story of Funes offers a parody both of Joyce's new linguistic experiments and of Nietzsche's claims. Joyce had requested for his "ideal reader" an "ideal insomnia" in *Finnegans Wake*. Borges feigns to take this literally and offers as an answer an ideal mnemonist who cannot forget anything. However, Funes cannot think: his mind is encumbered with the innumerable details of his copy-perfect memories. Embodying what Derrida has called Joyce's hypermnesiac machine with a vengeance, Funes can be the best of polyglots, but his mind, stacked with concrete particulars, will never grasp abstractions and relations.[61] This pathetic dreamer of indelible images is a debilitated Zarathustra, closer to the "idiot savant" of *Rainman* than to Nietzsche's *Uebermensch*.

In fact, Funes reiterates what Joyce said of Dublin, which was to become the city of all cities because it contained the accumulated garbage of universal history: "*I, myself, have more memories than all mankind since the world began*," he says, and "*My memory, sir, is like a garbage heap*" (CF, p. 135). Funes's insomnia turns him into a crippled suburban Nietzsche, whereas Joyce's claims smack of literary megalomania. The counterpart of Funes's parody is Pierre Ménard's project of copying *Don Quixote*, which runs parallel to *Ulysses* rewriting the *Odyssey* as a Dublin story. Ménard evinces contempt for modernized versions of classical stories and dismisses "those parasitic books that set Christ on a boulevard, Hamlet on La Cannebière, or Don Quixote on Wall Street" (CF, p. 90). Ménard's solution to the dilemma of modernity is well known. By literally copying page after page of *Don Quixote*, he creates a difference in an identical original text. This difference can be virtual – whereas Cervantes merely expressed the clichés of his age when he refers to history as the mother of truth, Ménard battles with all the clichés of universal literature, thus reaching a more comprehensive insight. Ultimately, the parable sends us to a theory of reading as translation displacing authorship: "Attributing the *Imitatio Christi* to Louis Ferdinand Céline or James Joyce – is that not sufficient renovation of those faint spiritual admonitions?" (CF, p. 95). Could we imagine a Pierre Ménard author of *Ulysses*?

Borges pretends to take Joyce's claims seriously, with an excessive seriousness that destroys them in the end. You needed an ideal insomniac reader? Here he is, Ireneo Funes, the prodigious mnemonist who will never forget anything. There is one slight problem: he cannot think at all! Similarly, Borges saw in the first essays devoted to Joyce's "Work in Progress" that it was based on Dublin's Phoenix Park. To this Irish park Joyce superimposed Heliopolis, the birthplace of the mythical Phoenix. In Joyce's recreation of Egyptian myth, the world was peopled by the god Atem, who masturbated on the primordial mud heap at Heliopolis.[62] Borges also plays with this legend in "The Cult of the Phoenix," a tale alluding to Heliopolis and deploying esoteric lore to trace an evasive sect. The secret signs by which its members recognize one another take us from Geneva to Israel, from Hungary to Chile, until we realize that the cult has spread throughout the world.

> The ritual is, in fact, the Secret. The Secret, as I have said, is transmitted
> from generation to generation, but tradition forbids a mother from

---

[61] Borges, "Funes, His Memory," in *Collected Fictions*, p. 137. Hereafter, CF and page number.
[62] James S. Atherton, *The Books at the Wake*, London, Faber, 1959, p. 133.

teaching it to her children, as it forbids priests from doing so; initiation into the mystery is the task of the lowest individuals of the group. A slave, a leper, or a beggar plays the role of mystagogue. A child, too, may catechize another child. The act is trivial, the matter of a moment's time, and it needs no description. (CF, p. 172)

Borges disclosed the "Secret" to Ronald Christ in 1968: it was none other than sex – that is, literally copulation, or the generative act.[63] Here, Borges meets Jung in a parody of Freud's "sexual obsession." For Freud, sexuality is every-where, as is the Secret: "The Secret is sacred, but that does not prevent its being a bit ridiculous; the performance of it is furtive, even clandestine, and its adepts do not speak of it" (CF, p. 173).

The Secret of sexuality, which unites all of humanity, while underpinning our quest for clues and meanings hidden since the foundation of the world, is out in the open. Joyce and Freud have blended in a similarly prophetic delirium marked by hubris: they wanted to "out" the secret too soon! In the end, however, Borges can make a truce with Joyce and with Freud, because they can commune with all the "others" who enjoy literature to the point that they can be saved by it. The door that they open leads to radical outside, even perhaps outside the library. In the collection *Elogio de la Sombra*, we find an "Invocation to Joyce." It concludes with these lines:

> Que importa mi perdida generación,
> Ese vago espejo, y si tus libros la justifican.
> Yo soy los otros. Yo soy todos aquellos
> Que ha rescatado tu obstinado rigor.
> Soy los que no conoces y los que salvas.[64]
> (What does it matter, my lost generation,
> that vague mirror, if your books justify it?
> I am the others. I am all those
> whom your obstinate rigor has saved.
> I am those you don't know and you save.)

"Yo soy los otros": I am the others. The Other of an absolute jouissance has been replaced by the small other of all the readers to come. Gnosticism over-comes its sexual repression via sublimation, while reaching out to an ethics of the other in a soteriologist sublime that is not without its barbs and puns.

---

[63] Ronald Christ, *The Narrow Act: Borges's Art of Allusion*, New York, New York University Press, 1969, p. 190.

[64] Jorge Luis Borges, *Obra Poetica*, Madrid, Alianza Editorial, 1972, p. 351.

Chapter 7

From the history of perversion to the trauma of history

Borges famously equated universal history with the history of a few metaphors. In the slight difference between almost identical sentences beginning and ending "Pascal's Sphere," we see a whole world of doubt, subjective performativity and unconscious agency creeping in. Borges begins: "Perhaps universal history is the history of a few metaphors." He ends: "Perhaps universal history is the history of the various intonations of a few metaphors"(SNF, pp. 351 and 353). Freud would not disagree: for him, universal history is the history of the various intonations of one metaphor, which is the primal murder of the Father of the horde, Freud's pure myth on which the construction of the Oedipus legend rests. Could Freud write a universal history that would not be a "history of infamy" or "a history of iniquity"?[1] How can one write a universal history if history is marked by a crime followed by concealment, forgetting, remorse, the election of a substitute for the murdered father, a better double with whom one can hope for atonement, and this at the very origin of historical time? This is the quandary in which Freud found himself at the outset of his most ambitious project, *Moses and Monotheism*, a book that that he planned as *ein historischer Roman*, his own "historical novel."[2] Besides the many problems posed by Freud's radical thesis – Moses was not a Jew but an Egyptian, he was a high official and priest of Aton, whose monotheistic faith had been rejected by Pharaonic priests, and who, defeated in Egypt, started a religious experiment in the wilderness with a band of freed slaves who happened to be Jews – the very narrative implies an intense struggle with the deferred temporality of *Nachträglichkeit*.

If the meaning of history arrives later, retrospectively, to an unspoken and unspeakable experience that remains outside history as a narrative, any narrative will have to start from indirect clues testifying to a repression. The

---

[1] I am quoting two translations of the title of Borges's first collection of tales, all based on real life stories; see CF, pp. 1–64.

[2] This was the subtitle of Freud's 1934 draft. See *Der Mann Moses und die monotheistische Religion: Drei Abhandlungen*, in *Studienausgabe, IX, Fragen der Gesellschaft, Ursprünge der Religion*, Frankfurt, Fischer, 1974, p. 457, introductory note.

founding event, the murder of Moses at the hands of the rebellious Jews, has been erased as literally unspeakable, and therefore it can only be retrieved indirectly. There are traces of the erasure in the tradition and a few rare texts (Ernst Sellin thought that he had found this in the book of Hosea[3]), but they have to be read against the grain of orthodoxy. Thus, if Moses stutters, it is a veiled admission that he could not speak the language of a foreign tribe he has chosen without belonging to it. He has to rely on Aaron, his interpreter and henchman, against whose rule of terror the freed slaves end up rebelling. There are many more revealing signs gathered by Freud, and my point here is not to discuss the validity of his interpretation of Biblical history, or his reasons for presenting it as he does.[4] Eliza Slavet's *Racial Fever: Psychoanalysis and the Jewish Question* tackles the vexed issue of Freud's belief in an unconscious heritage defining the concept of Jewishness. Jewishness cannot be defined as a "race," but the concept revisited by Freud implies a community of people linked by collective memories and a certain relation to their bodies. Memories are passed from generation, and thus the Jewish community is "embodied," which is why the role of bodily marks is crucial, with male circumcision always defined as symbolic castration by Freud. To understand how these Freudian concepts have underpinned most of the recent discussions about trauma, one should look at Cathy Caruth's eloquent book, *Unclaimed Experience: Trauma, Narrative and History.*[5]

Caruth's point of departure is Freud's notion of a "traumatic neurosis" that can be applied to history. Freud's analogy involves patients who suffer a shock as after an accident and then, only later, after a period of "latency" or "incubation," develop symptoms repeating the initial trauma.[6] Often the victim is not conscious of what happened and feels that everything is under control – only later do symptoms appear. This is taken as a hermeneutic paradigm for Caruth: if there is something like an "unclaimed experience," historical narratives cannot simply follow the experiential model defined by the sequence of events witnessed by observers and later consigned in chronicles.

[3] See Hosea, 12:14, where the "blood" of the prophet who has taken the Jews out of bondage will be avenged by God. The most lucid and informed discussion of Sellin's book and of its importance for Freud is to be found in the presentation by the Biblical scholar André Caquot, in an appendix to Jacques Lacan's *Seminar XVII, The Other Side of Psychoanalysis*, trans. Russell Grigg, New York, Norton, 2007, pp. 209–214.
[4] For all this, the best synthesis is Yosef Hayim Yerushalmi's *Freud's Moses: Judaism Terminable and Interminable*, New Haven, Yale University Press, 1991. See Eliza Slavet, *Racial Fever: Freud and the Jewish Question*, New York, Fordham University Press, 2009.
[5] Cathy Caruth, *Unclaimed Experience: Trauma, Narrative, and History*, Baltimore, Johns Hopkins, 1996. Hereafter, abbreviated as UE and page number.
[6] See Sigmund Freud, *Moses and Monotheism*, New York, Random House, 1967, p. 84, and UE, pp. 16–17. Hereafter abbreviated as MM and page number.

There is no immediate understanding when trauma is concerned. This will find a direct application to Holocaust studies.

Following Caruth's lead, Giorgio Agamben has taken Primo Levi's moving memoirs of Auschwitz as the starting point for a passionate meditation on the unspeakable in history.[7] As Levi argued several times, the real witnesses were not the survivors, they were those who had abandoned all hope in the camps, those who were called the *Müsselmänner* and who almost all died because they had gone deep into the horror. Two important critics have objected to the fetishization of the unspeakable. Ruth Leys has attacked Cathy Caruth for what she sees as a misreading of Freud on the concept of trauma and aims at showing that there are at least two models of trauma for Freud, one in which he believes in the reality of the event, the other in which it may just be a simulation.[8]

More recently, Thomas Trezise published a virulent attack on Agamben's account of Auschwitz. In *Witnessing Witnessing: On the Reception of Holocaust Survivor Testimony*,[9] he debunks the myth of the unspeakable event that cannot be inscribed either in subjective consciousness or collective memory. He attacks the rhetoric of pathos and awe that he sees in Adorno and Agamben and points out their dangerous results: if one can merely repeat the trauma, this will prevent any victim from giving a testimony about the cause of the trauma, its circumstances, and the ethical scandal it constitutes. In fact, what most victims insist on is their ability (or wish, at least) to provide a true account of their condition. I will return to this discussion at the end, and I will try to illuminate it with examples taken from Marguerite Duras, Robert Antelme, and Yann Martel.

I will simply note at this point that when Freud discusses the parallel he observes between traumatic neurosis and Jewish history, he makes a curious admission not mentioned either by Caruth of Leys: his own writing is caught up in the very *Nachträglichkeit* affecting historical phenomena. The English translation has downplayed the role of deferred temporality in the very writing of Freud's mythical history: "As an afterthought we observe that – in spite of the fundamental difference in the two cases, the problem of the traumatic neurosis and that of Jewish monotheism – there is a correspondence in one point. It is the feature which one might term *latency*" (MM, p. 84); the German original has "Nachträglich muss es uns auffallen."[10] Freud insists on the fact

[7] Giorgio Agamben, *Remnants of Auschwitz, The Witness and the Archive*, trans. Daniel Heller-Roazen, New York, Zone Books, 1999.
[8] Ruth Leys, *Trauma, A Genealogy*, Chicago, University of Chicago Press, 2000.
[9] Thomas Trezise, *Witnessing Witnessing: On the Reception of Holocaust Survivor Testimony*, New York, Fordham University Press, 2013.
[10] *Der Mann Moses und die monotheistische Religion: Drei Abhandlungen* in Freud, *Studienausgabe, IX, Fragen der Gesellschaft, Ursprünge der Religion*, p. 516.

that a similar delay marks individual trauma, the invention of monotheism, and his own narrative just as it aims at providing a solution. This solution entails a forceful demotion: his book aims at showing to the growing group of anti-Semites that they are wrong to identify a specific race with a religion that confers dignity on only a small group of human beings. For Freud, the formula of anti-Semitism is the Christian reproach: "You killed our God," meaning of course Jesus (MM, p. 114). The reproach is true, but it has to be interpreted as "[w]e killed our God." The one who was killed was Moses, whose rule had become tyrannical and his monotheistic God unbearable. After which, the rebellious Hebrews made peace with this murder by elaborating their own monotheism. Freud goes on, arguing that all those who reproach the Jews for the murder of Christ "are in fact suffering from a rejection of the very idea of a unique God – they have been badly Christianized, and still hanker after their barbaric and polytheist gods and goddesses." (MM, p. 117)). Hence, in a radical gesture, Freud will not hesitate to "deny" (*absprechen*) its greatest son and prophet to the community of the Jews. The bold move nevertheless entails a curious progression, indeed more reminiscent of a novel than of a history book, with a first chapter "Moses and Egyptian," followed by a second chapter, "If Modes was an Egyptian…" and a third chapter, "Moses, His People, and Monotheistic Religion." The story of the repetition of the murder of the father has to be repeated twice at least, which forces us to return to our initial question: How can one write a psychoanalytic history, if concealment and forgetting have been at work, silently, from the start?

History and perversion

This is an issue that has been tackled by Elizabeth Roudinesco when providing her own ambitious "history of perversion."[11] Can such a concept find successive incarnations and underpin a survey of premodern, modern, and contemporary history? Up to now, such a "history" was restricted to books such as Krafft-Ebing's *Psychopathia Sexualis*, with its notorious passages in Latin.[12] Krafft-Ebing offers something like an encyclopedia of perversion in countless absurd vignettes; who could forget the Parisian *coupeurs de nattes* who would snatch and cut locks from little girls out of school and not be disgusted by the unfortunates ones who would eat soggy bread full of urine left

[11] Elisabeth Roudinesco, *Our Dark Side: A History of Perversion*, trans. David Macey, Cambridge and Malden, MA, Polity Press, 2009.
[12] Richard von Krafft-Ebing, *Psychopathia Sexualis; mit besonderer Berücksichtigung der konträre Sexualempfindung*, Stuttgart, Ferdinand Enke Verlag, 1887.

in public *urinoirs*? Usually, this kind of survey belongs to popular literature. A good example of this is *Sordid Sex Lives: Shocking Stories of Perversion and Promiscuity from Nero to Nilsen.*[13] The roll call of famous people examined is as comprehensive as possible. Nigel Cawthorne surveys with unflappable equanimity the orgies, debaucheries, and sexual scandals that were rife from the Roman decadence, beginning with Cleopatra, to the modern times, continuing with usual suspects such as Marquis de Sade, Sir Richard Burton, Leopold von Sacher-Masoch, and Oscar Wilde. It ends with today's icons of popular culture such as James Dean, Elvis Presley, and Dennis Nilsen, the serial killer still alive today. And of course, he includes James Joyce (for his coprophilia and urophilia) and Marcel Proust (for his sadism).

If it seems that our culture has become more relativistic and tolerant, "perversion" calls up images of unspeakable practices rejected as so many social stigmata. One would then need a history of various conceptions of perversion, and it would correspond to varying notions of the "normal sexual aim." Perversions could be considered in an evolutionary way, as varied ideological projections about these standards and the rules to protect them. Each of them entails social reprobation and a nomenclature of practices deemed to be deviating from acceptable norms. For instance, in the thirteenth century, Aquinas's hierarchy of perversions posited that masturbation was far worse than "sodomy," which is not be the case today in most United States. For Aquinas, quite logically from his point of departure, Onan's sin was a refusal of sexual acts leading to the propagation of species. Sodomy implied an error as to the proper aim of sex: people were mistaken as to the right orifice or did not recognize their preordained sexual partners but were well meaning and thus should not be condemned too harshly.

The "perversion" invoked by the French judges who condemned Joan of Arc to the stake had little to do with the medical ideas that underpinned Oscar Wilde's notorious condemnation to jail, to take two famous examples analyzed by Roudinesco. She argues that, to study perversion, one should go beyond moralizing rejection; hence, one should remain historical, yet without falling into the trap of culturalist equanimity. She wants to avoid losing the conceptual contours of the term; therefore, she mixes theory and history, structure and genealogy. Her point of departure is the psychoanalytic definition of perversion. Freud and Lacan talk about perversion as a structure of the subject, and the three main paradigms they explore are fetishism, sadism, and masochism. Perversion is a structure that can be approached genetically.

---

[13] Nigel Cawthorne, *Sordid Sex Lives: Shocking Stories of Perversion and Promiscuity from Nero to Nilsen,* London, Quercus, 2010.

This disposition goes back to the evolution of young children as men and women. For Freud, paradoxically, perversion is somehow "natural": he speaks of children as "polymorphous perverse" in the *Three Essays on the Theory of Sexuality*.[14] For the male, fetishism corresponds to the negation of a castration glimpsed and then immediately rejected. It replaces the unseen phallus of the mother with substitute objects, such as shiny leather, furs, high-heel shoes, gloves, and so on. Such a simple pattern helps understand the Freudian approach to perversion. Freud added a very important note in 1915 in which he stated that psychoanalysis never separates subjects who have made a same-sex object choice from those who did not. He adds: "Thus from the point of view of psycho-analysis the exclusive sexual interest felt by men for women is also a problem that needs elucidating."[15] Freud was always aware of his own investments in male friends like Fliess, and he condoned his daughter Anna's lesbianism. However, his *Three Essays* tend to presuppose a linear teleology, a progression from oral to anal and then to phallic stages. Hence, sadism is often linked with a "regression" to an anal stage, which has led Melanie Klein to speak of the "anal-sadistic" stage.

Going further, Lacan sees perversion as a subject's individual way of avoiding the law of castration. Fetishism provides the model, but any perverse subject can illustrate in a creative or stereotyped manner the fundamentally transgressive nature of the sexual drive. Thus, contemporary libertinism, bisexual experimentations, fetishism, voyeurism, and exhibitionism are constitutive features of today's deployment of eroticism in popular culture, magazines, videos, and films. Literature is another site in which one can explore the analysis of perverse structures. Roudinesco gives vignettes and portraits similar to Emma Bovary's; the question of contemporary readers was, was she insane, hysterical or perverse? Roudinesco examines the files on Flaubert and Madame Bovary's trial or the notable perverse characters of Victor Hugo's *Les Misérables*, and, of course, Sade and Sacher-Masoch. Literature helps us understand what is at stake in sodomy, fetishism, masochism, and flagellation.

Roudinesco's category of perversion is thus transhistorical. She begins with two types of narratives. She finds that two main types of perversions have been documented in history: the excesses of Christian mystics and the abominable crimes of homicidal sadists. In the middle ages, characters such as Catherina of Siena, who loved to suck the pus of cancerous breasts, or Marguerite Mary Alacoque, still revered in Ireland, who would eat the turds left by dysenteric

---

[14] Sigmund Freud, *Three Essays on the Theory of Sexuality*, New York, Basic Books, 1975, p. 57. Children are compared with uneducated women who can then be exploited as prostitutes.
[15] Ibid., p. 12, note.

men in a hospice, were not uncommon. Such perverse practices were justified because they were thought to bring about an ecstatic communion with the body of Christ. The second half of the diptych comes from roughly the same period; it is represented by the history of Gilles de Rais, who ended up burned at the stake. The army general who saved France several times was exposed as a sadistic sodomite. He was discovered to have tortured and killed more than 300 children and young men. This confirms the possibility of a chronicle of historical perversion, which requires a fully fledged historiography buttressed on legal and psychiatric files.

After having sketched the possibility of a global historical narrative of perversion, Roudinesco addresses recent debates. The term "paraphilia," the condition of extreme and abnormal sexual desires, has officially replaced the term "perversion" in the recent versions of the *Diagnostic and Statistical Manual of Mental Disorders* (DSM). The term flaunts its scientific neutrality by avoiding the counter-idea of a norm. It limits its scope to observable behavior but never touches on issues of subjectivity. A so-called permissive culture will be loath to call perversion masturbatory practices sponsored by Internet pornography. Transsexualism and zoophilia appear as almost acceptable, if not recommended to all. According to the admonitions dispensed by Peter Singer, professor at Princeton, one ought to defend animals' lives, become strict vegetarians, and condone bestiality and zoophilia.

Against this apparent liberalism, Roudinesco insists that if a term like perversion is indeed a rigorous psychoanalytic concept, it should retain its theoretical valence and purchase. Its being able to address concerns of recent history begs the issue of the relevance of psychoanalytic discourse today. Thus she writes: "While the psychoanalytic movement has, over the last hundred years, developed a coherent clinical approach to psychosis and has succeeded in developing new approaches to neurosis … its almost exclusive concentration on structure in the clinical sense of the term has led it to overlook the historical, political, cultural and anthropological question of perversion"[16] (pp. 158–159). If one avoids talking about the cultural side of perversion, then "perverse" effects are generated in culture. The adjective "perverse" corresponds to "perversion" as well as to "perversity," a term liked by Poe and Baudelaire. It is as if our late capitalism could only recognize the results (that are often perverse) but denied the causes (perversion), simply because the cause is inherent to late capitalism itself. This program corresponds to the ambitions of psychoanalysis that Freud saw as capable of tackling a history of culture. Such a history will have to include its many aberrations. Beyond

---

[16] Roudinesco, *Our Dark Side: A History of Perversion*, pp. 158–159.

the structural concept of a repressive culture that generates "discontent," our current discontent derives most of the time from a naïve belief in science and progress. Science has a perverse side when it corresponds to our infantile fantasies about sex, gender, and sexuality.

One of recurrent dreams of psychoanalysis has been to elaborate a long-term history, which is why Freud ended his career with his "historical novel" in which the "hero" is Moses the Egyptian. Freud also enlisted the help of Senator Bullitt to write a similar historical novel in which there are no heroes but only one villain: the American President Wilson. Freud and Bullitt collaborated on psychobiography of President Wilson in 1932 with the intention of understanding the present crisis.[17] This book explains Freud's subsequent wish to dig deeper into the past of humanity to understand the roots of the problem. The main point of the biography is about religion, in fact. Freud and Bullitt argue that Wilson's main fantasy was an unconscious identification with Jesus. He thought that his father was God, and his passive libido facing a father that he wanted to imitate gave him the sense that he was invested with a sacred mission, hence, his idealism that made him incapable of confronting the schemes and manipulations of ruthless politicians such as Clemenceau and Lloyd George in 1919. Wilson believed he was ushering in a new alliance leading toward universal fraternity, whereas he stirred all nationalisms. Clemenceau, who mocked Wilson and described him as Christ come to earth to reform men, was right, according to Freud.[18] When Wilson had been warned of a risk of assassination, he replied: "I am immortal until my time comes."[19]

It was in the name of the League of Nations that Wilson abandoned piece by piece the international edifice he had constructed in 1918. Wilson's ignorance concerning the groups, ethnicities, and nationalities in central Europe was so great that he was never sure of what he was doing. The critical psychobiography of President Wilson demonstrates that it is possible to have at the same time a belief in a transcendent truth founded on the divine word and to allow practical sophisms giving free rein to the French and the British. He thus orchestrated monstrous births such as the creation of artificial states aiming at defusing Franco-British rivalries (among which was Irak, fabricated from the ruins of the ancient Ottoman Empire) and paved the way to the rise of Hitler in a deeply wounded and divided Germany. Thus the deluded megalomaniac would assist the rise to power of historical perverts such as Hilter, Eichmann,

---

[17] Sigmund Freud and William C. Bullitt, *Thomas Woodrow Wilson: A Psychological Study*, Boston, Houghton Mifflin, 1967.
[18] Ibid., p. 243.
[19] Ibid., p. 148.

Hoess, Goering, and many others. The religious delusion of one would feed the pagan and racist delirium of the others.

If it helps to learn from history's mistakes, psychoanalysis should not only complete Borges's *History of Infamy* but also promote a new enlightenment, as Freud imagined it. Such enlightenment will not be hampered by pure rationalism and will refuse to turn a blind eye to the obscure part in us. A historiography of perversion will lead to Georges Bataille's principle of "heterology," a principle that hesitates between the sublime and abjection in our culture. Hence, it is fitting that the French version of *La Part Obscure* should begin with an epigraph by Georges Bataille: "The greater the beauty, the deeper the stain."[20] As Roudinesco remarks, Freud had no illusion about human nature:

> Freud never read much of Sade, but without realizing it, he shared Sade's idea that human life was characterized not so much by an aspiration to the good and virtue, as by a permanent quest for the enjoyment of evil: the death drive, the desire for cruelty, a love of hatred, and an aspiration to unhappiness and suffering.... Being a thinker of the dark Enlightenment ... and not of the counter-Enlightenment, he rehabilitated the idea that perversion is an essential part of civilization to the extent that it is society's accursed share and our own dark side. But rather than grounding evil in the natural world order or seeing man's animal nature as the sign of an inferiority that can never be overcome, he preferred to argue that access to culture is the only thing that can save humanity from its own self-destructive drives.[21]

Freud's theory explores the darkest springs of our being; it leads to an awareness of unconscious fantasies that are shared by most. Hence, humanity's nightmarish history from which we are trying to awake, which is both the history of humanity (in us) and the history of inhumanity (in us too). This has also been explored in fiction – by Marquis de Sade.

The Sadean regime of literature

Lacan added something to Freud's analysis of perversion when he tackled the case of Marquis de Sade. His essay "Kant with Sade" stresses that even when Sade rejects the norms of "normal" sexuality, such norms remain active principles. Lacan's most obvious proof is the ending of the "Philosophy in the

---

[20] "Plus grande est la beauté, plus profonde est la souillure," Georges Bataille, quoted by Elisabeth Roudinesco, *La Part obscure de nous-mêmes, Une histoire des pervers*, Paris, Albin Michel, 2007, p. 7.
[21] Roudinesco, *Our Dark Side: A History of Perversion*, pp. 70–71.

Bedroom," when we see the mother, Madame de Mistival, who has tried to bring back home her debauched daughter Eugénie, leaving the castle with her sex sewn up by her perverse and depraved daughter. This outrage confirms for Lacan that the Mother will remain untouchable, forever forbidden.[22] The maxim, which could be called *Noli tangere matrem*, confirms that the perverse structure depends on the law that it negates. In the same manner, the teeming tortures imagined by Sade call up the absolute and limitless enjoyment of an evil god. Like Schreber's insane and libidinous God, Sade's Supremely Evil Being is a mere parody of the divine law. When dealing with Sade, one reaches a domain that is still today rather contentious – the excess of those who hate him having triggered a hero-worship as a response. Writers such as Monique David-Ménard denounced what appeared to them as Lacan's excessive complacency for the French writer.[23] One should never forget that Sade's main dream was to be acclaimed as a successful popular novelist or playwright. He only became a symbol of resistance to oppression because his writings, and not his sexual transgressions, sent him to jail for most of his life. In fact, Lacan's attitude is marked by extreme prudence facing the Sade cult. He does not hide strong reservations facing the "divine Marquis." Sade's figure nevertheless goes beyond the perversion that is associated with the term "sadism." Sade's main lesson for Lacan – and for psychoanalysis altogether – is what he teaches about excess, fantasy, and the law of nonreciprocity of desire.

Lacan's main insights about Sade had already been discussed in Maurice Blanchot's 1949 book *Lautréamont and Sade*. In the section devoted to "Sade's Reason," Blanchot describes the logical contradiction at the core of Sade's work. It has to do with the impossibility of generalizing or universalizing his maxims:

> At every moment (Sade's) theoretical ideas set free the irrational forces with which they are bound up. These forces both excite and upset the thought by an impetus of a kind that causes the thought first to resist and then to yield, to try again for mastery, to gain an ascendancy, but only by liberating other dark forces by which, once again the ideas are carried away, side-tracked and perverted. The result is that all that is said is clear but seems at the mercy of something that has not been said. Then, a little further on, what was concealed emerges, is recaptured by logic but, in its turn, obeys the movement of a still further hidden force. In the end, everything has been brought to light, everything has been

---

[22] Jacques Lacan, "Kant with Sade," in *Ecrits*, p. 607.

[23] For Monique David-Ménard, Lacan has misread Freud's theory of drives, which makes him believe that the pervert realizes better than anyone else the detour needed by desire. See *Les Constructions de l'universel*, Paris, Presses Universitaires de France, 1997, p. 10. Freud's earlier idea was that the pervert does not repress the way a neurotic does, but he was to change his mind later on.

> expressed, but equally everything has once more been plunged into
> the obscurity of undigested ideas and experiences that cannot be given
> shape.[24]

Blanchot sums up a maxim that can never become "universal": "Lend me the
part of your body that can give me an instant's satisfaction, and enjoy, if so
pleases you, the part of mine you prefer."[25] Lacan reformulates this more dras-
tically as follows: "I have the right of enjoyment (*jouissance*) over your body,"
anyone can say to me, "and I will exercise this right without any limit to the
capriciousness of the exactions I may wish to satiate with your body."[26]

Indeed, everyone will recognize here Sade's black humor, or an impercepti-
ble sliding from the rational to the reasonable and then to the pathological. At
least, the subversive impact of such a formulation lies in its debunking of any
"reciprocity" that would be taken as an ethical basis for intersubjectivity. Sade's
perverse and no doubt excessive enjoyment (it does not stop at mild tortures
and can entail the dismemberment of the chosen victim) shows that subjectivity cannot be equated to reciprocity. Perversion dispels that illusion; human
desire is marked by the Desire of the Other. The point of the formulation is
precisely its resistance to subjective reversal. The truth of Sade is that desire
negates reciprocity and that the drives know no ethical bounds, especially if
their main model is provided by the death drive. Sade radicalizes the part of
trauma that inheres to any sexual experience, and he plays with this, magnifying the attendant anxiety – but for the others.

Lacan's reading is above all in debt to Freud's analysis of sadism and masochism. Freud's thesis was developed in 1924 in "The Economic Problem of
Masochism." To deal with a type of masochism called "moral masochism,"
Freud presented Kant's "categorical imperative" as the most elaborate philosophical expression that can be given to the concept of the "cruelty" of the
superego. This is the genesis he sketched:

> This super-ego is in fact just as much a representative of the *id* as of
> the outer world. It originated through the introjection into the ego
> of the first objects of the libidinal impulses in the *id*. namely, the two
> parents, by which process the relation to them was desexualized, that
> is underwent a deflection from direct sexual aims. Only in this way
> was it possible for the child to overcome the Oedipus-complex. Now

---

[24] Maurice Blanchot, "Sade's Reason," in *The Maurice Blanchot Reader*, ed. Michael Holland, Oxford, Blackwell, 1995, pp. 75–76. The essay was first published in *Les Temps Modernes* in October 1947 under the title "A la rencontre de Sade."

[25] Blanchot, *Blanchot Reader*, p. 76. For a different translation, see Blanchot, *Lautréamont and Sade*, trans. Stuart Kendall and Michelle Kendall, Stanford, Stanford University Press, 2004, p. 10.

[26] *Ecrits*, p. 648, slightly modified.

the super-ego has retained essential features of the introjected persons, namely their power, their severity, their tendency to watch over and to punish.... The super-ego, the conscience at work in it, can then become harsh, cruel and inexorable against the ego which is in its charge. The categorical imperative of Kant is thus a direct inheritance from the Oedipus-complex.[27]

A "perverse couple" is thus created: the sadism of the superego and the masochism of the ego go hand in hand. Freud notes the paradox that the more people try to curb their aggressiveness facing others, instead of getting a more relaxed and gentle personality, the more inflexible, demanding, and dictatorial their conscience becomes.[28] In the same paper, Freud also evokes the characters of Russian novels, these "Russian character-types"[29] that one finds in Dostoevsky's novels. They multiply "sinful acts" to be punished by their sadistic conscience and often quickly and compulsively achieve their complete ruin. Here, Kant is clearly designated by Freud as the accomplice of Sade. The unlikely coupling of Sade and Kant poses all the problems associated with civilization's way of dealing with aggression. Freud shows that it is the renunciation to instinctual gratification that comes first; such renunciation then creates morality and not the reverse, as is often assumed.[30] Humans remain ambivalent facing what they have renounced, and the old libidinal aggression may flare up. This will be the point of departure of two parallel readings of Sade, one by Adorno and Horkheimer in the *Dialectic of Enlightenment*, and the other Lacan's essay "Kant with Sade."

However, Sade remains a literary author, and this cannot be subsumed by categories such as perversion or sadism, for that matter. Was Sade a sadist or a novelist? Pierre Klossowski has posed this question in *Sade My Neighbor*. Klossowski argues that Sade seems to be looking for purity in a cruel Nature dissociated from a no less cruel God.[31] Klossowski thus concludes that Sade was not a "pervert" or a monster but above all a writer – a boring and repetitive writer, for sure, but a writer obsessed with a few main themes. One of these concerns the link between fantasies created by a perverse imagination and reality. It is the very excess of Sade's imagination that misleads the reader who takes fiction for reality. Sade always stressed this distinction; he replied to a critic named Villeterque who thought that the theses of his *Crimes of Love* could be attributed to the author: "Loathsome ignoramus: have you not yet

---

[27] Freud "The Economic Problem in Masochism," *General Psychological Theory*, pp. 197–198.
[28] Ibid., p. 200.
[29] Ibid., p. 200.
[30] Ibid., pp. 200–201.
[31] Pierre Klossowski, *Sade My Neighbor*, trans. Alphonso Lingis, Evanston, Northwestern University Press, 1991, pp. 99–103. Hereafter abbreviated as SMN.

learned that every actor in any dramatic work must employ a language in keeping with his character, and that, when he does, 'tis the fictional personage who is speaking and not he author? ... Ah, Monsieur Villeterque, what a fool you are!"[32]

This point was not lost on Klossowski, a novelist of distinction, who comments:

> The parallelism between the apathetic reiteration of acts and Sade's descriptive reiteration again establishes that the image of the act to be done is re-presented each time not only as though it had never been performed but also as though it had never been described. This reversibility of the same process inscribes the presence of *nonlanguage* in language; it inscribes a foreclosure of language by language.
> (SMN, p. 41)

Sade's symptom is not the psychiatric category of "sadism," but of writing. This writing hesitates between the repetitive fantasy of an outrage to a Mother Nature who he abhors and a questioning of the function of the big Other's jouissance. Klossowski's concept of foreclosure evokes Lacan's translation of Freudian *Verwerfung* when defining the logic of psychosis. However, neither for Freud, nor for Lacan, was Sade a psychotic. Sade was not Schreber, although, like Schreber, he was above all a writer.

Sade's life as an individual was not a happy one: he was jailed for debauchery under the Old Regime from 1777 to 1790, imprisoned for a short time at the height of Terror in 1793–1794, which allowed him to see the mass slaughters; he was freed just before the date set for his execution because of Robespierre's downfall, then jailed again for his pornographic writings under the consulate and the empire (under direct orders from a puritanical Napoléon, it is said) between 1801 and 1814, when he died. Altogether he spent some twenty-seven years in prison – quite a record, at the time, for a noble man from an old family who had never killed anyone! Thus Sade was aware that the imposition of force on his passions had not restrained them but, on the contrary, exacerbated their violence. Here is what he writes to his wife in 1783, addressing less her person than those who had tried to censor and suppress his writings: "[Y]ou have produced a ferment in my brain, owing to you phantoms have arisen in me which I shall have to render real."[33] These specters have been embodied in the sense that they have been written, despite all types of censorship. Sade's scandalous

---

[32] Quoted by Marcel Hénaf in *Sade: The Invention of the Libertine Body*, Minneapolis, University of Minnesota Press, 1999, p. 7.
[33] Marquis de Sade, *Justine, Philosophy in the Bedroom and Other Writings*, trans. Richard Seaver and Austryn Wainhouse, New York, Grove Weidenfeld, 1965, p. 134.

reiterations of perverse fantasies that break all limits also explode the relatively staid category of Freudian "sublimation." Lacan compares Sade with Bataille, who of course placed Sade at the pinnacle of the "literature of evil." Lacan say this in his *Seminar on the Ethics of Psychoanalysis*:

> The fact that the book falls from one's hands no doubt proves that it is bad, but literary badness here is perhaps the guarantee of the very badness ... that is the object of our investigation. As a consequence, Sade's work belongs to the order of what I call experimental literature. The work of art in this case is an experiment that through its action cuts the subject loose from his psychosocial moorings – or to be more precise, from all psychosocial appreciation of the sublimation involved. (S VII, p. 201)

By insisting on writing as a chosen fate, Sade's life kept a coherence that no serial killer ever achieved. Sade forces readers to acknowledge that writing can explore its own limits and that it can stage perversion and also question the very possibility of its own foreclosure.

The foreclosed language of Sade's fictions opens up onto the space of the outside in a curious and ironical pragmatism of fantasy. Sade's well-known irony, so visible in his letters from the Bastille to his wife, or his savage and disturbing humor thus ultimately question the position of the superego. Moreover, his writings cannot be reduced to mere fantasies because they explore how fantasy is determined from the outside by the Law. Sade's sarcastic humor testifies to the division of the subject in the name of the superego, as Freud has pointed out very clearly in his essay on humor. Sade's works are not just templates for male fantasy because his readers are mostly neurotics who imagine that they are perverts. Sade points to the dark side of humanitarian ethics. He poses the question of man's universality (or lack of) in his relation to the unconditionality of the Law by presenting a gross caricature of the Law. Blasphemy remains caught up in the Law; like fantasy, it is determined by the Law of desire – here it is presented negatively as the obscene jouissance of the Other. Sade then becomes a hostage to an absolute jouissance, so excessive that only an evil God can experience it. This is why all Sadian libertines, whether men or women, will accumulate murders and transgression in an effort to approach absolute jouissance. However, they always feel inferior to it. Ultimately, if Sade is boring, it is because he needs to repeat endlessly these sexual scenes and these philosophical demonstrations. The repetition compulsion has devoured the space of fiction, which provides another reason for its foreclosure. Yet he embodied a radical change in history, redoubling revolutionary violence with his own attempt at a subversion of all values.

A history of trauma

Sade is a name whose echo calls up an irreversible turning point in French history: the revolution. Is it therefore possible to write a general history of perversion that will include the concept of sadism as a revolutionary notion? If this history includes successive distortions of the very concept of "perversion," it may seem more crucial to write a history of trauma. As we have seen, the field of trauma studies came into its own when Cathy Caruth took up a Freudian notion and applied it to the literature of the Holocaust and also to any type of memoir dealing with abuse, rape, murder, and extreme situations. In *Trauma: Explorations in Memory* and in *Unclaimed Experience: Trauma, Narrative and History*, Caruth starts from Freud's *Beyond the Pleasure Principle* to sketch a theory of the impossibility of registering or figuring certain events that can be called traumatic. The events being by definition "excessive," they cannot be inscribed either in the memory or consciousness, but they are bound to be repeated compulsively, literally, and mutely. Caruth takes her examples from Marguerite Duras (*Hiroshima mon amour*), Lacan, Kleist, and Freud. Each time, she insists on the missed experience, the inability to inscribe the trauma in a linear and coherent narrative.

A few years later, a formidable refutation was launched by Ruth Leys. Whereas Caruth was inspired by Paul de Man's mixture of materialist literality in the repetition of the trauma, and of rhetorical strategies of indirection that all kept a performative agency, Leys was influenced by Mikkel Borch-Jacobsen's deconstructive reading of Lacan and Freud. Leys attacks the convergence of theses of the physician Bessel van der Kolk and the critic Caruth, who both believe that the symptoms of traumas are literal and veridical repetitions of events that have happened but, being excessive in some way, were not fully registered. The consequence is that the Freudian concepts of repression cannot be applied to a traumatic experience.[34] The "wound" of the trauma has been so deep that it has contaminated the organs of perception and memory. She compares this thesis with the abundant medical and legal literature that began being produced about post-traumatic stress disorder (PSTD) in the 1980s (the term PSTD became official in the DSM III in 1980.) However, the two more recent versions of the DSM, she observes, were more cautious in attributing a literal and truthful nature to the traumatic phenomena. The growing number of persons suffering from recurrent memories, flashbacks, hallucinations, and recurrent nightmares, all generated by traumatic injuries or experiences, has left us with an enormous archive that is hard to interpret. For Freud, who was

[34] Leys, *Trauma, A Genealogy*, p. 230.

aware of the phenomenon, testified to the existence of a death drive beyond the pleasure principle. The suffering is no doubt real, but is the cause always a real event? We are going back to the initial interrogations of Freud when he was changing his views about the reality of the seduction of hysterical daughters by their "perverse" fathers in 1897.

Leys points out simplifications of the evidence in van der Kolk, and more damagingly, a contradiction in Caruth's main thesis. For Caruth, victims of traumas can only repeat them because they have no possibility of narrating them to themselves. They are literally happening over and over again. "The truth of the trauma (is) the failure of representation,"[35] she neatly summarizes. Thus Caruth interprets Claude Lanzmann's film *Shoah*, not as a representation destined to make people understand the Holocaust, the transportation toward death camps, but as a way of transmitting the trauma as such, in its incomprehensible horror. She calls the "pathos of the literal" this combination of scientism about overwhelmed neurotransmitters and a performative literary theory of the contagion of the unspeakable.

Leys's argument is founded on a critique of Caruth's simplifying or reductive reading of Freud. According to her, Caruth has tendentiously selected passages about the temporal aspect of the "traumatic neurosis," thus avoiding anything that resembles the castration model of the dialectics of trauma. Finally, it is Caruth's notion of the repetition compulsion that is biased. She thinks that Tancred, who kills Clorinda twice – once because he did not recognize her in combat, the second time after she has been metamorphosed into a tree – exemplifies a lack of awareness, whereas he was conscious of what he had done after the battle, and then states that Clorinda testifies to her wound when she is another subject of trauma. How can she both speak and not speak?

More damaging even is Thomas Trezise's violent refutation of Agamben's use of the same paradigm of trauma to discuss the Holocaust. Agamben exploits some of Primo Levi's hesitations about his own role. Levi felt that he was inadequate as a witness and left that role to those who could not fulfill it by definition because they were the glassy-eyed vanquished, the haggard mute shadows, those who had abandoned any hope. Trezise's main question is whether the way survivors have witnessed historical events can lead to a truth or whether the silenced speech of survivors can lead to a reconstruction. If, as Agamben avers after Primo Levi, the only true witness of the Shoah is the catatonic "Musselman" who believes that he or she will never return to the world of the living, abandons all hope, is barely human, and accepts to be killed in

---

[35] Ibid., p. 253.

the ovens, this does not leave much of a chance to those who try to narrate their experiences.

However, Trezise provides many examples of witnesses who wanted to be witnessing, for whom it was crucial to convey to those who were outside the extent and depth of the horror. For instance, he quotes Charlotte Delbo's moving *Auschwitz and After*. I will mention soon Robert Antelme's *The Human Species*, a book that begins by presenting all the survivors of the camps engaged in a frenzy of talk as soon they were able to return. For them, this endless low of discourse was the only attempt at eradicating the roots of the horror. Freud's concepts have been applied at times indiscriminately to accounts of the Holocaust. Following Freud, one might want to refuse the paradox of an account that is unspeakable and request a new accountability of the narrative of trauma. I will now turn to several narratives to test the validity of these theses. The first text is a fiction, but a fiction that narrates, or attempts to narrate, a traumatic experience.

Trauma and the ecstasy of abandonment

Marguerite Duras's novel *The Ravishing of Lol V. Stein* opens with a scene of "ravishing" – in fact, it is a psychological rape. The rest of the novel will consist in successive deployments of this primal abandonment. The opening scandal is disclosed in the first pages: in the city of South Thala, during a ball given for the engagement of Lol Stein, barely seventeen, Lola sees her fiancé, Michael Richardson, inexplicably attracted to Anne-Marie Stretter. Richardson falls under the spell of this seductive older woman. They dance all night and then leave together. Meanwhile Lol remains prostrate, mute, and catatonic. However, she says that she did not experience pain, as she stopped loving Michael the minute she saw him gaze at Anne-Marie Stretter. Michael and Anne-Marie never return to South Tahla, where Lol lives as a recluse. One day she marries on a whim, moves with her husband to another town, has children, and lives an orderly life. Ten years elapse, Lol and her husband return to live in South Thala, where Lol meets Jacques Hold. Hold is the lover of her school friend Tatiana Karl, now married to a doctor. Lol starts spying on the lovers as they meet for their trysts in the Forest Hotel. She obsesses about Tatiana, naked under her black hair. Jacques Hold starts falling in love with Lol, yet Lol insists that he continue making love to Tatiana. This he does, aware all the time that she is watching. Then Lol remembers her "ravishment." She goes with Jacques to the Casino and reenacts the night of the dance; at last, she experiences pain and talks about the past. At the end, however, she returns to the field to spy on the lovers. The novel finishes on an inconclusive note: "Lol had arrived there ahead of us. She was asleep in the field of rye, worn out, worn out by our trip."[36] As Marguerite Duras said several times (to me as well), at the end, Lol Stein has become incurably psychotic. We should not imagine a happy ending for her. Even if there has been a cathartic reenactment of the trauma, it will not make her progress or move away from her voyeuristic trance.

One important feature in the plot is absent from the English version. After the trauma of the abandonment, Lola decides to call herself simply Lol V. Stein instead of her full name Lola Valérie Stein. It is not clear whether the amputation of her names embodies her abandonment or introduces a new punctuation in a familiar signature. Nevertheless, her abbreviated names help her weather her severe depression. Duras would have loved the common abbreviation of "laughing out loud" as LOL, provided a good measure of hysteria be added to it. If her first name ominously echoes that of Nabokov's heroine discussed in the introduction, Lola Stein is no Lolita. The scansion of her names carries an emblematic weight. Every character in this novel is split, dedoubled by the pain of a lost love, caught up in triangular structures of desire mediated by a third person. The novel's plot consists less in the idea of repeating the traumatic event than in making a knot of its revolving patterns. In fact, the tale looks very much like Poe's "Purloined Letter," because "ravishing" means "stealing" as well. Lacan had asked Duras whether she had read him before writing this novel, but she refused to answer.[37]

There are three triangles in the novel. The first triangle posits Lol in one angle as the fascinated observer who cannot feel the enormity of her loss while Michael Richardson and Anne-Marie Stretter fall in love, caught in reciprocal passion. They "ravish" each other to the point that they forget the rest of the world, as in a mystical or erotic trance. This trance transfixes Lol's own gaze and "ravishes" her in turn, thus transforming her into an "unseeing" and unfeeling subject. Because she is not seen any longer by her lover, she cannot see anything when she looks at the scene of their ravishment. It is a sort of sudden hysterical blindness, the first sign of her trauma in excess of her ability to perceive it.

The second triangle repeats the first. Lol is watching in the field while Jacques and Tatiana make love in the hotel room. However, she cannot see much of the actual lovemaking from her vantage point, for she only sees the lovers emerge

---

[36] Marguerite Duras, *The Ravishing of Lol Stein*, trans. Richard Seaver. New York: Grove Press, 1966, p. 181. Abbreviated as RLS and page number. See also *Le ravissement de Lol V. Stein*, Paris, Gallimard, 1964.

[37] See my analysis of this encounter in *Jacques Lacan and the Subject of Literature*, Houndsmills, Palgrave, 2001, pp. 115–134. Given the density and complexity of Lacan's text on Duras, here I limit myself to summarizing certain aspects.

at intervals as they rest and come to the window. Jacques, aware that Lol is watching, does not divulge this to Tatiana. In fact, it is the presence of Lol in the field that makes him postpone a breakup with a mistress for whom he feels less and less attraction. The passionate words of love he whispers in her ear are meant for Lol.

In both triangles, there is a corner defined by an excessive jouissance that conjoins pain and desire while hollowing a space beyond. Lol occupies this place in the first triangle, whereas Jacques Hold occupies it in the second. Tatiana, who does not know what happens, has replaced Lol. This is why she falls more and more desperately in love with Jacques, precisely because she feels that he is a lover whom she cannot "hold." Meanwhile, Lol wants to continue believing in the fiction that Jacques Hold is a perfectly phallic lover with Tatiana, to whom he should bring the most intense sexual satisfaction.

The apparent overlapping of two triangles that, on closer inspection, do not repeat themselves fully generates narratological uncertainty. Relatively early in the novel, we discover a character seen through the eyes of Lol, who then turns out not to be Jacques Hold, Tatiana's lover, but the narrator of the novel who mentions his or her presence in the story without revealing more. When the narrator betrays his or her presence, there is a shift from the third to the first person ("Arm in arm, they ascend the terrace steps. Tatiana introduces Peter Beugner, her husband, to Lol, and Jack Hold, a friend of theirs – the distance is covered – me," RLS, p. 65). In a number of scenes, the narrative hesitates between the two:

> He tells Lol Stein: "Tatiana removes her clothes, and Jack Hold
> watches her, stares with interest at this woman who is not the woman
> he loves..."

But Tatiana is speaking:

> "But Tatiana is saying something," Lol Stein murmurs.
> To make her happy, I would invent God if I had to.
> "She utters your name"
> I did not invent that. (RLS, p. 123)

It could be Duras herself who appears through repeated mentions of "I see" that punctuate the narrative? "I see this ..." (RLS, p. 45), or "This I invent, I see: ..." (RLS, p. 46), "I invent: ..." (RLS, p. 46). When I asked Duras, a long time ago, what she meant with the last scene, she answered after a silence: "I don't know. I saw it." Thus, if Jacques Hold might be accountable for these moments, because we understand at the end that it is he who, out of love for Lol, has reconstructed her whole story, the presence of details and the mention of other characters imply that Jacques has a limited perception in his reconstruction.

Therefore, as in Lacan's reading of the "Purloined Letter," we have to posit a third triangle in which we readers figure as the fascinated voyeurs "ravished" by Marguerite Duras's narrative. The third triangle joining readers, Duras, and the novel establishes a grammar of fantasy in which all subjects are caught. It comes close to the model of what René Girard has called "triangular desire," or "mimetic desire" – that is, a triangle in which a third person always mediates the choice of the object of desire for the hero, as is often the case in Stendhal's or Proust's novels.[38] Here, the revolving triangles calculate the subject's determination by the Other. However, Duras's narrative is not a simple disclosure of the "truth" of mediated desire, because she also stages what we have to name trauma. Clearly, trauma defines what has happened with Lol: experiencing a mute trauma at the beginning, at the end, she will be swallowed by the Other. Only an excessive jou-issance can function as an equivalent of her excessive loss. The void into which she falls at the end is the hole of a letter, a love letter just limned or adumbrated by the whole novel. Here is Duras's lyrical evocation of this hole:

> What she does believe is that she must enter it [this unknown], that that was what she had to do, that it would always have meant, for her mind as well as her body, both their greatest pain and their greatest joy, so commingled as to be undefinable, a single entity but unnamable for lack of a word. I like to believe – since I love her – that if Lol is silent in her daily life it is because, for a split second, she believed that this word might exist. Since it does not, she remains silent. It would have been an absence-word, a hole-word, whose center would have been hollowed out in a hole, the kind of hole in which all other words would have been buried.... By its absence, this word ruins all the others, it contaminates them, it is also the dead dog on the beach at high noon, this hole of flesh. (RLS, p. 38)

The whole word would be the linguistic expression of the catastrophe experienced in a second during the ball: an absolute dereliction that shatters whatever imaginary certainty she had entertained until then, or, to quote Blanchot's book, a "writing of the disaster."[39]

---

[38] See René Girard's *Deceit, Desire and the Novel: Self and Other in Literary Structure*, trans. Yvonne Freccero, Baltimore, Johns Hopkins University Press, 1965. The original book was published in 1961 and gives a psychoanalytic approach to famous novels by Cervantes, Stendhal, Dostoevsky, Flaubert, and Proust, always showing how desire is mediated. The exhibition of such fictional mediation constitutes the "truth" of the novel, against the "deceit" of romantic poetry founded on the assumption that desire is immediate and transparent.

[39] See Maurice Blanchot, *The Writing of the Disaster*, trans. Ann Smock, Lincoln, University of Nebraska Press, 1995.

This word is thus impossible to utter, to write, or to read in any language, because it obscures a frozen vision:

> What Lol would have liked would have been to have the ball immured, to make of it this ship of light upon which, each afternoon, she embarks, but which remains there, in this impossible port, forever anchored and yet ready to sail away with its three passengers from this entire future in which Lol Stein now takes her place. There are times when it has, in Lol's eyes, the same momentum as on the first day, the same fabulous force. But Lol is not yet God, nor anyone. (RLS, p. 39)

And, indeed, Lol becomes "God," but only at the end, if we admit that by that time she has turned psychotic.

We can now understand why after the "primal scene" of the ball Lol will focus all her attention on one single wish: the desire to see Anne-Marie Stretter undressed by her fiancé, Michael Richardson. Such a desire defines the grammar of her fantasy. As we have seen with Freud's analysis of a fantasmatic scenario in "A Child Is Being Beaten," any subject can turn into an object, an active verb can become passive ("I am beaten" becoming "I am beating.") Thus by becoming a voyeur, Lol realizes a perverse fantasy that would repeat her fixation to another naked body fondled by another lover.

Here, we perceive a link between the perverse fantasy and the primal trauma. Perversion attempts a narrativization of what remained without any grammar. Thus Lol raises the gaze to the dignity of the Thing. The horror that was concealed in the Thing returns in Lol's final madness. The void contained by the mystical Word that she was hoping to find would be a sign that the catastrophe had always already happened. However, there is no one to tell her that. The void has been translated into a vision of nothing, in the pure memory of a blank stare, a fascinated expectation of what will have to remain off limits, outside the frame. If this account of Duras's main novel is accurate, it would seem to confirm Caruth's and Agamben's insights about trauma. Here, the unspeakable nature of the trauma cannot be lifted or sublimated. Lola is indeed a witness, but she is passive, catatonic at the beginning as at the end.

Another example, also discussed by Agamben, may allow us to qualify this conclusion. Duras has described in *La Douleur* the extreme pain of waiting for the return of her husband, Robert Antelme. She also narrates how, after having survived the shock of almost not recognizing Antelme and after having nurtured him until he retrieved his humanity, she did not hesitate to tell him that she was going to divorce him. The status of *La Douleur* corresponds indeed with a journal or diary of trauma: Duras had completely forgotten that she had written these pages, and in them she dares express what is deemed inexpressible, as the admission that she tortured a suspected collaborator, which leads me to Robert Antelme's book. Antelme is the author of one book only, his memoir of having survived various Nazi camps, entitled *L'Espèce Humaine*;[40] however, when one reads it, it usually sweeps clean all the other volumes remaining on the shelves of one's library.

I will note first that its title was mistranslated into English as *The Human Race*,[41] whereas, as Agamben states rightly, it should be *The Human Species*. Here is indeed Antelme's main theme: "For it is a matter of biological belonging in the strict sense ... not of a declaration of moral and political solidarity."[42] Agamben is quoting here Antelme's harrowing account of his stay in several concentration camps: Buchenwald, Gandersheim, and then Dachau. The intensity of his narrative and the sketches of the people he meets provide the sensation of an immediate immersion in that experience. Moreover, Antelme reconstructs the system of the *kapos*, whose authority over the prisoners was absolute. However, beyond the faithful and gripping account of the "bare life" in Nazi camps, and the extremities of pain endured at the end when they evacuated and moved along, with columns of straggling and exhausted skeletons who are shot one after the other by the guards, there is a definitive "message" in the book. It is the development of the title: "To say that one felt oneself contested then as a man, as a member of the human race (*comme membre de l'espèce*) – that may look like a feeling discovered in retrospect, an explanation arrived at afterwards. And yet it was that that we felt most constantly and immediately, and that – exactly that – was what the others wanted."[43] In several impassioned passages, Antelme insists on the unalienable fact of his being part of a common human species. The law of the *Lager* was that its inmates were not men but pigs or dogs, whose humanity could be obliterated by the SS. It is against this dangerous ideology of the "sub-men" that Antelme voices his obstinate resistance: "The SS cannot alter our species."[44]

In the end, Antelme does not simply assert a biological community; he wants to be a witness not just of the Nazi attempt at total obliteration of humanity but also of the possibility of an ethical resistance. This creates a counter-power: "They shall have burned children, they shall have done it willingly. We cannot have it that they did not wish to do it. They are a force, just as the man walking

---

[40] Robert Antelme, *L'Espèce Humaine*, Paris, Gallimard, 1957.
[41] Robert Antelme, *The Human Race*, trans. Jeffrey Haight and Annie Mahler, Marlboro, Vermont, 1992.
[42] Agamben, *Remnants of Auschwitz: The Witness and the Archive*, p. 58.
[43] Antelme, *The Human Race*, p. 5; *L'Espèce Humaine*, p. 11.
[44] Antelme, *The Human Race*, p. 74; *L'Espèce Humaine*, p. 83.

along the road is one. And as we are, too; for even now they cannot stop us from exerting our power."[45] The man on the road was an anonymous passerby who walked along the camp's barbed wires and preferred not to see the prisoners. Even those who try to do their best to help, the German woman who slips a chunk of bread to Antelme or the Rhinelander who one day shakes their hands without being seen, are accomplices if they do not claim openly their common humanity. Antelme stresses the courage to act together to embody ethics as the very foundation of politics. This is how biological commonality turns into history that denounces the mechanism of the most insane system of terror and dehumanization:

> By denying us as men the SS had made us historical objects that could no longer in any way be the objects of ordinary human relations. These relations could have such consequences, so impossible was it just to think of establishing them without being aware of the enormous prohibition against which one had to rebel in order to do so; so completely had one to have withdrawn oneself from the community whose grip in wartime was stronger, so ready had one to be to incur the dishonor, the ignominy of desertion, even of treason, that these relations could hardly be begun without turning at once into history, as if they were in themselves the paths, narrow and obscure, that history had been forced to follow.[46]

Antelme's book thus contradicts the theses about mute witnesses whose trauma has left them unable to assimilate or be conscious of what happened, so that they carry a message that they do not know, whose pathos can only be transmitted silently to the awed reader. As Trezise says, Caruth confuses consciousness and assimilation. There is a difference between a linear narrative and an ethical decision to be a witness to something that borders the unspeakable but that will find a logical order later, or even never. Perhaps because Antelme was a Communist militant (although he was excluded from the Communist Party soon after the Liberation), and not a Jew like Primo Levi, his experience of the Shoah was different. However, the events he documents would still carry the generic name of Auschwitz for Adorno or Agamben. And Antelme insists, much as Trezise implies, that there is a need to use a narrative to testify and overcome the trauma. Of course, the main difference between his testimony and that of his ex-wife, Marguerite Duras, is that he experienced the traumatic event directly, whereas she recreated it, making it resound creatively in her novels and films.

---

[45] Antelme, *The Human Race*, p. 74; *L'Espèce Humaine*, p. 84.
[46] Antelme, *The Human Race*, p. 75; *L'Espèce Humaine*, pp. 84–85.

The "I" in Pi

I will try to suggest a possible synthesis by taking a third example: the prize-winning novel by Yann Martel, *Life of Pi*. In the 2001 novel as in the 2013 film by Ang Lee, we soon understand that the beautiful but highly incredible scenes in which we see a young boy fending of a huge Bengal tiger in a lifeboat are not "facts" as in magic realism, but symbols or allegories. We do get the "true version" of the traumatic events at the end, when "Pi" Molitor Patel is interviewed by Japanese investigators. Inexplicably, the boat on which Pi's family and the animals of their were zoo has sunk in the sea. Only a few managed to survive, but they kill each other one by one until only Pi survives. In the accurate account that Pi ends up blurting out, there were just four people on the boat: a sailor with a broken leg, a cook, his mother, and himself. In the story that he spins for 200 pages, there are four animals, a zebra, am orangutan, a hyena, and a tiger. The most unforgettable image is that of Pi taming the tiger and reaching a truce with him.

The Japanese interrogators guess the truth: Pi has transposed the wounded sailor with a broken leg into a zebra with a broken leg, his mother is the fierce but weak orangutan, the cook is the hyena, and he is Richard Parker, the tiger with whom he struggles. In a twist similar to that of *Fight Club*, we see how subjective division and projections on a fantasmastic double can facilitate the experience of surviving a trauma. Pi needed the long fantasy, which veers off into opaque and even untranslatable images (the drifting island, full of weird meerkats, with the teeth of a long dead sailor, corresponds to archaic fantasies, perhaps allegorizing the traumatic and cannibalistic umbilicus of the dream, or a descent into the frightening whirlpool at the origin of all dreams, the inaccessible site where death drive can be experienced as such) to state the truth simply and quickly at the end. What Martel has shown us convincingly in this fiction full of literary allusions (it looks back to Poe's narrative of *Arthur Gordon Pym*, where he found Richard Parker – by a curious serendipity, Martel kept finding more sailors who had been killed, eaten by their comrades, or lost at sea whose name was Richard Parker) is that trauma can be overcome by a narrative provided it is not forced to stick to the facts – at first. Trauma is not accessible to experience directly, but it can somehow be reclaimed indirectly via metaphors.

Animals provide the best metaphors in this case because they follow the nomenclature of qualities and defects handed down by tradition (thus the cook is a hyena, which explains that he lets himself be killed by Pi after his shameful murder of the mother) while keeping all the unpredictable otherness that we associate with living beings that we cannot fully control. Animals are apt images for the recurrent feature of trauma literature: one key issue is the dehumanization of the victim, who can only project himself or herself into things or animals. The very logic that led to the worse cases of mass extermination (the Nazi's deliberate transformation of the Jews into "sub-men," the use of terms such as "cockroaches" by the Hutu leaders to justify the genocide of the Tutsi minority in Rwanda in 1994) can be used as a strategy for survival. This is the very spring of the dark humor of Kakfa's famous story "The Metamorphosis." When Gregor Samsa turns into a gigantic insect, his transformation is not only the literalization of the term used by anti-Semites for the Jews in Prague, but being an *Ungeziefer*, an abject monster that is half human, half animal, he can also entertain strategies of escape and even minimal enjoyment. It is only the negative reaction of his father that condemns him in the end.

The detour via a projection into animals allows Pi to bridge the gap between his previous life (in which he was fascinated by the zoo) and what has happened since the sinking. It is the unthinkable: terror, murder, cannibalism, the killing of his mother, his revenge, the bare life of survival. Mr. Okamoto only pretends to believe him at the end of his report, but as a wink and a homage to the determined resilience of the survivor. His was a situation in which it would have been insane not to become insane. The effect, nevertheless, is of strange exhilaration. Martel has accomplished with his novel the equivalent of what Beckett had enacted in his wonderful *Not I* in which the feminine character can only talk about her personal trauma (or come as close to it as she can) by avoiding to say "I." Pi can say "I" when he divides himself between a ferocious tiger and a nice young man. He cries bitterly when the tiger disappears into the wildness of Mexico, but he will slowly recover his speech and the ability to spin a tale or two. The tiger was also the carrier of the trauma, and he vanishes silently into the night of the unconscious; thus God will replace the tiger. Pi, who believes in God in spite of all his tribulations, is therefore the most rational of all irrational numbers.

Conclusion: Ambassadors of the unconscious

In February 2012, President Barack Obama wrote a letter to Yann Martel congratulating him on the powerful effect *Life of Pi* had on him and his daughter: "My daughter and I just finished reading *Life of Pi* together. Both of us agreed we prefer the story with animals. It is a lovely book – an elegant proof of God, and the power of storytelling."[1] Freud would have agreed with the second part of the assessment, not necessarily with the first – unless a belief in storytelling inevitably entails a belief in God. That would be Nietzsche's thesis: we still believe in God, he argued, just because we believe in grammar (hence, in logic and essences).[2] Freud believed in grammar, but he did not believe in God, at least if we trust the many statements he made to that effect. This was not just his personal disposition; it has to do with the whole effect of psychoanalysis. In a text originally written as an introduction to the works of Freud in Japanese translation, Jean-Luc Nancy has observed that psychoanalysis provides the only consistent atheistic discourse of the twentieth century, adding that, for this reason, it cannot even believe in itself.

Allegories of the Unconscious

Here is the gist of Nancy's argument: Freud's invention of psychoanalysis cannot be restricted to knowledge. Psychoanalysis is also a clinical practice, and as such its operative concepts rely on (and relay) the singularity of each case. He adds: "This is why Freud's invention is one of the most clearly and most resolutely non-religious of modern inventions. Also why it cannot believe in itself."[3] Nancy, who can be very critical of Lacan, has seen a fundamental

---

[1] Quoted in "Life of Pi Author Martel Hears from Obama," *Winnipeg Free Press*, Saskatoon Star Phoenix, reprinted April 8, 2010, accessed online August 31, 2013.
[2] Friedrich Nietzsche, "Twilight of the Idols," in *The Portable Nietzsche*, ed. Walter Kaufmann, London, Penguin, 1982, p. 483.
[3] Jean-Luc Nancy, *Adoration: The Deconstruction of Christianity*, II, trans. John McKeane, New York, Fordham University Press, 2013, p. 99.

200 Introduction to literature and psychoanalysis

feature of Freud's thought, which agrees with the internal division posited by Ruth Leys in her book on trauma. All his life, from the letters to Fliess to the analysis of the Wolfman, Freud continued to hesitate between the postulation of a real event and the postulation of a hallucinated event in any trauma.

Such a hesitation had a heuristic function: Freud's doctrine should never become a religion, not even a religion of science like Auguste Comte's nineteenth century doctrine of scientist positivism would have it. Nancy insists, talking once more of Freud's invention: "It is the most resolutely non-religious narrative – which is to say, also, the least disposed to give itself over to any set of beliefs whatsoever, even a belief in science."[4] Thus, if one danger is a quasi-religious enthusiasm for a theory that is supposed to cure everything and to explain everything, the other danger is the reduction to scientific axioms (a danger that many Lacanians have not avoided). I have often seen converts to Freud's or to Lacan's theories reject them rabidly five or ten years later. They would burn what they had adored. Their conversion had been religious, hence, situated at the wrong spot. However, the reductive account of Freud in introductory lectures to students in psychiatry is just as dismal. Given the baffling mixture of concepts and singular experience that psychoanalysis requires, one will have to plunge deep into oneself, into one's past first, so as to eradicate the adolescent dream of a new beginning. Freud always stated that one had to remain rational even when one explored the most irrational fears, anxieties of obsessions.

What did Freud believe in, then? It is likely that he "believed" in what he called his "mythology" – that is, the system of drives, especially the couple of libido and death drive established in *Beyond the Pleasure Principle*, when he had modified his metapsychology a last time. He believed in the soundness of the psychoanalytic clinical practice, and he also believed in art and literature as domains of exploration and discovery. The issue lies not in *what* we learn but in *how* we learn from literature and art. To conclude this survey, I will argue that literature teaches us something by making us play the role of an "ambassador" from the court of the Unconscious, if the formulation is not too presumptuous. This will lead me to connect three images: Freud's study and his couch, a famous historical painting, and a celebrated novel by Henry James. I want to link them because of a visual superposition: as soon as one looks at the carpet on Freud's couch and at Holbein's famous painting of *The Ambassadors* side by side, the resemblance is striking. The carpet on Freud's couch is almost identical with the carpet painted on a shelf covered with scientific instruments in *The Ambassadors*. Freud must have seen Holbein's *The Ambassadors* in the National Gallery when he visited London as a young man. Henry James saw it as well

---

[4] Nancy, *Adoration: The Deconstruction of Christianity, II*, p. 100.

when he drafted his novel, *The Ambassadors*. The allegorical objects that are clearly visible between the two French ambassadors look very much like the statues and curios displayed in Freud's study, now accessible to the public in what is the London Freud Museum. If this visual link teaches us something, it will be about the practice of psychoanalysis itself. A consideration of Freud's things, the objects of his material world, will lead us to examine several versions of *The Ambassadors*, from Holbein to Henry James.

Freud's decision to combine a lush Persian carpet on a couch facing a desk that held rows of antique statues obeyed hidden rules; they evoked either a private game to be played daily or a calculated pedagogical interaction with his analysands. Let us meditate on the setting chosen by Freud: on his writing desk there were always two or three rows of antique statues that he had collected patiently; these were also found above and around the couch. The couch was decorated with this rich, thick, oriental wool carpet. Immediately, two types of metaphors come to mind. On the one hand, the statues evoke the archeological metaphor systematically used by Freud to characterize the discovery of the Unconscious. His carefully chosen antiques embody antiquity; they point to the existence of an ancient and partly forgotten past, whose symbols can be understood thanks to some intellectual exploration. Freud told his patient whom he would call the Wolf Man: "The psychoanalyst, like the archeologist in his excavations, must uncover layer after layer of the patient's psyche, before coming to the deepest, most valuable treasures."[5] In this case, indeed, it is the psychoanalyst who does all the work: the patient will be "excavated" so as to bring back to light the treasures that were hidden through the layers of a given psyche.

A different notion is conveyed by the rug's oriental wool, the Qashqai Shekalu carpet. The exotic rug signals a more feminine process because it reminds us of the fact that in the Freud household, the women were adept at needlework, crocheting, knitting, and weaving. Throughout her life, Anna Freud used to make her clothes by hand. Her huge wooden loom has remained in the Freud Museum today. Anna Freud, like her father no doubt, thought that weaving was both useful and therapeutic. Her father commented on her "passion" in those terms: "If the day comes when there is no more psychoanalysis, you can be a seamstress in Tel Aviv."[6]

[5] The Wolf Man, "My Recollections of Sigmund Freud" in *The Wolf-Man by the Wolf-Man*, ed. Muriel Gardiner, London, Hogarth Press, 1971, p. 139. Quoted by Peter Gay in the introduction to *Sigmund Freud and Art*, State University of New York and Freud Museum, 1989, p. 16. See in the same volume the excellent article by Donald Kuspit, "A Mighty Metaphor: The Analogy of Archaeology and Psychoanalysis," pp. 133–151.
[6] Katja Behling, *Martha Freud, A Biography*, trans. R. D. V. Glasgow, Cambridge, Polity, 2005, p. 116.

Liliane Weissberg[7] has studied the images of weaving and unweaving in Freud's works, arguing that they had something to do with the textile professions in which so many of his family members distinguished themselves. This was especially the case of his half-brother Emanuel Freud and his brother Philip, who founded a cloth manufacture in Manchester. Freud's anglophile leanings (his preference for Shakespeare over Goethe is obvious) have something to do with the success story of that branch of his family. When in 1875, Sigmund visited Manchester as a student (he was 19 then) he was impressed by the possibility of such a career. He went back to Manchester in 1908 to visit Emanuel and Philip, and it was during this second trip that he visited the National Portrait Gallery. It was inevitable that he also visited the National Gallery, and we know that one of their prize paintings – only acquired in 1890, when the Earl of Radnor sold it to the museum, which required the help of rich donors – was Holbein's *Ambassadors*. The famous painting was then given pride of place, and its real life subjects had been divulged to the public by Mary F. S. Hervey's 1900 book, *Holbein's Ambassadors, The Picture and the Men*.[8]

What is important at this juncture is to note that the image of weaving suggests something different from that of excavating. In weaving a metaphorical piece of cloth on the couch, it is as if the patient was doing most of the work; the psychoanalyst more often than not unweaves by being silent or dropping punctual comments. This brings us closer to the constructivist view of interpretation put forward by Freud's later essays, such as "Constructions in Psychoanalysis" from 1937. There, Freud begins by quoting in English the motto, "Heads I win, tails you lose,"[9] only to dismiss the accusation that psychoanalytic interpretations can never be refuted. Even when people agree with one interpretation, a psychoanalyst will not accept this as a positive confirmation, but if a patient says, "I had never thought of that," something is revealed. Freud's imagined collaboration with an analysand puts him in the place of a Penelope who, inverting the Homeric paradigm, unweaves during the day what has been woven at night.

The same idea is developed beautifully by Freud in his speech of acceptance of the Goethe Prize in the summer of 1930. Because this address was delivered by Anna Freud, her father being ill at the time, he may have thought

---

[7] Liliane Weissberg, "Ariadne's Thread: Sigmund Freud, the Textile Industry, and Early Psychoanalysis," *MLN*, number 125, 2010, pp. 661–681, and "Freud, the Textile Industry and the Invention of Psychoanalysis" at http://www.en.uni-muenchen.de/news/newsarchiv/2009/weissberg.html, accessed April 20, 2014.

[8] Mary F. S. Hervey, *Holbein's Ambassadors: The Picture and the Men*, London, George Bell and Sons, 1900. After 1900, the painting was given the full title *Jean de Dinteville and Georges de Selve* ("*The Ambassadors*").

[9] Sigmund Freud, "Konstruktionen in der Analyse," in *Schriften zur Behandlungstechnik*, Frankfurt, Fischer Verlag, 1982, p. 395.

of his preferred daughter's hobby. Distinguishing psychoanalysis from pure biography, Freud wrote: "Psycho-analysis can supply some information which cannot be arrived at by other means, and can thus demonstrate new connecting threads in the 'weaver's masterpiece' spread between the instinctual endowments, the experiences and the works of an artist."[10] Freud literalizes Goethe's image of a *Gedankenfabrik* in *Faust*, I, 4. Mephistopheles talks about science and, above all, logic with a student. He tells him:

> Zwar ist's mit der Gedankenfabrik
> Wie mit einem Weber-Meisterstück,
> Wo ein Tritt tausend Fäden regt,
> Die Schifflein herüber hinüber schießen,
> Die Fäden ungesehen fließen,
> Ein Schlag tausend Verbindungen schlägt.
> Der Philosoph, der tritt herein
> Und beweist Euch, es müßt so sein:
> Das Erst wär so, das Zweite so,
> Und drum das Dritt und Vierte so;
> Und wenn das Erst und Zweit nicht wär,
> Das Dritt und Viert wär nimmermehr.
> Das preisen die Schüler allerorten,
> Sind aber keine Weber geworden.[11]

A literal paraphrase would be this:

> In fact the fabric of thinking / Is like a masterpiece of weaving, / One thrust of the foot moves a thousand threads / And back and forth shuttles fly, /Threads move quicker than the eye, /One stroke makes a thousand connections. /Then the philosopher comes, /And proves to you it had to be thus: /The first was so, the second so, / And hence the third and fourth are so; /But if there were no first and second /The third and fourth could never be. / Students applaud this everywhere,/ But never become weavers themselves.

Mephistopheles is Goethe's mouthpiece when he attacks Aristotelian logicians who trust the power of syllogism, separate all the elements, and kill the spirit, missing the dynamic weaving of all things. Weaving thus defines not only the process of intellection but also the production of matter in the universe. Freud agrees with Mephistopheles here and prefers the spirit, even if it is the spirit that "always negates," to dry logic. To follow the spirit implies learning to become a weaver.

[10] Sigmund Freud, "The Goethe Prize," in *Writings on Art and Literature*, p. 262.
[11] Johann W. Goethe, *Faust, Gesamtausgabe*, Frankfurt, Insel, 1992, pp. 193–194.

Freud had already used these lines from *Faust* in an important passage of the *Interpretation of Dreams*: the analysis of the dream of the Botanical Monograph. There, it is the dream that is compared to a weaver's work, and one signifier, botanical in this case, functions like a knot in a tapestry: "Thus "botanical" was a regular nodal point in the dream. Numerous trains of thought converged upon it.... Here, we find ourselves in a factory of thoughts."[12] Once more, the concept of "nodal points" leads to the principle of "overdetermination." We see that the dream process works like a weaver's factory: the greater the number of points of intersection is, the richer the fabric of interrelated thoughts will be. Such a process, which captures the productive logic of the dream work itself, will be allegorized by the carpet.

Let us pause at the threshold or at the frame of the loom, so as to stress links between the collection of antiques, clearly meant to embody a mythical audience, and the oriental carpet on the couch. Freud would rearrange the rows of figures every day, recreating another gaze bearing on the analysand and on him. He described to Fliess a statuette of Janus he had just bought in those terms: "The ancient gods still exist, because I obtained a few recently, among them a stone Janus who looks at me with his two faces in a very superior manner."[13] The divine, human, and animal representations that he arranged thus were to incarnate an Other audience. Through their juxtapositions, he would sketch new constellations. The whole apparatus combines three features: the embodiment of a vertical past, the present agency of a collaborative work of weaving, and a gaze coming from elsewhere to see people and things in a different light. Freud's office implied a triangulation between culture (all his books), the statues, and the rug on the couch. If archaeology betrayed Freud's belief in a hidden truth rising from psychic depths, the process of weaving suggests a continuous intermeshing of the patient's psyche with the psychoanalyst's own. Such an "interweaving" calls up the etymology of *text*, deriving, as Walter Benjamin and Roland Barthes often pointed out, from Latin *textum*, *texere*, hence, to weave.[14]

The orientalism of the Qashqai Shekalu wool rug might be situated in the context of a fascination with the Orient that was dominant in Europe before

---

[12] Freud, *The Interpretation of Dreams*, p. 317.

[13] Letter to Fliess from July 17, 1899, in *The Complete Letters of Sigmund Freud to Wilhelm Fliess*, p. 361. It is in this letter that Freud quotes the epigraph of the *Interpretation of Dreams*, "Flectere si nequeo superos, Acheronta movebo" (If I cannot bend the Powers Above, I'll move the Infernal Regions).

[14] Walter Benjamin compares the work of Proust in *In Search of Lost Time* with a web in which "the day unravels what the night has woven," and links this process with the etymology of "text" as "web." See "The Image of Proust" in *Illuminations*, trans. Harry Zohn, New York, Schocken Books, 1969, p. 202.

the First World War. The craving for the oriental under all shapes, whether it came via Venice, Saint Petersburg, or Tokyo, enhanced the pleasure of the imagination. Thus Proust could transform a Breton port like Balbec into a Persian temple via the magic of its name. Similarly Walter Benjamin points out that the invention of psychoanalysis was inseparable from a material arrangement of rooms, plush sofas, thick curtains, and deep armchairs, in short from a whole bourgeois "philosophy of furniture" elaborated at the end of the nineteenth century:

> It is one of the tacit suppositions of psychoanalysis that the clear-cut antithesis of sleeping and waking has no value for determining the empirical form of consciousness of the human being, but instead yields before an unending variety of concrete states of consciousness conditioned by every conceivable level of wakefulness within all possible centers. The situation of consciousness as patterned and checkered by sleep and waking need only be transferred from the individual to the collective. Of course, much that is external to the former is internal to the latter: architecture, fashion – yes, even the weather – are, in the interior of the collective, what the sensorial of organs, the feeling of sickness in health, are inside the individual. And so long as they preserve this unconscious, amorphous dream configuration, they are as much natural processes as digestion, breathing and the like. They stand in the cycle of the eternally selfsame, until the collective seizes upon them in politics and history emerges.[15]

In this context, Freud's careful arrangement of his couch and of his favorite treasures would play the role of dream machines, or more precisely, of dream-catching machines. By insisting on the private nature of his own assemblages, Freud brought to the fore his process of selection: "To live in these interiors was to have woven a dense fabric about oneself, to have secluded oneself within a spider's web, in whose toils world events hand loosely suspended like so many insect bodies sucked dry."[16] However, Freud let some air in by producing something like a private arcade, a "passage Viennois," one might say. This, according to Benjamin, would be a space in which the inside and the outside always communicate: "Arcades are houses or passages having no outside – like the dream."[17]

[15] Walter Benjamin, *The Arcades Project*, trans. H. Eiland and K. McLaughlin, Cambrige, MA, Harvard University Press, 1999, pp. 389–390.
[16] *The Arcades Project*, p. 216.
[17] *The Arcades Project*, p. 406.

Anamorphic ambassadors

As in the densest and most significant dream of *The Interpretation of Dreams*, the dream of Irma's injection, the stuffy Viennese interior presents a riddle that brings along its own "solution." The riddle and the solution derive from a visual clue, the superposition, nay, the quasi identity of Holbein's oriental carpet on the shelf between the French ambassadors and the famous Qashqai Shekalu wool carpet with which Freud covered his couch. Holbein's *Ambassadors* depicts two French courtiers, Jean de Dinteville and Georges de Selves, who met briefly in London in the spring of 1533. At the time, Holbein was already the main court painter in England when he painted the double portrait. Jean de Dinteville, soon to fall out of favor with the French king, brought the painting back home and hung it in the castle of Polisy, where it remained for several centuries. De Dinteville was portrayed several times; he is the Moses of the wonderfully enigmatic *Moses and Aaron before Pharaoh: Allegory of the Dinteville Family* in the New York Metropolitan Museum of Art.[18]

This celebrated double portrait is familiar to readers of Lacan, who used it to illustrate his theory of the gaze in *Seminar XI*. I will briefly allude to his commentary. In *Seminar XI*, Lacan takes his point of departure in an analysis of the strange anamorphic skull that dominates the foreground of the painting. His remarks are inspired by Jurgis Baltrusaitis's book *Anamorphoses*. Lacan states:

> The two figures are frozen, stiffened in their showy adornments. Between them is a series of objects that represent in the painting of the period the symbols of *vanitas*. At the same period, Cornelius Agrippa wrote his *De vanitate scientiarum*, aimed as much at the arts as the sciences, and these objects are all symbolic of the sciences and art as they were grouped at the time in the *trivium* and *quadrivium*. What, then, before this display of the domain of appearance in all its most fascinating forms, is this object, which from some angles appears to be flying through the air, at others to be titled? You cannot know – for you turn away, thus escaping the fascination of the picture. // Begin by walking out of the room in which no doubt it has long held your attention. It is then that, turning round as you leave – as the author of the *Anamorphoses* describes it – you apprehend in this form.... What? A skull.[19]

Lacan compares the anamorphic skull with Salvator Dali's soft watches, before moving from the skull to death and negativity. Holbein would have made

[18] See Susan Foister, Ashok Roy, and Martin Wyld, *Making and Meaning: Holbein's Ambassadors*, London and New Haven, National Gallery Company and Yale University Press, 1998, p. 24.

[19] Jacques Lacan, *The Four Fundamental Concepts of Psychoanalysis*, trans. Alan Sheridan, New York, Norton, 1981, p. 88.

visible an emblem of both erection and castration, hence, made the phallus appear in such a way that it speaks directly to our gaze. Our gaze is pinned and imprisoned, caught in this "pulsatile, dazzling and spread out function."[20] Lacan generalizes this function to all pictures and concludes: "This picture is simply what any picture is, a trap for the gaze. In any picture, it is precisely in seeking the gaze in each of its points that you will see it disappear."[21] To reach these insights, Lacan's relay has been Merleau-Ponty's *The Visible and the Invisible*, a book in which the exploration of the visible opens up to an investigation of the "prose of the world." Merleau-Ponty's phenomenology of the eye and the gaze leads Lacan to posit the existence of a materialization of the gaze of the Other in some detail of the painting – here, a disquieting skull distorted by anamorphic projection. The gaze of the Other comes from the Unconscious via the suggestion of the power of death and castration embodied in the skull. Thus one can say that Holbein's painting projects also a material allegory of the psychoanalytic situation.

Lacan does not gloss all the details of the painting. There is one that often escapes the eye of art critics: the little brooch that Jean de Dineville has pinned to his black hat. We may need a magnifying glass to see that the figure it carries is a little skull in gold. It is not only a smaller skull that is almost invisible, but also the slanting orientation of the beret on which it is pinned rigorously parallels the plane of the anamorphic skull. Those two "details," both skulls, one in precious metal, the other in bone, but partly hallucinated, suggest that death traverses the painting in an oblique diagonal. Why does the anamorphic skull project its shadow to the left, whereas the objects referring to the sciences, and allegorizing *vanitas* on the shelves, project their shadows to the right? Holbein implies that the skull's origin is otherworldly: the symbol of death is bathed in the light of a different sun.

Is this other sun Dürer's celebrated "black sun" of melancholy, another variation on the *vanitas* theme? Jean de Dineville was melancholy, ill at ease, and homesick during his stay in London in 1533: thoughts of death were never far from him. He complained in May 1533: "I am the most melancholy, weary and wearisome ambassador that ever was seen." And again in a letter of June 4: "I am, and have been, very weary and wearisome."[22] Besides, the time was rife for huge changes – this was the summer when the British king married an already pregnant Ann Boleyn. Henry VIII was divorcing Catherine of Aragon, thus precipitating a schism with the Catholic Church. Peace reigned for once between France and England, but the situation was fraught with tensions. The

[20] Ibid., p. 89.
[21] Ibid., p. 89.
[22] Quoted in Foister et al., *Holbein's Ambassadors*, p. 16.

two French gentlemen were made to witness this shift and were conscious that disunity was looming, hence, the lute with a broken string and the curious presence of a Lutheran hymnbook.

In Holbein's painting, the rug is a setting for the most precise mathematical instruments of the day, a celestial globe, a shepherd's dial, two quadrants, a small dial, a polyhedral sundial, and a *torquetum*. The lower wooden shelf, with the lute, a book of mathematics, another globe, and the hymnal, remains bare. Above, the oriental rug frames a dialogue between the left hand of Jean de Dineville, which curves downward openly, and the right hand of Georges de Selve, who clutches his gloves and holds his coat. The triangulation of the two men's gazes and the gaze of the Other calls up the setup chosen by Freud for the psychoanalytic session: Freud, seated in his deep armchair, gazes in front of him, while the analysand, lying on the couch, talks or is silent. All those frames and props are necessary if one wants to materialize the locus of the Other – in other words, prepare for an unlocking of unconscious knowledge.

The textual Unconscious at work

A similar triangulation takes place in Henry James's *The Ambassadors*. To understand it, we do not have to put Henry James on Freud's couch: true to Freud's own dictum, James had understood the process by himself. The fact that he decided the make a novel of this shows that a painting is already a text, at least insofar as it can generate innumerable texts. James had seen Holbein's double portrait in London while he was thinking of his novel.[23] This took place when Freud had just published his *Interpretation of Dreams* and when Mary F. S. Hervey had proved definitively that the two characters depicted by Holbein were French ambassadors.[24] We need another novelist, J. M. Coetzee, to verify that James's novel indeed provides a sketch of the Freudian Unconscious. Coetzee analyzes the text itself, letting its semantic structure speak, to show how *The Ambassadors* is a text that works with the Unconscious. He discusses the relationship between form and meaning in passive constructions. Briefly considering the plot of *The Ambassadors*, Coetzee adds:

> In Henry James's *The Ambassadors*, Lambert Strether, out for a day in the country, spies the guilty lovers Chad Newsome and Madame de

---

[23] Adrian Poole, "Introduction" to Henry James, *The Ambassadors*, New York, Penguin Classics, 2008, p. xxxi. Abbreviated as A and page number.

[24] It is likely that James knew Mary Hervey's book, *Holbein's Ambassadors*, as is argued by Adeline R. Tintner in her excellent analysis of this "pictorial source" for *The Ambassadors* in *Henry James and the Lust of the Eyes*, Baton Rouge, Louisiana State University Press, 1993, pp. 88–89.

Vionnet boating down the river. // "It was suddenly as if these figures, or something like them, had been wanted in the picture, had been more or less wanted all day, and had now drifted into sight ..." The passive *wanted*, stressed by repetition, has a double signification: (1) The lovers in the boat reveal that the rural scene, considered as a picture, has in fact been aesthetically incomplete until this moment. (2) The appearance of the lovers solves a mystery, adds the last piece (the piece that was wanting) to a puzzle which Strether, up to this minute, has not wanted to admit he wants solved, since life is so much easier if lies are believed. In the complex play that James performs here, the absence marked by the agentless form is the absence of a drive to find out the truth; and that drive has been suppressed by a hitherto stronger agency, the desire in Strether for the easy, the beautiful, the romantic. What is marked at this instant of the narrative is therefore a moment of self-realization at which ... the moral agent supplants the aesthetic in Strether. And all without Strether's yet being aware of it: the drama takes place in the vacant arena where the agent phrase might have been – as good a syntactic representation of the unconscious one is likely to find.[25]

Space lacks to engage with this detailed discussion of the famous novel, but one will readily concede that, being contemporary with Freud's exploration of the Unconscious, *The Ambassadors* attempts something similar through fiction. Strether, our "hero," is a clumsy "ambassador" sent by a mother, who is also his fiancée, in the hope of bringing back to the fold Chad, the wayward son seduced by European manners. Strether betrays his mission by falling in love twice, and twice without fully realizing it: first with the seductive and playful Miss Gostrey, then with Chad's own lover, the beautiful Madame de Vionnet. The fact that Strether is unaware of his own feelings creates an exquisite game of hide-and-seek with the reader. The reader becomes a psychoanalyst and guesses the truth before the hero faces it, which happens only close to the end, as we have seen.

This game of detection presupposes something like an Unconscious, whether Freudian or not; the importance of the concepts is made manifest by the recurrence of the adjective "unconscious," which is repeated six times in the novel. The truth of Chad and Madame de Vionnet's sexual relationship is something that had been obvious for some time but that Strether could not face, preferring to lie to himself by believing the couple's deliberate equivocations. An indication of this process of revelation is provided early in the novel by an

[25] J. M. Coetzee, "The Agentless Sentence as Rhetorical Device" (1980), in *Doubling the Point: Essays and Interviews*, ed. David Attwell, Cambridge, Harvard University Press, 1992, pp. 174–175.

exchange between Strether and Miss Gostrey. They discuss the consequences that Strether's trip to Paris cannot fail to have on Chad's attitude:

> "You see more in it," he presently returned, "than I."
> "Of course I see *you* in it."
> "Well then you see more in 'me!'"
> "Than you in yourself? Very likely. That's always one's right." (A, p. 69)

This dialogue explains what his novel, like most important novels and paintings, is doing. It presents a knowledge about us that we have not yet discovered, realized, or formalized. This is why knowledge is the only thing that Strether will gain in the end. The outcome of his melancholy trip is that he loses both the prospect of getting rich by marrying Mrs. Newsome or the prospect of mutual love when he refuses to stay in Paris with Maria Gostrey, who has all but offered marriage to him. However, Strether decides to return to Woollett, Massachusetts, choosing a drab bourgeois life devoid of any illusion. It may be that Strether wants to return to die. How can we guess this? The idea is suggested by a comparison with a short story that James wrote at about the same time and in which a Holbein painting figures prominently.

"The Beldonald Holbein," written in 1899, published in 1903, tells the story of the vain and beautiful Lady Beldonald who wants to have her portrait painted by the unnamed narrator, an artist. Lady Beldonald likes being accompanied by a plainer friend or relative whose role it is to serve as a "foil" to her striking looks. When the story begins, she has chosen a very ugly cousin from America, Louisa Brash, invited to England as her obliged confidante. True to her function, she is quite ugly. However, at a party, the French painter Paul Outreau notices the older lady and exclaims: "*Que cette vieille est donc belle!*"[26] (How beautiful is this old crone.) Outreau, whose name clearly suggests *outré*, implies that Louisa Brash has transcended her plainness just because she looks exactly like the portrait of an old woman by Holbein. Louisa Brash soon becomes the object of general attention as she is praised everywhere as a true "Holbein." This triggers the spite and hatred of Lady Beldonald; although she remains polite, she begins resenting Louisa until it becomes a matter of life and death: "The whole thing was to be the death of one or the other of them but they never spoke of it at tea."[27] Finally, their fight to the death is solved when Lady Beldonald sends Louisa back to the United States. The decision comes suddenly, of course, before her portrait can be painted. Having lost her newly discovered source of power and interest, the old cousin soon dies in her provincial American town. The short story ends by extending the metaphor that

[26] Henry James, *The Beldonald Holbein*, London, Macmillan, 1922, p. 5.
[27] Ibid., p. 14.

equated her with a Holbein painting – but this time the painting will be turned against the wall:

> [T]he poor old picture, banished from its museum and refreshed by the rise of no new movement to hang it, was capable of the miracle of a silent revolution; of itself turning, in its dire dishonour, its face to the wall.... Mrs. Munden continues to remind me, however, that this is not the sort of rendering with which, on the other side, after all, Lady Beldonald proposes to content herself. She has come back to the question of her own portrait. Let me settle it then at last. Since she *will* have the real thing – well, hang it, she shall![28]

Her death following her social repudiation leads to the reconciliation between the painter-narrator and the Lady. He will paint her portrait, and we can guess that it will not be a Holbein. However, James had in mind a Holbein when he wrote this; it was the portrait of Lady Margaret Butts painted in 1543 and bought in 1899 by Isabella Stewart Gardner for her famous Boston collection, because we know that Isabella Gardner was a model for Lady Beldonald. The unnamed American city to which Louisa Brash returns to die with her face turned to the blank wall also evokes Woollett, Massachusetts. It is the place to which Strether returns, having failed as an ambassador and having been replaced by the more efficient Jim Pocock. Just as we never learn the name of the mysterious object that is mass-produced in Woollett (could it be a toothpick, as some critics think?) and is the origin of the wealth of the Newsomes, we will never fathom the rationale for his return home. James did not want us to guess what the diminutive object was. His allegorical scheme implies that the Thing (the looming death skull, the *memento mori*) can find an enigmatic counterpart in the part object, the small thing, which is also the unnamable emblem of triumphant capitalism. The painting of the ambassadors and James's novel display the same structure: a parallel mirroring of mementos, from the tiny part object to the looming allegory of death.

Learning from the other side

One possible lesson to be drawn from James's novel is that the loss of everything is not too great a price to pay if one can attain knowledge. This disappointing knowledge goes beyond the "truth" about sexuality and love; it has to comprehend life and death. Strether will return to face death, having rejected all hedonistic seductions. The vision of a good life in Paris remains a fantasy,

---

[28] Ibid., p. 16.

a reminder of a past irrevocably lost. We are just told that he will go back to "a great difference" (A, p. 469), which, with a wink in the direction of Derrida, we can interpret as having to do with writing. No epithalamium is expected, just the unfolding of text as process.

This melancholic truth of the novel is an issue that Freud faced at the end of his life, having settled in London. His stoicism before death allows us to answer a question I have left dangling: From which court do the ambassadors come? Apparently, Freud gave an answer in a letter written in December 1938 to thank the novelist Rachel Berdach, who had sent him *The Emperor, the Sages and Death*, a novel in which death figures prominently. The setting of her novel[29] calls up the historical situation of Holbein's *Ambassadors*. Freud wrote:

> Your mysterious and beautiful book [*The Emperor, the Sages and Death*] has pleased me to an extent that makes me unsure of my judgment. I wonder whether it is the transformation of Jewish suffering or surprise that so much psychoanalytical insight should have existed at the court of the brilliant and despotic Staufer which makes me say that I haven't read anything so substantial and poetically accomplished for a long time.... [W]ho are you? Where did you acquire all the knowledge expressed in your book? Judging by the priority you grant to death, one is led to conclude that you are very young.[30]

Berdach's novel is situated in the thirteenth century, when the Holy Roman Emperor Frederick II and Rabbi Jacob Charif Ben Aron were intimate friends despite everything that separated them. The novel begins and ends with the rabbi's death. His ethical concerns and religious piety clash with the scientific optimism of Friedrich II von Hohenstaufen. At the time, Friedrich was trying to bring together scientists from various parts of the world – Arabs, Greeks, Jews, and Christians – and made them exchange views on medicine, astronomy, and astrology. Three centuries later in London, those sciences would become emblems piled up on two shelves by the worried French ambassadors. In Berdach's novel, given the "heretic" complicity between the ruler and the rabbi at the end, the latter's death is represented as a peaceful surrender to the Angel of Death. Azrael, the Angel of Death who takes him in his wings while the whole world appears to him as deprived of any life, might also be figured twice by Holbein's anamorphic skull and Jean de Dinteville's hat brooch with a gold skull.

---

[29] Rachel Berdach, *The Emperor, The Sages and Death*, trans. William Wolf, New York, Thomas Yoseloff, 1962.
[30] *The Letters of Sigmund Freud*, selected and edited by Ernst L. Freud, London, Dover, 1992, p. 1192.

Freud imagined Rachel Berdach to be a young person because she tended to see death everywhere. His wrong guess baffled Max Schur.[31] In fact, Berdach was middle-aged at the time she wrote the book, although she had drafted it when she was younger, after the loss of a dear friend. Freud's thesis is exposed in *Beyond the Pleasure Principle.* When we are young, we think that death is a result of a sad but common fate, an *anangke* against which there is nothing to do. A young person tends to see death as the ultimate truth of life so as to find comfort in advance, to anticipate future losses. An older person has less to lose and everything to gain by betting on knowledge, which, for Freud, meant "science." Like Strether, they will be less afraid of dying, less tempted to take death as a final answer. And perhaps they will appreciate more readily the intimate connection between death and writing. Freud, who owned a beautiful Egyptian statue of Thoth, the god of writing, knew this: the process of textualization that constitutes the Unconscious is tributary to the death drive, a drive that acquires more and more importance in his metapsychology.

This insight was shared by Joyce when he presented Stephen Dedalus in the Irish national library, meditating on Thoth during a pause in his speech about Shakespeare. In this passage, Stephen muses on literary ghosts, on the power of dead writers once their thoughts have been "coffined" in books:

"Coffined thoughts around me, in mummycases, embalmed in spice of words. Thoth. God of librariries, a birdgod, mooncrowned. And I heard the words of the Egyptian highpriest. *In painted chambers loaded with tilebooks.*

They are still. Once quick in the brains of men. Still: but an itch of death in them, to tell me in my ear a maudlin tale, urge me to wreak their will."[32]

Significantly, Stephen quotes an Irish orator who had portrayed Moses talking to an Egyptian priest as a pointed allusion to the way the Irish were kept in bondage by the English. Moses chose exile with his chosen people but armed with the wisdom gleaned among Egyptian hieroglyphics. One should read the entire episode of *Ulysses:* it shows why a psychoanalytic reading of literature needs the fallacy of biographical criticism (even if, as with Shakespeare, we may wonder whether the man we are discussing is the famous writer of the plays and sonnets) to go beyond it, before reaching a point when any great writer will appear to be "all in all in all of us."[33]

Thus, the knowledge provided by literature, when filtered through psychoanalysis, is not a knowledge about biographical facts, or just about emotions or feelings, or is it about the correlation between fact and theory, or even between affects and ideation. It will not bring new insights about anger or guilt, as when

---

[31] Max Schur, *Freud: Living and Dying,* New York, International Universities Press, 1972, p. 516.
[32] Joyce, *Ulysses,* p. 159.
[33] Ibid., p. 175.

we rail against parents on the couch. It does not consist in a more accurate evocation of passions. It is not a method, but it combines several features that we have observed in all these readings. First, it is a reading of the letter; a literalist approach that is not all that formalist. Then, because a lot of ancient history has been deposited in the letters, the reader turns into a detective searching for clues. At the same time, the reader is not neutral but steeped in a world of affects: anxiety, enjoyment, boredom, and transference love will be broached; issues of sexual identity will be traversed. Finally, the ultimate questions can be posed – not "what is Truth?" because we have seen with Kant and Freud that this question presupposes all the rest – but questions posed by Socrates and Freud, since the beginning: "Is it worth living an unexamined life?"[34]

What are the concepts needed to establish a solid bridge between fiction and so-called real life? What can our dreams and nightmares tell us? Can we pose questions of life and death? Freud did, and this is nowhere more relevant than in an old Jewish joke presented in his book on Jokes and the Unconscious: "The *Schadchen* has assured the suitor that the girl's father is no longer living. After the engagement, it emerges that the father is still alive – and serving a term in prison. The suitor then accuses the *Schadchen*. 'So?' says the *Schadchen*. 'What did I tell you? That you call *living*?'" (JU, p. 44.) Do we call that "living"? Do we know what we mean when we talk about living? The knowledge gained by linking psychoanalysis and literature is admittedly an obscure knowledge. The audacity needed to pose these questions will have an impact on the *form* that the acquisition of any knowledge will take. Like literature, this knowledge touches on the agency of death and writing, a writing that underpins the working of our own psychic apparatus. Such knowledge mobilizes the countless dead speakers, myriad dead words that we revive each time we read a text. Here is a paradoxical knowledge because it is a knowledge that does not know, or at least does not know all. It does not apply to anything nor can it be applied. Instead, it "deploys" and unfolds. By unfolding its images continuously, it transgresses its limits as soon as they appear. If we work psychoanalytically with literature, exploring those darker spaces, we will learn to work with unknowing, which means we will learn to trust our Unconscious. Even if we plunge deeper into an abyssal "Other" scene, there will be a disembodied voice telling us that we can return. And if, having returned all the wiser from our voyage of exploration, we keep on acquiring more knowledge and even turn the process into a method, then we can indeed call ourselves the ambassadors of the Unconscious.

---

[34] I am alluding to Socrates' famous remark that "the unexamined life is not worth living," in Plato's *Apology of Socrates*, 38 a. See Plato, *The Collected Dialogues*, ed. Edith Hamilton and Huntington Cairns, Princeton, Princeton University Press, Bollingen Series, 1973, p. 23.

Abjection

Term proposed by Julia Kristeva to add a third pole to the dichotomy of "subject" and "object." The "abject" is what has been rejected from the symbolic order as impure and debased. Its referents encompass objects such as the skin on heated milk, filth, waste, excrement, and subjects or persons. The term applies to whoever has been excluded as impure from a social group. The novels of Jean Genet offer a powerful meditation on the convoluted dialectics of abjection.

Affect

The term covers the psychoanalytical description of emotions. Since Aristotle, we know about the power of terror, pity, or anger and how these negative affects find a social use via catharsis or purgation. Freud's method was first called a "cathartic method." Starting from the basic opposition between pleasure and displeasure, Freud studies other negative affects, such as anxiety, shame, fear, disgust, and positive affects such as love, joy, compassion, and the "oceanic feeling," the sense of self-dissolution in the world.

Andreas-Salomé, Lou (1861–1937)

Born into an aristocratic German family in Russia, Lou Andreas-Salomé became a devoted friend of Freud, after having briefly been Nietzsche's lover (in a complex triangle with Paul Rée) and then Rilke's lover. She met Freud in 1911, and she decided to devote her life to psychoanalysis. However, Andreas-Salomé had warned Rilke not to begin a therapy that might make him lose his creative neurosis. She wrote many novels, penned several important essays on psychoanalysis (including an essay on anal eroticism praised by Freud), and explored the question of feminine sexuality thoroughly.

Animus/Anima

This couple of related figures has been elaborated by Carl Gustav Jung as two complementary archetypes of the unconscious mind: anima is the female principle, and animus, the male principle. They both coexist in any person's mind. Although the two organize different images and characters, the anima is distinguished by Jung for its four stages or paradigms: Eve, Helen, Mary, and Sophia.

Anxiety

One of the main symptomatic affects dealt with in psychoanalysis, with a recognizable series of bodily manifestations. Freud opposes it to fear, which has an immediate object, whereas anxiety would have no clear object, or very distant sources of worry, such as the fear of dying. Lacan reverses this opposition and argues that anxiety is an affect that never deceives. It has a specific object: the lack, absence as such, or the pure form of a-symbolizable objects.

Anzieu, Didier (1923–1999)

A French psychoanalyst who had the distinction of being the son of "Aimée," the paranoid patient treated by Lacan and discussed in his dissertation. Anzieu's original contributions to psychoanalysis bore on Freud's self-analysis, on the study of groups, and on the concept of the "skin-ego." He also discussed literature, most notably Beckett's work and painters such as Francis Bacon.

Bataille, Georges (1897–1962)

A French writer, anthropologist, sociologist, and economist, and a dissident of Surrealism who opposed Breton's rigorism in the name of "base materialism." He was psychoanalyzed by Doctor Adrien Borel in 1925, learning to write freely about his erotic obsessions. His essays offer a materialist critique of Freud's dualism. The concepts that he coined, such as the "accursed share," "sovereignty," and "expenditure," combine Hegel, Nietzsche, and Freud and deeply influenced Jacques Lacan, whose second wife happened to have been Bataille's first wife.

Bettelheim, Bruno (1903–1990)

The contested personality of Bettelheim became public news after his death. He had had the rare experience of knowing internment in the Dachau and Buchenwald concentration camps in 1938–1939. Freed by amnesty, he emigrated to America, where he founded a school in Chicago. His work on fairy tales, *The Uses of Enchantment*, is strictly Freudian. He showed that dark or horrific stories of injustice, abandonment, and mutilation were not dangerous but rather trained children to cope with real life problems: they fostered emotional growth. He drew on his experience as a camp survivor to tackle autism in *The Empty Fortress*. He committed suicide in 1990.

Bion, Wilfred Ruprecht (1897–1979)

Born in India of an Indian mother and a British father, Bion moved to England as a child. He became a disciple of Melanie Klein but rejected parts of her dogmatic approach to elaborate a more philosophical system detailing links between "beta elements" (raw affective experiences) and "alpha elements" (thoughts that are available to the subject). Besides his theory of thinking, Bion elaborated an original theory of group dynamics. He was Samuel Beckett's psychoanalyst and wrote several novels himself. He had a large impact in California, Argentina, and Brazil.

Bonaparte, Marie (1882–1962)

A distant descendant of Napoléon Bonaparte, Princess Marie Bonaparte became a disciple of Freud in 1925, when she was still preoccupied with her frigidity. She became one of the main founders of the French psychoanalytic association. Bonaparte's fortune and connections helped Freud emigrate to London during the Nazi period. Her work explored feminine sexuality, the works of Poe, and her own autobiography.

Castration

For Freud, this is the irrational fear of most children as a consequence of the Oedipus complex. Boys fear that their father or a figure of authority will cut off their penis; girls fear having lost an already severed penis. Note that Freud, who never lived on a farm, confused castration (the ablation of testicles) and eviration (getting rid of the genitals). Such a confusion does not pose a problem because the idea of castration remains an infantile sexual theory, or a threat, and never a fact. Thus, Freud speaks of female castration, the fiction that women lack something essential, which can be compensated by having children, for instance. Melanie Klein uses the term in a broader sense, talking about the castration of the breast as a primal deprivation.

Cathartic Method

The term used by Aristotle to describe the therapeutic function of tragedy, which works by the purgation (*catharsis*) of passions. It was extensively discussed by Jakob Bernays, the uncle of Freud's wife, in 1857 and 1880. It was Breuer who used the term for the first time, followed by Freud, in their *Studies on Hysteria*. There, language was proposed as a tool for the possible "abreaction" (the experience of reliving a strong emotion) of affects.

Cixous, Hélène (Born 1937)

Born in Algeria to an Ashkenazy mother and a Sephardi father, Hélène Cixous taught in Bordeaux and Paris, where she was one of the founders of the experimental university at Vincennes (Paris-8). Her abundant work is comprised of novels, plays, and essays on literary criticism. In her manifesto "The Laugh of the Medusa" (1975), Cixous introduced the term of "feminine writing" so as to reject dogmatic Freudianism and dogmatic feminism (because Joyce and Genet are said to be representatives of it). She has incorporated in an original manner the teachings of Lacan and Derrida.

Culture/Civilization

Freud calls "civilization" (*Kultur*) the sum of shared human achievements, which defines a collective spirit for a given period. Its social institutions and archives constitute a specific history. Civilization entails a renouncing of a number of archaic urges, drives, and desires. Because it asks too much from its human subjects, they often resent it, for they feel trapped and constrained by it. Lacan pushes the term toward anthropology and sees in its basic rules as organizing exchanges of words, people, goods, and values – the making of the "Symbolic."

Deferred Action (*Nachträglichkeit*)

A type of retrospective arrangement of the past, exhibited most markedly by hysterics, but with universal application. Deferred action implies the idea of a reinscription of previously repressed excitations, often sexual in nature. Its temporality is thus not linear but recursive and complicates the work on memory that psychoanalysis presupposes. It also pertains to the temporality of literature.

Derrida, Jacques (1930–2004)

Born into a Jewish family in Algeria, Jacques Derrida came to Paris as a student of the Ecole Normale Supérieure, where he later taught philosophy. Derrida is best known for having ushered in deconstruction, a philosophical survey of a metaphysical tradition defined by its rejection of writing in what he called "phonocentrism." His wide-ranging investigations examined Freudian texts while applying some of their procedures to literature and philosophy. His work provides a sharp but constructive critique of Lacanian theories of the sign, language, and literature.

Desire

Freud began his career by stressing the agency of unconscious desire: a dream is the manifestation of indestructible desire. Desire is then either *Wusnch* (wish) or *Begierde* (desire, craving, in the philosophical tradition). The term is a key concept for Lacan for whom desire cannot be reduced to neither biological need nor an infinite demand of love but remains as a principle of negativity that sets the dynamics of subject-formation in motion.

Drive

The term drive (*Trieb*) has often been mistranslated as "instinct," which misses its specificity by reducing it to Darwinism. Freud generally distinguishes between *Instinkt* and *Trieb*; the latter corresponds to a general force accounting for the upsurge of erotic energy in human beings. Freud rigorously defined the term in 1915 and analyzed it according to its pressure, source, object, and aim. In the 1930s, Freud opted for a stronger dualism between the erotic drive (Eros) and the death drive (Thanatos), a notion that has been rejected by some psychoanalysts. Lacan saw in the death drive the model for the structure of all drives.

Family Romance

A phrase coined by Freud and Otto Rank to describe a process of idealization by neurotics. They imagine that they have had better parents, whether of noble origins or endowed with heroic features. Most "heroes" of various cultures exhibit similar features of having been abandoned, exposed, or found somewhere, before being adopted by a humbler family (Moses, Oedipus, Paris, Romulus, Lohengrin, and Christ). Neurotics participate in the foundational myths of various cultures and religions.

Fantasy

Early on, Freud realized that the memories of hysterics were partially fabricated, and all did not record traces of real abuse. Fantasy is thus both understood in opposition to reality and seen as a systematic unconscious construction that underpins reality. Fantasy is organized: it often boils down to the subject being engaged in a certain mode of access to pleasure, a stylized scenario that can be written in a single sentence. A fantasy will then mesh with other fantasies to create the imaginary of a given subject. Fantasies are not solipsistic, however, as they function as frames through which subjects relate to the world and to others.

Ferenczi, Sandor (1873–1933)

The main Hungarian psychoanalyst, and Freud's closest disciple, whose example in Hungary inspired Melanie Klein, Geza Roheim, and Michael Balint. Ferenczi's many essays and rich correspondence with Freud explore clinical issues, such as countertransference, a term that he elaborated in 1908. He accompanied Freud and Jung during their visit to America in 1909. Ferenczi revised Freud's seduction theory and came close to supporting Rank's dissident theories but never renounced his allegiance to Freud. His main work, *Thalassa: A Theory of Genitality* (1924), examines the wish to return to the womb.

Fliess, Wilhelm (1858–1928)

Freud's closest friend during the years of Freud's elaboration of psychoanalysis, Fliess was a physician in Berlin and focused his research on the links between the nose and sexual organs. He met Freud in 1887, and they exchanged letters for almost two decades. Freud owes to him many concepts (such as the idea of bisexuality) but above all the possibility of conducting a form of auto-analysis via their correspondence. Fliess became jealous of Freud and accused him of plagiarism, which provoked their breakup.

Freud, Anna (1895–1982)

Anna was Freud's sixth and last child, the only one who followed her father's example and became a psychoanalyst. At 18, she was courted by Ernest Jones during a trip to London with her father, who prevented anything from happening. She remained devoted to her father, never married, and was analyzed twice by him. All her life, she was Freud's confidante and nurse. She became a noted child psychoanalyst. Later, she developed a version of Freudian doctrine that took the ego as the main site of psychoanalytical work, as one sees in her main work, *The Ego and the Mechanisms of Defense* (1936), whose theses clashed with the British school, led by Melanie Klein.

Freud, Sigmund (1856–1939)

Freud was born in Moravia but moved with his family to Vienna in 1860. He was a remarkable medical student but discovered the psychosomatic disease called "hysteria" when he went to Paris to study with Charcot in 1885. When he came back to Vienna, he met hostility or indifference. He settled in 19 Berggasse, where he resided until he was forced to leave Vienna in 1938. His major book, *The Interpretation of Dreams*, published in 1899 but dated 1900, combines self-analysis via his own dreams and the description of a general mechanism: dreams exemplify the Unconscious, understood as having been produced by the repression of illicit desires. Freud's immense corpus of psychoanalytical texts is rendered in English in twenty-four volumes called the "Standard Edition," under the supervision of James Strachey. It was first published in London by Virginia and Leonard Woolf's Hogarth Press.

Groddeck, Georg (1866–1934)

Groddeck was a German physician interested in psychosomatic phenomena. His books strongly influenced Freud, above all, the *Book of the Id* (1923) but also his whimsical novel *The Soulseeker, a psychoanalytical novel* (1921). Groddeck would combine in an original manner suggestion, massage, hypnosis, and psychoanalytic treatment. His fulsome and enthusiastic works show how man is inhabited by the Unconscious and how organic diseases can be cured or helped by psychological analysis—and by laughter.

Hysteria

One of the main neuroses analyzed by Freud, who invented psychoanalysis when treating Viennese hysterics after having been Charcot's student and disciple in Paris. As soon as he came back to Vienna, Freud shocked his audience when he made room for male hysteria, contradicting the common opinion that it was only a feminine disease. This type of structure can include any speaking subject divided by desire. Clinical hysteria as in the Dora case consists of exhibiting an unsatisfied desire, or the horror of being the object of another's desire.

Id (*Es*)

A term introduced in 1923 by Georg Groddeck in his *Book of the Id*, then immediately added to Freud's theory of the drives when he replaced a first division between the Conscious, the Unconscious, and the Preconscious, with a new trinity: the ego, the superego, and the id. The id is a reservoir of unconscious drives, including the death drive and Eros. Freud ends lecture XXXI of his *New Introductory Lectures on Psycho-Analysis* by stating: "Wo Es war, soll Ich werden," ("Where Id was, there Ego shall be"). It can be interpreted as leading to an "ego psychology," or, as Lacan thought, as sketching a grammar of pronouns, one neutral and the other subjective, the "I" intervening on the site of an "it" that speaks through language ("It speaks").

Imaginary (the)

One of the three "orders" or realms distinguished by Lacan along with the Real and the Symbolic, it corresponds to the essential connection between the ego and the specular image discovered during the "mirror stage." The term is then generalized to include a linguistic dimension as well as all personal and cultural identifications. It is also the site of ideological formations as explored by Louis Althusser.

Imago

A term introduced by Jung in 1911 to refer to images used by people to shape their personalities by identifying unconsciously with key figures of their families (father, mother, elder sibling) or archetypes of the collective unconscious. Freud, acknowledging Jung's coining, used the term at the time, especially when founding the review *Imago* in 1912 with Hanns Sachs and Otto Rank. *American Imago* was the title chosen by Freud and Hanns Sachs in 1939 when they launched an American journal of psychoanalysis, which also explored anthropology, art history, culture, and mythology.

Jones, Ernest (1878–1958)

A Welsh psychoanalyst, founder of the British school of psychoanalysis, and author of Freud's first biography. His book on *Hamlet and Oedipus* was published in 1910 and popularized Freud's thesis about the Oedipus complex in literature. He was at one time very close to Anna Freud. His numerous essays developed the idea of applied psychoanalysis to domains such as art, literature, religion, and culture.

Jouissance

Lacan's translation of Freud's "pleasure" (*Lust*), pushed closer to a sexual limit (orgasm) and to the more radical enjoyment at the cusp between pleasure and pain. The term has legal connotations and economic implications, because it implies the rights an owner may have over objects or persons. Lacan opposes it to desire insofar as desire accepts the function of castration. Jouissance stays undivided and can be linked to a feminine position via the "Jouissance of the Other" that Lacan identifies in mystics and in writers such as Marguerite Duras.

Jung, Carl Gustav (1875–1961)

Jung had begun his career as a psychiatrist in Zurich, experimenting with word association, when he found a kindred spirit while reading Freud. The years 1906–1913 saw an intense exchange of theories and concepts between the two thinkers. Freud wanted Jung to be his successor so as to move psychoanalysis out of a Jewish ghetto. However, the differences in their positions were enormous: Jung was more religious than Freud, and he disliked the stress on sexuality and biology. Their paths split, and Jung coined terms such as "imago," "animus" and "anima," and "archetypes." If he has lost most of his clinical followers, his readings of literary and religious texts are still influential.

Klein, Melanie (1882–1960)

Born in Vienna, Klein moved to Budapest where she discovered Freud's ideas in 1910. She started an analysis with Ferenczi and analyzed her own five-year-old son. She moved back to Berlin in 1921 and to London in 1926, where she dominated the psychoanalytic scene. She brought several innovations to Freudian psychoanalysis, changing the conception of the inception of the Oedipus complex and elaborating different "positions," such as the "schizoid-paranoid" position. Her influence led to the rise of the object-relation school, which was opposed by the ego psychologists led by Anna Freud. A remarkable clinician, Klein kept refining her concepts, such as "envy" and "gratitude."

Kristeva, Julia (born 1941)

Born in Bulgaria, Kristeva moved to France and became an influential literary critic and psychoanalyst. Her works combine cultural theory influenced by Roland Barthes and Mikhail Bakhtin with feminism and psychoanalysis. The concepts that she has popularized, such as intertextuality, abjection, and the semiotic, have had a huge impact on psychoanalysis-oriented literary criticism.

Lacan, Jacques (1901–1981)

Lacan blended philosophy, mostly Spinoza and Hegel, literature (he was close to the Surrealists and wrote poetry) and psychoanalysis. He began as a psychiatrist and first published papers on hysteria and paranoia. His 1932 doctoral thesis was an analysis of a case of paranoia. Lacan came to psychoanalysis via the clinic of psychoses. He then explored the "mirror stage." Having spent two months training with Jung in 1930, which blacklisted him, Lacan came to hold strong opinions, which had him excluded from the International Psychoanalytical Association. Under the motto of a "return to Freud," Lacan led the battle against dogmatic Freudians by using linguistics as a new tool. He combined a Heideggerian mediation on being as language with a rhetoric of the Unconscious founded on the couple signifier/signified. The Unconscious was "the discourse of the Other" but structured as a language. In the last decade of his long and inventive career, Lacan focused on James Joyce so as to go beyond the Trinitarian scheme of his three interlocked realms of the Real, the Symbolic, and the Imaginary, to introduce the Symptom. The Symptom would embody a subject's singularity and should be simply enjoyed. Psychoanalytic cures had to work through puns and linguistic equivocation, following the example of Joyce's *Finnegans Wake*.

Laplanche, Jean (1924–2012)

Laplanche was all at once a famous wine maker in Burgundy, a philosopher who taught psychoanalysis, and a psychoanalyst. He clarified many concepts of Freud, including the seduction theory, which he expanded into drama stemming from the Otherness of desire and not necessarily from actual sexual traumas. He negotiated between Lacan, from whom he took the notion of drive as opposed to instinct, and the classical Freudians. His book on the German poet Hölderlin remains a model of literary analysis influenced by psychoanalysis.

Libido

Sexual energy as defined by Freud that can only be desexualized through sublimation. It finds its culmination in the figure of Eros in *Beyond the Pleasure Principle*: here, it becomes identical with the drive to live and survive. It can branch off into an "ego-libido" and an "object-libido."

Marcuse, Herbert (1898–1979)

A Marxist philosopher from the Frankfurt school, Marcuse moved to the United States in 1934. He followed Adorno's critique of the adaptive and meliorist drift of American psychoanalysis in the 1950s and modified Freud's theory of the drives in *Eros and Civilization* (1955) moreover. He coined the phrase of "repressive desublimation" to argue that postwar mass culture had reinforced political repression by condoning sexual provocations. He delivered a scathing critique of the "one-dimensional" nature of life in bourgeois society, calling for a renewed and more authentic rebellion against conformity.

Mauron, Charles (1899–1966)

Trained as a scientist, he became a translator of English authors. A close friend of Roger Fry and of the members of the Bloomsbury group, he launched psycho-criticism in the thirties, a structural method of reading canonical authors by studying the recurrent or "obsessive" metaphors that would constitute a private mythology.

Mimetic Desire

An expression used by French literary critic René Girard to describe a triangular structure in canonical novels in which one character needs the model of another person's desire to fall in love with a given person or want to possess a given object. Desire is thus always mediated by a previous desire. The desiring subject identifies with the other person chosen as a model. Therefore, there is no "natural" object of desire. This analysis is indebted to Lacan's concept of a "mirror stage."

Mirror Stage

Henri Wallon was the first to study the effect of one's reflection in the shaping of personality. In 1936, Lacan transformed this into a Freudian "stage," to be traversed to stabilize one's sense of identity. The process shapes the ego through the subject's identification with her image in a mirror. As the mirror stage only produces an imaginary sense of fullness and completion of the reflected being, Lacan insists on the precariousness of ego-identity and highlights the aggression often triggered by the recognition of a rival image.

Mourning

Often contrasted by Freud with melancholia, the process of mourning (*Trauerarbeit*) implies that after a certain period of time, the subject has processed a given loss and is ready to move on and invest in new objects of desire. Because such a process entails "killing the dead person," it can be refused by the subject. If it is halted, blocked, or inhibited, one obtains the melancholic position: the lost object cannot be abandoned when the ego narcissistically identifies with the lost object.

Name-of-the-Father

A key Lacanian concept linking the cornerstone of the Symbolic realm (going from one's father's name to the Name of God) and the resolution of the Oedipian drama (the phrase sounds as the "No of the Father"). Given this degree of condensation, Lacan often calls it the "paternal metaphor."

Object a

Object a is Lacan's term for the part-object of Kleinian metapsychology. Generated by a reading of Plato's *Symposium*, in which the object is described as "agalma," hidden, and precious ornaments that make Socrates desirable, its appearance is a condition for the emergence of love and desire. Object a is thus both the object of all fantasies and the absent cause of desire, a pure remainder that will be dropped or will "fall" as mere junk or refuse at the end of the talking cure. Lacan provides a limited list of objects a – the breast, the face, the gaze, and the voice; later, he adds the "nothing" and the "phallus" to the list.

Oedipus Complex

This is the "complex" combination of sexual desire and murderous hatred developed in children toward their parents that is incompatible with the foundational law of culture and must therefore be repressed. This inevitable repression conditions the elaboration of unconscious wishes, hence the development of the Unconscious as such. Later theoreticians have proposed the idea of an "Electra complex" and even of a "Jocasta complex" to differentiate the evolution of male and female subjects, whereas Freud talks about a universal Oedipus complex as "nuclear complex" explaining all the rest. The concept of Oedipus was questioned by Deleuze and Guattari in their canonical *Anti-Oedipus*. For Lacan, the Oedipus complex is Freud's main myth, along with that of the Father of the Horde in *Totem and Taboo*.

Overdetermination

Freud used this term to explain why dream images or dream words have to be interpreted at several levels: each of them is generated by a multiple determination. In other words, each element of a dream has been caused by several chains of associations. Louis Althusser later implemented the concept to describe how multiple chains of rational determination cause historical events.

Paranoia

This is a term Freud inherited from classical psychiatry (Kraepelin) to describe the loss of reality one experiences in psychosis with usual symptoms of persecution delirium and self-aggrandizing delusions, often religious in kind. The case of Schreber is Freud's main analysis of a case of paranoia. Melanie Klein uses the term to define a developmental position often distinguished from the depressive position and coupled with schizophrenia as in the "schizo-paranoid" position that marks the earliest moments of a baby's psychic life.

Perversion

The idea of perversion is founded on a deviation from "normal" sexual acts, which begs the question of the "norm" and contradicts Freud's idea of a "polymorphous perverse disposition" traversed by all children. For Freud, the norm is not genital heterosexuality, because he did not consider homosexuality as pathological. The "norm" is human desire marked by the law of castration. Hence, fetishism, masochism, and sadism are the main perversions because all three attempt to bypass this law. "Perverse" also generates "perverseness" or "perversity," terms not to be confused with perversion. They mean a wish to behave against acceptable norms or to do the contrary of what one should be doing, as shown in Edgar Allan Poe's "The Imp of the Perverse." Such contrarian impulses may lead to the delusion that there can be a "gratuitous act," as exemplified by André Gide's Lafacadio, who murders a man in a train for no particular reason.

Pfister, Oskar (1873–1956)

A Swiss Lutheran minister and psychoanalyst, he engaged Freud on the question of religion in a famous controversy around *The Future of an Illusion*. He remained a disciple of Freud in spite of their difference of opinion and refused to follow Jung, with whom he had worked. He thought that Freudian psychoanalysis and Christianity were compatible. He wrote books on art, faith, and pedagogy, which were considered from a psychoanalytic point of view.

Phallus

A symbol representing a tumescent male sexual organ, often displayed in gardens and in front of houses in ancient Greece and Rome, and used by Freud and the main theoreticians of psychoanalysis as a reminder that psychic castration is a necessary stage and that the representation of phallic power is a way of warding off ancient terrors. If the phallus is a key concept in Freudian psychoanalysis, it does not mean that Freud fell into the trap of "phallocentrism." The phallus is linked with the idea of a female "castration": the penis never existed in women's nature or bodies and, hence, can be relegated to the domain of fantasy. The "phallus" (not to be confused with the penis as organ) is a cultural construct preventing real or imagined threats of castration. The phallus functions in a symbolic logic working via substitutes, as we learn from Freud who shows that a child can play the role of the phallus for a mother. A sports car or chiseled abdominals can have a phallic function for a man.

Play

Term used by D. W. Winnicott to sketch the space of creativity as opposed to reality. Playing first derives from an exchange between inner worlds and outside reality, when the imagination reshapes the world. Playing as an activity brackets out anxiety, whether for adults or children. A psychoanalytic treatment should enhance the sense of playing with one's past and not focus on the unveiling of a tragic truth.

Psychosis

Freud used a term that had been current since 1845 to define madness when it entailed a loss of reality, as encountered in schizophrenia, paranoia, and manic-depressive syndromes. Psychosis is usually differentiated from neurosis, under the assumption that neurosis does not create a delusional universe, and is more curable than psychosis. Melanie Klein supposed an early form of psychosis in infants when she postulated the sequence of a paranoid-schizoid stage and a depressive stage between the ages of three and six months when infants attempt to make sense of the world. Lacan began his career by studying clinical psychosis. He used the term "foreclosure" (Freud's *Verwerfung*) as a mechanism allowing for a comprehension of psychosis: a primary signifier, quite often the name of the father, cannot be symbolized, hence will return in the Real as hallucination or delirium.

Rank, Otto (1884–1939)

Rank, born Rosenfeld, had been self-taught as a young man, and he was only twenty-one years old when he gave Freud his first book, *The Artist*, which impressed Freud. Soon, Rank would become the preferred disciple of the Viennese circle. In 1924, Rank's *Trauma of Birth* nevertheless signaled that he was taking some distance from orthodox Freudianism, because for him everything hinged around the separation from the mother, much before the Oedipus complex. He was the first to break with Freud's exclusive attention to the father, an idea that would impact both the Kleinians and the Lacanians. Sensing "heresy," Jones and then Freud excluded him. He had a complex relationship with Anais Nin. After moving to the United States, Rank continued a brilliant career outside the official institutions.

Reality / Real

Freud's dualism opposes the reality principle to the pleasure principle from the point of view of psychic reality. For psychic reality, there is often no difference between real events, memories, and hallucinations. Hence, reality is not a stable foundation for psychoanalysis but has to be constructed consciously. It does not exist for the Unconscious, which is why the Unconscious does not know time or death, the mortal limit set for real human life. Lacan differentiated the term "Reality," a world of images and representations projected by the ego and made up of wishes, fantasies, and delusions, from the "Real" as a pure outside intractably resistant to symbolization and reached as the "Thing." The Real is commonly experienced by psychotic patients via hallucinations. Psychosis is defined as the return to the Real of what cannot be symbolized, as one sees with Schreber's "impossible" father.

Reich, Wilhelm (1897–1957)

Best known as the founder of Freudo-Marxism, Reich attempted to combine the teachings of Freud and those of Marxism. His 1927 book *The Function of Orgasm* had a huge impact on the counterculture of the sixties. Reich saw a revolutionary potential in the orgasmic release from repression. An unleashing libido was a weapon against neurosis and capitalism. His position was the exact opposite of Jung's rejection of sexuality, but like Jung he soon endowed his genital revolution with a mystical dimension. He can be seen either as a martyr of antipsychiatry, excluded from psychoanalytic institutions because of his political views, or as a delirious paranoiac. He moved to the United States, where he was later accused of fraud for having invented and sold "orgone boxes" – accumulators of cosmic energy supposed to cure cancer. He was sentenced to two years in prison, his publications were burned by order of the court, and he died in jail of heart failure.

Repetition

Appearing first under the guise of the *Widerholungszwang* in Freud, the neurotic "compulsion to repeat," repetition becomes a key concept in *Beyond the Pleasure Principle*. The repressed content seeks to return; hence, it creates a symptom. The compulsion to repeat neurotically – that is, to recreate situations that can be embarrassing or disagreeable – led Freud to the hypothesis of a death drive. This is also a clinical principle, because transference to the analyst leads the analysand to repeat symptomatic behavior, which can then allow patients to understand their nature.

Reverie

A term used by W. R. Bion to describe an ability that most mothers have but some lack (with negative effects for their children) of sensing intuitively what their infants feel or experience before language by letting their fantasies accompany the child's development. This maternal empathy can become a tool for the psychoanalyst who will play along with the patient's images and fantasies.

Sharpe, Ella Freeman (1875–1947)

Sharpe began her career as a teacher of English literature in England, having been introduced to the reading of Shakespeare very early by her father. She went to Berlin, where she had an analysis with Hanns Sachs, and when she came back to London, she joined the British Psychoanalytical Society and followed the teachings of Melanie Klein. Her work concerns both clinical issues (particularly sublimation, transference, and countertransference) and literature (she wrote several articles on *Hamlet* and on poetry).

Signifier

A term borrowed by Lacan from Ferdinand de Saussure's structural linguistics also used by Jean-Paul Sartre in *Sketch of a Theory of Emotions* (1938) so as to define the material part of language used in a psychoanalytic cure; within a word, it is one half of the meaning (or signified), and it is conveyed either as a verbal phoneme or as written sign. If psychoanalysis works by and through language in the "talking cure," the materiality of the signifier will precipitate unconscious meanings and associations. Psychoanalysts work through equivocations that send back key signifiers to the analysand in an effort to let them grasp hidden undertones. Furthermore, Lacan would repeat that "a signifier represents a subject for another signifier," thus highlighting the determining impact of language on subjectivity.

Sinthome

Lacan used an old French word already found in Rabelais to describe James Joyce's position as the symptom of literature. The term combines sin, tomes, Aquinas (saint Thomas d'Aquin), and symptom. The sinthome consists in a re-knotting of the registers of the Real, the Symbolic, and the Imaginary, thus ultimately providing permanence and subsistence to the writer's ego.

Slip

Flaubert's *Dictionary of Received Ideas* would have it that a slip is always Freudian. To be preferred, in any case, to "parapraxis," the cumbersome rendering of *Fehlleistung* ("faulty functioning") – an umbrella expression covering slips of the tongue, slips of the pen, misreadings, mis-rememberings, forgetting of proper names, screen memories, and even superstitions, all the inadvertent actions that betray a symptomatic origin. Freud's *Psychopathology of Everyday Life* gives a very entertaining compilation of parapraxes, with subtle interpretations of those common psychic disturbances.

Sublimation

Freud's term for the transformation of sexual drives into acceptable social achievements. For instance, a boy's youthful sadism may lead him to choose a medical profession and become a surgeon. This process underpins the logic of art or science as they sublimate childish interrogations about sexuality. The study of Leonardo da Vinci led Freud to speculate that Leonardo's *libido sciendi* had blocked his artistic creativity. Is sublimation a desexualization or a radical transformation of the object of libido? Lacan offered a critique of this notion, whereas Jean Laplanche found it operative.

Symbolic

The Symbolic is Lacan's term for cultural phenomena organized as an unconscious linguistic system. The concept is extrapolated from Claude Lévi-Strauss's structural anthropology in which a culture is read as a system of signs, words, and practices through which unconscious prohibitions underpin social division and the management of goods. Art, marriage regulations, science, religion, and mythologies are all symbolic systems. Altogether they constitute the Symbolic whose laws determine the makeup of a given culture. The term of symbolism is often used by Jung in a different sense to describe powerful and recurrent images found in all cultures that belong to the class of archetypes, the alphabet of a collective Unconscious.

Symptom

A psychoanalytic symptom is not like a medical symptom, because it belongs to the grey zone of "psychosomatic" manifestations. Hence, Dora's cough in Freud's analysis of a case of hysteria is not the sign of a bad cold but of her unconscious identification with her father, whose sexual life she imagines to be limited to oral sex. Neurotic symptoms are formations of the Unconscious and can be interpreted; everyday parapraxes, such as forgetting the name of someone whom one is introducing, are common symptomatic manifestations of the psychopathology of everyday life described by Freud.

Thing

A term introduced by Freud in the *Project for a Scientific Psychology* to define a degree of exteriority of objects that cannot be processed by consciousness and later used by Lacan to conceptualize the process of sublimation. Sublimation will be defined in Seminar VII as "raising an object to the dignity of a Thing."

Transitional Object

Term invented by Winnicott to describe objects that children often choose for comfort, such as a teddy bear, and that adults use as well when they are playing. A transitional object is both real and imaginary at the same time, and it helps cope with separation, as in Freud's example of a bobbin his one-year-old grandson played with, hiding it and making it reappear, all the while saying *fort ... da ...* ("away ... here") so as to control the pain of his mother's absence.

Trauma

Often used by Freud in the context of "traumatic neurosis," the term refers to a psychic "wound" that cannot heal and, hence, triggers endless repetitions. The notion of trauma implies a break in the integrity of the psychic apparatus, to the point that it cannot not absorb, register, or process the shocking or excessive event. If such excess is neither controllable nor even fully perceptible, it generates either intolerable anxiety or endlessly repetitive symptoms.

Uncanny

A term meaning roughly "uncomfortably unfamiliar" in German and introduced by Ernest Jentsch in 1906. It was taken over and systematized by Freud to make sense of a variety of psychic manifestations, from the fear of dead people, ghosts, and doubles, to the involuntary repetition of certain actions. It is most obviously deployed in fantastic literature. The term itself is double because it superimposes the "homely" and the "unhomely," both working together to produce anxiety.

Unconscious, (The)

Freud's key concept, often surprisingly mistaken for the "subconscious," which is merely a subcategory. It looks like a logical contradiction, because "consciousness" excludes by definition what is not conscious, which was Jean-Paul Sartre's justification of his repudiation of the term. The German *Unbewusst* adds a nuance unavailable in English, namely that the Unconscious has to do with knowledge, with the root of *wissen* ("to know"). Freud often speaks of the "unconscious knowledge" contained in dreams, for instance. Freud describes it at length in his metapsychological essays: the Unconscious does not know time, negation, or death. It has a certain dimension, yet the Unconscious itself seems unaware of that feature. Lacan will push the concept to the *une-bévue* so as to insist on the parapractical side of the Unconscious, even when defined as structured as a language.

Von Hartmann, Karl Robert Eduard (1842–1906)

Von Hartmann was a German philosopher who published *The Philosophy of the Unconscious* in 1869, a book that contributed to the dissemination of the concept of the Unconscious. There, von Hartmann produced the synthesis of two previous philosophies: that of Arthur Schopenhauer, who saw the universe underpinned by a "Will" defined as an obscure ground for all existence, and that of Hegel, whose history of consciousness left a great agency to unconscious desire. His work had a strong impact on Jung, whereas Nietzsche thought that his "philosophy of unconscious irony" was the work of a mere "parodist," as he writes in *Untimely Meditations*.[1]

---

[1] Friedrich Nietzsche, *Untimely Meditations*, trans. R. J. Hollingdale, Cambridge University Press, 1983, pp. 108–109.

Winnicott, Donal Woods (1896–1971)

Winnicott was a pediatrician and a child psychoanalyst at the Paddington Green Children's Hospital in London for forty years. He rose to prominence at the time of the conflict between Anna Freud and Melanie Klein. He belonged to the "Middle Group," even if he acknowledged the crucial influence of Klein, with whom he remained in dialogue. Having come to psychoanalysis from pediatrics, Winnicott treated his work with children as central, leading him to invent several concepts, such as "holding," "transitional object," and "the true self." His idea of a "good-enough mother" was a de-idealized version of the role of the mother, finding in the ordinary mother a usable model. A central theme running through his work is the idea of play: for Winnicott, playing was the key to emotional and psychological well-being. He held that in playing, people are entirely their true selves. Psychoanalysis had to be conceived as a mode of playing. Playing could also be seen at work in the use of a "transitional object," because it is both real and imaginary at the same time.

Witz (joke)

The English translation of *Witz* as "joke" misses one part of the sense of the German term, which is closer to *mot d'esprit* in French. In Freud's famous analysis of the "joke-work," he shows how "wit" at the same time reveals and conceals repressed meanings, whether sexual or aggressive. Fundamentally, the book on jokes demonstrates that the Unconscious is "witty."

Žižek, Slavoj (born 1949)

A prolific philosopher from the school of Ljubljana, Slovenia, Žižek has authored many books and essays that have popularized Lacanian psychoanalysis as a mode of cultural critique. Blending Marx, Hegel, and Lacan, Žižek often discusses films, television series, science-fiction novels, and icons of popular culture. Taking his cue from the later Lacan, his dissertation on psychoanalysis supervised by Jacques-Alain Miller contains the seeds of all his subsequent work: a Hegelian version of Lacanian psychoanalysis combined with a political critique of ideology and a revisited communism presented as a radical alternative to bourgeois liberalism.

Bibliography

Adams, Laurie Schneider. (1993). *Art and Psychoanalysis*. New York: Harper and Collins.

Adams, Parveen, ed. (2003). *Art: Sublimation or Symptom*. New York: The Other Press.

Agamben, Giorgio. (1999). *Remnants of Auschwitz, The Witness and the Archive*, trans. Daniel Heller-Roazen. New York: Zone Books.

Antelme, Robert. (1957). *L'Espèce Humaine*. Paris: Gallimard.

(1992). *The Human Race*, trans. Jeffrey Haight and Annie Mahler. Marlboro, VT: Marlboro Press.

Aristotle. (1967). *Prior Analytics*, trans. Hugh Tredennick. Cambridge: Harvard University Press.

(1982). *The "Art" of Rhetoric*, trans. J. H. Freese. Cambridge: Harvard University Press.

Atherton, James S. (1959). *The Books at the Wake*. London: Faber.

Aubert, Jacques, ed. (1987). *Joyce avec Lacan*. Paris: Navarin.

Barthes, Roland. (1977). *Image-Music-Text*, trans. Stephen Heath. London: Fontana-Collins.

(1980). *La Chambre Claire. Note sur la photographie*. Paris: Gallimard/Seuil.

(1981). *Camera Lucida*, trans. Richard Howard. New York: Noonday Press.

(2012). *Mythologies*, trans. Richard Howard and Anette Lavers. New York: Hill and Wang.

Baudelaire, Charles. (1961). *Oeuvres Complètes*, vol. 1. Paris: Gallimard, Pléiade.

Bayard, Pierre. (2004). *Peut-on appliquer la littérature à la psychanalyse?* Paris: Minuit.

(2007). *How to Talk about Books You Haven't Read*, trans. Jeffrey Mehlman. New York: Bloomsbury.

Beckett, Samuel. (1953). *Watt*. New York: Grove Press.

(1957). *Murphy*. New York: Grove Press.

(1982). *En Attendant Godot / Waiting for Godot*. New York: Grove Press.

(1983). *Disjecta*. London: Calder.

(1986). *The Complete Dramatic Works*. London: Faber.

(1991). *Three Novels*. New York: Grove Press.

(1995). *The Complete Short Prose, 1929–1989*, ed. S. E. Gontarski. New-York: Grove Press.

(2009). *Letters*, vol. I. Cambridge: Cambridge University Press.

Behling, Katja. (2005). *Martha Freud, A Biography*, trans. R. D. V. Glasgow. Cambridge: Polity.

Bellemin-Noël, Jean. (1979). *Vers l'inconscient du texte*. Paris: Presses Universitaires de France.

(1983). *Gradiva au pied de la lettre*. Paris: Presses Universitaires de France.

Benjamin, Walter. (1969). *Illuminations*, trans. Harry Zohn. New York: Schocken Books.

(1999). *The Arcades Project*, trans. H. Eiland and K. McLaughlin. Cambridge, MA: Harvard University Press.

Berdach, Rachel. (1962). *The Emperor, The Sages and Death*, trans. William Wolf. New York: Thomas Yoseloff.

Bergler, Edmund. (1950). *The Writer and Psychoanalysis*. Garden City, NY: Doubleday.

Berman, Jeffrey. (1987). *The Talking Cure: Literary Representations of Psychoanalysis*. New York: New York University Press.

Bersani, Leo. (1986). *The Freudian Body: Psychoanalysis and Art*. New York: Columbia University Press.

Berthold-Bond, Daniel. (1995). *Hegel's Theory of Madness*. Albany: State University of New York.

Bettelheim, Bruno. (1982). *Freud and Man's Soul*. New York: Knopf.

Bion, Wilfred Rupert. (1965). *Transformations: Change from Learning to Growth*. New York: Basic Books.

(1993). *Second Thoughts: Selected Papers on Psycho-Analysis*. Northvale: Jason Aronson Inc.

(1997). *Taming Wild Thoughts*. London: Karnac.

Biswas, Santanu, ed. (2012). *The Literary Lacan: From Literature to Lituraterre and Beyond*. London and Calcutta: Seagull Books.

Blackman, Jackie. (2007). "Beckett Judaizing Beckett." *Samuel Beckett Today/ Aujourd'hui*, "All Sturm and no Drang", no. 18, ed. Dirk Van Hull and Mark Nixon, pp. 325–340.

Blanchot, Maurice. (1995). *The Maurice Blanchot Reader*, ed. Michael Holland. Oxford: Blackwell.

(1995). *The Writing of the Disaster*, trans. Ann Smock. Lincoln: University of Nebraska Press.

(2004). *Lautréamont and Sade*, trans. Stuart Kendall and Michelle Kendall. Stanford: Stanford University Press.

Block, Marcelline, ed. (2009). *The Many Ways We Talk about Death in Contemporary Society*. Lewiston: Edwin Mellen.

Bloom, Harold. (1982). *Agon: Towards a Theory of Revisionism*. New York: Oxford University Press.

Bloom, Harold, ed. (2004). *Bloom's BioCritiques: Jorge Luis Borges*. Philadelphia: Chelsea House.

Boehlich, Walter, ed. (1990). *The Letters of Sigmund Freud to Eduard Silberstein, 1871–1881*, trans. Arnold J. Pomerans. Cambridge: Harvard University Press.

Bonaparte, Marie. (1949). *The Life and Works of Edgar Allan Poe: A Psycho-Analytic Interpretation*, trans. John Rocker. London: Imago.

(1953). *Female Sexuality*. New York: International Universities Press.

(1995). "Cahiers d'enfance, séquence du Crayon de Bouche, Vaga et les petits cahiers noirs." In Jean-Pierre Bourgeron, Daniel Ferrer, and Jean-Michel Rabaté, eds. *Genesis*, 8, *Psychanalyse*. Paris: Jean-Michel Place, pp. 149–178.

Borges, Jorge Luis. (1972). *Obra Poetica*. Madrid: Alianza Editorial.

(1993). *Oeuvres Complètes*, vol. 1, ed. Jean Pierre Bernès. Paris: Gallimard, Pléiade.

(1998). *Collected Fictions*, trans. Andrew Hurley. New York: Penguin.

(1999). *Selected Non-Fictions*, trans. Eliot Weinberger. New York: Penguin.

Breger, Louis. (2009). *A Dream of Undying Fame: How Freud Betrayed his Mentor and Invented Psychoanalysis*. New York: Basic Books.

Breton, André. (1960). *Nadja*, trans. Richard Howard. New York: Grove Press.

(1972). *Manifestoes of Surrealism*, trans. Richard Seaver and Helen R. Lane. Ann Arbor: University of Michigan Press.

(1988). *Oeuvres Complètes I*, ed. Marguerite Bonnet. Paris: Gallimard, Pléiade.

(1990). *Communicating Vessels*, trans. Mary Ann Caws and Geoffrey T. Harris. Lincoln: University of Nebraska Press.

(1992). *Oeuvres Complètes II*, eds. M. Bonnet, P. Bernier, E.-A. Hubert, and J. Pierre. Paris: Gallimard, Pléiade.

(1993). *Earthlight*, trans. Bill Zavatsky and Zack Rogow. Los Angeles: Sun and Moon Press.

(1999). *Oeuvres Complètes*, vol. III, ed. Marguerite Bonnet. Paris: Gallimard, Pléiade.

Brooke-Rose, Christine. (1996). *Remake*. Manchester: Carcanet.

Brooks, Peter. (1984) *Reading for the Plot: Design and Intention in Narrative*. New York: Knopf.

(1993). *Body Work: Objects of Desire in Modern Narrative*. Cambridge, MA: Harvard University Press.

(1994). *Psychoanalysis and Storytelling*. Oxford: Wiley-Blackwell.

Burgin, Richards. (1969). *Conversations with Jorge Luis Borges*. New York: Holt, Rinehart and Winston.

Canetti, Elias. (1984). *Crowds and Power*, trans. Victor Gollancz. New York: Farar, Strauss and Giroux.

Caquot, André. (2007). "Appendix." In Jacques Lacan, *Seminar XVII: The Other Side of Psychoanalysis*, trans. Russell Grigg. New York: W.W. Norton & Company, pp. 209–214.

Caruth, Cathy. (1996). *Unclaimed Experience: Trauma, Narrative, and History*. Baltimore, MD: Johns Hopkins.

Cavell, Stanley. (1987). *Disowning Knowledge*. Cambridge: Cambridge University Press.

Cawthorne, Nigel. (2010). *Sordid Sex Lives: Shocking Stories of Perversion and Promiscuity from Nero to Nilsen*. London: Quercus.

Cervantes, Miguel de. (1998). *Exemplary Stories*, trans. Lesley Lipson. Oxford: Oxford University Press.

(1998). *Don Quixote*, trans. Charles Jarvis. Oxford: Oxford University Press.

Christ, Ronald. (1969). *The Narrow Act: Borges's Art of Allusion*. New York: New York University Press.

Coetzee, J. M. (1992). *Doubling the Point: Essays and Interviews*, ed. David Attwell. Cambridge: Harvard University Press.

(2013). *The Childhood of Jesus*. London: Harvill Secker.

Cohn, Robert Greer. (1949). *Mallarmé's Un Coup de dés: an exegesis*. New York: AMS Press.

Critchley, Simon, and Jamieson Webster. (2013). *Stay Illusion: The Hamlet Doctrine*. New York: Pantheon Books, Random House.

Dalí, Salvador. (1998). *Oui. The Paranoid-Critical Revolution: Writings 1927–1933*, ed. Robert Descharnes, trans. Yvonne Shafir. New York: Exact Change.

David-Ménard, Monique. (1997). *Les Constructions de l'Universel*. Paris: Presses Universitaires de France.

Davis, Michael Thomas. (1995). "Jacques Lacan and Shakespeare and Company." *James Joyce Quarterly*, vol. 32, no. 3–4, pp. 754–758.

Derrida, Jacques. (1978). *Edmund Husserl's Origin of Geometry: An Introduction*, trans. J. P. Leavey. Stony Brook: Nicholas Hays.

(1978). *Writing and Difference*, trans. Alan Bass. Chicago: Chicago University Press.

(1982). *Positions*, trans. Henri Ronse. Chicago: University of Chicago Press.

(1987). *The Post Card: From Socrates to Freud and Beyond*, trans. Alan Bass. Chicago: University of Chicago Press.

(1989) *Edmund Husserl's Origin of Geometry: An Introduction*, trans. John P. Leavey, Jr. Lincoln: University of Nebraska.

Duras, Marguerite. (1964). *Le ravissement de Lol V. Stein*. Paris: Gallimard.

(1966). *The Ravishing of Lol Stein*, trans. Richard Seaver. New York: Grove Press.

Eliot, T. S. (1972). *The Sacred Wood*. London: Methuen.

(1996). *Inventions of the March Hare, Poems 1909–1917*, ed. Christopher Ricks. New York: Harcourt and Brace.

Ellmann, Richard. (1977). *The Consciousness of Joyce*. London: Faber.

(1982). *James Joyce*, 2nd ed. Oxford: Oxford University Press.

Ellmann, Maud, ed. (1994). *Psychoanalysis and Literary Criticism*. London: Longman.

Evans, Dylan. (1996). *An Introductory Dictionary of Lacanian Psychoanalysis*. London and New York: Routledge.

Fédida, Pierre. (1984). "La paranoïa comme théorie de la communication." In *Le Temps de la réflexion*, V. Paris: Gallimard.

Fink, Bruce. (1996). "Reading Hamlet with Lacan." In Willy Apollon and Richard Feldstein, eds. *Lacan, Politics, Aesthetics*. Albany: SUNY Press, pp. 181–198.

Fitch, Noel Riley. (1983). *Sylvia Beach and the Lost Generation*. New York: W.W. Norton & Company.

Foister, Susan, Roy Ashok, and Martin Wyld. (1998). *Making and Meaning: Holbein's Ambassadors*. London and New Haven: National Gallery Company and Yale University Press.

Freud, Ernst L., ed. (1992). *The Letters of Sigmund Freud*. London: Dover.

Freud, Sigmund. (1946). *Totem and Taboo*. New York: Random House.

(1950). *The Question of Lay Analysis*, trans. Nancy Procter-Gregg. New York: W.W. Norton & Company.

(1953–1974). *The Standard Edition of the Complete Psychological Works of Sigmund Freud*, 24 vols., ed. James Strachey. London: Hogarth Press and Institute of Psycho-analysis.

(1954). *The Origins of Psychoanalysis, Letters to Wilhelm Fliess, Drafts and Notes 1887–1902*, eds. M. Bonaparte, A. Freud, and E. Kris, trans. Eric Mosbacher and James Strachey. New York, Basic Books.

(1958). *On Creativity and the Unconscious*, ed. B. Nelson. New York: Harper and Row.

(1959). *Collected Papers*, vol. 5, ed. James Strachey. New York: Basic Books.

(1963). *General Psychological Theory*. New York: Collier Books.

(1963). *Therapy and Technique*, ed. Philip Rieff. New York: Collier Books.

(1965). *The Interpretation of Dreams*, trans. James Strachey. New York: Avon Books.

(1967). *Moses and Monotheism*. New York: Random House.

Freud, Sigmund, and William C. Bullitt. (1967). *Thomas Woodrow Wilson: A Psychological Study*. Boston: Houghton Mifflin.

Freud, Sigmund. (1970). *Studienausgabe, X, Bildende Kunst and Literatur*. Frankfurt: Fischer.

(1971). *Studienausgabe, VI, Hysterie und Angst*. Frankfurt: Fischer.

(1973). *Studienausgabe, VII, Zwang, Paranoia und Perversion*. Frankfurt: Fischer.

(1974). *Studienausgabe, IX, Fragen der Gesellschaft, Ursprünge der Religion*. Frankfurt: Fischer.

Freud, Sigmund (1975). *Three Essays on the Theory of Sexuality*. New York: Basic Books.

Freud, Sigmund. (1977). *The Origins of Psychoanalysis*, trans. Eric Mosbacher and James Strachey. New York: Basic Books.

(1978). *Sexuality and the Psychology of Love*. New York: Collier Books.

(1980). *Die Traumdeutung*, Studienausgabe II. Frankfurt: Fischer.

(1982). *Studienausgabe, III, Psychologie des Unbewussten*. Frankfurt: Fischer.

(1982). *Studienausgabe, Ergänzungsband, Schriften zur Behandlungstechnik*. Frankfurt: Fischer.

Freud, Sigmund. (1985). *The Complete Letters of Sigmund Freud to Wilhelm Fliess, 1887–1904*, ed. and trans. Jeffrey Moussaieff Masson. Cambridge, MA: Harvard University Press.

Freud, Sigmund. (1989). *Beyond the Pleasure Principle.* New York: W.W. Norton & Company.

(1989). *New Introductory Lectures on Psycho-Analysis,* trans. James Strachey. New York: Norton.

(1993). *Dora, An Analysis of a Case of Hysteria.* New York: Collier Books.

(1997). *Writings of Art and Literature,* ed. Neil Hertz. Stanford: Stanford University Press.

(1998). *The Interpretation of Dreams.* New York: Avon Books.

(1999). *The Interpretation of Dreams, the Original Text,* trans. Joyce Crick. Oxford: Oxford University Press.

Freud, Sigmund, and Josef Breuer. (2000). *Studies on Hysteria,* trans. James Strachey and Anna Freud. New York: Basic Books.

Freud, Sigmund. (2002). *The Joke and Its Relation to the Unconscious,* trans. Joyce Crick. London: Penguin.

(2002). *The Psychopathology of Everyday Life,* trans. Anthea Bell. New York: Penguin.

(2002). *The Schreber Case,* trans. Andrew Weber. London: Penguin.

(2003). *The Uncanny,* trans. David Mclintock. London, Penguin.

(2006). *The Psychology of Love,* trans. Shaun Whiteside. London: Penguin.

Fry, Roger. (1996). *A Roger Fry Reader,* ed. Christopher Reed. Chicago: University of Chicago Press.

Gardiner, Muriel, ed. (1971). *The Wolf-Man by the Wolf-Man.* London: Hogarth Press.

Gay, Peter. (1988). *Freud: A Life for Our Time.* New York: Doubleday.

Gay, Peter, ed. (1989). *The Freud Reader.* New York: Norton.

Gide, André. (1948). *Journals,* trans. Justin O'Brien. New York: Knopf.

(1951). *Journal 1889–1939,* Paris: Gallimard, Pléiade

(1972). *The Counterfeiters,* trans. Dorothy Bussy. New York: Knopf.

(2001). *Souvenirs et Voyages,* ed. Pierre Masson. Paris: Gallimard, Pléiade.

(2009). *Romans et Récits,* vol. I. Paris: Gallimard, Pléiade.

Gilbert, Stuart. (1955). *James Joyce's Ulysses, A Study.* New York: Vintage.

Girard, René. (1965). *Deceit, Desire and the Novel: Self and Other in Literary Structure,* trans. Yvonne Freccero. Baltimore: Johns Hopkins University Press.

Goethe, Johann W. (1992). *Gesamtausgabe: Faust.* Frankfurt: Insel.

Gorman, Herbert. (1939). *James Joyce.* New York: Farrar and Rhinehart.

Grinstein, Alexander. (1990). *Freud at the Crossroads.* Madison, CT: International Universities Press.

Grosskurth, Phyllis. (1991). *The Secret Ring: Freud's Inner Circle and the Politics of Psychoanalysis.* London: Jonathan Cape.

Gunn, Daniel. (1988). *Psychoanalysis and Fiction.* Cambridge: Cambridge University Press.

Guyomard, Patrick. (1992). *La jouissance du tragique: Antigone, Lacan et le désir de l'analyste.* Paris: Aubier.

Harari, Roberto. (1995). *How James Joyce Made His Name: A Reading of the Final Lacan*, trans. Luke Thurston. New York: The Other Press.

Hardack, Richard. (2013). "Revealing the Bidder: The Forgotten Lesbian in Pynchon's *The Crying of Lot 49.*" *Textual Practice*, vol. 27, no. 4, pp. 565–595.

Hart, Clive. (1962). *Structure and Motif in Finnegans Wake*. London: Faber.

Hegel, Georg Wilhelm Friedrich. (1957). *The Phenomenology of Spirit*, trans. A. V. Miller. Oxford: Oxford University Press.

Hervey, Mary F. S. (1900). *Holbein's Ambassadors: The Picture and the Men*. London: George Bell and Sons.

Hoffmann, Ernst Theodor Amadeus. (2006). *Fantasiestücke*. Frankfurt: Deutscher Klassikder Verlag.

Hofman, Frederick John. (1957). *Freudianism and the Literary Mind*. New York: Grove Press.

Hulak, Fabienne, ed. (1992). *Folie et Psychanalyse dans l'expérience surréaliste*. Nice: Z'éditions.

Huyssen, Andreas. (1986). *After the Great Divide*. Bloomington: Indiana University Press.

James, Henry. (1922). *The Beldonald Holbein*. London: Macmillan.

(2008). *The Ambassadors*. New York: Penguin Classics.

Jensen, Wilhelm. (1903). *Gradiva*. Leipzig: Kamm & Seemann.

Jolas, Eugène. (2009). *Critical Writings, 1924–1951*, eds. Klaus H. Kiefer and Rainer Rumold. Evanston: Northwestern University Press.

Jones, Ernest. (1949). *Hamlet and Oedipus*. New York: Doubleday.

(1953). *The Life and Work of Sigmund Freud*, vol. 1. New York: Basic Books.

(1955). *The Life and Work of Sigmund Freud: Years of Maturity, 1901–1919*, vol. 2. New York: Basic Books.

Joyce, James. (1939). *Finnegans Wake*. London: Faber.

(1975). *Selected Letters*, ed. Richard Ellmann. London: Faber.

(1986). *Ulysses*, ed. H. W. Gabler. New York: Random House.

Jung, Carl Gustav. (1909). *Die Bedeutung des Vaters für das Schicksal des Einzelnen*. Leipzig and Vienna: Deuticke.

(1972). *The Spirit in Man, Art and Literature*. Princeton: Princeton University Press.

(1974). *The Psychoanalytic Years*, trans. R. F. C. Hull. Princeton: Princeton University Press.

Kafka, Franz. (1977). *Letters to Friends, Family and Editors*, trans. Richard and Clara Winston. New York: Schocken.

(2007). *Selected Stories*, ed. Stanley Corngold. New York: W.W. Norton & Company.

Kant, Immanuel. (1998). *Critique of Pure Reason*, ed. and trans. Paul Guyer and Allen Wood. Cambridge: Cambridge University Press.

Klossowski, Pierre. (1991). *Sade My Neighbor*, trans. Alphonso Lingis. Evanston, IL: Northwestern University Press.

Knowlson, James. (1996). *Damned to Fame*. New York: Simon & Schuster.

Kofman, Sarah. (1988). *The Childhood of Art, An Interpretation of Freud's Aesthetics*, trans. Winfred Woodhull. New York: Columbia University Press.

Krafft-Ebing, Richard von. (1887). *Psychopathia Sexualis; mit besonderer Berücksichung der conträre Sexualempfindung*. Stuttgart: Ferdinand Enke Verlag.

Kuspit, Donald. (1989). "A Mighty Metaphor: The Analogy of Archaeology and Psychoanalysis." In *Sigmund Freud and Art*. New York and London: State University of New York and Freud Museum, pp. 133–151.

Lacan, Jacques. (1966). *Ecrits*. Paris: Seuil.

(1971). "Lituraterre." In *Littérature*, no. 3. Paris: Larousse, pp. 3–10.

(1975). *De la psychose paranoïaque dans ses rapports avec la personnalité suivi de Premiers écrits sur la paranoia*. Paris: Seuil.

(1975–1976). "R.S.I." In *Ornicar?*, no. 5. Paris: Le Graphe, pp. 17–66.

(1981). *The Four Fundamental Concepts of Psychoanalysis*, trans. Alan Sheridan. New York: W.W. Norton & Company.

(1982). "Desire and the Interpretation of Desire in Hamlet," trans. James Hulbert. In Shoshana Felman, ed. *Literature and Psychoanalysis. The Question of Reading: Otherwise*. Baltimore: Johns Hopkins University Press, pp. 11–52.

(1992). *The Seminar of Jacques Lacan: The Ethics of Psychoanalysis, Book VII*, trans. Dennis Porter. New York: W.W. Norton & Company.

(1993). *Seminar III: The Psychoses*, trans. Russell Grigg. New York: W.W. Norton & Company.

(1994). *Le Séminaire IV: La Relation d'objet*. Paris: Seuil.

(1998). *Seminar II: The Ego in Freud's Theory*, trans. S. Tomaselli and J. Forrester. New York: W.W. Norton & Company.

(1998). *Seminar XX: On Feminine Sexuality, The Limits of Love and Knowledge*, trans. Bruce Fink. New York: W.W. Norton & Company.

(2005). *Le Séminaire, Livre XXIII, Le Sinthome*, ed. Jacques-Alain Miller. Paris: Seuil.

(2006). *Ecrits*, trans. Bruce Fink. New York: W.W. Norton & Company.

(2013). *Le Désir et son Interprétation*, ed. Jacques-Alain Miller. Paris: Editions de la Martinière et le Champ Freudien.

Lacoue-Labarthe, Philippe, and Jean-Luc Nancy. (1988). *The Literary Absolute: The Theory of Literature in German Romanticism*, trans. Philip Barnard and Cheryl Lester. Albany: State University of New York Press.

Ladenson, Elisabeth. (1999). *Proust's Lesbianism*. Ithaca: Cornell University Press.

Laplanche, Jean. (1980). *Problématiques III. La Sublimation*. Paris: Presses Universitaires de France.

(2006). *Problématiques VI, L'après-Coup*. Paris: Presses Universitaires de France.

Lejeune, Philippe. (1996). *Le pacte autobiographique*. Paris: Seuil.

Leys, Ruth. (2000). *Trauma: A Genealogy*. Chicago: University of Chicago Press.

"Life of Pi Author Martel Hears from Obama." (2010). Saskatoon: *Winnipeg Free Press*, April 8, 2010.

Lupton, Julia Reinhard, and Kenneth Reinhard. (1993). *After Oedipus: Shakespeare in Psychoanalysis*. Ithaca: Cornell University Press.

Mallarmé, Stéphane. (1945). *Oeuvres Complètes*, eds. H. Mondor and G. Jean-Aubry. Paris: Gallimard, Pléaide.

(1994). *Collected Poems*, trans. Henry Weinfield. Berkeley: University of California Press.

Masschelein, Anneleen. (2011). *The Unconcept: The Freudian Uncanny in Late-Twentieth-Century Theory*. Albany: SUNY Press.

Mauron, Charles. (1963). *Introduction to the Psychoanalysis of Mallarmé*, trans. Archibald Henderson, Jr., and Will L. McLendon. Berkeley: University of California Press.

Mauss, Marcel. (1967). *The Gift: Forms and Functions of Exchange in Archaic Societies*, trans. Ian Gunnison. New York: W.W. Norton & Company.

McGuire, William, ed. (1994). *The Freud/Jung Letters*. Princeton: Princeton University Press.

Merkin, Daphne. (October 2008). "I Think, therefore I'm Art." *New York Times Sunday Magazine*, pp. 18–20.

Messac, Régis. (1929). *Le "Detective Novel" et l'influence de la pensée scientifique*. Paris: Honoré Champion.

Meyer, Conrad Ferdinand. (1976). *Complete Narrative Prose*, vol. II, trans. David B. Dickens and Marion W. Sonnenfeld. Lewisburg: Bucknell University Press.

Michaud, Henriette. (2011). *Les Revenants de la Mémoire: Freud et Shakespeare*. Paris: Presses Universitaires de France.

Miller, Ian, and Kay Souter. (2013) *Beckett and Bion: The (Im)Patient Voice in Psychotherapy and Literature*. London: Karnac.

Mitchell, Andrew J. and Slote, Sam, eds. (2013). *Derrida and Joyce: Texts and Contexts*. Albany: State University of New York Press.

Moorjani, Angela. (2009). "Whence Estragon?" *Beckett Circle*, vol. 32, no. 2, pp. 7–8.

Muller, John P. Muller, and William J. Richardson, eds. (1988). *The Purloined Poe: Lacan, Derrida and Psychoanalytic Reading*. Baltimore: Johns Hopkins University Press.

Nabokov, Vladimir. (1962). *Pale Fire*. New York: Putnam.

(1966). *Speak Memory*, rev. ed. New York: Putnam.

(1980). *Lectures on Literature*. New York: Harcourt.

(1997). *Lolita*. New York: Vintage.

Nancy, Jean-Luc. (2013). *Adoration: The Deconstruction of Christianity*, II, trans. John McKeane. New York: Fordham University Press.

Neri, Louise. (April 2009). "Sophie Calle" in *Interview Magazine*, at http://www.interviemagazine.com/art/sophie-calle, accessed April 20, 2014.

Nietzsche, Friedrich. (1982). *The Portable Nietzsche*, ed. Walter Kaufmann. London: Penguin.

Orlando, Francesco. (1978). *Toward a Freudian Theory of Literature*, trans. Charmaine Lee. Baltimore: Johns Hopkins University Press.

Piling, John. (2007). "From an Abandoned Work: All the Variants of the One." In *Samuel Beckett Today*, no. 18, *All Sturm and No Drang*, pp. 173–183.

Plato. (1973). *The Collected Dialogues of Plato*, eds. Edith Hamilton and Huntington Cairns. Princeton: Princeton University Press.

Poe, Edgar Allan. (1983). *The Complete Tales and Poems of Edgar Allan Poe*. Harmondsworth: Penguin.

Politzer, Heinz. (1974). *Hatte Oedipus einen Oedipus-komplex?* Munich: Piper.
    (2006). *Freud and Tragedy*, trans. Michael Mitchell. Riverside, CA: Ariadne Press.

Potts, Willard, ed. (1979). *Portraits of the Artist in Exile: Recollections of James Joyce by Europeans*. Seattle, WA: Wolfhound Press.

Pound, Ezra. (1986). *The Cantos*. London: Faber.

Pynchon, Thomas. (1986). *The Crying of Lot 49*. New York: Harper and Row.
    (2013). *Bleeding Edge*. New York, Penguin.

Rabaté, Jean-Michel. (1996). *The Ghosts of Modernity*. Gainesville: University Press of Florida.
    (2001). *Jacques Lacan: Psychoanalysis and the Subject of Literature*. Houndsmills: Palgrave.
    (2007). *Given: 1° Art, 2° Crime. Modernity, Murder and Mass Culture*. Eastbourne: Sussex Academic Press.
    (2007). *The Ethics of the Lie*, trans. Suzanne Verderber. New York: The Other Press.
    (2014). *Crimes of the Future*. New York: Bloomsbury.

Ross, Ciaran. (2011). *Beckett's Art of Absence: Rethinking the Void*. Houndsmills: Palgrave Macmillan.

Roth, Michael S., ed. (1998). *Freud, Conflict and Culture. Essays on His Life, Work and Legacy*. New York: Knopf.

Roudinesco, Elisabeth. (1990). *Jacques Lacan & Co. A History of Psychoanalysis in France, 1925–1985*, trans. Jeffrey Mehlman. Chicago: University of Chicago Press.
    (1997). *Jacques Lacan*, trans. Barbara Bray. New York: Columbia University Press.
    (2009). *Our Dark Side: A History of Perversion*, trans. David Macey. Cambridge and Malden: Polity Press.

Roustang, François. (1996). *Comment faire rire un paranoïaque*. Paris: Odile Jacob.
    (2000). *How to Make a Paranoid Laugh, or What is Psychoanalysis?*, trans. Anne C. Vila. Philadelphia: University of Pennsylvania Press.

Royle, Nicholas. (2003). *The Uncanny*. New York: Routledge.

Sade, Marquis de. (1965). *Justine, Philosophy in the Bedroom and Other Writings*, trans. Richard Seaver and Austryn Wainhouse. New York: Grove Weidenfeld.

Salgado, César Augusto. (1998). "Barocco Joyce: Borges's and Lezama's Antagonistic Readings." In Karen R. Lawrence, ed. *Transcultural Joyce*. Cambridge: Cambridge University Press, pp. 63–94.

Santner, Eric L. (1996). *My Own Private Germany: Daniel Paul Schreber's Secret History of Modernity*. Princeton: Princeton University Press.

Schatzman, Morton. (1973). *Soul Murder: Persecution in the Family*. London: Penguin.

Schopenhauer, Arthur. (2009). *The Art of Always Being Right*, trans. T. Bailey Saunders. London: Gibson Square Books.

Schreber, Daniel Paul. (1973). *Denkwürdigkeiten eines Nervenkranken*, ed. Samuel Weber. Frankfurt: Ullstein.

(2000). *Memoirs of My Nervous Illness*, trans. Ida MacAlpine and Richard A. Hunter. New York: New York Review of Books.

Schur, Max. (1972). *Freud: Living and Dying*. New York: International Universities Press.

Shakespeare, William. (1985). *Hamlet*, ed. Philip Edwards. Cambridge: Cambridge University Press.

Sharpe, Ella Freeman. (1950). *Collected Papers on Psycho-Analysis*. London: Hogarth Press.

Shloss, Carol Loeb. (2005). *Lucia Joyce: Dancing in the Wake*. London: Picador.

Slavet, Eliza. (2009). *Racial Fever: Freud and the Jewish Question*. New York: Fordham University Press.

Sloterdijk, Peter. (1987). *Critique of Cynical Reason*, trans. Michael Eldred. Minneapolis: University of Minnesota Press.

Steiner, Ricardo, ed. (2003). *Unconscious Phantasy*. London: Karnac.

Stewart, Elizabeth. (2010). *Catastrophe and Survival: Walter Benjamin and Psychoanalysis*. New York and London: Continuum.

Tintner, Adeline R. (1993). *Henry James and the Lust of the Eyes*. Baton Rouge: Louisiana State University Press.

Trezise, Thomas. (2013). *Witnessing Witnessing: On the Reception of Holocaust Survivor Testimony*. New York: Fordham University Press.

Trotter, David. (2001). *Paranoid Modernism*. Oxford: Oxford University Press.

Weissberg, Liliane. (2010). "Ariadne's Thread: Sigmund Freud, the Textile Industry, and Early Psychoanalysis." *MLN*, no. 125, pp. 661–681.

Williamson, Edwin. (2004). *Borges: A Life*. New York: Viking.

Wilson, J. Dover. (1959). *Hamlet*, 2nd ed. Cambridge: Cambridge University Press.

Woscoboinik, Julio. (1998). *The Secret of Borges: A Psychoanalytic Inquiry into his Work*, trans. Dora Carlisky Pozzi. Lanham, MD: University Press of America.

Yerushalmi, Yosef Hayim. (1991). *Freud's Moses: Judaism Terminable and Interminable*. New Haven: Yale University Press.

Žižek, Slavoj. (1991). *Looking Awry: An Introduction to Jacques Lacan through Popular Culture*. Cambridge: MIT Press.

(1992). *Enjoy your Symptom!* New York: Routledge.

(1999). *The Žižek Reader*, eds. Elizabeth and Edmond Wright. Oxford: Blackwell.

Zweig, Stefan. (1987). *Briefwechsel mit Hermann Bahr, Sigmund Freud, Rainer Maria Rilke und Arthur Schnitzler*, eds. Jeffrey B. Berlin, Hans-Ulrich Lindken, and Donald A. Prater. Frankfurt: Fischer.

Index

Abraham, Karl, 98, 126–27
Achilles, 138
Adler, Alfred, 156
Adorno, Theodor Wiesengrund, 57, 105, 176, 185, 196, 226
Agathon, 111
Agamben, Giorgio, 176, 189, 194, 196
Agrippa, Cornelius, 206
Alacoque, Marguerite Mary, 179
Allais, Alphonse, 29
Allan, John, 123–24
Allégret, Marc, 149
Altenberg, Peter, 7
Andreas-Salomé, Lou, 215
Antelme, Robert, 176, 190, 194–96
Animals, 66–69, 197–98
Animus-anima, 151–52, 166, 216
Antigone, 37
Anzengruber, Ludwig, 52–53
Anzieu, Didier, 61, 216
Apollo, 74–75
Apuleius, 56
Aquinas, 32, 178, 232
Aragon, Louis, 99, 101
Archetypes, 153, 166, 233
Aristotle, 82, 111–14, 203, 215, 218
Artaud, Antonin, 98
Atherton, James, 172
Aton, 174
Atreus, 140
Aubert, Jacques, 161, 165
Auriti, Marino, 94

Babinski, Joseph, 95, 99, 101, 106
Bacon, Francis, viscount, 2, 169

Bacon, Francis, 216
Badiou, Alain, 1, 65
Bahr, Hermann, 7
Bakhtin, Mikhail, 234
Balzac, Honoré de, 87
Balint, Michael, 220
Barca, Hannibal, 27
Barthes, Roland, 59, 84–88, 204, 224
Bataille, Georges, 98, 102–4, 182, 187, 216–17
Bateson, Gregory, 13
Baudelaire, Charles, 85, 123–24, 131, 136, 180
Bauer, Ida (Dora), 19–24, 29, 234
Bayard, Pierre, 2–6
Beach, Sylvia, 160
Beckett, Samuel, 14, 60–71, 163, 198, 216, 217
Bellemin-Noël, Jean, 4, 75
Benjamin, Walter, 171, 204–5
Berdach, Rachel, 212–13
Bergler, Edmund, 1
Bergson, Henri, 4
Berman, Jeffery, 1
Bernays, Jakob, 218
Bernès, Jean-Pierre, 168
Bettelheim, Bruno, 78, 217
Bion, Wilfred Ruprecht, 6, 60–66, 68–69, 71, 217, 232
Blanchot, Maurice, 183–84, 193
Block, Marcelline, 88
Bloom, Harold, 167
Boleyn, Ann, 207
Bonaparte, Marie, 1, 4, 122–28, 131, 133, 136, 141, 217

Borch-Jacobsen, Mikkel, 188
Borel, Adrien, 216
Borges, Jorge Luis, 29, 150,
    167–74, 183
Boudinet, Daniel, 87
Brancusi, Constantin, 128
Brandes, Georg, 27
Breger, Louis, 18–19
Brentano, Franz, 70
Breton, André, 93–107, 117, 121, 216
Breuer, Josef, 15, 18–19, 218
Brody, Daniel, 163
Brooke-Rose, Christine, 60
Browne, Thomas (Sir), 169
Bullitt, William Christian, 181
Burgin, Richard, 167
Burton, Richard Francis, 169, 178

Calle, Sophie, 84, 88–92
Callot, Jacques, 10
Can Grande della Scala, 53
Canetti, Elias, 118
Caquot, André, 175
Carlyle, Thomas, 13
Carus, Carl Gustav, 159
Caruth, Cathy, 175–76, 188–89,
    194, 196
Castration, 65, 103, 125, 127–28, 131,
    139, 147–48, 175, 218
Catharsis, 82–83, 215, 218
Catharina of Siena, 179
Catherine of Aragon, 207
Cavell, Stanley, 45
Cawthorne, Nigel, 178
Cazotte, Jacques, 44
Céline, Louis Ferdinand, 172
Cervantes, Miguel de, 9–10, 12–14,
    16–17, 24, 170, 172
Charcot, Jean-Martin, 6, 95, 99,
    221, 222
Christ, Ronald, 173
Christie, Agatha, 5
Claudel, Paul, 166
Clémenceau, Georges, 181
Cleopatra, 178

Clifford, Charles, 84
Cixous, Hélène, 3, 79, 218
Coetzee, John M., 80–82, 208–9
Coleridge, Samuel Taylor, 40, 169
Cohn, Robert Greer, 131
Comte, Auguste, 200
Conrad, Joseph, 35, 117
Copernicus, Nicolaus, 8
Cooper, Paula, 88
Corngold, Stanley, 79
Crébillon, Prosper J. de, 137, 140

Dalí, Salvador, 1, 99, 102–4, 108, 206
Dallo, Marcel, 61
Dante Alighieri, 53, 62
Darwin, Charles, 8
David-Ménard, Monique, 183
Da Vinci, Leonardo, 7–8, 122, 233
Davis, Michael Thomas, 160
Daydreaming, 52–54, 232
Dean, James, 178
Death Drive, 56, 189, 200, 213
De Gourmont, Remy, 146
Delay, Jean, 142, 164
De la Nux, Marc, 145
Delbo, Charlotte, 190
Delboeuf, Joseph Rémi Léopold, 96
Deleuze, Gilles, 228
Delusion, 72, 75, 80, 82, 94, 101,
    106–7, 114, 118, 153, 182
De Man, Paul, 188
De Rais, Gilles, 180
Derrida, Jacques, 3, 78–79, 131,
    136–41, 161–62, 171, 218
Descartes, René, 65, 69, 145
De Dinteville, Jean, 206–8, 212
De Saussure, Ferdinand, 232
De Selves, Georges, 206, 208
Dickinson, Emily, 169
Diogenes, 14
Dionysus, 74–75
Dostoevsky, Fyodor, 4, 118, 122, 185
Douglas, Alfred (Lord), 145–46
Duchamp, Marcel, 83, 91, 93–94
Dumas, Alexandre, 129

Dupin, Charles, 129
Duras, Marguerite, 176, 188–94, 196
Dürer, Albrecht, 207
Duthuit, Georges, 71

Ego, 162, 167
Eichmann, Adolf, 181
Eliot, Thomas Stearns, 30, 32, 34–35,
    40, 105, 160, 168, 169
Ellmann, Richard, 33, 151, 163, 166
Eluard, Paul, 101, 104
Euclid, 63

Family Romance, 51–52, 220
Fantasy, 40, 42, 52–55, 57–60, 63, 72,
    85, 115, 140, 187, 220
Fedida, Pierre, 120
Ferenczi, Sandor, 6, 15, 220–21, 224
Fetishism, 178–79, 228
Feuerbach, Ludwig, 11
Fink, Bruce, 45, 135
Flaubert, Gustave, 6, 169, 179, 233
Flechsig, Paul, 115, 118
Fliess, Wilhelm, 15, 17, 25, 27, 28, 48,
    50, 113, 119, 140, 179, 200, 204, 221
Foucault, Michel, 164
Fraenkel Théodore, 95
France, Anatole, 7–8
Frazer, James (Sir), 167
Frederick II, Emperor, 212
Freud, Anna, 15, 31, 179, 201–2, 221,
    223, 224, 236
Freud, Emmanuel, 202
Freud, Philip, 202
Freud, Sigmund, 1–4, 6–30, 35–39,
    45–46, 48–60, 63, 66, 68, 71–79, 82,
    85, 91, 92, 94–99, 103–4, 110, 112–
    16, 119–20, 122–23, 127–28, 132,
    140, 141, 147, 148, 154–59, 163–64,
    167–69, 173–76, 178–82, 184–85,
    188, 199–205, 208, 212–15, 217–18,
    220–25, 227–31, 233–36
Fromm, Erich, 1
Fry, Roger, 130, 132, 226
Fuss, Gisela, 11–12, 16

Gabin, Jean, 61
Gardner, Isabella Stewart, 211
Gautier, Théophile, 132
Gay, Peter, 201
Genet, Jean, 165, 215, 218
Geulincx, Arnold, 69–70
Gide, André, 4–5, 44, 141–50, 229
Gide, Madeleine, 142–44, 147–49
Gilbert, Stuart, 160, 171
Gillet, Louis, 33–34
Gioni, Massimiliano, 94
Girard, René, 193, 226
Glover, James, 31
Goering, Hermann, 182
Goethe, Johann Wolfgang von, 3, 8, 40,
    50, 81, 122, 159, 202–3
Gomperz, Theodor, 7
Gorman, Herbert, 163
Grimm, Jacob and Wilhelm, 55, 72
Grinstein, Alexander, 7
Groddeck, Georg, 222
Guibert, Hervé, 90
Guattari, Félix, 228
Guyomard, Patrick, 36

Hardack, Richard, 108
Hart, Clive, 165
Hegel, Georg Wilhelm Friedrich, 20,
    86, 117, 131, 137, 159, 217, 225,
    235, 236
Heidegger, Martin, 225
Heine, Heinrich, 3
Heinroth, Johann Christian
    August, 120
Heller, Joseph, 107
Hénaf, Marcel, 186
Henry VIII, King, 207
Hertz, Max, 113
Hervey, Mary F. S., 202, 208
Hesse, Hermann, 7
Highsmith, Patricia, 59
Hinton, Charles Howard, 171
Hitler, Adolf, 118, 181
Hoess, Rudolf, 182
Hofman, Frederick John, 1

Hoffmann, Ernst Theodor Wilhelm, 10, 76, 78
Holbein, Hans, 200–2, 206–8, 210–12
Hölderlin, Friedrich, 159, 225
Homer, 5, 8, 12, 29, 42, 57
Hopkins, Gerard Manley, 169
Horkheimer, Max, 57, 185
Hosea, 175
Hugo, Victor, 179
Hume, David, 130
Husserl, Edmund, 162
Huyssen, Andreas, 105
Hysteria, 6, 17–24, 95, 98, 101–6, 112–14, 116–17, 222

Ibsen, Henrik, 6
Imaginary (the), 165, 223, 226–27, 229

James, Henry, 117, 200–1, 206–13
Janet, Pierre, 95, 147
Janus, 204
Jean Paul (Richter), 10–11, 13
Jensen, Wilhelm, 71–77, 93–94, 121–22
Jentsch, Ernst, 235
Jesus, 151, 220
Joan of Arc, 178
John, the Baptist, 131
John, of the Cross, 66
Johnson, Barbara, 136, 138
Jokes, 12, 109–11, 119, 168–69, 214, 236
Jolas, Eugène, 63, 158, 162
Jolas, Maria, 158
Jones, Ernest, 18, 30, 42, 72, 98, 152, 223, 230
Joseph II, Emperor, 164
Jouissance, 116–17, 124, 127, 145–48, 150, 164, 168, 169, 173, 186, 187, 192, 223–24
Joyce, James, 4–5, 30, 32–33, 38, 46–47, 108, 131, 150–55, 158, 160–73, 178, 213, 218, 223–24, 225, 232
Joyce, John, 166

Joyce, Lucia, 33, 108, 151–53, 166, 178
Joyce, Patrick Weston, 160
Julius II, Pope, 158
Jung, Carl Gustav, 6, 15, 33, 62–63, 71, 94, 98, 119, 147, 150–60, 163, 166–68, 171, 216, 223, 224, 225, 229, 231, 235

Kafka, Franz, 23, 54–55, 79–80, 125, 198
Kant, Immanuel, 65, 71, 83, 86, 97, 119–20, 182, 184–85, 214
Keats, John, 168, 170
Keller, Gottfried, 7
Kipling, Rudyard, 7
Klein, Melanie, 31, 32, 35, 61–66, 156, 179, 217, 218, 220, 221, 224, 227, 230, 232, 236
Kleist, Heinrich von, 188
Klossowski, Pierre, 185–86
Knowlson, James, 60
Kodama, Maria, 169
Kofman, Sarah, 4
Kraepelin, Emil, 107, 228
Krafft-Ebing, Richard von, 177
Kristeva, Julia, 3, 162, 215, 224
Kronos, 27, 131
Kuspit, Donald, 201

Lacoue-Labarthe, Philippe, 159
Ladenson, Elizabeth, 146
Lacan, Jacques, 2, 4, 5, 19–21, 35–47, 65, 77, 78, 82–84, 87, 103–4, 116–17, 127–28, 133–44, 148, 150, 159–69, 171, 175, 178, 182–88, 191, 193, 200, 206, 216–20, 223, 225–27, 230, 232–33, 235, 236
Laclos, Pierre Choderlos de, 5
Laplanche, Jean, 49–50, 225, 233
Lautréamont (Isidore Ducasse), 183–84
Lavater, Johann Kaspar, 63
Lenin, Vladimir, 61, 97
Levi, Primo, 176, 189, 196
Lévi-Strauss, Claude, 19, 21, 22, 233

Leys, Ruth, 176, 188–89
Libido, 30, 118, 128, 156, 158, 200, 225
Lichtenberg, Georg Christoph,
    10–11, 109
Lloyd George, David, 181
Locke, John, 130
Lucian of Samosata, 119
Lutpton, Julia, 45

Macaulay, Thomas Babington, 7–8
Mach, Ernst, 7
Machiavelli, Niccolò, 8
Mallarmé, Stéphane, 34, 130–33, 145
Marcuse, Herbert, 226
Martel, Yann, 176, 197–99
Marx, Karl, 59, 97, 103, 231, 236
Masschelein, Anneleen, 79
Maupassant, Guy de, 5–6
Mauron, Charles, 4, 130–33, 226
Mauss, Marcel, 22
McCormick, Edith, 151
McGreevy, Thomas, 63
McLintock, David, 77
Mehlman, Jeffrey, 139
Melancholia, 30, 31, 37, 207–9, 227
Merezkhovsky, Dmitri, 7–8
Merleau-Ponty, Maurice, 207
Messac, Regis, 129
Meyer, Conrad Ferdinand, 7,
    48–51, 53–54
Michelangelo di Lodovico
    Buonarroti, 122, 157–58
Michaud, Henriette, 25
Miller, Jacques-Alain, 161–62, 236
Mitchum, Robert, 59
Molière (Jean-Baptiste Poquelin), 20
Mondor, Charles, 130
Montaigne, Michel de, 6
Moses, 154–55, 157–58, 174–75, 177,
    181, 206, 213, 220
Mourning, 31, 42, 227
Mozart, Wolfgang Amadeus, 90
Muller, John, 136
Multatuli (Eduard Douwes
    Dekker), 7

Nabokov, Vladimir, 1–2, 19,
    23–24, 191
Nachträglichkeit (deferred action),
    48–51, 90, 112–14, 174, 176–77, 219
Nadar (Gaspar-Félix Tourmachon), 87
Nancy, Jean-Luc, 159, 199–200
Napoléon Bonaparte, 186
Neri, Louise, 89
Nero, 178
Nietzsche, Friedrich, 6, 74, 115, 145,
    147, 154, 171–72, 199, 215, 217, 235
Nin, Anaïs, 230
Novalis (von Hardenberg), 159

Obama, Barack, 199
Objet a, 40–43, 63–64, 227
Oedipus, 26, 36–38, 44–46, 58, 66–69,
    80, 116, 126–27, 131, 143, 156, 174,
    185, 220, 223, 224, 227–28
Onan, 178
Orpheus, 133
Ortega y Gasset, José, 171
Other (the), 36, 39, 40, 43, 70, 84, 108,
    116, 140, 148, 173, 184, 186–87, 193,
    204, 207–8, 214
Overdetermination, 100, 204, 228

Pappenheim, Bertha (Anna O), 15, 18
Paranoia, 95–98, 101–9, 115–21,
    224, 228
Pascal, Blaise, 108
Paulhan, Jean, 107
Perversion, 57, 116, 144, 148–49, 154,
    165, 178–88, 189, 228–29
Phallus, 21, 39–44, 126–28, 136,
    138–39, 144, 147–48, 150, 227, 229
Picasso, Pablo, 170
Pfister, Oskar, 1, 104, 229
Phillips, Adam, 2
Pilling, John, 66–67
Pithius, 111
Plato, 15, 113, 227
Pliny, 167
Poe, Edgar Allan, 5, 78, 122–31,
    133–37, 180, 191, 193, 197, 217, 229

Politzer, Heinz, 46
Poole, Adrian, 208
Popper-Lynkeus, Josef, 52
Pound, Ezra, 105, 146, 167
Presley, Elvis, 178
Prôton pseudos, 112–14, 117
Proust, Marcel, 5, 86, 146, 178, 193, 204, 205
Pseudo-couple, 14–15, 61–62
Pynchon, Thomas, 108

Rabelais, François, 165, 232
Rancière, Jacques, 1
Rank, Otto, 1, 6, 52, 98, 221, 223, 230
Reich, Wilhelm, 231
Real (the), 116, 165, 230–31
Rée, Paul, 215
Reich, Wilhelm, 231
Reinhard, Kenneth, 45
Renoir, Jean, 61
Repetition, 56–57, 76–77, 134, 231
Richardson, William, 136
Rilke, Rainer Maria, 215
Rimbaud, Arthur, 103
Rivière, Jacques, 147
Robespierre, Maximilien de, 186
Rodker, John, 163
Roheim, Geza, 220
Ross, Ciaran, 60–61
Roth, Michael, 94
Roudinesco, Elisabeth, 104, 160, 177–82
Rousseau, Jean-Jacques, 63
Roustang, François, 109
Royle, Nicholas, 3, 78–79

Sacher-Masoch, Leopold von, 178–9
Sachs, Hanns, 31, 98, 223
Sade, Donatien Alphonse François, Marquis de, 178–79, 183–88
Sadism, 178–88, 228
Salgado, César Augusto, 170
Santner, Eric, 118
Sartre, Jean-Paul, 86, 165, 232, 235
Schatzman, Morton, 119

Schelling, Friedrich Wilhelm Joseph, 159
Schizophrenia, 151, 154, 166
Schlegel, August, and Friedrich, 159
Schniztler, Arthur, 7
Schopenhauer, Arthur, 97, 111, 235
Schreber, Daniel Paul, 104, 107, 114–22, 183, 228
Schur, Max, 213
Sellin, Ernst, 175
Shakespeare, William, 2–5, 8, 25–47, 55–57, 82, 122, 152, 202, 213
Sharpe, Ella Freeman, 31–32, 35, 39, 43, 46, 232
Shloss, Carol, 152
Silberstein, Eduard, 9–16, 25, 110
Singer, Peter, 180
Slavet, Eliza, 175
Sloterdijk, Peter, 13
Socrates, 15, 214
Sokolnicka, Eugenie, 147–48
Sollers, Philippe, 162
Sophocles, 8, 25–26, 28, 30, 35–37, 45, 82–83
Soupault, Philippe, 98
Spinoza, Baruch, 225
Stalin, Jospeh, 149
Stein, Gertrude, 162
Stendhal (Henri Beyle), 193
Stevenson, Robert Louis, 6
Strachey, James, 222
Sublimation, 82–84, 90–91, 233, 234
Surrealism, 1, 92, 94–105, 159
Symbolic, the, 165, 233
Szasz, Thomas, 118

Tasso, Torquato, 16
Taylor, John, 154, 213
Thing (the), 82–84, 92, 211, 231, 234
Thoth, 213
Thyestes, 140
Tintner, Adaline, 208
Tiresias, 46
Todorov, Tzvetan, 5, 79
Trauma, 67, 188–98, 200, 234

Trezise, Thomas, 176, 189–90, 196
Trotter, David, 105
Tutankhamen, 73
Twain, Mark, 7–8

Uncanny (the), 68, 71–92, 235
Uranus, 27

Valéry, Paul, 96, 107
Van der Kolk, Bessel, 188–89
Vico, Giambattista, 161
Vidocq, Eugène François, 129–30, 135
Villeterque, Alexandre-Louis de,
    185–86
Volkelt, Johannes, 96–98
Von Hartmann, Karl Robert
    Eduard, 235
Von N., Elizabeth, 17
Von Scheffel, Joseph Victor, 11

Weier, Johann, 8
Weiss, Ottocaro, 151

Weissberg, Liliane, 202
Wellington, Duke of, 110
Whitman, Walt, 170
Wilde, Oscar, 145–46, 178
Wilson, John Dover, 30
Wilson, Woodrow, president, 181
Winnicott, Donald Woods, 61, 229,
    234, 236
Wolf Man (the), 201
Woolf, Leonard, 222
Woolf, Virginia, 222
Wordsworth, William, 169
Woscoboinik, Julio, 167–8

Yerushalmi, Yosef Hayim, 175

Zeno, 138
Zeus, 27
Zizek, Slavoj, 1, 58–59, 87, 94,
    138–40, 236
Zola, Emile, 7–8
Zweig, Stefan, 18

Cambridge Introductions to Literature

Authors

Margaret Atwood   Heidi Macpherson

Jane Austen   Janet Todd

Samuel Beckett   Ronan McDonald

Walter Benjamin   David Ferris

Lord Byron   Richard Lansdown

Chekhov   James N. Loehlin

J. M. Coetzee   Dominic Head

Samuel Taylor Coleridge   John Worthen

Joseph Conrad   John Peters

Jacques Derrida   Leslie Hill

Charles Dickens   Jon Mee

Emily Dickinson   Wendy Martin

George Eliot   Nancy Henry

T. S. Eliot   John Xiros Cooper

William Faulkner   Theresa M. Towner

F. Scott Fitzgerald   Kirk Curnutt

Michel Foucault   Lisa Downing

Robert Frost   Robert Faggen

Gabriel Garcia Marquez   Gerald Martin

Nathaniel Hawthorne   Leland S. Person

Zora Neale Hurston   Lovalerie King

James Joyce   Eric Bulson

Thomas Mann   Todd Kontje

Christopher Marlowe   Tom Rutter

Herman Melville   Kevin J. Hayes

Milton   Stephen B. Dobranski

Toni Morrison   Tessa Roynon

George Orwell   John Rodden and John Rossi

Sylvia Plath   Jo Gill

Edgar Allan Poe   Benjamin F. Fisher

Ezra Pound   Ira Nadel

Marcel Proust   Adam Watt

Jean Rhys   Elaine Savory

Edward Said   Conor McCarthy

Shakespeare   Emma Smith

Shakespeare's Comedies   Penny Gay

Shakespeare's History Plays   Warren Chernaik

Shakespeare's Poetry   Michael Schoenfeldt

Shakespeare's Tragedies   Janette Dillon

Harriet Beecher Stowe   Sarah Robbins

Mark Twain   Peter Messent

Edith Wharton   Pamela Knights

Walt Whitman   M. Jimmie Killingsworth

Virginia Woolf   Jane Goldman

William Wordsworth   Emma Mason

W. B. Yeats   David Holdeman

Topics

American Literary Realism   Phillip Barrish

The American Short Story   Martin Scofield

Anglo-Saxon Literature   Hugh Magennis

Comedy   Eric Weitz

Creative Writing   David Morley

Early English Theatre   Janette Dillon

The Eighteenth-Century Novel   April London

Eighteenth-Century Poetry   John Sitter

English Theatre, 1660–1900   Peter Thomson

Francophone Literature   Patrick Corcoran

Literature and the Environment   Timothy Clark

Modern British Theatre   Simon Shepherd

Modern Irish Poetry   Justin Quinn

Modernism   Pericles Lewis

Modernist Poetry   Peter Howarth

Narrative (second edition)   H. Porter Abbott

The Nineteenth-Century American Novel   Gregg Crane

The Novel   Marina MacKay

Old Norse Sagas   Margaret Clunies Ross

Poetics   Michael Hurley and Michael O'Neill

Postcolonial Literatures   C. L. Innes

Postmodern Fiction   Bran Nicol

Romantic Poetry   Michael Ferber

Russian Literature   Caryl Emerson

Scenography   Joslin McKinney and Philip Butterworth

The Short Story in English   Adrian Hunter

Theatre Historiography   Thomas Postlewait

Theatre Studies   Christopher B. Balme

Tragedy   Jennifer Wallace

Travel Writing   Tim Youngs

Victorian Poetry   Linda K. Hughes

Made in the USA
Middletown, DE
23 May 2016